T0314131

A EUROPE MADE
OF MONEY

A volume in the series
Cornell Studies in Money
edited by Eric Helleiner and Jonathan Kirshner

A list of titles in this series is available at
www.cornellpress.cornell.edu.

A Europe Made of Money

The Emergence of the European Monetary System

Emmanuel Mourlon-Druol

CORNELL UNIVERSITY PRESS   ITHACA AND LONDON

First published 2012 by Cornell University Press
Printed in the United States of America

Library of Congress Cataloging-in-Publication Data

Mourlon-Druol, Emmanuel.
    A Europe made of money : the emergence of the European Monetary System / Emmanuel Mourlon-Druol.
        p. cm. — (Cornell studies in money)
    Includes bibliographical references and index.
    ISBN 978-0-8014-5083-9 (cloth : alk. paper)
    1. Monetary policy—European Economic Community countries.
2. European Monetary System (Organization)—History.   I. Title.
II. Series: Cornell studies in money.

    HG930.5.M68 2012
    332.4'94—dc23   2012005416

Cornell University Press strives to use environmentally responsible suppliers and materials to the fullest extent possible in the publishing of its books. Such materials include vegetable-based, low-VOC inks and acid-free papers that are recycled, totally chlorine-free, or partly composed of nonwood fibers. For further information, visit our website at www.cornellpress.cornell.edu.

Cloth printing   10 9 8 7 6 5 4 3 2 1

Contents

Abbreviations

AAPD	*Akten zur Auswärtigen Politik der Bundesrepublik Deutschland*
ACS	Archivio centrale dello stato, Rome
AdsD	Archiv der sozialen Demokratie, Bonn
AMAE	Archives du ministère des affaires étrangères, La Courneuve
AN	Archives nationales, Paris or Fontainebleau
ASBI	Archivio storico della Banca d'Italia, Rome
BAK	Bundesarchiv, Koblenz
BB	Bundesbank Archiv, Frankfurt
BdF	Archives historiques de la Banque de France, Paris
BoE	The Bank of England Archive, London
CAEF	Centre des archives économiques et financières, Savigny-le-Temple
CADN	Centre des archives diplomatiques de Nantes
CAP	common agricultural policy
CDU	Christlich-Demokratische Union Deutschlands
CMA	Council of Ministers Archives, Brussels
COREPER	Comité des Représentants Permanents
CSCE	Conference on Security and Cooperation in Europe
CSU	Christlich-Soziale Union
DG	Directorate-General, European Commission
DGSE	Direction générale des services étrangers (Banque de France)
DM	deutsche mark
EC	European Community
ECB	European Central Bank
ECHA	European Commission Historical Archives, Brussels
ECJ	European Court of Justice
ECOFIN	EEC Council of Economics and Finance Ministers
ECSC	European Coal and Steel Community
ECU	European Currency Unit
EEC	European Economic Community
EIB	European Investment Bank
EMCF	European Monetary Cooperation Fund
EMS	European Monetary System
EMU	Economic and Monetary Union
EMUA	European Monetary Unit of Account

EPU	European Payments Union
EUA	European Unit of Account
FDP	Freie Demokratische Partei
FF	franc français
GNP	gross national product
HAEU	Historical Archives of the European Union, Florence
HSA	Helmut-Schmidt-Archiv
IMF	International Monetary Fund
LECE	European League for Economic Cooperation
MCA	monetary compensatory amount
MTA	Margaret Thatcher Archive
MTFA	medium-term financial assistance
NAI	The National Archives of Ireland, Dublin
PAAA	Das Politische Archiv des Auswärtigen Amtes, Berlin
PS	Parti socialiste
RPR	Rassemblement pour la République
SDR	Special Drawing Right
SGCI	Secrétariat général du Comité interministériel pour les questions de coopération économique européenne
SPD	Sozialdemokratische Partei Deutschlands
STMS	short-term monetary support
TNA	The National Archives, Kew
UA	unit of account
UCE	Unité de compte européenne
UCME	Unité de compte monétaire européenne
UDF	Union pour la démocratie française
UNICE	Union des industries de la Communauté européenne
ZBR	Zentralbankrat (Bundesbank)

Multilevel Governance, History, and Monetary Cooperation

> Since the Werner Plan a dozen years ago and since the days of the
> snake, since the founding of the EMS in particular, different bodies
> and groups have done enormous preparatory work for further mon-
> etary cooperation. This work resembles a hidden treasure: all the
> papers are written by monetary experts and for the use of monetary
> experts; they therefore hardly ever have reached the attention of the
> leaders or heads of state or government; in most cases they have not
> even been given full attention and full reading by finance ministers.
>
> —Helmut Schmidt

The creation of the European Monetary System (EMS) is traditionally considered one of the landmarks of postwar Western European history. Many textbooks stress that it was an example of how European elites coped with global
economic change. The advent of floating exchange rates, following the collapse of
the Bretton Woods system in the early 1970s, was harmful for Western European
economies, and the EMS constituted a European response. The EMS represented,
indeed, the first serious attempt at reintroducing a semifixed exchange rate system on a European basis. And most important, that European response would
have a strong influence on the economic and social policies of many participating European countries from 1979 onward. The EMS would be an external constraint—lauded or criticized—for the domestic economic policy choices of many
European governments. Further adding to the importance of the EMS, countless
European policymakers would present it as the first necessary step on the road
to economic and monetary union (EMU). The European Currency Unit (ECU),
the argument goes, was the forerunner of the euro. Though both of these asser-
tions are certainly debatable, they do hint at one of Western Europe's perennial
problems: the need to stabilize monetary relations in a geographical zone where
internal trade is intense. From the nineteenth-century Latin Monetary Union
to the present-day euro, organizing currency fluctuations within Europe has remained a central issue for European policymakers.

But the EMS was more than just an exchange rate system. The inception of the EMS was part of a wider trend toward the tentative affirmation of the European Economic Community (EEC) as an international actor amid the profound economic, political, institutional, and social transformations of the 1970s. The EEC, created in 1957, had specific competences, multiple levels of governance, and a record of diverse successes and failures. But in the course of the 1960s and '70s, it witnessed a steady enlargement of its sphere of influence. The EEC became a major international trade actor, set up diplomatic relations, and concluded a trade agreement with the People's Republic of China; the European Political Cooperation (EPC) process, created in 1970, attempted to give a single voice to the EEC in foreign policy, with many failures but one important success at the Conference on Security and Cooperation in Europe (CSCE) in 1975.[1] The emergence of the European Council, created in 1974, was itself a clear attempt to provide some form of European leadership.[2] In addition to the European Council, the EEC's complex political system was further developed with the first direct elections to the European Parliament in 1979.[3] Nonstate actors increasingly tried to lobby the EEC to support new policies or reform older ones, thereby showing that the EEC increasingly mattered in terms of public policy choices.[4] The successive enlargements (with the addition of Britain, Denmark, and Ireland in 1973; Greece in 1981; Portugal and Spain in 1986) further increased the size and importance of the EEC as a regional bloc.[5] And finally, a new generation of policymakers had progressively replaced those who had first created the new institutions of Western European cooperation after the Second World War, showing that the EEC was something more than just a short-lived experiment. If the story of European monetary cooperation in the 1970s was, in many ways, the story of a regional attempt to provide an answer to global problems, there were also other solutions. Social, regional, industrial, and development policies, and the institutionalization of summitry (the G7 and European Council), to name but a few, were part of a response to the dramatic challenges posed by the collapse of the Bretton Woods system, the oil shock, the global recession/stagflation, the Third World and emerging countries, and the ongoing cold war.[6] However imperfect and limited it was, the EEC of the 1970s was an affirmed polity, with a life of its own, more than a decade after its creation.

Among all these attempts, monetary cooperation was arguably both the most unsuccessful and the most pressing issue. Monetary fluctuations put at severe risk the key achievements of the EEC, namely, the common agricultural policy (CAP) and the common market. The creation of a European monetary identity would also consolidate the European polity. Some mechanism aimed at stabilizing monetary relations in the European Economic Community was therefore needed. The Werner Plan, an ambitious three-stage proposal for EMU put forward in 1970, suffered the breakdown of the Bretton Woods system and the advent of generalized floating, and was quickly abandoned. Monetary cooperation was in a paradoxical situation: its improvement was urgently necessary, but it appeared to be caught in an inextricable deadlock.

Yet this should not be taken to mean that further EEC monetary cooperation, let alone integration, was bound to happen. To the contrary, I will argue that if indeed a European polity was emerging, the central problematic was how a regional level of cooperation could fit into global developments. The historical reconstruction of the EMS creation invites us to show the alternatives that existed at the time. In other words, monetary relations did not respect the strict boundaries of the EEC. The snake—the first EEC exchange rate system, created in 1972—was not seen as an obvious instrument for EEC integration by all member states. Some saw it as merely an instrument of monetary policy stability, and were therefore quite keen to associate non-EEC member states with it. That an exchange rate system would become an instrument for furthering European integration per se was certainly not obvious in 1974, just when the first concrete attempt at EMU—the Werner Plan—had failed.

Deus ex Machina?

The conventional reading of the years 1974–1979, in terms of monetary cooperation in Europe, is well-known, and can be summarized briefly.[7] The Werner Plan was quickly abandoned and nothing happened until late 1977, when Roy Jenkins, president of the European Commission, had the controversial idea to call for a European monetary union in a famous speech in Florence. This revived the debate about EMU. West German Chancellor Helmut Schmidt, upset by the dollar's fall, then adopted this theme, and, once the French government had been reappointed following the March 1978 general elections, he presented his plan in close cooperation with his French counterpart, Valéry Giscard d'Estaing, at the Copenhagen European Council of April 1978. A few months later, French and German leaders set out the terms of the EMS in the so-called Bremen Annex attached to the conclusions of the July 1978 Bremen European Council. Negotiations over the details of the scheme lasted until the Brussels European Council in December of that same year, when the EMS was agreed on, and finally entered into force in March 1979 following a last-minute French obstruction coming from their request for reform of an obscure technical aspect of the CAP's functioning—the monetary compensatory amounts (MCAs). Compared to the snake, the EMS is usually interpreted as a considerably improved scheme with a major new technical device (the divergence indicator), the embryo of a future common currency (the European Currency Unit, or ECU), and the planned inception of a European Monetary Fund (EMF). Overall, the EMS appears a deus ex machina of European monetary cooperation: after years of stagnation, the EMS suddenly appeared and was intensely but swiftly negotiated. It provided an EEC answer to the so far intractable problem of monetary instability thanks to the intervention of the divine "fathers of Europe," who this time were Jenkins, Giscard, and Schmidt in place of Monnet, Schuman, and Adenauer.

There is some truth in that simplified story—and not all the EMS literature tells it in this way.[8] Yet each of these events, taken separately, deserves some nuance, and the most problematic element is the link among them. The underlying assumption of such periodization—that is, an almost exclusive focus on the creation of the EMS in 1978—is that the EMS negotiations alone form a coherent and autonomous whole. This is highly misleading in that it downplays the influence of other, mid- to long-term trends preceding and underlying the EMS creation, and it also tends to reinforce some sort of European integration mythology surrounding the EMS inception. This traditional reading therefore gives us a retrospective simplification of what had been an uncertain, protracted monetary cooperation, and thereby overestimates the originality of the EMS (earlier, ill-fated plans suggested similar ideas) and downplays the role of other actors and processes (notably transnational), as well as other motivations (notably those that cannot be reduced to "material interests"). The EMS in the history of European monetary cooperation of the mid- to late 1970s plays the role of the deus ex machina in Greek tragedy: a previously intractable problem is suddenly solved due to a divine intervention—but at the expense of the story's internal logic.

I focus, by contrast, on the internal logic of that story. By moving away from an exclusive focus on the EMS, I challenge a rather simplistic interpretation of its creation and shed new light on the wider trends in European monetary cooperation. A long period of brainstorming, from the collapse of the Bretton Woods system and the failure of the Werner Plan to the Schmidt Plan of early 1978, led to the emergence of several themes—policy against the dollar, symmetry of interventions, role of a currency unit in the exchange rate mechanism—that would return, in one form or another, in the EMS negotiations. The book is thus about the "hidden treasure" mentioned by Schmidt and why, how, and to what extent it had (or had not) reached the attention of European decision makers. I suggest that the peculiarity of European monetary cooperation between 1974 and 1979—and interest in the wider perspective of post-1945 international economic history—rests in the interweaving of transnational, intergovernmental, and supranational dimensions as well as the interaction among economic, political, political-psychological, and technical dimensions.

International History and European Integration History

The last decade has witnessed the refinement of methodological approaches to the history of European integration. Partly in reaction to the first writings on European integration by federalists, Alan Milward stressed the role of economic interests and national governments in his analysis of the origins and later development of the integration process.[9] Yet some scholars felt that two types of actors were missing in his analysis: supranational institutions (the European Commission in particular) and transnational actors (nonstate actors, political parties, formal and informal networks). Wolfram Kaiser, Ann-Christina Knudsen, and Piers Ludlow, among others, have—with different time frames and different topics—attempted to use a different methodology in order to make up for these shortcomings.[10] As Piers Ludlow's book on the EEC in the 1960s has shown, an approach such as supranational history can better trace the development of the EEC by taking into account the role of the Commission in particular, and the peculiar development of EEC institutions in general. Wolfram Kaiser has shown that transnational actors—transnational political parties and interest groups—influenced European decision making and should therefore not be overlooked. Furthermore, he argued that social science concepts should be taken into greater consideration in writing this history.[11] It has thus become increasingly fashionable in the last decade to assert that brand-new approaches are needed in the study of European integration. While this book does not deny the merits of these works and the significant contributions they have made, I aim to bring two important qualifications to this general methodological discourse.

It is, first of all, striking to note that historiographical developments in the area of European integration history largely happen without regard to the wider field of international (economic) history, to which I think this book belongs. Perhaps because this niche is at times too anglophone-centered, it is often overlooked that French and Italian historians have developed *l'histoire des relations internationales/la storia delle relazioni internazionali*, which, in reaction to diplomatic history, also aimed to go beyond the nation-state and include other actors (nongovernmental) and other dimensions (the so-called *forces profondes*: perceptions, economy, power, psychology, *mentalités*, and so forth).[12] In the case of European economic and monetary history, francophone and Italian historians have long stressed the importance of transnational networks and nongovernmental actors.[13] Even using social science concepts is certainly not an invention of the past decade, as the Annales School, from the 1920s and 1930s onward, attempted to improve cooperation not only between historians and sociologists or political scientists but also between geographers and anthropologists. This book tries to demonstrate that an application of these older methodologies still brings many rewards. It focuses on the European level of cooperation; many studies have so far focused on one member state's policy *toward* the EEC.[14] It also includes some of the debates that interested mostly economists and political scientists. It is of vital importance to bring in, for instance, the debate about optimum currency areas (OCAs) initiated by Robert Mundell—and thereby the question of economic convergence—in the discussion on European monetary cooperation.[15] Similarly, given that the creation of the EMS is an interesting case study about the policymaking of the emerging EEC polity, it appears also very important to include some political science debates—constructivism, systemic perspectives on US policy, neofunctionalism, liberal intergovernmentalism, and the notion of epistemic communities.

Second, and even more important, this book aims to show that study of transnational or supranational phenomena alone does not suffice to explain why some European states decided on further (monetary) cooperation. Recent advances stressing the role of supranational and transnational actors are welcome and needed. Yet an exclusive focus on these dimensions cannot provide a comprehensive answer to problems of multilevel governance. At times, as we will see, supranational institutions were impotent, informal nongovernmental networks irrelevant, or governments powerless—or just the opposite. It is an analysis of the *combination* of these strands that helps us understand the EMS story, not their compartmentalized, isolated study. In order to render a comprehensive picture of European discussions and decision making, research for this book has been carried out using eighteen archives in six countries, including Britain, France, Germany, Ireland, Italy, and the EEC.[16]

Combining Intergovernmental, Supranational, and Transnational Approaches

My central question is, how was a European consensus built regarding European monetary cooperation in a world of floating currencies? This book tries to break new ground by analyzing a story where *simultaneously* transnational, intergovernmental, and supranational phenomena mattered, and by explaining why, how, and to what extent attention shifted from one level to another. "Intergovernmental" refers to the cooperation between states at world or European level (be it bilateral or multilateral, as in the G7 or the European Council). "Transnational" refers to processes above and beyond the structures of the nation-state, the central idea being, as Badie and Smouts put it, "the bypassing of the state" (*le contournement de l'État*).[17] This typically means informal networks of academic economists in addition to a monetary elite not exclusively relying on its national allegiances but also reacting to various institutional logics, such as the EEC. "Supranational" refers to power transferred to a nonnational common authority (typically the European Commission, the European Court of Justice, or today's European Central Bank), this common authority having in turn exclusive or shared competence in certain policy areas. A key question of European monetary debates therefore relates to whether a central institution will have authority over EEC member states—who would thus lose part of their sovereignty.

One actor "belonging" to one of the three categories outlined above can also play a role in another. Hence the European Council could deal with supranational issues, like the CAP, for instance—an intergovernmental institution could have implications for Community affairs. A transnational nongovernmental actor (an academic economist, for instance) could suggest creating a supranational EEC institution in charge of monetary policy. An intergovernmental institution (the Bank for International Settlements, or BIS) could serve as a forum of socialization, of exchange of ideas, for a transnational monetary elite. Members of the supranational Commission could have transnational links (with academic economists, for instance), or be themselves part of both categories.

Rendering the complexity of European decision-making processes prevents me from delving into more specific issues linked to European monetary cooperation. Hence there is no space here to explore in detail the consequences of a potential break between the British and Irish pounds, to carry out an in-depth study of the perennial debate about the respective merits of fixed and flexible exchange rates, or to analyze the German Christian Democrats' opposition to the EMS. This book will nevertheless make the following arguments:

1. There was much more than simply a financial story at stake. Technical developments mattered, of course, but technicalities mattered economically *and* politically, in the sense that technical proposals—whether accepted or rejected—reflected the way in which European governments thought about European monetary cooperation and EMU. Technical suggestions were not politically innocent. Even more important, one of my central themes is the complex interlinkage between domestic politics, economic policy, international developments, institutional issues, economic thought, and even apparently remote topics such as defense issues and memory. Different policy areas all had an impact, of greater or lesser extent, on European monetary developments. Many historians have stressed the complexity of the history of international monetary relations and the

need to think of it in global, comprehensive terms.[18] Schmidt famously quipped that "monetary policy is (also) foreign policy."[19] This book is an attempt to reconstruct these complex interconnections, and thereby render the multifaceted nature of monetary issues.

2. Monetary stability is not an end in itself. Indeed, aiming to stabilize monetary fluctuations also had a lot to do with the *perception de puissance*, as Robert Frank put it.[20] Monetary issues—and their wider implications for economic and financial strength—are one of the elements of this perception, with respect both to each member state and to the EEC as a whole. For example, through the *perception de puissance* we can find an implicit (rather than explicit) link between the cold war and European monetary cooperation.

3. Discussing European monetary cooperation led the EEC to think about its own identity, not only in terms of image (the symbol of a single currency) but also in defining what it wanted to achieve (EMU), and to what extent its members were committed to it. This was in a sense comparable to the challenge posed by EEC enlargement in the 1960s. The parallel is striking, since in strict monetary terms, the crux of the problem in the 1970s was the *enlargement* of the snake. In addition, the story of monetary cooperation in the 1970s is a story of the fight by the Commission and some member states for the integration of the snake in an explicit *EEC* framework.

4. Monetary cooperation was not only a story of "material interests." It would be impoverishing to portray the European monetary story exclusively in terms of interests. "What is the interest of actor X in doing Y?" leads us to overlook many other significant factors like the influence of trust, ideas, or even sentiments (pro- or anti-Europeanism for instance). The attempts to improve European monetary cooperation often reactivated a sort of European integration mythology that cannot be reduced to interests.[21] The importance of trust (or mistrust) in politics is a case in point. Good examples can be found in the Giscard-Schmidt relationship (or the Schmidt-Carter relationship), the perception of the Barre government by the Germans, or the perception of Giscard by his EEC counterparts. Still, the Giscard-Schmidt friendship should not lead us to take for granted their agreement on all topics, even those where they claimed they had a common vision.[22] Quite often their agreement *de façade* hid differing interpretations that help explain the time it took to negotiate the EMS and the limited outcome of the negotiations.

5. The mid- to late 1970s provide a good example of learning among a transnationally connected monetary elite. These years were character-

ized by a fascinating circulation of monetary ideas that would remain on the European/EEC monetary agenda in the following decades. This transnational monetary elite was made up of networks both formal (Committee of Central Bank Governors, Monetary Committee, snake members meetings) and informal (Clappier-Schulmann-Couzens group; academic economists, notably around Robert Triffin). Central bankers and academic economists, and the extent to which they could be seen as epistemic communities (a transnational network of knowledge-based experts), will be of particular interest.[23] Their cohesion, their real intentional influence, their conscience as a group is uneven, as the following pages will show. Yet they provided crucial anchors for the volatile circulation of monetary ideas in the 1970s. This transnational transfer of ideas was not limited to Europe nor to political circles. It also went from the United States to Europe, and from academic to administrative and political circles (for example, monetarist ideas or the debate about the introduction of a parallel currency). The Monetary Committee and the Committee of Governors, as well as contacts between (monetary) officials outside these official channels, contributed to the slow formation of a common language among European monetary experts. In a period of crisis, the policy learning and common language slowly built between experts (particularly snake members) provide a basis on which they can lean, in an atmosphere of uncertainty. This transnational learning process was centripetal in that it resulted in the formation of a consensus around the core Bundesbank-led snake members; or, to put it differently, the periphery of non-snake members progressively (and with the exception of Britain) joined the central group of snake members.

6. This transnational learning process was protracted and tortuous, but continuous, and led to the rethinking of the motivations, aims, and scope of European monetary cooperation. The outcome was the setting up of the EMS. I stress in particular that the EMS was more the outcome of what was "in the air" already, rather than a sudden qualitative leap forward. Although the 1970s were years of stagnation and crisis, the decade was also a period when a new economic and monetary consensus began to emerge, which would influence later developments in the EEC. Regular references to the so-called economists versus monetarists debate have a heuristic value; they help us better map the place of the mid- to late 1970s in the wider history of European monetary cooperation.

7. The improvement of administrative and political cooperation, largely in reaction to the challenges posed to the nation-state, was a constant trend of the 1970s, and its impact goes well beyond a purely institutional story.

The fact that monetary cooperation remained on the EEC agenda was, for instance, facilitated by the European Council, which had become, over the second half of the 1970s, the most visible EEC agenda setter. The emergence of the European Council as a case study of the functioning of the EEC as an emerging polity is central to this book. The furthering of administrative cooperation happened at various levels: domestic (Barre's new weekly consultations with his administrations: Trésor, Budget, Prix); bilateral (Franco-German "mini-convergence" experiment from 1977 onward); EEC (European Council); international (G6/7). All these changes had deeper roots, yet they were all, to different extents, thought of as institutional cooperative answers to international economic and monetary challenges.

8. In more general terms, a clear distinction must be borne in mind, particularly in monetary affairs, between actual phenomena and their perception by the actors of the time. For instance, the preservation of EEC internal trade was often given as a motivation behind stabilizing EEC exchange rates. Yet as Otmar Emminger underlined, unstable exchange rates did not prevent EEC internal trade from continuing to grow.[24] Hence, the problem lay also in the *perception* that the erratic fluctuation of exchange rates would hinder trade rather than simply its actual wrongdoings. Similarly, there is an important difference between inflation *perceived* and *actual* inflation, as well as between an anti-inflationary economic policy and its perception as a credible policy. In a similar vein, I stress that the existence of pertinent policy solutions or economic models did not mean that decision makers would use them.

9. The story of European monetary cooperation in the mid- to late 1970s was not a one-way street. I challenge the view of a unitary process: there existed different ways to reach monetary stability in Europe, and the following pages explore how different strands of thinking developed in Europe in the 1970s. Alternative options included parallel currency, an "economist" approach, and a "monetarist" approach. The EMS option eventually managed to attract a consensus, in which only one EEC member state refused to take part. Furthermore, the views of each EEC government should not be seen as monolithic.

10. More generally, European monetary cooperation in the mid- to late 1970s was one of the European responses to international economic and monetary crisis. It should be considered in the wider history of globalization in the twentieth century. For instance, a parallel with the great interwar crisis should be kept in mind, although of course the nature of the problems was different. As Robert Boyce put it, "Midway through

the interwar period the international economic *and* the international political system simultaneously broke down."[25] Coincidence or not is the subject of intense debate, but the simultaneous occurrence of both crises, economic *and* political, marked decision makers for generations. The concurrent collapse of the Bretton Woods system, the oil crisis, stagflation, and the ongoing cold war provoked widespread fear that history might repeat itself and that Western liberal democracy might well collapse. Schmidt's constant stress that Western liberal democracy was vulnerable is an example, even though his fears were often considered exaggerated.[26]

European Monetary Cooperation in the 1970s

"European" here is Western European—excluding the countries under Soviet influence—but not exclusively the EEC.[27] My main focus is on the nine EEC members, but I do not ignore the position of or interest shown by non-EEC members, such as Switzerland. Most important, a central theme of this book relates to the nature of the EEC exchange rate mechanism, and whether it was—or was not—a *Community* instrument. What was often described as a Community exchange rate mechanism was managed by central bankers in meetings at the BIS in Basel, in Switzerland, and included only some EEC members. As in the field of technology, "European" did not necessarily equate with "EEC."[28] I focus on the European level of monetary cooperation, but other levels—domestic, bilateral, Community, continental European, and international—are important in the story. One of my central tasks is to depict a set of interlinked types of cooperation, shifting quickly from one level to another, from domestic politics to European finance ministers, central bankers, academic economists, and heads of government.[29] Finally, I note the impact of the newly created European Council. In December 1974, the European Council was created in order to tackle at heads-of-government level the problems of an interconnected world.[30] It was critical in the international monetary/economic/energy crisis of the 1970s. If it did not always reach remarkable decisions, it manifested, at the very least, the will of EEC member states to *attempt* cooperation within an EEC forum.

Money has three commonly accepted functions. It is a means of exchange, a unit of account, and a store of value. Consequently, *monetary* cooperation, particularly in the 1970s, means not only projects of EMU but also the (superficially) lower-key story of the European Unit of Account (EUA), born in 1950,[31] reformed in 1975, and renamed in 1978.[32] In more general terms, I draw particular attention to the meaning attributed to "monetary" questions. Talking about an EMU is *not* the same as devising an exchange rate mechanism. The former is much more ambitious than the latter. An EMU implies a common or single currency; it can mean the inception of some stabilization systems involving important resource transfers, or imply a high degree of financial harmonization and the development of a significant common budget. In other words, full EMU implies important transfers of sovereignty to a supranational body, a move that is very different from an intergovernmentally managed exchange rate mechanism. That many actors of the time used these expressions interchangeably should lead the historian to be careful. There were, moreover, alternative routes to further European monetary cooperation or to reach monetary stability: the discussion about economic reflation from surplus countries, the debate about the creation of a substitution account at the IMF to absorb dollar surpluses, plans for reaching a European monetary union all at once, plans advocating a step-by-step approach, a reform of the snake, or the creation of a parallel currency. All of these options were considered in the 1970s, which ended with the implementation of a further option, the creation of a "new" exchange rate mechanism akin to the snake. The story of European monetary cooperation in the 1970s was a slow realization that EMU was not achievable in the short run, that reform of the snake was not acceptable to snake members, and that a new system—the EMS—was needed. The extent to which the EMS was truly new will be a central question in chapters on the EMS negotiations. Finally, I stress that the stability of monetary relations and the type of exchange rate system (flexible or fixed) are separate issues. There is no necessary link between the stability of a monetary system and the fixity of exchange rates: "fixed" is not a synonym for "stable." A floating system might (or might not) prove stable—and looking for the fixity of exchange rates might (or might not) cause economic and monetary stability.

I prefer "cooperation" to "integration" inasmuch as the latter has now become a catchword for a complex and confusing set of ideas. "Integration" often implies the melding of competences into some sort of supranational body. The use of the word raises the issue of a teleological interpretation of European monetary developments—and of postwar European cooperation in more general terms. Mark Gilbert has recently delved into the narration of the "process" of European integration, often done with the underlying conception that "the institutions of the EU are the outcome of a historical process whereby national institutions are being superseded and replaced by supranational ones."[33] The EMS is a good case in point. Not only is the EMS traditionally seen as the only significant event of the mid- to late 1970s but its inception is presented in a progressive and determinist way. It is, for instance, a problematic shortcut to state, as Marie-Thérèse Bitsch does, that it was in monetary affairs that "the Community achieved the most striking progress."[34] This means first that it was *the Community* that did something (this is highly debatable), then that it was *a progress* (that the EMS was better than the snake also is debatable, as is the notion that further monetary cooperation or integration per se were desirable objectives),[35] and finally that it was *striking* (in mythological terms perhaps, but closer analysis does not necessarily leave such an impression).

In the wider perspective, the use of the word of "integration" is deeply problematic since we all know where the story ended: in the creation of the euro. We all know that many EEC/EU members have monetarily *integrated* themselves, simply because we witness it in our everyday life. Yet this should not lead us to conclude that the EMS was a necessary step on that road: alternative routes existed. As Gilbert puts it, such a "progressive conception has blinded authors to the possibility that alternative narratives of European integration are possible."[36] Hence, for instance, some people, particularly some academic economists, thought that the most promising way for further "integrating" "Europe" was the introduction of a parallel currency, not the progressive narrowing of fluctuation margins.

"Cooperation" by contrast, carries less teleological weight. It also characterizes much better the work of monetary experts in the 1970s. Richard Cooper identifies six degrees of central bank cooperation.[37] To sum up, the first is "simply to exchange information"; the second is "to standardise concepts and fill gaps of information"; the third is "to exchange views on how the world works and on objectives of central bank policy"; the fourth is "to share information on the economic outlook"; the fifth is a more sophisticated version of standardization than in the second, involving the consequence that "the data collected by different central banks can be directly compared, even added up"; and the sixth "and what many people think of as the sole form of cooperation, is commonly agreed actions." As I stress, cooperation does not only mean commonly agreed actions. An important dimension of cooperation, not confined to central banks, is more sociological: the progressive development of interpersonal trust, of a habit to work in concert, in a European framework.

Finally, the teleological interpretation is particularly risky for the 1970s. This was a time of economic and monetary uncertainty due to a new type of crisis, namely stagflation. This crisis undoubtedly had a logic, but its logic was not necessarily yet intelligible to the people living it. On many occasions, as we will see, European officials simply did not understand what was going on. A teleological interpretation risks interpreting events with the benefit of hindsight. Hence if it is true that the EMS is a European response to international economic and monetary problems, its inception was not obvious, and does not concern only one year, 1978, at the end of the decade.

What types of cooperation does "monetary cooperation" exactly entail? Money normally being the creation of a state, and monetary affairs being arguably the second-most-sensitive issue for a state after defense, monetary cooperation is centered on interstate relations.[38] European monetary cooperation asks the question of how to go *beyond* the nation-state. These relations involve various state actors (heads of government, finance ministers, central bankers) as well as non-state (academic economists), EEC, and international actors. It is noteworthy that the independence of a central bank from a government, as in the case of the Bundesbank, crucially changes decision-making roles, as I will show. Moreover, the existence of the EEC renders the nature of monetary cooperation more complex by introducing other levels, transnational and supranational. The book therefore centers on the constant interplays in this multilevel governance. If academic economists are part of the story, pressure groups and civil society during this period and for this topic were by and large deprived of influence, and it is therefore hoped that their absence is understandable.

EMU had been the EEC's major internal objective since 1969.[39] The early 1970s are already well covered in the historiography, and so I take spring 1974 as a starting point.[40] That moment was marked by the almost simultaneous coming to power of Harold Wilson in Britain, Giscard in France, and Schmidt in Germany, and is more generally the beginning of a new era after the breakdown of Bretton Woods and the oil shock. Other factors justify the choice of 1974. That year marked the almost official abandonment of the Werner Plan; it also saw the creation of the European Council, which significantly changed the EEC decision-making process. The book ends with the entry into force of the EMS in March 1979. By adopting a time frame that does not coincide with the EMS negotiations, the book in a sense confirms what Peter Ludlow cursorily suggested in the first detailed study of EMS negotiations: "It is, in fact, arguable that the EMS negotiations can only be properly understood if they are seen within the context of a longer-term trend towards the emergence of a European monetary bloc."[41] He probably meant a longer-term trend than five years. Yet it is very much the spirit of this book to place the EMS negotiations in the wider context of the 1970s, and particularly to conduct a detailed study of the post-Werner, pre-EMS attempts to further European monetary cooperation.

EUROPEAN MONETARY COOPERATION, 1945–1974
Background and Debates

> If the international monetary system was itself based on fixed exchange rates and on currency convertibility, the problem would have been much less acute. You know that there has been a historical coincidence between the progressive organization of economic and monetary union in Europe and the progressive dislocation of the international monetary system.
>
> —Valéry Giscard d'Estaing

This first chapter recalls several key ideas necessary to understand the working of monetary coordination. A first important one is the so-called triangle of compatibilities, or trilemma. According to Mundell, of the three components of his "holy trinity"—high capital mobility, fixed exchange rates, and independent monetary policy—only two can be met at the same time. For instance, under the Bretton Woods system, fixed exchange rates and autonomous monetary policies were able to coexist thanks to low levels of capital mobility. The rising of capital mobility from the late 1960s onward rendered unsustainable the maintaining of fixed exchange rates, and the Bretton Woods system collapsed. In the specific European case, this "trilemma" is of particular interest. Indeed, seeking fixed (or semifixed or adjustable) exchange rates means that either international capital mobility should be restrained, or that the autonomy of monetary policy should be surrendered. Even more interesting, as will be discussed in the next section on EEC law, it would seem theoretically logical to surrender monetary policy autonomy, since the freedom of capital mobility within the EEC is provided for in the Treaty of Rome.

A second important debate, also associated with Mundell, was that of optimum currency areas (OCAs). The start of the OCA debate is usually associated with the publication of Mundell's eponymous article in the early 1960s.[1] As its name suggests, the OCA debate is about determining in what area (group of countries) the use of a common currency would be optimum (that is, would not create any loss of well-being). Mundell listed a series of factors that identify such an area. Subsequently, other authors—Ronald McKinnon, Peter Kenen, James

Ingram, Gottfried Haberler, Marcus Fleming, Charles Kindleberger—added new
ones to the list. In a nutshell, the first two factors identified by Mundell were
the mobility of the factors of production (labor and capital) and the symmetry
of external shocks (i.e., the entire group must receive identical shocks). Other
factors added to these two are varied: McKinnon stressed the openness of the
economy, Kenen the diversification of production, Ingram the financial dimension, Haberler and Fleming the convergence of inflation rates, Kindleberger the
homogeneity of preferences within the zone.[2] To what extent Europe forms such
an OCA, then and now, is the subject of long and heated discussions. What the
OCA debate highlights, however, is the profound implications of a full monetary
union, in particular in fiscal and budgetary terms. As the Marjolin Report would
stress in March 1975, it is not certain that European policymakers, while talking
about the desirability of EMU, had realized its full implications.[3]

Underlining the uncertainties of the time, the mid-1970s also witnessed a re-
surgence of critiques about the economic idea of rational expectations and the
stability of theoretical macroeconomic relationships. The so-called Goodhart
Law in 1975 and the so-called Lucas Critique in 1976 are the most famous cases
in point.[4] Charles Goodhart, a chief economic adviser at the Bank of England,
pointed out that once an indicator is chosen as a policy target, it loses its validity
and reliability. In a similar vein, the economist Robert Lucas pointed out that
econometric models used to conceive future economic policies are built on past
behaviors, with the expectations that these past behaviors will repeat themselves
in the future. Lucas argued, however, that this premise is mistaken since economic
agents may well adapt their expectations in a new way and thereby undermine
the initial theoretical validity of the economic policy model being implemented.
Central bankers underlined their difficulty in choosing between these economic
theories. "Monetary policy is not a matter of dogma, be it Friedmanite, Keynesian, or Marxist; it is a matter of trying to understand the mechanisms and their
application to the conditions of the moment," explained Renaud de La Genière,
sous-gouverneur in the French central bank, in 1979.[5] Of course, other central
bankers might have had more clear-cut views. Yet, crucially, de La Genière's remark underscores the uneasy position of the central banker having to choose
among various, sometimes contradictory, monetary theories.

The variety of approaches to EMU reflected the academic divisions in economic and monetary theories. The most famous one is through the narrowing of exchange rates, examples of which can be found with the snake or the
EMS. Another option is that of currency competition, and in particular the
inception of a parallel currency. Nearly all those who defended this position,
as the next chapters will show, were academic economists. In early April 1974,
Robert Mundell argued, for instance, that the only antidote to current global

problems (inflationary pressures) "would be a further currency issued and managed by a regional political entity."[6] He argued that a new currency unit—the "Europa"—would need a political base, which Europe could provide. Similarly, in 1974, Giovanni Magnifico published a book tellingly entitled *L'Europe par la monnaie*.[7] He had earlier advocated the creation of a European Currency Unit (ECU).[8] These interpretations remained almost permanently confined to academic experts' circles, with the partial exception of the European Commission. The option of exchange rate unification was, by contrast, mostly associated with governments. It emerged most famously with the Werner Plan and the creation of the snake in 1972. Subsequently, one of the central underlying questions of European monetary discussions was whether this was a correct strategy.

As far as the method was concerned, there also existed different views. A first basic methodological difference lay in the strategy to be used: An incremental approach or a "big leap forward"?[9] The former implied progressive steps, such as harmonizing policies and narrowing exchange rates, while the latter implied more immediate steps, such as establishing a full monetary union or introducing a parallel currency. Most famously, the perennial dichotomy between the "economists" and the "monetarists" nurtured European monetary discussions from the 1960s onward. The economists believed that the convergence in the economic situation of the member states should come before monetary union. Economic strategies and performance would have to be harmonized and coincide before Europe could proceed to monetary union. Economic convergence meant lowering inflation rates, synchronizing economic cycles, and eliminating excessive debts and deficits. The economists could agree that the creation of a common currency was a significant and desirable objective, but they totally rejected the idea that it would be *the* dynamic element of the integration process. This was also referred to as the "coronation theory," in the sense that the locking of the exchange rate once and for all resembled the coronation of a king or a queen after a time of preparation.[10] By contrast, the monetarists claimed that monetary constraints could induce economic convergence. This is, of course, not to be confused with Milton Friedman's brand of monetarism. Monetarists believed that fixing exchange rates would itself cause macroeconomic convergence, and that as a consequence monetary unification would proceed sooner or later. Indeed, the need to maintain predetermined exchange rates would exert pressure on member states to make their own domestic economic policies compatible with the policies at Community level.[11] It would also have the advantage of focusing on the most salient, symbolic, and politically attractive aspect of EMU, namely, the creation of a common currency. This has also been referred to as the "Nike approach": "the best way to lock the exchange rate . . . was to 'just do it.'"[12] It is also called the "institutionalist" approach, since it could induce an increased development of common policies such as regional or budgetary.[13] A monetarist strategy would thus start by the narrowing of exchange rate fluctuation margins. Admittedly, the position of both camps was not always clear-cut. Since each strategy had some internal coherence, the lines between the two were sometimes somewhat blurred. And indeed, in order to reach a European consensus, proposals often had to reach a compromise between the two options. It is hence often said that the Werner Plan had managed to strike a good balance between the two approaches—its own strategy thus being dubbed the "parallel approach."[14] The failure to implement the second stage of the Werner Plan in 1974 thus meant the end of the economists versus monetarists cease-fire, as the next chapters will show. A good example of these methodological disputes can be found in the different interpretations of the meaning of the word "symmetry." At times, it means that surplus and deficit countries must share the burden of adjustment; but it is also used in a more ironic way, to mean that the richest must pay. An illustration of this can be found in the definitions David Marsh gives to the term. When used to describe the "Fourcade plan for 'greater symmetry,'" Marsh defines "symmetry" as "the French code word for reduced German influence."[15] But when he explains that "Britain and Italy would want 'symmetry' in the new system [the EMS]," "symmetry" is suddenly diplomatically defined as meaning that "deficit and surplus countries would be equally obliged to reduce balance of payments disequilibria."[16] "Symmetry," in the French, British, Italian, but also Irish cases, in fact meant both: a genuine and legitimate quest for a more balanced EEC economic and monetary development, but also an excuse aimed at hiding the inability to follow an economic and monetary policy consistent with European ambitions. With the perceived failure of the snake in the mid-1970s, the above-mentioned debates and dichotomies would be felt even more keenly during the next few years.

As far as monetary cooperation in the 1970s is concerned, the EEC institutional framework can be seen at three levels: the Finance Council, the specialized committees, and their alternates and groups of experts. The Council of Ministers of the EEC brings together, according to the topic tackled, the relevant ministers of each EEC member state. Of interest to us, therefore, is the Council of Ministers of Economics and Finance (hereafter, Finance Council), which met roughly once a month.

A second level concerns the specialized EEC committees.[17] Three of them are relevant: the Monetary Committee, the Committee of Governors, and the Economic Policy Committee. The Monetary Committee, enshrined by the Treaty of Rome (article 105) and set up on 4 June 1958, was the regular institution for weighing decisions in monetary affairs. It was composed of two members chosen by the Commission and two members nominated by each member state (one representative of the central bank, usually its "number two," and one representative of the Finance Ministry/Treasury). The Monetary Committee was therefore the place where the two institutions of the modern state dealing with monetary issues (central bank and finance ministry/treasury) regularly met up, in a specifically EEC framework. The Committee of Governors of the central banks of the EEC (hereafter, Committee of Governors) was created by a decision of the Council of Ministers on 13 April 1964. The central bank governor and an alternate (or two) took part in the meetings. The Committee of Governors included both snake and non-snake members. It met monthly in Basel at the Bank for International Settlements (BIS), which provided the Committee of Governors with its secretariat. The snake members also met separately to discuss snake matters. The Committee of Governors was therefore where snake *and* non-snake members socialized. Admittedly—and this does matter in a longer-term perspective—central banking cooperation has a much longer history starting in the 1920s. It has a history different from that of the EEC. Third, the Economic Policy Committee (whose acronym, EPC, should not be mixed up with another EPC, European Political Cooperation) was established by the Finance Council on 18 February 1974. It represented the fusion of three former committees (Short-Term Economic Policy Committee, Medium-Term Economic Policy Committee, and Budgetary Policy Committee). Its mission was to contribute to the coordination of short- and medium-term policies in the EEC. Its role is much less significant in monetary affairs, but since it was intended to improve coordination of the member states' economic policies, it cannot be overlooked. In particular, it would be central to the "concurrent studies" during EMS negotiations.

The third level concerns the alternates of the Monetary Committee and Committee of Governors, as well as their own specialized groups of experts. Cursory references to these groups will be made in the following pages. The main task of the alternates was to prepare the groundwork of their parent groups, while the expert groups carried out more technical work, often aimed at harmonizing the working methods of member states' monetary authorities, or to monitor financial developments. The alternates of the Monetary Committee shared the same makeup as its parent group, namely, one representative of each finance ministry and one representative of each central bank. The Monetary Committee had established two more specialized groups, the Working Party on Short-Term Capital Movements and the Working Party on Securities Markets. The Committee of Governors was similarly assisted by a Committee of alternates, and two specialized subcommittees, the Heyvaert Group (dealing more specifically, but not only, with exchange rate issues) and the Bastiaanse Group (aimed at harmonizing the intermediary objectives of monetary policy). More revealing was the inception in February 1974 of a group entitled "harmonisation of monetary policy instruments." The Monetary Committee and the Committee of Governors set it up jointly. The wording of its mandate was extremely careful, as, for example, in its second task: "The experts will detail the principal indicators and parameters that are used by the Member States when they formulate their monetary policy objectives. They will try to establish a common base for these indicators and parameters."[18] It was still clearly a child of the Werner Plan, as its seventh task showed: "The group will conduct its work in the light of the progressive achievement of economic and monetary union within the present decade, notably in order to indicate how far and at what rate the progress towards this union requires the harmonisation of monetary policy instruments." This was an early sign of the ongoing learning process in the EEC, which will be detailed in the next chapters.

Besides these institutions, a couple others will regularly appear in the following pages. The European Monetary Cooperation Fund (EMCF, but often known under its French acronym, FECOM) was set up in April 1973 as part of the Werner Plan. Among its main tasks was to narrow the EEC currencies' margins of fluctuation and to manage EEC monetary support. The question of its reinforcement and improvement regularly resurfaced in the second half of the 1970s. The European Investment Bank (EIB), also enshrined in the Rome Treaties, was set up in 1958. It financed, and still finances, a number of specific projects aimed at contributing to the balanced economic development of the EEC member states. It was to be central to the EMS "concurrent studies." Finally, it must also be remembered that the Commission had power of proposal and expertise in economic and monetary affairs thanks to the eponymous Directorate-General (DG) II. As the brief historical survey of pre-1974 monetary discussion will recall below, early initiatives in monetary affairs emanated from the Commission (Marjolin, Barre) and the institution was to carry on defending its expertise and leadership on these affairs, with varying degrees of success.[19]

On top of these three levels—Finance Council, specialized committees, and their alternates and groups of experts—in 1974 the European Council appeared. In an attempt to fill the EEC's leadership vacuum, the EEC heads of state and government decided to institutionalize the meetings of EEC heads of government to discuss EEC affairs.[20] Very soon after its inception, the European Council became an increasingly central institution in the EEC institutional setup, particularly with regard to economic and monetary affairs. In a decade dominated by economic issues, the regular meetings of EEC heads of government became the privileged forum where they could discuss these topics.

A final point that deserves careful attention is the legal basis of European monetary cooperation. The crucial importance of EEC law is here of course more implicit than explicit. There was no new regulation or directive imposing monetary cooperation. Nevertheless, the legal framework of the emerging EEC polity in which monetary discussions were taking place was increasingly binding and also had far-reaching, and sometimes unexpected, consequences. It therefore does matter that direct implementation of EEC law was confirmed and reinforced in the period we are looking at. That is not to say that—in contrast to the learning process idea—there was direct mention of it anywhere in the course of monetary discussions.[21] It is instead to argue that it lay somewhere in the background of EEC cooperation in more general terms, and that European decision makers would have to sooner or later cope with that dimension. A first important aspect lay in the continued affirmation of EEC law over national laws. The breakthrough of the *Van Gend en Loos* and *Costa v. ENEL* cases, in 1963 and 1964 respectively, was confirmed and expanded in the mid- to late 1970s.[22] The Van Duyn case of 12 December 1974 further confirmed this jurisprudence. The Court indeed recognized the direct effect not only of the provisions of the Treaties but also of the directives laid down for their application. And again in March 1978, the Simmenthal case further reinforced this jurisprudence. The Court recalled the implication of the direct applicability of EEC law, and added that national judges had the obligation to fully apply EEC law, by leaving unimplemented any contradictory disposition of a national law.[23] The Treaty of Rome is, however, famously silent on monetary cooperation.[24] The articles concerning monetary cooperation—103 through 109—were under the headings "Conjunctural Policy" and "Balance of Payments." As the headings suggest, the articles did not specifically evoke an exchange rate mechanism, let alone a monetary union. Instead, they confined themselves to economic and monetary consultation and other declarations of principles. More interesting—in particular with respect to Mundell's "trilemma"—the freedom of capital movements was one of the four freedoms, along with the free movement of persons, goods, and services, provided for in the Treaty of Rome.[25] The ultimate objective was the abolition of all restrictions and practices discriminatory to the freedom of capital movements within the EEC. Were this provision to be implemented, it would mean that member states would have to surrender the autonomy of their monetary policy, or the fixity of their exchange rates. Admittedly, however, the first steps toward the liberalization of capital movements had been timid. The complete liberalization of capital movements would indeed only be decided as part of the Single Market Programme in the second half of the 1980s.

The Search for Monetary Stability in Europe

European monetary cooperation has been a preoccupation of European governments since well before the 1969 Hague summit or the 1970 Werner Report.

Monetary cooperation in Europe indeed existed before the founding of the EEC, thereby underlining once more that Europe and the EEC are not necessarily interchangeable. The European Payments Union (EPU) had been created in 1950 by the Organisation for European Economic Cooperation (OEEC) in order to move from the bilateral trade patterns of the immediate post–Second World War period to a multilateral trade of peacetime reconstruction. It is noticeable that the first secretary general of the OEEC, Robert Marjolin, would have his name associated with later initiatives in the monetary field, not least with a report bearing his name.[26] Even before the EPU, and even before the Second World War, central bank cooperation had tentatively started in the 1920s, with the informal meetings between the governor of the Bank of England, Montagu Norman, and that of the Reichsbank, Hjalmar Schacht.[27]

Paradoxically, the issue of monetary cooperation had a relatively low profile in the early years of the EEC. It was only in the 1970s that this issue really gained prominence. As Loukas Tsoukalis argues, the history of the discussions about EMU can be divided into three principal phases.[28] The first phase, between 1958 and 1969, witnessed the emergence of ideas about monetary cooperation while the EEC was busy with other projects, such as the customs union or the CAP. The second phase extends from the December 1969 Hague conference until the summer of 1971 that was marked by the international monetary crisis. The first serious efforts at furthering monetary cooperation in Europe were then made, albeit unsuccessfully, partly because of an unpropitious international context. The third period stretches from 1971 until 1974. The creation of the snake was the landmark of this time.

The creation and implementation of the Common Market and the CAP dominated the first ten years of activity of the EEC.[29] Monetary cooperation was of course not entirely absent from the EEC's agenda.[30] As early as 1958, when he took up his post of commissioner in charge of economic and monetary affairs, Marjolin thus prioritized monetary cooperation. Yet there already existed a functioning international monetary system, that of Bretton Woods. In spite of its deficiencies, it provided sufficient monetary stability so that the quest for a regional zone of stability in Europe was not the most pressing issue.

The situation changed in the late 1960s, and the goal of monetary cooperation regained prominence. The Barre memoranda in 1968 and 1969 were aimed partly at resurrecting the discussions initiated by Marjolin a few years earlier but also at simply improving EEC economic and monetary coordination.[31] Indeed, various disturbances in the international monetary system took place. In 1969, the French government devalued the franc, and a few months later, the German government revalued the DM. This proved to be a first major test for the EEC's CAP. The CAP required policy action if intra-EEC exchange rates moved. Indeed, the prices of many agricultural products were fixed on the basis of a common unit, and this common unit was defined as the gold content of one US dollar.[32] In practice therefore, exchange rate changes endangered what was then the EEC centerpiece. Two years later, in August 1971, Nixon suspended the convertibility of the dollar and imposed a "temporary surcharge" on imported goods. He thus put a de facto end to the Bretton Woods system. In addition, the Yom Kippur War between Israel and neighboring Arab states in 1973, and the subsequent oil shock, pushed the Western world into recession and high inflation. Needless to say, this was an inauspicious backdrop.

At the end of the 1960s, the EEC had completed the customs union ahead of schedule and had established a CAP. It therefore not only seemed time for a further move forward, but more generally a new project seemed needed in order to maintain or recapture the élan of the first years of the EEC. In December 1969, the EEC member states met in The Hague and affirmed the wish to move forward to EMU while opening the EEC to three new members. They commissioned a group chaired by Pierre Werner to write a report, released in 1970. This report, known as the Werner Report, detailed how EMU could be attained in stages by 1980. The EEC member states initially endorsed the Werner Report, and the Finance Council embarked on the attainment of EMU by stages.

Implementing one of the measures intended to be part of the Werner Plan's first step—narrowing the fluctuation margins between EEC currencies—the EEC members decided in 1972 to create an exchange rate system dubbed "the snake." The system entered into force on 24 April 1972. The four EEC candidates took part in the snake negotiations and joined the scheme (and remained associated with it even if they did not enter the EEC, as, for example, Norway). Austria, Spain, Switzerland, and Sweden sooner or later expressed an interest in the snake, partly because of their strong commercial relationship with this monetary zone.[33] Sweden was the only country to formally ask for an association with the exchange rate system, while the other three maintained a de facto stable exchange rate relationship with the snake.[34] The only limitation for the non-EEC members was obviously that they could not benefit from EEC monetary support mechanisms. Their association took the form of bilateral agreements with each and every snake central bank. Fluctuations between currencies were restricted to a certain limit (2.25%) by intervening on the currency market. For a short period, the snake undulated in a dollar tunnel. Indeed, between 1972 and generalized floating in 1973, the snake currencies respected established bands of fluctuation vis-à-vis the dollar (4.5%). Over time, however, the overall snake system became a DM zone since the British pound, the French franc, and the Italian lira quickly fell out.

The Werner Plan's overall implementation quickly ran into difficulties, principally because the plan implicitly relied on a functioning Bretton Woods system—which was collapsing at precisely the time the Plan's first stage was being implemented. The Werner Plan, its goal and its method, would, however, continue to haunt European monetary cooperation in the second half of the 1970s, as the following chapters will show.

European Disintegration?

Beyond monetary issues, a more general sense of crisis dominated the EEC in 1974. Concerned that the very existence of the Community was endangered by the economic and monetary crisis, the Commission published an "*appel solennel*" to the EEC heads of government and, through them, to "all Europeans," on 31 January 1974.[35] In May, Giscard warned against the "dislocation of Europe."[36] At their first meeting in June, Giscard and Schmidt stated that their first priority for Europe was "to maintain all the *acquis* of European integration and to call a halt to the ongoing process of weakening."[37] This crisis had two main general aspects: political and institutional on the one hand, economic and monetary on the other.

The inefficiency of the Council of Ministers was the first of these institutional problems. To be sure, this was a long-standing complaint originating in the 1960s.[38] Giscard and Schmidt raised similar issues during the informal dinner between the EEC heads of government held in Paris on 14 September.[39] Seeking to fill this lack of leadership, and to resolve these institutional problems, EEC leaders decided, in December 1974, to meet three to four times a year, in a "European Council."[40] Besides these institutional issues, the solidarity of the EEC member states was called into question. Beyond the almost traditional economic nationalism that regularly appears in times of economic crisis, each EEC member state had a different agenda regarding European integration in late 1974. The British government clearly posed the most pressing problem for the EEC—the expression *l'hypothèque britannique* even reappeared.[41] The Italian government, as well as the Irish and Dutch, focused on regional policy.[42] The German government pointed to the problem of energy,[43] while the Benelux governments wanted to address the question of the direct election of the European Parliament, and naturally did not favor institutional developments in an intergovernmental fashion.[44] This state of disarray was further reflected by the reappearance of the "two-speed Europe" theme. Willy Brandt, for example, argued that the EEC needed a policy of gradual integration. This debate about a two-speed EEC would come back with the discussion of the Tindemans Report.[45] Brandt suggested that the member states that were faring well economically would integrate further and sooner, while other countries, given their less positive situation, would take part in integration at varying degrees.[46] Although this in fact described an already existing situation—such as the snake—it provoked numerous objections of principle.[47]

Interlinked with this political-institutional disarray, the economic and monetary crisis was the second important dimension of the EEC's problems in 1974. Following the collapse of the Bretton Woods system and the start of the oil crisis, a deep economic crisis developed, with inflation and growing unemployment. The occurrence of these two phenomena together—inflation and recession—was particularly worrying since these two had never been simultaneously experienced so far—and, as Schmidt put it, were not dealt with in economic textbooks.[48] The economies of the EEC member states were drifting apart, to such an extent that many feared—member states and Commission alike—the disintegration of the EEC itself.[49] Some limited or unsuccessful efforts were made in order to overcome this gloomy situation. The EEC did attempt to solve its two main problems, namely, the economic divergence of its member states and monetary turbulence. As for the latter, the Finance Council agreed in principle to the text of a resolution on the implementation of the second stage of the Werner Plan on 17 December 1973.[50] This second stage was meant to start on 1 January 1974. A few points were still to be rewritten, however, before the eventual adoption of the text settling this second stage. The only actual achievement concerned the first aspect, namely, economic coordination. The Finance Council indeed adopted a directive on economic convergence on 18 February 1974. As mentioned above, this directive notably created the EPC and called for further coordination of economic policies.[51] Overall, however, the member states failed to agree on how to proceed to the Werner Plan's second stage, and its implementation thereby was unofficially abandoned.[52] In addition, numerous obstacles appeared on the road to monetary union in early 1974. First and foremost, the snake had lost many of its members. Britain and Ireland left in 1972, Italy in 1973, and France in January 1974.[53] The remaining snake was therefore a large DM zone, and it did not leave much hope for the future of European monetary cooperation. As the American Embassy in Paris reported, the spirit itself of European monetary cooperation seemed to be hit.[54] Second, the British government openly called into question EMU at the Council of Ministers on 1 April for the objective (1980) was too early and the modalities (fixed exchange rates) were too strict.[55] Third, and more generally, the above-mentioned issues—institutional deadlock, diverging economic situations, the economists versus monetarists debate—represented further obstacles on the road to EMU.

If the warnings about the dangers of an EEC collapse were numerous, calls for action were no less so. Precisely because of this state of disarray, requests for new initiatives multiplied—even if the content of such requests was often not detailed.[56] A head of unit in the DG II of the Commission, Jean-Claude Morel, thus personally supported the idea of the creation of a European monetary asset—dubbed "Europa."[57] Giscard, then French Finance Minister, and the French Treasury were reported to be envisaging alternative forms of snake in March 1974.[58] EEC and member state officials were not alone in calling for a European reaction. Academic economists did so as well. Robert Triffin, long-standing advocate of European monetary integration, and long-standing critic of the Bretton Woods system, had already called for such a reaction well before 1974. Already in 1972, he argued that the EEC should "define *as a matter of emergency* a European monetary organisation capable of preserving its very existence."[59] His final objective was the institution of a stable constellation of intra-Community exchange rates, allowing only limited fluctuations within margins intended to be gradually narrowed until their total suppression.[60]

If most people agreed on the diagnosis—European integration was threatened by economic and monetary turbulences—and on the need to do something, a further question appeared: at which level should action be directed? Indeed, since the problems were not European in origin, it was not obvious that the best level of action would be the EEC. Furthermore, was it more sensible to act through the EEC (institutionally blocked) or at the international level, where it would be even more difficult and take longer to find a solution? The Quai d'Orsay thus noted the "Atlantic vision" of Bonn and London, leading them to look for global solutions with the United States rather than Europe-centered ones.[61] Considering the urgency of the situation within the EEC, the Quai d'Orsay argued that the issue was "to affirm the existence of a European monetary personality and to bring the most efficient contribution possible to the sorting out of the international monetary system."[62]

New Leaders, New Trust?

In spite of this gloomy context, the almost simultaneous coming to power of two rather pro-European leaders gave birth to new hopes of advances in European integration, if not simply of new trust in EEC affairs, and, still more important, to a renewal of the Franco-German entente. True, Harold Wilson's return to power in Britain in February 1974 was not promising for the EEC, since the Labour Party manifesto for the general election had pledged a renegotiation of Britain's accession agreement. In May, however, Willy Brandt left power and Helmut Schmidt replaced him. That same month, in France, Valéry Giscard d'Estaing was elected president of the Republic after the sudden death of Georges Pompidou. In the French case, it is particularly striking that economic and monetary experts close to Giscard had taken the main posts.[63] The new economic and finance minister, Jean-Pierre Fourcade, was known to be close to the new president; the new holder of the Treasury, Jacques de Larosière, was a former head of cabinet of Giscard at the rue de Rivoli; Bernard Clappier, closer to Giscard, replaced Olivier Wormser as governor of the Banque de France in 1974. The situation would be even more striking in 1976 when Raymond Barre, a university professor in economics, was appointed both prime minister and minister of economics and finance. All this should not be overestimated, of course. The strong emphasis of this new administration on economic and monetary affairs did not mean from the outset that a monetary plan would necessarily be designed in the next year. But this did show, however, a propensity to act in a certain fashion, and this right from the beginning of Giscard's *septennat*. This was particularly important in a system where, in contrast with other EEC member states, the real power, particularly in the case of foreign policy, lay in the hands of the Élysée not the Foreign Ministry.[64]

Another important dimension was Schmidt's and Giscard's personal expertise in financial and monetary issues. This started well before their ministerial careers, since Schmidt wrote his *Diplomarbeit* in the late 1940s comparing German and Japanese monetary reforms after the Second World War, and Giscard's father had published a book on the economic unification of Europe in the early 1950s.[65] Of course, this is not to suggest that writing a master's thesis on monetary reform or having a father who wrote about the monetary unification of Europe would necessarily lead them to search for monetary integration in Europe twenty or thirty years later. Rather, it gives a good idea of their intellectual formation— their "*outillage mental,*" as Lucien Febvre put it—or their personal interests.[66] The effect of this specific interest was well captured by Jenkins in his account of a meeting with Giscard in 1978:

> Giscard rather impressively received us two minutes ahead of time, and we talked for about an hour and a half. It was one of the best conversations I have had with him. . . . We went on to monetary arrangements in Europe, in which Giscard was extremely hard and firm and clearly determined to go ahead. The curious effect of this was that, perhaps because he was more interested, because we were discussing something more closely, interrupting each other a good deal, he became, if anything, rather smaller, less like a would-be Louis XIV, or even General de Gaulle, and more as I remember him as a Finance Minister; less making pronouncements as a head of state, more discussing a real subject.[67]

In more concrete terms, Giscard, and to a lesser extent Schmidt and Barre, had a natural inclination toward fixed exchange rates system over flexible ones. In describing Giscard's monetary ideas, the French Treasury considered that Giscard "was thinking of the creation of islands of monetary stability centred on leading currencies, which would provide the way back to an eventual system based on par values."[68] It is also important to note that for both Giscard and Schmidt, monetary problems largely belonged to politics. Giscard thus declared at the IMF that "the monetary problem must be situated at its level, which is that of politics," while Schmidt repeatedly said that monetary policy was foreign policy.[69]

With Giscard's arrival in office, a new trust seemed to appear in EEC affairs, as his election marked the end of la République gaullienne. Giscard had been elected on the motto "libéral, centriste, et européen." France's EEC partners could therefore hope that the French government would be more flexible and open-minded in European affairs. This sense of new trust was confirmed during the preparation of the 1974 Paris summit. As Émile Noël recognized, the informal dinner held in Paris on 14 September had one main objective: to establish "a climate of greater mutual trust."[70] Compared to the atmosphere of the 1960s, this was certainly not the least important change.

Almost immediately after taking office, Giscard and Schmidt made public their good personal relationship, thereby confirming the return of a strong Franco-German axis, in particular in EEC affairs. The Franco-German partnership, reinforced by the personalities and the personal entente of the two national leaders, was also strategically a logical answer to the replacement of Heath by Wilson. Since Wilson was not likely to adopt a pro-European stance, Giscard and especially Schmidt were not tempted to see in the new British prime minister a natural partner, or the third member of a would-be troika. On the contrary, this replacement showed clearly to Giscard and Schmidt that they alone could exercise European leadership. In diplomatic words, this meant that Franco-German cooperation was the natural basis of European integration.[71] Giscard and Schmidt met in Paris on 1 June, in the framework of the Élysée Treaty, in order to have a general discussion about Europe.[72] It helped to observe that the French and German governments shared, generally speaking, a common view on European problems, that greater economic stability should be attained. All this did not bring about concrete decisions, but it did show, beyond the conventional diplomatic discourse, a good entente, and a willingness to take coordinated initiatives. The importance of a close Franco-German partnership was made plain by Schmidt to François-Xavier Ortoli already in June 1974.[73] The feeling that, given the international and European economic and political crisis, any Franco-German initiative would be welcomed, and was likely to succeed, further reinforced it.[74] Economic and monetary affairs in particular were likely to be at the center of new initiatives. Giscard had said as much as early as May, shortly after both he and Schmidt had taken office.[75] The central issue that such an initiative would have to deal with, however, was how to carry it out. The implementation of the Werner Plan having failed, what type of new step could any European government hope to take? Should it revise the method employed? Or should it instead modify the objective (EMU by 1980, EMU at all)? Was the snake the most viable instrument to advance European monetary cooperation, or should one be looking for some other, more efficient, form of monetary cooperation? In the following chapters I will explore how the Western European governments and the EEC itself tried to cope with these difficulties and move on after the failure of the Werner Plan, starting with the 1974–1975 initiative of the French government.

SHIFTING AWAY FROM THE WERNER APPROACH, MAY 1974–MAY 1975

Until 1975, the European Community, which was nearing its twentieth anniversary, still did not have any monetary identity.

—Jean-Yves Haberer

The agreement that the heads of government meet regularly in the future, but in particular the idea, which has now settled in the heads of nine governments, of the necessity for parallel, better articulated, complementary orientations of their respective economic policies, is an indisputable step forward, with which one must confront incorrigible pessimists.

—Helmut Schmidt

Despite the snake's failures and the abandonment of the Werner Plan, monetary discussions did not stop in 1974. On the contrary, that year saw the multiplication of initiatives in the monetary field. This chapter examines the extent to which the partial buildup of consensus about the need for action at the European level and about the need to adopt stability-oriented economic policies permitted the Nine to take several steps forward in European monetary affairs. I will first describe the context in which these various proposals appeared. Second, I will analyze in detail the parallel attempts of the Commission and, crucially, the French government, to set out an improved version of the EEC exchange rate system. Third, I will scrutinize the second attempt of the French government to achieve such reforms following the reentry of the French franc in the snake. Taken together, the three parts of this chapter illustrate how, though they failed for the most part, these proposals—and the Fourcade memorandum in particular—introduced at an EEC level a whole set of issues that would remain on its agenda for years to come.

A Partial Consensus

From the very beginning of their new political mandates, Schmidt and Giscard did not hesitate to make known their close understanding. Whether it was a close friendship or not, the fact that they apparently shared views on various problems gave the impression that they had come to an agreement regarding the need to pursue stability-oriented economic policies.

An Agreement on Stability-Oriented Economic Policies

While the preference of the German government for such economic policies was not a novelty, the French government's decision to prioritize the fight against inflation was more of a surprise. On 12 June 1974, Jean-Pierre Fourcade, French minister of economics and finance, announced an ambitious "cooling-off plan."[1] It included, among other things, an income tax surcharge, a tightening of credit, an increase of savings interest rates, and various energy-saving measures. Fourcade hoped to bring the French inflation rate down to 1 percent per month—an ambitious goal since it was currently at 1.5 percent per month. The plan was backed by the French government's clear and unequivocal political discourse both at home and abroad. During the July 1974 Franco-German consultations held in the framework of the Élysée Treaty, Giscard even made ironical reference to the previous stop-and-go practices of the French government, and how they contrasted with the newly determined policy.[2] The times had changed, inflation was the enemy, and the French government was officially following the German model. Franco-German agreement on the fight against inflation was described as "the most important result" of the meeting.[3] Schmidt himself stated that he was "very satisfied" with the French anti-inflationary measures of July 1974, as much as he was reassured by the series of Italian measures against inflation.[4] The German chancellor even hoped that Giscard would put France on the road to economic stabilization within the next six months.[5] By contrast, it was not really surprising to see the German government prioritizing the fight against inflation. In this case also political discourse was very strong, but it merely confirmed a long-standing economic preference, as Schmidt stressed in his reaction to the Italian prime minister's announcement of his new stability-oriented policy.[6] Even when faced with the increasing demand from the left of the SPD for more Keynesian policies, Schmidt maintained the focus of his economic policy on stabilization.[7]

Monetary Initiatives as an Answer to the Crises

A new climate of greater economic convergence, both in words and in deeds (but not yet totally in outcome), had thus progressively developed in the EEC over the summer of 1974. Since the EEC member state so far best weathering the international economic crisis was also the chief defender of the "economist" approach to European monetary cooperation, the convergence of economic policy beliefs presented above was likely to open the door for new monetary initiatives. Schmidt constantly told his European partners that economic convergence was a precondition to monetary integration.[8] The Finance Council of 15 July 1974 confirmed this impression that a new Europe-wide consensus had been born.[9] In suggesting to his colleagues that a list of objectives should be drawn up on how to make progress on the road to EMU, Fourcade picked as the first one the need to reach better results for the harmonization of economic policies so as to be able to envisage a greater consultation of exchange rate policies. Economic convergence was therefore seen as a precondition to further monetary cooperation. This was not an insignificant step in the evolution of French thinking on the subject. The French government's conversion to the fight against inflation was all the more important since it was presiding over the Council for the second half of 1974. The French government was indeed willing to use the opportunity of its presidency to take new initiatives at the European level. Not only Giscard but also Jacques de Larosière, head of the French Treasury, made statements to that effect.[10] The details of this initiative will be the subject of the next section.

The atmosphere in Brussels also seemed propitious for action. The confederation of European business (Union des Industries de la Communauté européenne) and the European League for Economic Cooperation (ELEC) openly defended the idea of a European (monetary) relaunch. The UNICE worried about the current situation of the EEC, and called for concerted actions, especially in the economic and monetary field.[11] However, it limited its proposal to the control of parities at the international and EEC level. But the last sentence of the communiqué called for implementation of the decisions taken at the Copenhagen and Paris summits—in other words, reference was made to the ambitious "EMU by 1980" target. On 13 May, the ELEC issued a "monetary resolution" similarly encouraging EMU.[12] If it blamed external conditions for having complicated the process of EMU, the League especially accused "the lack of political will on the part of its Member States." It first proposed general economic measures: to grant the Commission a prior right of judgment as to the compatibility of national economic policy measures with the EEC interest; to improve communication and cooperation between EEC countries maintaining the snake; and to create an EEC system for financing balance of payments deficits resulting from the increase in the prices of oil and raw materials. Then it advanced more concrete and ambitious monetary measures, among which was the pooling of reserves. Similarly, the rapporteur for EMU at the European Parliament, Brandon Rhys Williams, wrote a report on EMU on 22 May 1974, showing that the European Parliament also kept an interest in the subject.[13] Of course, the impact of these three initiatives should not be overestimated. The European Parliament, in particular, had no direct means of action on the EEC economic and monetary decision-making system. They do show, however, that the will of the French government to act in the monetary sphere was not isolated.

A COMMISSION INITIATIVE

Of still greater significance was a number of declarations from the Commission itself seeming to indicate a readiness to take new measures in the monetary field. Already in February, the president of the Commission, together with the president of the Council, had encouraged the search for ways not only to consolidate the snake but also to bridge the snake with other floating currencies.[14] In May, the Committee of Governors adopted a resolution calling for a strengthening of the coordination of the central banks' monetary and credit policies.[15] In parallel, the Committee of Governors adopted a decision aimed at improving the information exchanged in the framework of the coordination of central banks' monetary policies—information that was so far fragmentary, according to the Governors.[16] Even more important, the Commission presented on 5 June 1974 a communication to the Council titled "urgent measures in economic and monetary affairs."[17] The Commission identified four areas in which action should be taken: the fight against inflation, international economic and monetary cooperation, balance of payments deficits, and the inception of a system of joint floating for the EEC currencies floating freely and for those belonging to the snake. Such a system would allow, the Commission argued, better coordination of efforts regarding monetary policy, interest rates, and capital movements.

The list of symptoms and cures outlined by the Commission was quite traditional, and perceived as such by EEC member states.[18] The plan of the Commission was also very vague, since it only gave a few hints at possible solutions, without detailing them further. The Commission, however, managed to reaffirm its expertise in economic and especially monetary issues. Even though this communication was not implemented, it did show that the Commission was willing to provide some leadership on this type of issue. Incidentally, the Commission tended to adopt a "monetarist" approach to European monetary cooperation, by focusing on monetary arrangements in order to reach EMU. Naturally, the Commission also insisted on economic convergence. But it actually suggested starting to improve the snake even before actual convergence had been achieved. This tendency was confirmed a few months later, when Ortoli stated that "despite the crisis, the continuing existence of what is known as the little snake . . . testifies to the usefulness of a mechanism that, by the imposition of monetary discipline, implies economic discipline as regards credit, of course, but also budgetary matters of taxation."[19] It was doubtful, however, that monetary discipline implied economic convergence, as Ortoli put it, since the French franc had pulled out of the snake earlier in the year precisely because the French government was not yet ready to adopt a stability-oriented economic policy.

THE BIRTH OF THE ECU

The interest of the Commission in the improvement of the European Unit of Account also was a good indicator of its monetarist thinking. Ortoli proposed, for instance, the creation of "a new monetary unit, which we could call the ECU, as the Latin countries would quickly be familiar with this now defunct continental currency, while the Anglo-Saxons would be happy to see the English initials of the 'European Common Unit' for the common European currency."[20] With the benefit of hindsight, it is of course amusing to see this acronym naively put forward by the Commission president. Though Ortoli seems to have been the first to make a conscious and explicit parallel between the ECU acronym and the old French currency, this acronym did not first appear in Ortoli's speech, nor was it a sudden bright inspiration of Giscard in Bremen.[21] It was, in fact, regularly mentioned in financial circles at least since the early 1970s. On 20 November 1970, the European Coal and Steel Community (ECSC) announced that it planned to issue loans denominated in "European Currency Units" (also with the acronym ECU).[22] This was a unit of account equal to the US dollar at its then parity, and composed of all EEC currencies (but with no gold value). It was alternatively (and indifferently) called "European Monetary Unit."[23] In mid-1971, too, the British Gas Council envisaged ECU (also meaning "European Currency Unit") loans.[24] ECUs again comprised the national currencies of the EEC members. One of the main advantages of the operation, the argument went, was that under current market conditions, the coupon for an issue in ECUs would be cheaper than for a similar issue in dollars or D-marks. The Rothschild & Sons Investment Bank also used various acronyms and composite currency schemes in the early 1970s. It suggested, on 2 August 1971, the creation of "a new unit 'CECU,' or Composite European Currency Unit." The acronym ECU, referring to the ECSC loans, appeared earlier in the letter. This unit amounted to "a fixed number of units of each of the selected currencies."[25] The Rothschild Bank even explicitly suggested that the CECU "might be described as a putative EEC currency." On 16 May 1973 it suggested the same idea, but this time dubbed the composite European currency a "Euro-Unit."[26] A few days later, Rothschild & Sons had already redubbed the composite unit—but the principle of its composition remained the same, that is, "a 'basket' of European currencies, comprising fixed amounts of the currencies of each of the nine members of the European Economic Community"—which became the Eurco ("European Composite Unit").[27]

The same is true for the technical dimension of the ECU (and even the future EUA adopted in April 1975). A composite unit of account—that is, a unit based on a weighted basket of EEC currencies—had already been considered and implemented at least since the early 1970s by some private banks as well as the EIB. A group of European banks (Barclays Bank International Ltd., Algemene Bank Nederland N.V., Banca Nazionale del Lavoro, Banque de Bruxelles, Banque Nationale de Paris, Bayerische Hypotheken und Wechselbank A.G., Dresdner Bank, Österreichische Landerbank) also considered "possibilities of promoting a European Monetary Unit, to be used as a monetary reference or index for the purpose of expressing prices of goods and services in commercial contracts."[28] The unit to be used was the Eurco, "which is the one drawn up for the planned European Investment Bank Bond Issue." The EIB eventually issued its first bond in Eurco in September 1973; the second one was in January 1974.[29] Similarly, in late 1973 and early 1974, the composite "B-Unit" was being researched and outlined by the International Money Management section of Barclays Bank International.[30] The real impact of these schemes is difficult to assess, however. A Bank of England official sensibly commented on these schemes that

> The Euro-Unit is an ingenious variation on the theme of multi-currency/unit of account issues; . . . potential subscribers must by now be fairly well sated with the number and variety of schemes of this sort which have been evolved. . . . It would seem wise not to raise exaggerated hopes for the Euro-Unit as the solution to the current antipathy to dollar-denominated bonds. . . . It is a pity that the houses concerned do not coordinate their ideas.[31]

Hence, if there was indeed an emerging European monetary identity, this very identity was still fragile, and emanating so far mainly from private banks, not from governments.

This observation about the unit of account's acronym leads logically to another potential feature of this unit, namely, its development into a parallel currency. Some academic economists regularly argued for such a case. The so-called Kiel Report, conceived under the auspices of the Kiel Institut für Weltwirtschaft, issued on 5 December 1974, was a case in point.[32] The central idea of this report, written by Alec Cairncross, Herbert Giersch, Alexandre Lamfalussy, Giuseppe Petrilli, and Pierre Uri, was to create a unit of account and composite currency that would be "a complement to, rather than . . . a substitute for, existing European currencies. . . . A new currency, the 'europa,' might be issued to circulate side by side with the currencies of member countries and gradually replace them as it came to be seen as a more convenient unit of account and store of value."[33] Giersch, one of the authors of the Kiel Report, who also participated in the Marjolin Group, reiterated this proposal in March 1975 in the individual contributions attached to the Marjolin Report.[34] Giersch further suggested the creation of an "exchange-equalization account." "An exchange-equalisation account," he wrote, "would absorb foreign currencies when money flowed in and would sell foreign currencies when people sought to make withdrawals. The account would hold a portfolio of currencies, including the currencies of member countries. According to whether it was faced with an inflow or outflow, it would switch its portfolio so as to make available the currencies in demand at a fairly steady price, at the same time taking up into its portfolio the currencies on offer."[35] Interestingly, this idea echoes in many respects the Witteven-de Larosière proposal for an IMF substitution account.[36] In the following pages we will see that this idea of a parallel currency supported by academic economists regularly resurfaced, but still with limited actual influence.

THE FOURCADE MEMORANDUM: *LA RELANCE MONÉTAIRE EUROPÉENNE*

Regarding monetary affairs, however, the most important initiative was to come from Paris.[37] The attitude of the French government concerning a European monetary relaunch was paradoxical: the desire for such a relaunch was unequivocal, but its timing, its coherence, and its scope were fairly vague, at least at the beginning. Despite the fact that Fourcade announced on 15 July that the franc would remain outside the snake, and although he observed that the member states' economies were too divergent to allow a narrowing of exchange rates, he declared on the same day that France was determined to carry out with its partners all the necessary studies to progressively reach a greater stability of exchange rates within the EEC. This was an important policy statement since less than a month before, in his departing speech, Olivier Wormser, then governor of the Banque de France, explicitly talked of a failure of his mission as *gardien du franc* before the conseil général of the French central bank, because he had been unable to contain the high French inflation rate.[38] Yet in spite of these difficulties, Fourcade supported a reform of the current functioning of the snake.[39]

This declaration was evidence of wider reflection on this topic within the French Finance Ministry as well as in the Banca d'Italia. Earlier in August, Jacques de Larosière had identified two causes that rendered even more difficult the European enterprise, namely, the generalization of floating exchange rates and the ill adaptation of the snake to international monetary problems.[40] This did not mean that the endeavor should be abandoned, however. For the future of European integration in general, de Larosière argued, progress in monetary cooperation was needed. Indeed, monetary disorder put at risk what had been gained in other fields, as, for instance, the free movement of goods. Moreover, since it was the French government that, in Europe, insisted most on monetary unification, its current passivity could be interpreted as a meaning that, given the difficulties, it was distancing itself from the project—or even that it had completely changed its mind.

The French Treasury identified three major types of obstacles—political, economic, and institutional—on the road to monetary integration. The political obstacle was the independence of the member states: monetary integration requiring various transfers of resources or creation of common institutions implied, in turn, loss of sovereignty. De Larosière of course concluded that there was not much to do about this matter, apart from not ignoring these important implications. More worrying was the economic obstacle, which arose from the heterogeneity of economic conditions within the EEC. De Larosière noted that the overall economic cohesion in the EEC had been greater in the 1960s than it was today, rendering any far-reaching and perfectionist plans hopeless. Still more important was the institutional obstacle, namely, the complexities and inadequacies of the EEC's institutional system. De Larosière criticized the fact that no significant progress could be made on monetary union if advance went on being linked to the simultaneous progress of other questions, like sectoral policies.[41] The head of the Trésor then pointed at the overall slow and complex decision-making process in Brussels in a rapidly evolving international situation. As a consequence, the EEC appeared impotent. Although de Larosière was critical of the EEC's institutional setup, he explicitly proposed *in fine* to use it, and to present the Council with a memorandum sketching out as realistic a proposal as possible. Even before the memorandum was actually presented to the Finance Council, the French government seemed quite confident with regard to its reception.[42]

Given the perceived urgency, the communication of the president to the Council on 16 September on *la relance monétaire européenne* proposed that these actions could be implemented before the end of the year.[43] Fourcade set out four measures: an EEC loan, a unit of account, the adaptation of the intra-EEC exchange rate system, and coordinated action on the Euromarkets. The second and the third steps, which more directly interest monetary cooperation, will be analyzed here. According to Fourcade, the revision of the unit of account was necessary because the official price of gold no longer had any significance. The adoption of a basket-SDR on 1 July 1974 officialized the abandonment of gold at world level.[44] It thereby rendered the then European unit of account obsolete, and prompted the EEC to adapt its own unit of account—hence Fourcade's suggestion. This new European Unit of Account (EUA) could be defined on the basis of a "basket" composed of different European currencies. Two problems were left open: the question of the weighting of currencies and the question of the conditions of variation of the value of the unit (the system needed to be adjustable in order to take into account the possible variation of the value of each currency). As far as the reform of the snake was concerned, Fourcade presented the same ideas as those exposed by de Larosière in late August: to set an adjustable EEC level of the dollar and allow currencies to fluctuate with respect to adjustable reference rates; to permit a temporary departure of a currency from the system should the markets necessitate it; to define the (adjustable) margins of fluctuation of each currency without the use of a maximum differential between the two currencies, but instead with reference to the value of the European Unit of Account; and to diversify the modes of intervention and payment by central banks. It is also worth noting at this stage that the idea, suggested above, of organizing an exchange rate system around the unit of account would be central to the EMS negotiations.[45]

The French government then detailed these guidelines before the Monetary Committee in the following weeks. Jean-Yves Haberer, a senior official in the French Treasury, outlined a possible solution to the current inadequacies of the snake: the creation of a second system that would act as a "waiting room" for the currencies that could not yet rejoin the snake.[46] Since it was virtually impossible to fight against the tendencies of the market, especially when the market was well informed about the fixed line followed by the currencies, the new system would have to be flexible and secret. Everything in the new system was therefore to be adjustable—which did not mean that it would always be adjusted—thereby guaranteeing both the flexibility and the secrecy of the system. The objective of this new system was to create a "welcome structure" aimed at facilitating the reintegration of non-snake currencies in the snake, and thus to reestablish a single exchange rate system for the whole EEC. The French experts explained that the steps leading to the final reintegration of the currencies could not be described and planned with precision since they were very much dependent on unforeseeable external factors. Haberer did distinguish, however, two main phases: a preliminary one (*le flottement de concert*) and an ultimate one (*le flottement concerté*). The first step would have a nonbinding character: the governors of the central banks of the currencies that freely floated would make a secret declaration of intent stipulating that they aimed at making their currency float "*de concert*"— that is to say, as parallel as possible—with those of the snake. This step would therefore essentially be a step of coordination (*concertation*). The second step, *le flottement concerté*, would lead to the reintegration of a floating currency within the exchange rate regime. It would necessitate the stability of each central rate, the progressive narrowing of the margin of fluctuation (which would of course, at the beginning, be wider than the one used within the snake), and reciprocal and simultaneous interventions in European currencies.

To a very large extent the French preoccupations and proposals were similar to those of the Banca d'Italia and the Commission. Already in March 1973, the Banca d'Italia had put forward proposals for "concerted floating": "We do not think it desirable, either technically or politically, to maintain for long a two-tier arrangement, whereby some EEC currencies float more or less independently while others tend to gravitate around the deutsche mark."[47] Rinaldo Ossola, deputy director general in the Banca d'Italia, suggested "a multiphase approach to achieve a stable Community exchange rate mechanism." Ossola outlined four phases: first, the non-snake currencies would coordinate their interventions so as to closely follow the snake; second, all EEC currencies would move into a single Community system, more flexible than the snake, with larger fluctuation margins (3%–4%); third, the band would be narrowed and EEC currencies would basically return to the old, stricter snake. "Over time, this would lead to phase four, the elimination of fluctuations altogether among EEC currencies, i.e., the creation of a European Monetary and Economic Union." The proposal purposely did not mention any precise timetable so as to increase its operational flexibility—and avoid one of the pitfalls of the Werner Plan. Yet the Italian government did not formally reformulate these proposals at the European level in 1974, presumably because of the French initiative.

Unlike the Banca d'Italia, the Commission put forward its own proposal. In a note on concerted floating written in October, the Commission first recalled that "an indispensable ingredient of any scheme of concerted floating is that there should be full, frequent, and effective coordination of *all* aspects of macroeconomic policy between participating countries."[48] The Commission noted, for instance, that the top officials (such as finance ministers and central bank governors) of the present snake countries all meet together informally at frequent intervals to discuss (and coordinate) their economic policies. Such arrangements should be extended to the EEC as a whole. As for exchange rates policy, the Commission agreed to the common idea that no return of non-snake currencies could be envisaged in the short term, and not until more economic convergence had been achieved. It also underlined a new sensitivity of the Commission to the "economist" theses. The Commission then argued that for the moment, in order to improve the situation, there was no alternative to simply accepting wider fluctuation margins. The Commission insisted, however, that this was an interim solution, not a permanent one. It was keen on establishing a new fluctuation system that, "while avoiding the excessive rigidity that characterized the snake in its original form, will nevertheless push countries in the direction of greater convergence of economic policies than is being achieved, or is likely to be achieved, under the present system." The Commission then refused to provide a detailed description of such a system, claiming that it was still too early to do so. It did, however, ask a list of questions that actually tally with some points of the French initiative—for instance, the organization of the new exchange rate regime and a coordinated attitude vis-à-vis the dollar.

Three further objectives dominated the French proposal for a new fluctuation regime as detailed at the Monetary Committee.[49] The first was to reestablish a link between the European currencies and the international environment. Concerted interventions in dollars would therefore restart, but without formal reestablishment of a "tunnel." The second objective was to create a better adapted system of fluctuations: the margins could be enlarged, the fluctuations could be organized around pivot rates, and a currency could be allowed to float freely until new margins had been adjusted. The last objective was to share the burden of intervention more equitably (since it usually fell on the weakest currency) and to reexamine the mode of payment, mainly to increase the time of payment. In order to apply a new fluctuation regime regrouping all the European currencies, two mechanisms could be established immediately. A modifiable threshold of intervention vis-à-vis the dollar could be first agreed on. It would consequently create *un tunnel déformable*. In addition to this new tunnel, a new European fluctuation margin, independent from the current snake, could be launched. The limit could be equal to or greater than 2.25 percent. It would differ in two key ways from the existing snake: the margins would be adjustable and interventions could be made either in dollars or in European currencies. In the longer term, the French note was keen on envisaging the European margin as based on a new unit of account. This was of course the idea exposed by de Larosière: the margin would not be defined as the instantaneous differential between two currencies, but instead by the maximum differential, for each currency, with respect to its value in EUA. This EUA would be composed as a basket where all European currencies would be represented according to their significance. As a consequence, the fluctuation margin between two currencies taken separately would be significantly increased. To ensure the maximum of secrecy within the new system, the note used Haberer's reasoning: the system would be set up to be permanently revisable—which did not mean that it would necessarily be revised.

As for the specific case EUA, the French members of the Monetary Committee argued that a new one was needed for two reasons.[50] First, the reform of the international monetary system was likely to put an end to the official price of gold, which would provoke ample—and economically unjustified—variations in the value of the UA. Second, the floating of European currencies made it practically difficult to determine the value of each European currency in the UA. That said, two methods could be envisaged to define a new EUA: a par value of central rate grid approach (*méthode des parités*) or a standard basket approach (*méthode de l'échantillon*). The first would aim at fixing the value of each European currency in EUA without worrying about the very definition of the EUA itself. The second consisted of defining the EUA as the sum of an appropriate number of units of each of the EEC currencies. This debate recalled the reserve debate and the creation of the Special Drawing Right (SDR) in the 1960s.[51] There was, however, an important distinction: the SDR was created to meet the need for additional reserves, a reason that did not appear in the French initiative.[52] At that time the French government had preferred *la méthode des parités*; it was now, given the circumstances, ready to defend *l'échantillon*. It was indeed much easier to use the basket approach rather than the parities since a number of European currencies were floating. Moreover, given that a new EUA would prefigure a European currency, the point was to find an average marker, especially since the current attempt to harmonize economic policies should in the end eliminate any risk of divergence in the relative value of the currencies. Last, the note explained that the EUA could have an active role in the functioning of an EEC exchange rate system and constitute the pivot of the system. All these proposals, of the Commission, the Banca d'Italia, and the French government, above all reflected their continuing preoccupation with EMU, and particularly their focus on its monetary dimension—which was not shared by others, chiefly the German government, as the next section will show.

Monetary Cooperation in an Impasse?

In late 1974, monetary affairs came to be discussed in two main channels: first, in the usual EEC decision-making process—this included the discussion, and eventual failure, of most of the proposals contained in the Fourcade memorandum—and second, although in a much more limited manner, during the preparation of the Paris summit of December 1974, and the corresponding ad hoc group set up on this occasion.

The Fourcade Memorandum: A Trial Balloon?

Though the French initiative did not provoke much enthusiasm, it would be quite unfair to say that all of the proposals were completely rejected. The fact that the intentions of the French government were understood—and shared—led to some of their ideas being discussed and redefined. This section analyzes first the proposals that were rejected—the new fluctuation regime and the suggestion of organizing it around a new EUA—and second, the aspects of the French plan that attracted more support within the specialized committees—the question of the interventions against the dollar and the redefinition of the EUA.

After Fourcade's communication to the Council on 16 September, the French proposals were analyzed by the two specialized committees (Monetary Committee and Committee of Governors).[53] As early as 2 December, Fourcade observed in a note to Giscard that the proposals had received the support of no other country.[54] Virtually all the first reactions of the specialized committees were indeed skeptical.[55] As long as France and those countries that had fallen out of the snake still had macroeconomic outcomes that were significantly different from those of the countries within the snake, no amount of monetary trickery was likely to bridge the gap between the weak currency countries and the strong. Too ambitious a project, with too much publicity, would in the end provoke new setbacks that would, in turn, alarm the markets and public opinion. On more technical points, the experts were strongly opposed to any system of fixed relations with the dollar, since this possibility had already been studied in 1972 and had been found to be too difficult to put into practice. The experts of the snake countries were opposed to the redefinition of the exchange rates system, since the snake, as it was, had to remain the only objective.[56]

More specifically, the French plans concerning the temporary exchange rate system in charge of the reintegration of non-snake currencies in the EEC system were not welcomed. The Théron group report criticized the French plans for setting up a "kind of boa around the snake" given the still strong economic differences across the EEC.[57] This also was in essence the core of the German Finance Ministry's position.[58] The group then concluded that the member states whose currencies were floating and that wanted to rejoin the snake had to do so on their own. Unsurprisingly, Bernard Clappier, governor of the Banque de France, reacted curtly: "It is really the least to say of country that it can do what it wants."[59] He then defended the French proposal by making clear that it was not aimed at denaturing the snake but rather at generalizing it across the EEC. Seemingly upset, he went on: "It is possible that they [the French proposals] are not perfectly appropriate, but one should then not reject them without making any effort, especially in the experts group, to find another formula, perhaps better adapted to the objective envisaged." No one, however, tried to improve either the French proposal or the very similar one from the Commission.

But why did the members of the two Committees refuse this proposal, even "just to have a try," as the French members suggested? In general terms, it seems that the members of the snake were worried by proposals for any new/modified/alternative exchange rate regime. This was clearly noted by the Monetary Committee: "All members of the existing Community exchange rate system (the 'snake') attached great importance to avoiding all action that would in any way diminish its significance or impair its operation."[60] Curiously enough, the Monetary Committee noted at the same time that the French insisted that their proposal was not an alternative to the present snake arrangement, but that it could well coexist. And it remains quite unclear in what ways this "boa" could really have affected the normal functioning of the snake.

Concerning the proposal to build a new exchange rate regime around this new EUA, the opinions were here also negative—as would indeed be the case during the EMS negotiations. The Committee of Governors considered it too radical a change and invoked the complexity of the creation of such a system as a reason to reject it.[61] More specifically, a note of the *Banque nationale de Belgique* already pointed out two of the major weaknesses of an exchange rate system based on the unit of account (the so-called ECU-based option of the EMS negotiations), namely, that the question of the currency of intervention was left open, and that such a system tended to discriminate between currencies of bigger and smaller countries.[62] The Monetary Committee did not even mention it in its reports of 29 November and 4 December. It seemed anyway that the French members had abandoned their project (or understood that it was hopeless), since they did not reiterate it in their last note to the Monetary Committee on 28 November. This attitude helps explain why the French officials during the EMS negotiations—and chiefly Clappier—would again quickly abandon this very same idea over the summer of 1978.[63]

The skepticism and reluctance shown by most EEC members toward the proposals of the French government and the European Commission should not, however, be allowed to obscure two important advances based on these initiatives. Indeed, the EEC Committees left the door open not only to the idea of coordinating interventions against the dollar but also to the redefinition of the unit of account. The proposal of setting an EEC level for the dollar was transformed into a less ambitious but more concrete coordinated policy vis-à-vis the US currency.[64] After having criticized the idea of setting an EEC level of the dollar, the experts indeed looked more positively on the idea of finding a flexible mechanism reestablishing a link between the currencies of the snake and those that had left it. In particular, they unanimously agreed on the necessity of reaching better parallelism on the foreign exchange market, notably vis-à-vis the dollar. The goal was not to fight against long-term trends but rather to regulate current movements in order to avoid unjustified erratic fluctuations that perturbed the market and nurtured speculation. Furthermore, such a policy was part of the normal responsibility of central banks to stabilize the evolution of foreign exchange markets, and it could aim at ensuring greater cohesion among EEC currencies. This policy would therefore have three advantages: it would avoid important and economically unjustified changes between European currencies, it would ensure a better division of the cost of interventions between the different countries, and it would perhaps dissuade speculation. Such a policy, even if of limited impact, would come within the framework of the objective of the return of the floating currencies to the intra-EEC exchange rate system, and should therefore be encouraged. Concretely, the report of the Théron group suggested that only a few rules should be adopted in applying this idea so that the functioning could be as discreet and flexible as possible. It proposed first to set a margin regarding maximum daily variations of the dollar (between 0.75% and 1%). It then warned about the need to be highly reactive, namely, to be ready to augment the margin, diminish it, or even abandon the experiment according to the circumstances, and to be able to do so within a very short time. The Monetary Committee showed the same level of interest.[65] The final policy would be decided in January 1975.

By contrast, the outcome of the debate about the new unit of account was still extremely uncertain in early December. Though it was agreed that the current pegging of the unit of account to gold was anachronistic, it was believed that the suppression of this link would not bring any change in practice. To further complicate the French initiative, no unanimity was found on the definition of this new EUA (parity grid system, standard basket approach, or SDR model), especially since three camps existed: those happy with the current definition (mainly the snake countries), those in favor of a EUA defined with the standard basket approach (some non-snake countries, plus the Commission), and those wanting to keep all options open.[66] The Monetary Committee warned, in its report of 4 December, that a unit of account would not help solve all of the operational problems in the EEC, and refused to give any specific recommendation. A unit of account could accommodate but not prevent changes in the relative values of currencies, these changes being large and unpredictable.[67] On 13 December, the Commission also stressed that the present UA no longer reflected the market exchange relations.[68] This was particularly problematic for the EEC, since the UA served both as a guarantee of exchange (it maintained financial amounts at a fixed rate in terms of a common denominator) and as an expression of price uniformity (for a particular economic sector—agriculture, for instance—at the EEC level). The Commission favored the French option of the standard currency basket since it "would not only constitute a technical arrangement to solve financial problems arising among the Member States, but would also represent a step towards a Community monetary identity." The Commission confirmed this position during the Council of 19 December, and encouraged the Council to continue studies on that topic—a position of course backed by Fourcade.[69] Yet the Eight all concluded that it was premature to take new decisions on the issue. At the time of the Paris summit, the debate about the reform of the EUA was hence still very much in its infancy.

Monetary Cooperation and the Paris Summit

Monetary cooperation was an issue not only in the EEC Council of Ministers and the specialized committees but also among heads of state and government.

The issue came up at three stages in late 1974: at the informal dinner in Paris on 14 September, then during the *travaux préparatoires* leading to the conference of heads of state and government, and finally on the occasion of the summit itself on 9 and 10 December.

In order to have an initial discussion of European problems, Giscard invited his European partners to an informal dinner in Paris on 14 September. From the outset, Giscard reaffirmed that his priority in foreign affairs was Europe, and that political decisions could be taken in the fall.[70] Though discussion did start with economic and monetary affairs, this topic was not the most talked about during the meeting, and it did not begin well. Schmidt warned that it was too early to constitute an EMU, as the convergence in economic beliefs had not yet produced a convergence in economic outcomes. However, common disciplines already agreed on had to be maintained, as, for instance, that of the snake.[71] Leo Tindemans, the Belgian prime minister, also said that he was rather pessimistic about the prospect of EMU. The very fact that there was not a more detailed discussion was in itself telling about the attitude of the heads of government toward the topic. The *travaux préparatoires* leading to the Paris summit confirmed this trend. After the first two meetings of the foreign ministers on 16 September and 15 October, it was decided to focus the summit on two main themes, political and institutional questions on the one hand, and "questions de fond" on the other (the latter being themselves divided in two topics: first inflation, unemployment, and regional policy, and second, energy).[72] Two ad hoc groups were created to organize the *travaux préparatoires* on each of these topics. Monetary issues were thus not included as a subject in their own right but were to be discussed merely as a subset of the discussions planned on inflation.

The discussions about economic affairs started in early November.[73] In the second report of the ad hoc group to the foreign ministers on 21 November, after the joint declaration stating that EMU was still the EEC objective, the French delegation suggested the inclusion of a paragraph encouraging the reinforcement of the EMCF.[74] The French delegation remained isolated, however. Instead of this sentence, the German government (followed by the British and Irish ones) wanted to state that the EMCF would become an instrument to coordinate monetary policies, while the Commission (backed by the Belgian, Danish, and Luxembourg governments) wanted to affirm that in addition to being reinforced, the EMCF would also become an instrument for the coordination of monetary policies and would contribute to the equilibrium of balance of payments, and that, in fine, all these steps would allow the reestablishment of a link between snake and non-snake currencies. The German government withdrew its draft wording in the report of 5 December, and only the versions suggested by the Commission and the French government remained for a moment, and eventually disappeared.[75]

The British government put a reserve on the text related to EMU, and was in part backed by the Benelux governments.[76] As a consequence, on 3 December, the pursuit of the project of EMU was still presented as an "open question."[77] The French government, however, backed by the governments of Germany, Italy, and Ireland, managed to maintain the initial text, with only the British reserve. The Italian and Irish governments, according to Burin des Roziers, gave their backing because the summit linked together the issues of regional policy and EMU. More generally, both the Italian and the Irish governments constantly insisted on the need for parallel progress on economic (reducing structural imbalances within the Community) and monetary (exchange rate stability) fronts.[78] This was an interesting foreshadowing of the EMS negotiations, during which, in a similar fashion, the same two governments (plus this time the British government) would stress the link between the EMS Exchange Rate Mechanism (ERM) discussions and the "concurrent studies."[79]

On the whole, the *travaux préparatoires*, as far as monetary (and economic) affairs were concerned, were quite disappointing. As Émile Noël, the secretary general of the Commission, rightly noted, apart from establishing a common diagnosis of the economic situation, it became quickly obvious that the ad hoc group would not be able to do more than write up an inventory as detailed as possible of the points of convergence, and especially of the points of divergence.[80] In addition, given that from the beginning, the British government unsurprisingly contested the objective itself of EMU, and that, crucially, it was still maintaining suspense about its participation in the EEC, the discussions were greatly restrained from the very start.

On 18 November the Finance Council devoted its session to the preparation of the summit, and drew up a list of questions to be submitted to the heads of government, from which the main issues raised by the Fourcade memorandum (joint floating, EUA) were totally absent.[81] In spite of Clappier's further defense of the Fourcade proposals, as well as his call for confirming the line of the 1972 Paris summit at the next conference, his partners did not back him.[82] Fourcade himself, writing a note to Giscard summarizing the positions that he thought should be defended at the summit, included only his proposal for a newly defined unit of account, leaving out the arrangements on joint floating and the policy vis-à-vis the dollar.[83] Yet most interestingly, Fourcade showed an awareness that, in order to reach an agreement on a proposal, one needed to override Council deadlock by making effective use of the European Council. Such effective use was, however, not possible in the case of the Fourcade memorandum, not least because convergence in economic thinking was yet too fragile.

The crux of the problem lay in the ongoing British renegotiation. Not only was there a general *hypothèque britannique* looming over the EEC debates in

1974, but this *hypothèque* hit monetary affairs particularly hard. As de Larosière noted, the British government's general reserve on the principle itself of EMU largely discouraged any attempt to discuss it.[84] Moreover, as I will later explain with regard to the 1975 referendum, the French president did not want to interfere with the British domestic debate by adding a topic—monetary affairs—that would clearly not help the case for continued British participation in the EEC.[85]

Although other issues—the institutionalization of summitry, the elections of the European Parliament by universal suffrage, the regional fund, and the British renegotiation—dominated the summit, monetary cooperation was indeed the first topic to be discussed.[86] Wilson naturally expressed doubts that the EEC would be able to realize EMU by 1980, and James Callaghan further explained that the British position on EMU was based on "a dislike of intellectual dishonesty"—that is, of affirming EMU would happen in the near future.[87] While Schmidt thought the same, he stressed, however, that it was not possible to retract ones' predecessors' statements. Giscard concurred, observing that, given the present circumstances, hardly any progress toward EMU could be made. He did not even dare to mention the Fourcade proposals. Schmidt, however, had underlined the symbolic importance of the orientation given by heads of government statements, which would be considerably reinforced by the regularity of the European Council's meetings.[88] Overall then, heads of government agreed that EMU was unlikely to happen soon, but they also agreed that officially abandoning the EMU objective itself would be dangerous. The conclusions thus dropped only the 1980 target while reaffirming the long-term ultimate goal: "The heads of government, having noted that internal and international difficulties have prevented in 1973 and 1974 the accomplishment of expected progress on the road to EMU, affirm that in this field their will has not weakened and their objective has not changed since the Paris Conference."[89]

In opening the Finance Council on 19 December, Fourcade curiously declared that the conclusions of the conference were positive, and that it had reinforced the will to achieve EMU according to the timetable set at the Paris conference in 1972.[90] It is doubtful that EMU was *reinforced* after the summit, especially since the official target of EMU by 1980 was no longer mentioned, and it was even more doubtful that concrete actions would be taken soon, since Fourcade's own proposals had not even been discussed. The summit had, however, one important result: it showed that EMU was not buried but definitely remained on the agenda. Should this be interpreted as success? A document written by the general secretariat of the Council judged it to be "neither a success, nor a failure."[91] But although no progress toward EMU was made in Paris, given the gloomy context the mere fact that it appeared in the final communiqué was not insignificant. The EMU project was at least not (yet?) officially dead. The year 1975 would, however, prove to be even more difficult.

A Second Try

In contrast to the French presidency, the Irish presidency, beginning on 1 January 1975, did not prioritize monetary issues.[92] In fact, the European monetary context was ambiguous. True, the EMU ambition had clearly been reduced at the Paris summit, and the international economic situation was still extremely worrying. However, some concrete, smaller steps were being taken by EEC member states regarding monetary affairs. Still more important, the altered French economic policy bore its first fruits with the announcement of the reintroduction of the French franc into the snake in May. In analyzing these developments, I will first investigate the extent to which some parts of the Fourcade memorandum were adopted by the EEC. I will then explain how spring 1975 saw the shelving of the EMU project by the EEC heads of government. Finally, I will argue that even if the EMU project seemed to have been adjourned, technical studies about how to improve the European exchange rate system were still—and even more intensively—carried out.

The Follow-Up to the Fourcade Memorandum

Although rejected in its most innovating parts (notably the proposal for a new exchange rate system centered around a weighted basket of European currencies), the Fourcade memorandum did see the partial success of two of its proposals: the common policy vis-à-vis the dollar and the reform of the unit of account.

The issue of setting a common policy vis-à-vis the dollar was settled over the winter. A verbal agreement on the principle of trying to take common action vis-à-vis the dollar was reached among EEC central bank governors on 10 December.[93] The most important measure was to decide that the daily range of fluctuations of the dollar should not exceed, in principle, 0.75–1 percent either way. A meeting in Washington on 3 and 4 March with the Federal Reserve Board removed any lingering doubts.[94] The Federal Reserve confirmed that it would operate in harmony with the EEC plan, and that it would not do anything to jeopardize EEC currencies. The system eventually entered into force on 12 March 1975.[95] It was, however, quite unlikely that the newly designed system of intervention against the dollar would considerably change the situation. For a start, the agreement contained a clause allowing any participating central bank, in the case of "exceptional circumstances," to temporarily suspend application of the new system's rules.[96] For this reason, Clappier openly wondered whether the system would ever actually work.[97] As for the daily range of fluctuations, it was quite large—0.75 to 1 percent—and hence would confine the interventions to a limited number of cases. Clappier also made this point, warning that with such a limit, the interventions would be rare and consequently the experience limited.[98] Despite those qualifications, however, the creation of this new system stressed the continuity of the dollar concern in the EEC. This preoccupation indeed was not born with the sudden decline of the dollar in 1978. Quite the contrary, the need for a concerted, if not common, policy vis-à-vis the dollar originated quite obviously in the disappearance of the "tunnel" in 1973, if not simply in the breakdown of the Bretton Woods system. The arrangement of 12 March 1975 was hence an indirect attempt at reconstructing the tunnel in which the snake used to undulate. After a six-month trial period, the governors concluded that for various reasons the arrangement was not fully satisfying.[99]

The negotiations about the creation of a new European Unit of Account had, as seen above, made an unpromising start but ended well. From the outset, the idea of modifying the definition of the unit of account, launched by the French government in the Fourcade memorandum and strongly backed by the Commission, was agreed on in principle but rejected in practice. Of the three options that existed—the current one ("parity grid unit") with the dropping of the reference to gold, the adoption of the SDR, or the basket of European currencies—the Monetary Committee recommended the basket type.[100] A reference to the dollar in European affairs was hence avoided. That would certainly not have been the case had the SDR been adopted, within which the EEC currencies constituted less than half the total weight. The French government underscored the political dimension of redefining the unit of account, with Fourcade talking about "the birth of a European monetary identity" that would reinforce the credibility of the EEC as a whole.[101] Once redefined, it did not mean that the new EUA would be automatically widely used, however. A further question was actually to determine where it would be appropriate to use it. For instance, the EMCF had only to deal with snake currencies, hence the new EUA based on all EEC currencies would not really suit its operation. Using the new EUA for the budget would also open two questions: How often would the EUA be recalculated? And how would this affect the contribution of each member state to the EEC budget?[102] As a consequence, the use of the new EUA was at first limited to express the amounts given in the ACP-EEC Lomé Convention (with a provisional British reservation) and the EIB.[103] This partly derived from the fact that the French government understood that in order to obtain an agreement on the basket-type unit of account, it should concede from the outset to limit its scope.[104] Other EEC activities progressively adopted its use, such as the ECSC in 1976 and the EEC budget in 1978. The EUA nonetheless existed well before March 1975 but in the form of a financial instrument in the banking sector. Indeed, the Kredietbank of Luxembourg created an original version of the EUA in 1961.[105] It was a multicurrency denomination, initially based on a complex association of gold and the value of seventeen

European currencies. The 1973 version, however, was simpler and closer to the EEC-EUA, since it was based on a basket of the nine EEC currencies.[106] Interestingly, the progressive character of the extension of the EUA's use—and the progressive sharing of the same unit of account in a given economic and political system—was a good example of advanced monetary cooperation. It was even sometimes believed—as would be more famously the case with the ECU—that the gradual extension of the EUA's use would lead to the sharing of a common currency.[107] This underlines the point made above about the link between the unit of account and the parallel currency debate. The EUA creation was therefore of crucial importance at least in four respects. First, in theoretical terms, a unit of account is by definition the basis of monetary cooperation. Second, in technical terms, it was a composite unit, the definition of which would be used for the ECU in 1978. Third, the EUA born in March 1975 was in some ways a European SDR, and thereby underlined the strong influence of global developments on the European story. Finally, on a symbolic, psychological, and political note, it marked the birth of a distinct European monetary identity, as noticed by Haberer.[108] Overall, then, if there is a single date to remember in the story of the unit of account, it is 1975, rather than 1978.

The Shelving of EMU at the Heads of Government Level

While the last section delved into rather technical aspects, attention should also be paid to the more general trends of early 1975 in high politics. In that period, EEC attention focused on the first European Council in Dublin and the release of the Marjolin Report. The issue of the British renegotiation attracted most of the attention for this first European Council for two connected reasons. To start with, the renegotiation process had been haunting the EEC for about a year. Many began to feel that international concerns were already serious enough, and that the EEC did not need an extra worry of this type. Consequently, both the British government and the Eight sought a quick and fair solution to the problem. But the discussion of this topic was also seen as a first life-size test of the efficacy of the newly created European Council. Created to facilitate the decision-making process in the EEC, the European Council faced an experiment that could justify—or invalidate—its inception. The European Council passed this first test. Even though the referendum validating the outcome of the discussions was still to be held, the British renegotiation issue was for the most part settled, and Wilson even declared that the renegotiation process had ended.[109] This constituted the most significant political result of the meeting. As for economic and monetary affairs, they were, as the diplomatic language stated, "discussed." But the final communiqué, in contrast with that of Paris in

December 1974, did not reaffirm the commitment of the EEC member states to the goal of monetary union. Did it really matter that EMU did not appear in the final communiqué? In the current context, two obstacles hindered any progress: the economic situation and the fact that most member states preferred maintaining the status quo to taking the risk of modification. As a consequence, the SGCI—as the French Treasury had done before—observed that the best strategy for the French government was, in the present circumstances, to carry on looking for concrete advances, such as the EUA, instead of devising long-term plans and objectives—such as the announcement of the achievement of an EMU in a communiqué.[110]

The publication of the Marjolin Report, on 8 March, came as a confirmation of this situation. Appointed in early 1974 by the Commission in order to carry out a study on EMU, the group of experts, presided over by Robert Marjolin, former vice president of the Commission in charge of economic and monetary affairs, submitted its report in March 1975.[111] In drawing up an evaluation of the efforts made since the Hague summit, it formulated the oft-quoted expression "Europe is no nearer to EMU than in 1969. In fact if there has been any movement it has been backwards."[112] Characterizing the Marjolin Report with this sentence alone would be quite misleading, however. The report did not deny "certain progress of a technical nature," although these tiny improvements did not prevent the group from painting a bleak picture of EMU. It did not consider the situation to be entirely hopeless either. It actually proposed a short- and long-term agenda for action. Finally, if the Marjolin group formulated this statement with strength, it was not the first one to make it but only perhaps the first one to say it and be remembered for doing so. Already in September 1974, for instance, the Commission president himself, Ortoli, said that "not only Economic and Monetary Union, based above all on a narrowing of currencies, had regressed, but the concept itself had even declined."[113]

Though the Marjolin Report reached relatively broad and accepted conclusions, it interestingly stressed an additional little-noticed failure in the implementation of the Treaties of Rome, namely, the liberalization of capital movements.[114] Given Mundell's famous theory of the "holy trinity," it was always surprising not to see this point mentioned more often in discussions about EMU. The Marjolin Report did refer to it, although without directly relating it to progress toward EMU. The group identified three main causes explaining the failure of EMU so far: "unfavourable events, a lack of political will, and insufficient understanding in the past of the meaning of an EMU." The "unfavourable events" amounted to the international monetary crisis; the "lack of political will" referred to the reluctance of most member states to act in a *Community* manner; and the last point criticized the fact that most member states failed to grasp the implications of an

EMU (namely, the creation of common institutions, or even of a system akin to that of a federal state).

The Marjolin Report slightly digressed from most conventional analysis when looking to the future of EMU. If it painted a bleak picture of the situation, it did not describe it as hopeless, but instead as difficult. This did not amount to playing on words, since it suggested some new measures. Crucially, and this was quite a novelty, it stated from the outset that "further progress [in EMU] requires the manifestation of a political will." This was an interesting statement because EMU was usually confined to economic and monetary issues. The Marjolin Report argued instead that it was primarily a *political* problem. Significantly, it underlined a change of attitude, distancing itself from the Werner Plan. Accordingly, EMU was not a scheme to be coldly implemented through a step-by-step plan, but rather a sort of ideal, meant to be patiently and imperfectly followed.

The Quest for Technical Improvements

Contrary to what is often said about the Marjolin Report, the study did propose that some decisions be taken in order to "bring nearer the time when the creation of an EMU might be seriously envisaged." It first quickly mentioned the most urgent problems menacing the EEC—inflation, unemployment, and balance of payments deficits—and suggested some measures to fight them. With regard to economic policy, it insisted that stimulation by aggregate demand measures was not currently appropriate. Instead, investments should be supported.

The Marjolin group sketched out a short-term program with a view to EMU.[115] The Marjolin Report recommended three types of action: an increase in cooperation between the intra-EEC exchange rate system and domestic monetary policies; the creation of an Exchange Stabilisation Fund (which would in fact be an improved version of the existing EMCF),[116] together with increased possibilities to raise joint loans; and finally, the creation of a new European unit of account that it (presciently) called a European Currency Unit. None of these three measures were radical, and most of them could be implemented through the development of existing mechanisms, as was the case with the EMCF. They were also not brand-new: even to dub a European unit of account an "ECU" had already been suggested earlier by Ortoli. Yet all three actions confirmed the tendency outlined above, which privileged an incremental process over a qualitative leap forward.

Trying to compensate for the lack of clarity it had earlier criticized about what was actually meant by an EMU, the Marjolin Report outlined the conditions for such a union.[117] These were both psychological ("large parts of the population having a feeling of belonging to a union") and concrete and far-reaching (the creation of a single central bank, a sizable EEC budget). Quite logically, the group refused to give more details about, for instance, the distribution of competences. But it did list a number of policies that ought to be implemented in order to render an EMU feasible: industrial policy, energy policy, capital market policy, budgetary policy, and Community unemployment policy. Interestingly, this type of proposal was quite uncommon in a plan discussing EMU. Usually the story was more about pivot rates and the width of fluctuation bands. Instead, the Marjolin group adopted a more comprehensive approach including various economic issues. Hence, while it remained relatively "parallel" in its presentation, it seemed to have much more sympathy for the "economist" approach to monetary integration.

This economist approach had been backed by the fact that, since early June 1974, the French and German governments officially shared a common ambition to fight against inflation. Some slight doubts began to surface from the French side, however. They originated from the different hierarchy of priorities of the finance minister and the prime minister.[118] While Fourcade was described as almost obsessed by inflation and trade balance, Chirac had much more political preoccupations. Chirac observed that these anti-inflationary measures were obviously not popular and was concerned not to hurt his electorate. Since recession seemed imminent, the French government tolerated some small exceptions to the anti-inflation rule, first in December 1974 and then in April 1975, in the form of easier credit ceilings and an increase in government expenditure.[119] Jean-Pierre Ruault, one of Giscard's economic advisers, criticized this economic policy course.[120] He warned that a changing, or softening, of the economic policy after only six months would be the wrong signal to send to economic actors. The objectives assigned were far from being reached, and modifying the course of action would put at risk the achievements already banked.

And indeed, as Ruault noticed, just as the French government began to slightly soften its stability program, it actually started to reap the benefits of the fight against inflation it had begun in June 1974. As a consequence of the decrease in the inflation rate and an improved external trade balance, the French franc had indeed been getting closer to the snake as of December 1974.[121] Interestingly, Fourcade acknowledged this "economist" thesis, according to which the return of the French franc was the result of the economic policy pursued by the French government since June 1974: economic convergence had induced monetary convergence.[122] By mid-May 1975, the French franc had de facto rejoined the European exchange rate mechanism. Giscard announced the future de jure return of the French franc in the snake on 9 May. Needless to say—especially given the fact that it was Giscard's decision—the announcement of the return of the French franc to the snake on the date of the anniversary of the Schuman declaration was highly symbolic.[123] By timing the announcement this way, however, Giscard was

attracting unnecessary attention to a risky bet. Not only was his own administration not convinced by this decision, as I will discuss below, but his European
partners were not really persuaded either. Schmidt, in particular, was aware of the
acute risk taken by Giscard in terms of prestige were the French franc forced to
leave the snake again later on.[124] The French president, meanwhile, did not seem
to be aware of this. As a result, his decision clearly shattered the already fragile
governmental French consensus on European monetary cooperation.[125]

In a note to Fourcade about the possibility of a return of the French franc
in the snake, de Larosière abruptly—and in retrospect, presciently—had indeed
warned of such a measure. According to the head of the Treasury, such a return
was premature and would not last long.[126] While he again criticized the inherent drawbacks of the snake, he argued that "it has become clear to everyone that
there is no possible monetary solidarity between European countries without
a convergence of their economic policies." And de Larosière openly wondered
whether the current similar hierarchy of economic priorities across the EEC was
likely to last. De Larosière did not believe that rejoining the snake would bring
many rewards. On the one hand, the snake was no longer an *EEC* mechanism,
since four EEC members had already left (Britain, Ireland, Italy, and France) and
three non-EEC members had joined (Norway, Sweden, Austria, and even perhaps
Switzerland). In addition, the snake had become a mere club of strong currencies, thereby shelving most of the political ambitions of the project. Hence returning into this monetary arrangement would not mean much with regard to
European—understood as EEC-linked—monetary cooperation especially since
a similar move was still not in sight for the pound or the lira. On the other hand,
concerning the stabilization of external trade, a return to the snake would also
not bring much since France had more trade in the EEC than with the snake
members alone. For these reasons, remaining outside the snake was, according to
the head of the Trésor, the solution that was "technically the best, psychologically
without problem, and politically the most secure."[127] In virtually identical terms
the Banque de France opposed the return of the French franc to the snake, both
in December 1974 and in May 1975.[128] Even Fourcade himself, in line with his
earlier memorandum, favored a two-tier system accommodating the lira and the
pound.[129] It is therefore clear that the return of the French franc to the snake was
Giscard's personal decision.

Of particular significance was the fact that in spite of these internal disagreements, the French Treasury carried on thinking that the snake needed some
technical improvements. The constant support received from the Commission
certainly reinforced French endeavors.[130] And given that the French franc was
able to reenter the snake anyway, this second series of proposals thus appeared
as a genuinely consistent belief that the inner flows of the European exchange

rate mechanism were an obstacle to further monetary cooperation. The French government was therefore seemingly not seeking to trick or denature the system instead of reforming its economy, particularly since the French franc's reentry in the snake was not made conditional upon acceptance of the proposals for reform of the snake of the French government.

This second French initiative in European monetary affairs in less than a year was of course much inspired by the first.[131] It accordingly reformulated a triptych similar to the first one: improved mechanism of interventions, common policy vis-à-vis the dollar, and more technical considerations. It restated the long-standing French complaint of the lack of symmetry of interventions in the snake, since the burden of adjustment always fell on the weakest currency. This was problematic because the responsibility for the divergence between two currencies can sometimes be due to speculation on the strongest currency. In addition, the obligation of intervention falls on only one currency, the weakest, excluding all the others. Finally, the interventions limited to the only two currencies reaching the limits of fluctuation might be too late. Earlier interventions, symmetrical and in dollars, could have the advantage of slowing down some tendencies of the market, without leaving the entire burden of adjustment on the weakest currency. It restated that "it might be envisaged to define the European margin as a maximum gap for each currency, with respect to its value in the European unit of account."[132] It also proposed the increase of short-term monetary support (up to 10 billion units of account), as well as medium-term financial support (to be increased "accordingly"). Interestingly, these last two points patently bear a lot of similarity to the ECU-based option and the discussion about the credit mechanisms of the EMS negotiations.

In half a year, however, most of the EEC member states had not changed their opinion. For instance, the Danish government was opposed to any widening of the fluctuation margins, since both the functioning of the CAP and the EMU perspective required, in principle, a relatively strict system.[133] The Italian government shared again the basic ambition of the French proposals, not least because some were similar to some of its own, but once more rejected the EUA-centered exchange rate system.[134] If the French proposals were again widely analyzed, it seemed this time that they were given much less attention than in September 1974. It was no great surprise that the Committee of Governors rejected the French proposals. While it politely promised that they would be reexamined in the next six months, it seemed more flexible than before concerning the evolution of the snake, describing it as "still provisional in character."[135] This was relatively new, since the snake countries had tended so far to refuse *any* modification of the snake, as had been the case during the discussions in September 1974. Whether this matter of fact was likely to bring changes soon was still an open question. But it was already apparent that any changes made would not be carried out through an implementation of the second Fourcade memorandum.

Conclusions

There were more than simply technical issues at stake in all these failed attempts at relaunching European monetary cooperation. Detailed examination reveals much about the way in which the EEC member states defined the problem, the extent to which institutional issues could affect monetary affairs, and finally, the centrality of a whole set of technical issues. This concluding section looks closely at these three points.

Defining the Contours of the Problem

The attempts at relaunching European monetary cooperation in 1974–early 1975 revolved around five main questions. The first concerned the European dimension of monetary cooperation. In June 1975, Karl-Otto Pöhl, the German finance minister, explained: "Perhaps the concept of a monetary world was too ambitious. . . . That's why I wonder whether it is not more realistic, under these circumstances, to imagine the monetary world of the future as it is currently developing: regions with similar basic performances in economic policy, which are bound among themselves with fixed exchange rates, but are more or less freely floating toward the rest of the world."[136] This declaration shows the extent to which European policymakers were simply unsure about the monetary future. In that sense, the Fourcade memorandum and the proposals of the Commission managed, with partial success, to attract the attention of the EEC member states back to intra-European monetary issues. Indeed, if the stability of the Bretton Woods system had ruled out the need for European monetary integration, the collapse of the Bretton Woods system, and the quest for a new and stable one, had also somewhat distracted European policymakers from the EEC negotiations. Interestingly, the two dimensions—Europe and the world—were not mutually exclusive. Quite the contrary, international discussion nurtured European debates. There were very conscious parallels between the conception of the SDR and the EUA. The influence of international monetary discussions was particularly striking in the case of the second Fourcade memorandum, which drew an explicit parallel with IMF discussions.[137] Moreover, the whole issue of the dollar policy stressed how extra-European developments could be central to European monetary cooperation.

But what did "European" actually mean in this context? A second question brought up by the 1974 monetary debates in the EEC regarded the definition of "Europe." Was the existing snake a Community mechanism? In legal terms, the Community character of the snake was ambiguous.[138] Though the EEC was very much involved in the functioning of the snake (with the EMCF, for instance), it was actually born out of a simple intergovernmental agreement. Furthermore, in 1974, many EEC member states were outside the exchange rate system (France, Britain, Ireland, Italy), while non-EEC member states were in, informally associated, or willing to join (Norway, Sweden, Finland, Austria, Switzerland, Spain). In addition, it must be noted that as regards the two successes derived from the Fourcade memorandum—namely, the new EUA and the dollar policy—*all* the EEC member states were involved in the schemes from the outset. Clappier shrewdly summed up the crux of the problem by saying that the European exchange rate mechanism contained in fact two ambitions at the same time.[139] One was properly *communautaire*: to reinforce the existing EEC. Another was monetary: to create a *regional* zone of monetary stability in order to palliate international difficulties. It was, however, noticeable that the Fourcade memorandum was the first of many attempts in the next few years to explicitly bring back all EEC currencies in a single EEC framework.

A third question central to the attempt at relaunching European monetary cooperation regarded the way in which monetary issues ought to be dealt with: Was monetary cooperation a political question or a mere technical one? Taking a political approach would imply more discussions at the intergovernmental level, while a technical approach would certainly confine monetary affairs to the debates within specialized committees. This tension appeared during the debate in the Committee of Governors about the common policy vis-à-vis the dollar.[140] The German member, Karl Klasen, insisted that the rules of intervention were a technical question. The efficacy of the modifications to the existing rules ought to be judged after a six-month trial. By contrast, the French member, Clappier, very much insisted on the political side of the decision. Hence he repeated three times in his (short) intervention that the measures in question "take on also a psychological and political importance" since they highlighted that the burden of adjustment should not always fall on the weakest currency. The debate concerning the new unit of account also was strongly political. In particular, the issue of a European monetary identity was clearly behind the choice between the SDR type or the European-basket type of unit of account. The fact that the Commission—and also to some extent the French government—was stubbornly against the SDR option was of course a good sign of this. Hence the definition of a new unit of account, although not yet christened ECU in spite of Ortoli's and others' suggestion, and although still limited in usage, was clearly a political step. "The affirmation of the personality of Europe," Ortoli argued, happened "through and by progress in economic and monetary integration."[141]

A fourth question clarified by the 1974 debates concerned the strategy to adopt in order to make progress on the road to EMU. While some believed that a qualitative leap forward should be taken, others thought that technical, pragmatic measures would better improve the situation. After the discussions over the European monetary relaunch, and given the difficult international context, a consensus emerged in favor of the incremental process. The Bundesbank, the French Treasury, and the Irish government were, for instance, clearly in favor of an incremental process based on what already existed.[142] Official reports also endorsed this new thinking, much different from the earlier Werner Plan strategy. Accordingly, the Marjolin Report insisted on the need to separate long- and short-term objectives. The implementation of the latter was indeed meant to help the realization of the former.[143] Even the alternative approaches placed themselves in opposition to the Werner method. Giersch, in making his point for the inception of a "Europa," explicitly said that "the case for creating a European Parallel Currency is based on the case against the Werner Plan."[144]

A fifth and last question also concerned strategy but in more theoretical terms. Regarding the evolution of the debate between the two strategies to reach EMU, economist and monetarist, the period 1974–mid-1975 is revealed to be extremely ambiguous. With the arrival in office of Giscard and Schmidt, a rapid convergence in policy beliefs emerged, centered around the need for stability-oriented economic policies—and hence an economist strategy for EMU. In early December 1974, before the Paris summit, de Larosière went to Bonn in order first to affirm the French government's engagement in pursuing stability-oriented economic policies, and second to try to overcome the French government's isolation on monetary issues.[145] As far as the French monetary proposals were concerned, the meeting did not manage to convince the German monetary authorities, but interestingly, the French Treasury and the German monetary authorities seemed close on economic matters.

Even if a certain degree of economic rapprochement did exist, notably between France and Germany, the German government wanted stronger commitments. During the preparation of the Paris summit, Hans-Dietrich Genscher, the German foreign minister, declared that the need to follow stability-oriented policies should no longer be called into question. It must here be underlined that the position of the German government was certainly not characterized by flexibility.[146] Yet this lack of flexibility, although understandable, was likely to turn out to be interpreted as arrogance by those countries—including France—faring much worse in the economic crisis. In addition, the extent to which the proposals of Fourcade or the Commission would have really loosened the discipline of the snake was rather uncertain. Nevertheless, the intransigent German position soon came to be justified. A further problem was indeed that the initiatives of the French government regarding the fight against inflation were clearly not set in stone. As explained above, they started softening in early 1975. The German chancellor seemed well aware that Giscard had to face a difficult domestic situation that did not guarantee that he could pursue such an economic policy for long. For instance, as early as June 1974, in a meeting with Ortoli, Schmidt wondered how long Giscard could maintain a stability-oriented economic program, since 49 percent of the French electorate had voted against him in May.[147] With this remark, Schmidt underlined how much domestic politics could influence the course of European integration. The second half of 1975 would offer a good example of this—and confirm Schmidt's fears.

Overall, in spite of an agreement to fight inflation, an only partial convergence in policy outcomes ensued. This permitted, for instance, the return of the French franc to the snake. But it was not yet enough to reach a consensus over the Fourcade proposals or those of the Commission. A convergence in policy beliefs did not mean a convergence in policy outcomes.[148] Although this could be seen as a truism, it was certainly the most important lesson learned by the French government through the Fourcade memorandum negotiations.

The Weaknesses of the EEC's Decision-Making System

The analysis presented in this chapter is of course an artificial structure, designed to give a more understandable picture of the fate of the Fourcade memorandum and other initiatives. As a consequence, it might give the impression that the Fourcade memorandum, in particular, went through a relatively smooth decision-making process. It must be underlined, however, that this process was slow and complicated. First, an impressive number of committees were involved in the whole decision-making process. This did not produce much clarity. The Monetary Committee, the Committee of Governors, their alternates, and various experts all produced innumerable notes, often without recommending any specific solution. The Council of Ministers often spent more time speaking about procedures than content. This explains a stupefying remark in a report about the Council of 19 December: "The session has been characterized by a very relaxed atmosphere, mostly explained by the fact that no debate on the substance of the problems has taken place."[149] The decision-making process was further hindered by the multiplication of preliminary reports. For instance, the Council of 16 September invited, among others, the Monetary Committee to carry out the necessary studies about the unit of account that might lead to proposals for a decision;[150] and the decision was, once this study had been examined during the Council of 19 December, to instruct the Monetary Committee to carry out further studies, while the Committee of Governors already had given a competent and detailed opinion![151] Of course this is not to suggest that the committees involved were incompetent, but that the decision-making process had reached such a degree of complexity that it resembled, in the end, a discreet and proper attempt to bury the initiative, or at the very least to postpone any decision, rather than a way of conducting useful preliminary discussion. Another case in point was the Finance Council of 21 October.[152] Although Fourcade clearly suggested that reports should relate the advantages and disadvantages of the solutions studied, he had been obliged, after the examination of the report of the Monetary Committee on the unit of account (in which it said that it "found itself unable to make recommendations in favor of any particular unit of account"), to ask *again* for a report stating the advantages and disadvantages of the different options concerning the unit of account. At worst, this was the mistake of the Monetary Committee, which did not strictly follow the mandate given by the Council; at best, it did not help simplify and accelerate the decision-making process.

These two interlinked issues—the multiplication of procedures and a slow decision-making process—were not new symptoms of the institutional problems in the EEC. They originated in the general perception of a lack of leadership, which the creation of the European Council in December 1974 was meant to palliate. The track record of the new institution was of course still limited. Its first session in Dublin was regarded as positive, since it contributed to the settling of the British renegotiation issue. But it was certainly still too early to draw more far-reaching conclusions. Its mere existence was, however, considered a positive step. The potential of the new institution as both an agenda-setting body and a decision-making one was recognized, and it was generally recognized also that it was worth continuing the "experiment." The *méthode communautaire* was not seen as severely threatened by the new intergovernmental institution. Actually the main danger facing the European Council was that of excessive expectations.[153] These could indeed bring correspondingly great disappointments.

Another significant variable in the European monetary cooperation equation was that of the British position. This chapter covered a period when the EEC was coping with a somewhat unfinished enlargement to Britain. That country was divided over its continued EEC membership, from the time Wilson became prime minister in early 1974 until June 1975—the whole period of the Fourcade memorandum discussions, in other words. The uncertainty about continued British EEC membership had two consequences. On the one hand, it kept the French government from pressing ahead fully with its monetary initiative. The referendum prospect prevented any clear position taking of the British government before mid-June. The British government would actually face a very similar situation in 1978, with the prospect of the general elections in the midst of the EMS negotiations. As a consequence, Giscard, well aware of the British government's uneasy situation, refrained from mentioning in public interviews the type of topics that might cause trouble in the British debate.[154] On the other hand, the unclear British position cleared the way for the Franco-German tandem. To be sure, Giscard and Schmidt did not need an external impetus for reinforcing their bilateral cooperation. The British renegotiation nonetheless drew attention to the Franco-German partnership. Schmidt was aware very early on of the risk of such a de facto exclusion of the British government from the Franco-German duo, and tried to reassure Wilson.[155] In many respects, the newly created European Council would be one way to overcome these risks.

A New Monetary Agenda

Finally, and perhaps most significant for the EMS negotiations, the Fourcade memorandum and the proposals of the Commission introduced a number of key issues that would stay on the monetary agenda of the EEC in the coming years. This was, of course, the case of the two measures that were eventually adopted from the Fourcade memorandum: the EUA and the dollar policy. The new EUA in particular, the definition of which the 1978 ECU was based on, was regarded as a useful new tool. It technically made sense, and those who were willing to could see in it the embryo of a common currency. The acronym "ECU" was even coined by Ortoli in September 1974, and used in the Marjolin Report. Of course, its use was at first limited to the EIB. But it marked the beginning of a movement of increased affirmation of the monetary personality of the EEC. Another innovation was the French proposition of giving a greater role to the EUA in a revised exchange rate system. In retrospect, it obviously recalls the EMS debates about the role of the ECU as center of the system. As of 1974, this desire would remain the French position until the EMS negotiations. The Fourcade memorandum was the first explicit criticism in the EEC context of the asymmetric distribution of the burden of support operations required in order to keep currencies inside the margins of fluctuation of a fixed exchange rates system. The central idea of this memorandum was indeed that the costs of intervention must be spread more fairly. This idea would also remain central to all subsequent monetary discussions in the EEC. Finally, the idea of rectifying the inward-looking nature of the snake would also remain, in one form or another, on the EEC monetary agenda. Fourcade suggested the idea that setting wider fluctuation margins in order to narrow the distance of non-snake currencies from the exchange rate mechanism—the "boa"—would be worth trying. The political will to take such a risk was not yet present, however, and the proposal got buried. A similar debate would resurface on the occasion of the EMS negotiations, with the proposal made to the Irish and Italian governments to let their currencies benefit from a wider bandwidth (with the same hope that in the medium term they might join the normal fluctuation margins).

Even more important, the "Fourcadery," as Michael Balfour nicknamed the French proposal, was part of a wider and more profound ongoing transnational learning process about the reasons, modes, and extent of European monetary cooperation.[156] As of 1974, monetary policy learning had to answer one straightforward question arising from the failure of the Werner Plan: Is the strategy of reaching monetary union through a progressive narrowing of exchange rate fluctuation margins misguided? Some said yes, and proposed either a parallel currency (mostly academic economists) or stressed economic convergence to the expense of the snake reform (chiefly the German government). Others replied no, and proposed various plans for monetary cooperation (Fourcade memorandum) that were in essence variations (though meant to be an improvement) on the theme of the snake system. Ortoli thus told Denis Healey, Chancellor of the Exchequer, in early 1975 that he thought "that the doctrine of EMU needed to be revised."[157] A stage-by-stage approach no longer made sense according to him. And Ortoli—as would be the case in 1977—wanted above all to make concrete progress in a number of specific areas, such as economic coordination. The way in which de Larosière reported the state of the discussion of the Fourcade memorandum in the EEC machinery clearly shows that it was about testing new ideas: "These proposals [were] aimed at *provoking a reflection in the Community* about a number of easing measures or improvements to bring to the snake mechanism."[158] The impact of these ideas and the way in which they were progressively recycled, amended, or rejected will become even clearer in the next chapters.

On a sociological note, it is also striking to see the socialization of this monetary elite, and the way in which its members were progressively trying to get acquainted with each other's working methods and interpretations. A good example of this is found in the visits of central bank officials to one another's institutions. The way in which a Bank of England official recounted his visit to the Bundesbank in May 1974 is telling:

> I spent three weeks with the Bundesbank in Frankfurt. My aim was to see how they analysed and forecast conjunctural developments in Germany (and abroad), to learn more about German monetary policy in theory and see it working in practice, and to improve my knowledge of the country at first hand. I feel that I achieved these aims most satisfactorily and I am very grateful to the Bank for sending me.[159]

Although archival traces of such visits are quite difficult to find, it is very likely that many other such examples exist. At a higher level, the way in which de Larosière valued his bilateral contact with Pöhl is even more revealing. De Larosière had visited Pöhl in December 1974 in order both to explain the French government's anti-inflationary policy and to defend the French monetary proposals. The French head of the Treasury concluded: "This meeting allowed an exchange of views freer than those that happen during or on the occasion of usual committee meetings in Brussels. One cannot expect from meetings of this sort, where civil servants do not commit their governments, anything but better mutual information. But this can, on a number of points, contribute to the dispersal of distrust and misunderstandings."[160] Hence a member of this transnational monetary elite revealingly described both the significance and limits of bilateral contacts with his foreign counterpart. Finally, at EEC level, the inception of the group "Harmonisation of the Instruments of Monetary Policy" was in itself a good example of this monetary learning process. On the request of this group in September 1974, central banks produced notes explaining their own monetary policy and instruments.[161] The Commission then summarized this monetary stocktaking in a detailed note.[162] The group would later produce various reports.[163] The conclusions drawn related to how the various instruments and objectives could be made compatible, mutually improved—the impact of which was uncertain and would certainly deserve a highly technical study of its own. What did matter here was the incremental process, the will to cooperate and exchange information in a time of diplomatic intergovernmental standstill.

Another striking feature of the 1974–1975 monetary discussions was the close connections between all the monetary elite involved in the discussions. As it will become even more obvious in the next chapters, the same names keep coming up in two different and separate areas: those (academics) defending the parallel currency approach and those (mostly practitioners) negotiating in the EEC institutions. The identity of the authors writing the numerous "expert reports" is a case in point. In late 1974, for instance, the Commission invited a group of economists (Dieter Biehl, Arthur Brown, Francesco Forte, Yves Fréville, Martin O'Donoghue, Theo Peeters, Russell Mathews, Wallace Oates), under the chairmanship of Donald MacDougall, to work on the role of public finance in European economic integration.[164] Three of these—Forte, MacDougall, and Peeters—had also been members of the Marjolin study group. It is also noticeable that the MacDougall group was serviced by Paul Van den Bempt and Michael Emerson, director and head of division, respectively, in the DG II; Emerson would indeed be the central figure in the devising of Jenkins's ideas about monetary union in 1977.[165] These interconnections, particularly noticeable in the Marjolin Report, irritated the French head of the Treasury.[166] Not only was de Larosière annoyed by the fact that the report contradicted the French thesis (it rejected the "reform of the snake" approach) but he did not appreciate that the report of the group was exclusively associated with its (French) president's name, particularly since the then governor of the Banque de France, Bernard Clappier, took part in the work until his appointment as head of the French central bank in June 1974. The effect of this was quite obviously to put at risk the overall consistency of the French position. The U-turn made in the French government's economic policy would even more seriously damage this consistency in late 1975, and will be one of the topics of the next chapter.

EMU OFF THE AGENDA?
JUNE 1975–JUNE 1976

> When in 1976 France left for the second time, it was clear to us that
> it was hardly likely that it would decide to join the "snake" again for
> a third time. It was in the air that, for this to occur, something else
> would have to be created.

—Otmar Emminger

Why and how did economic divergences induce only the partial disappearance
of monetary cooperation from the European Community's agenda between
June 1975 and June 1976? In this chapter I first concentrate on the development
of a more positive EEC climate after the settlement of the British renegotiation
issue. The change in the British position gave a renewed psychological impetus to European (monetary) cooperation, although only for a moment. On this
occasion the hope of a European relaunch lasted until the French government
abandoned its stability-oriented economic policy in favor of a new, Keynesian-
inspired economic plan. I then concentrate on this turning point, underlining
how far domestic politics can influence the course of European (monetary) cooperation. In the third part of the chapter I analyze the EEC-wide consequences
of these economic divergences. In doing so, I examine their impact on the EEC's
structure, in terms of both agenda (abandoning EMU?) and institutions (what
role for the European Council?). In the concluding section I present a balanced
assessment of what was clearly the lowest point in terms of monetary cooperation. I suggest that these times of crisis allowed the emergence of a clearer
sense of what still needed to be done in order to improve European monetary
cooperation. In addition, this period, although marked by conspicuous failures,
continued to see the flourishing of various studies about monetary union in the
EEC, thereby underlining that EMU did remain, in one form or another, on the
European agenda.

Promising Steps?

The result of the referendum in Britain came as relief in the chancelleries of many EEC member states. The renegotiation episode was over, and the EEC could now concentrate more easily on trying to cope with the international economic crisis. In this section I will examine the new political climate that developed over the summer of 1975. I will first discuss the end of the *hypothèque britannique* and analyze to what extent it reinvigorated European (monetary) cooperation. I will then concentrate on the second European Council, held in Brussels in July 1975, which offered an interesting discussion on economic and monetary matters among EEC heads of government.

The EEC after the British Referendum

"The (future of the) EEC after the British referendum" was a relatively banal formula employed as the title of numerous notes about EEC affairs circulated in the governments of the Eight.[1] However banal, it nevertheless was an accurate reflection of the general mood in June 1975 in the EEC member states. That new steps would be taken in European integration was still uncertain, but at least it would be done with *nine* EEC members: "The United Kingdom is now completely engaged in Europe," declared Wilson at the beginning of his intervention at the European Council in Brussels in July 1975.[2] This was a welcome confirmation. The most widely used image to describe the situation was the "removal of a question mark" over British EEC membership. This image had been revived in the mid-1970s after its first uses in the 1960s. It also represented the removal of one of the reasons for the slowdown in EEC development.[3] True, as the German government recalled, it did not remove the tangible obstacles to economic integration.[4] But some governments formulated the hope that the end of this *hypothèque* would have result in the psychological relaunch of the European integration process.[5] The French government insisted on introducing a special topic of discussion for the next European Council concerning "the future of European integration after the British referendum."[6] What type of initiatives could be taken remained unclear, however. Keeping Britain within the EEC was not necessarily good news for EMU, since the British government had repeatedly declared its reluctance—to say the least—toward monetary integration. The European Council of Brussels in July was meant to clarify the options open to the Nine.

The improved atmosphere in the EEC nearly coincided with the official return of the French franc into the snake. The return was no surprise, since it had been announced in early May by Giscard. Nevertheless, it put monetary cooperation back in the spotlight.[7] This time it did not incite the French government to produce a new memorandum, but rather to revive its internal monetary brainstorming. To start with, the French government confirmed that the European exchange rate system should be preserved and reinforced.[8] Far from despairing at the failure of his proposals, Fourcade still showed some willingness to improve European monetary cooperation. He thus asked de Larosière to sketch out reflections on the future of EMU. Interestingly, the Treasury produced divergent opinions: the note produced by the services of the Treasury recommended a Werner-type plan for economic and monetary union, while the head of the Treasury forwarded the note but made clear his strong disagreement with most of its content.[9] Instead, de Larosière underlined two important aspects of European monetary cooperation: its numerous political implications and the inextricable interconnections between its technical, political, psychological, and institutional aspects.[10] The head of the Trésor explained that EMU was usually presented as implying drastic economic and institutional changes. Of course, no single European government would be ready to take the risk to implement such changes today. As a consequence, when so described, reflections on EMU were met with hostility, not only because they implied a loss of sovereignty but also because they raised the question of a political union given the extent of the changes they asked for. From a totally different perspective the note of de Larosière aimed at showing that it was possible, in the next five years, to realize substantial progresses regarding European monetary organization without binding the governments with radical decisions. Such a *démarche* was likely to satisfy both the member states that were willing to go further and those that were reluctant to do so. De Larosière recalled that the criteria for monetary union were the following: the suppression of fluctuation margins, the irrevocable fixing of parities, and the creation of a European (but not necessarily single) currency. Such a situation, de Larosière observed, seemed to be compatible with the objectives of the French government: namely, the existence of a zone of stability and the development of the EEC as a more homogeneous entity vis-à-vis the rest of the world. Crucially, de Larosière did not think that such a monetary union would imply a total loss of sovereignty, since the economic situation varied so much from one member state to the other and it would hence be impossible to govern it with a single institution.

Of still greater value was the analysis of the Commission regarding monetary affairs in its *Report on European Union*, published on 26 June 1975. Ortoli addressed the report, written at the request of heads of government at the Paris summit of October 1972, to Liam Cosgrave in his capacity as president of the European Council, which in 1974 began holding regular and frequent meetings of these heads of government.[11] This underlined, as did several other points that will be looked at later, that one of the central tasks of the European Council was the

orientation of future endeavors of the EEC as a whole—of which monetary matters formed a significant part. The aim of the Commission's report was to analyze
the "transformation of the whole complex of the relations of Member States into
a European Union."[12] With this report the Commission reaffirmed its "monetarist" conception of EMU: "The achievement in due course of Monetary Union
is a *precondition* for economic integration within the Union and its cohesion in
the world at large."[13] Within a European Union, the Commission believed that
monetary policy would become an exclusive field of competence of the Union,
"just as the common external tariff is already." This would entail the creation
of a European central bank, or an EEC system of central banks, with a "fairly
high degree of independence." Concerning the crucial question of how to achieve
these aims, the Commission clearly opted for an improvement of already existing
mechanisms instead of pursuing a whole new creation. A first method envisaged
by the Commission was that of the parallel currency, coined for that occasion
"a new monetary instrument peculiar to the Community."[14] This meant that a
common, European currency would circulate, while the national currencies—
and hence the snake—would carry on functioning as normal. The EMCF would
be in charge of the introduction of this currency, and would hence become "the
forerunner of the future monetary authority." The Commission did not provide
many detailed justifications for its choice of this parallel currency approach. It
simply stated that such a parallel currency approach would avoid "an unduly
rapid freezing of intra-Community exchange relationships," thereby allowing
more flexibility for national policies. More interestingly, the Commission argued
that this method would allow more room for "adjusting the rate of advance toward monetary union to the progress made in bringing economic, industrial,
and regional structures into line."[15] Although the Commission had adopted a
monetarist position, this statement somewhat softened its position by showing
that it paid attention to the economist point of view. If the *Report on European
Union* started out as a renewed endorsement of the monetarist approach, it thus
ended with a careful remark on the merits of the parallel approach.

As for institutional issues, apart from the EMCF, the Commission proposed
the creation of a European executive: "European Union means nothing if it
does not involve the development of a European governmental executive."[16] The
Commission suggested a relatively complex institutional setup that would see
the coexistence of this European executive together with the Commission and
the European Council. In contrast with its thinking on monetary affairs, the
Commission was much more keen on creating a whole new comprehensive
model regarding institutional structure. Hence, contrary to the later Tindemans
Report, for instance, the *Report on European Union* did not attach great importance to the European Council. It recognized the need for its creation, which was

attributed to two factors: the weaknesses of the existing structures and "the need for political agreement at the highest level." The Commission was much less clear, however, regarding the future role of this institution. Given the additional creation of a European executive, its significance would clearly be reduced, or at least overshadowed, by this proposed European government. The Commission maintained, though, that "once the institutions have been set up, meetings of Heads of Government should be limited to dealing with the most difficult political problems that will continue to arise."[17]

The First Ordinary European Council

Interesting and thought provoking though it may have been, this monetary brainstorming could not conceal the fact that the economic situation of the EEC was not encouraging. The heads of government of the EEC member states convened in July 1975 for the second European Council. With the international economic situation what is was, this summit meeting was more like group therapy than anything else: the patients met up in Brussels and described and discussed their problems together. This Brussels European Council was the first that was not dominated by a single issue, as had been the case in Paris (dominated by the European relaunch) and then Dublin (British renegotiation) a few months earlier. In addition to this, the French government insisted on organizing a low-profile summit meeting: it was not "a high point of world diplomacy," Jean Sauvagnargues argued.[18] Since no single theme emerged, the preparation of this summit meeting was characterized by uncertainty: uncertainty about the number of topics to be tackled, uncertainty about whether they would really be tackled, and uncertainty about the outcome of the discussions. The risk identified—in particular by Gabriel Robin—was that the meeting would lack excitement.[19] For a young institution like the European Council, still not enshrined in legal texts, this did matter. It was indeed likely to appear as merely a traditional Council of Ministers, but with heads of state and government, and more media. Here was the key: a new equilibrium had yet to be found for the European Council, which ought to offer serious and informal discussion conditions to its members, without being either too influenced by or contemptuous of media attention. This new equilibrium to be created in the EEC institutional machinery was also directly influenced by the opinions of its members: some governments that considered the European Council an improved EEC Council were not really concerned with the way in which its meetings were becoming routine, while others, like the French government, believing it ought to become "the real leading institution of European integration,"[20] were more troubled by this evolution. The first issue concerned the attendants at the European Council session. Some governments (Benelux, Denmark, Ireland) pressed for the participation of the permanent representatives and the political directors.[21] The British and French governments explicitly and immediately rejected this proposal, insisting that the issue had already been settled in Dublin earlier in March. A second issue was the fear that the European Council would become a mere "instance of appeal" of the Council of Ministers.[22] Here again it was a question of equilibrium: the European Council ought to settle issues that could not be sorted out in the Council of Ministers, but this feature should not become systematic. Indeed, it would have, in short, the double disadvantage of paralyzing the Council of Ministers (which would tend to refuse to make decisions on problematic dossiers) and downplaying the role of the European Council itself (which would become a super Council of Ministers).

In the course of this European Council session, Giscard clearly sought to lead the overall discussion concerning economic and monetary affairs, and was always closely followed by comments from Schmidt. The overall impression was the existence of a Giscard-Schmidt partnership on economic and monetary issues. Giscard's speaking time was particularly impressive. In the course of discussion he twice stated his own conclusions about the situation: the need for a more stable international structure for consultation, the need for improvements of the snake (and reinforcement of its Community character), and finally, the need for taking measures to support economic activity.[23] In this overall discussion, the Commission found itself in an awkward position. It could obviously not deny that action ought to be carried out at the global level, but was at the same time seemingly aware that such actions would not put the EEC—and the Commission itself—at the forefront of the negotiations. It would instead tend to diminish further its influence over the course of events. Yet the Commission sought to maintain EEC leadership in monetary affairs. In this field it insisted that action should be taken first between European countries, and then maybe at the global level. Although it eventually was not the case, it was initially reported that the Commission considered putting a paper on economic and monetary issues before the European Council in Brussels in July 1975.[24] The Commission would have envisaged a mere call for increased cooperation, particularly between snake and non-snake countries. The most important point, however, was that the Commission's efforts were geared toward the European Council and no longer the Finance Council. This was an important move, although no formal step had yet been taken; it was, however, merely a question of months, as the Commission would present a paper to the European Council in April 1976. The French president defended a line close to that of the Commission. He declared, for instance, that the Community character (instead of the European character) of the snake ought to be reinforced. On the whole, the group therapy experiment revealed itself to be of limited effectiveness. No agreement had been found on economic on monetary issues. The EEC had yet to find a good therapy.

More worrying for European cooperation, the common Franco-German understanding was not as deep-rooted as commonly suggested.[25] There are several possible explanations as to why the apparent harmony between the French and German governments on monetary issues turned out to be illusory. One of them is that the French and German governments actually had a tendency to misunderstand each other economically. To begin with, Giscard and Schmidt differed slightly in their analysis of the crisis. According to Giscard, "This crisis, described as a crisis of the Western economic system, is, in fact, above all a monetary crisis."[26] For Schmidt the situation was slightly different. Of course, he did not deny Giscard's thesis, but placed the emphasis instead on the economic side of the crisis, not the monetary. The divergent analyses of the two leaders thus represented a variant of the economist versus monetarist debate.

Of still greater significance was the fact that while Giscard and Schmidt constantly reaffirmed that they agreed with what each other had just said, it was striking to see that each of them somewhat misinterpreted what the other was actually saying. The difference was striking with regard to economic policies. On the one hand, Schmidt expressed his doubts regarding "deficit-spending" policies aimed at supporting internal consumption, and instead called for a backing of investment. Furthermore, he repeatedly said that isolated measures by individual EEC member states would be very insufficient. In place of this, what was needed was an increase of *worldwide* demand. On the other hand, while Giscard said he agreed with Schmidt, he announced that the French government was about to take measures comparable to "deficit spending" *alone*, and that the most urgent task at a world level was to organize the increased consultation of Western leaders. Of course, this is not to say that the opinions of the French president and the German chancellor were at odds. But it did show, however, that the hierarchy of priorities was not the same on each side of the Rhine. The French president tended to remain monetarist in his thinking, while the German chancellor inclined more toward the economist approach. And for an economist like Schmidt, the measures taken by the French government in April 1975 in order to stimulate the economy were certainly worrying.[27] These measures mainly consisted of a partial reimbursement of the supplementary income tax levied in 1974. Quantitatively, they were not alarming. But with respect to the internal battle in the French government between those encouraging *la relance* (Chirac) or those supporting *la rigueur* (Fourcade), the prime minister appeared to have won some points. If this episode was not yet decisive, it did underline the increasing uncertainty of the French government's commitment to a stability-oriented economic program.

Another issue that revealed Franco-German divergence was the possible participation of the Swiss franc in the snake. This constitutes an interesting case study of the interplay between specifically EEC matters and Europe-wide dimensions of monetary cooperation. In early 1975, following the appreciation of the Swiss franc vis-à-vis the DM and the dollar, the Swiss government formally applied to join the snake arrangement.[28] The crux of the problem lay in the fact that the Swiss franc was a relatively strong currency and would oblige weaker currencies to intervene in the markets to defend their parity. Moreover, the strength of the Swiss franc was partly due to a capital inflow motivated by the privileged rules of the Swiss fiscal system. To sum up, while the German government favored the entry of the Swiss franc, the French government was much more reluctant, and set as a precondition some fiscal reforms. The Swiss government, in December 1975, eventually abandoned its application. What was of particular interest, however, were the remarks made by Schmidt to Giscard in arguing for the Swiss case. True, Schmidt argued, including Switzerland would mean an increased influence of non-EEC countries in an EEC mechanism. But this had already been the case before. Revealingly, what mattered in Schmidt's eyes was the additional support for his stability-oriented economic policies that he thought he would find in the Swiss participation (among others).[29] The snake was therefore, so far, not only an EEC mechanism but a mechanism aimed at encouraging monetary stability in Europe in general.

The French Government's Economic U-Turn

The major event of late 1975 was, as far as monetary affairs were concerned, the economic U-turn executed by the French government. Opting for an economic strategy at odds with the German one, the French government indirectly dashed all hopes of progress in European monetary affairs, at least in the short run. This section will delve into this mind-boggling decision and analyze its consequences. I will try to explain why, how, and for what purposes such a Keynesian-like plan was adopted in late 1975. I will then broaden my analysis to the wider European and international context to show that many factors—including the salience of international issues, like the Rambouillet meeting, or simply the declarations of some member states—indicated a (provisional?) abandonment of the issue of monetary integration in the EEC.

La Rupture

That the commitment of the French government concerning its fight against inflation was increasingly insecure was no cause for surprise. By contrast, it was much more astounding that the French president would implement such a far-reaching plan of economic relaunch in September 1975. Part of the explanation lies in the French domestic political situation. Since May 1974, the French government had been formed around a heterogeneous majority, composed of the Gaullists, led by Jacques Chirac, and the centrists and liberals, led (indirectly) by Giscard. During the 1974 presidential elections, Chirac, who unexpectedly supported Giscard and managed to bring an extra Gaullist support to his candidacy, had thwarted the campaign of the official Gaullist candidate, Jacques Chaban Delmas. Hence, even after Giscard had been elected, some of the Gaullists in the parliament did not support the new president with much enthusiasm. Once Giscard nominated Chirac for prime minister in May 1974, a covert battle, which quickly became overt, was waged between the two. The parliament became another arena within which this struggle could be played out. Giscard therefore had to face a paradoxical situation in his first two years in office—and arguably during most of his *septennat*—in which his most ardent opponent did not necessarily come from his parliamentary opposition, but instead from his own majority.

With local elections to be held in March 1976, however, the greatest danger came more traditionally from the rise of the left. Since 1974, the French government had opted, more or less constantly, for a stability-oriented economic program to fight the consequences of the world economic crisis. This choice opened up a political avenue for the left, which criticized the government for refusing to redistribute money to its citizens while inflation was still high. Numerous reports from the *préfets* described an increasingly pessimistic country discontent with the executive.[30] In addition, some in the presidential majority even started to doubt the efficiency of this policy. Chirac himself began to be, as of late 1974 and early 1975, the principal advocate of an economic *relance*.

It must be said here that the roles and responsibilities in deciding this strategy are somewhat unclear. The idea of an expansionist program would have initially been strongly backed by Chirac and strongly opposed by Fourcade, with Giscard undecided and accordingly stuck in the middle.[31] The debate and the indecision of the French president lasted through the spring and part of the summer of 1975. He took his decision in late July, set out in detail the plan in late August and early September, and Parliament voted for it in early September. In the meantime, the plan became very much Giscard's child. Although it originated as Chirac's idea, the president himself and his collaborators sketched it out.[32] This is quite paradoxical, since to this day the plan is still referred to as the "Chirac plan." Another slight paradox lay in the fact that although the general approach of the French economic relaunch was quite clearly incompatible with the goal of European monetary cooperation, the French government actually did not seem to be fully aware of the potential consequences of its economic plan. It simply did not know whether the stimulus given to the French economy would be too little, about right, or too much.[33] Even more revealing, no direct and explicit reference to European monetary cooperation was ever made in the discussions. Domestic political and economic considerations and European monetary cooperation were still very compartmentalized.

In substantive terms, the plan envisaged a number of measures aimed at immediately stimulating aggregate demand. Numerous measures were taken to sustain domestic consumption, such as the so-called *aides exceptionnelles* aimed at giving nontaxable financial assistance to families, disabled persons, and elderly people, and an easing of credit facilities.[34] In addition to this, various projects were launched directed at developing public infrastructure. The total cost was estimated at 30 million French francs, or more than 2 percent of GNP.[35] The scope of the relaunch appears even greater in retrospect. Indeed this conservative/liberal plan actually cost twice as much as the relaunch carried out by the socialist government of Mitterrand in 1981.[36] This episode was, of course, to have significant domestic consequences in addition to an important effect at the EEC level.

The Confirmation of the Break

Two types of event confirmed the existence of a break in European monetary cooperation, starting with the French decision. First, the Rambouillet meeting—the first world economic and monetary summit that gathered the leaders of the six most industrialized countries—attracted most of the monetary attention, and this somewhat to the detriment of European monetary cooperation. Second, the German government, following its "economist" thinking, did not consider European monetary arrangements to be a pressing issue in the short run given the growing economic divergence within the EEC. International uncertainties—monetary instability, economic recession, protectionist measures—were higher than ever on the agenda in mid-1975. International negotiations, of various types, dominated the agenda of 1975, from Helsinki (30 July–1 August 1975) to Rambouillet (November 1975) and even to Jamaica (January 1976).[37] Of course, such discussions at the international level did not prevent the EEC from adopting new initiatives. But they did show that an important degree of dynamism, and the focus of attention, were not centered around the EEC but rather the international (monetary) system.

These international monetary negotiations also provided a good opportunity to observe the consistency of the monetary proposals of the French government. Interestingly, it put forward a proposal aiming at progressively restoring a system of "stable but adjustable" parities at the international level.[38] In particular, the two steps of the plan patently recalled some of the ideas contained in the

Fourcade memorandum. The first step would allow currencies to float freely during a short period of time, until they could rejoin the new international monetary system. The second step would consist in the determination of pivot rates between the group of currencies with stable exchange rates and those that still floated freely. These parities could be periodically revised. Finally, after this system had been in operation for a year or two, the participating countries would examine the possibility of definitively restoring a universal system of stable but adjustable parities. Two ideas were here characteristic of those of the Fourcade memorandum—or indeed of the monetary thinking of the French government during that period: the possibility for a currency to temporarily float and the possibility to revise, without drama, the pivot rates. While the Keynesian relaunch of the French government underlined the interlinkage between domestic politics and European integration, this example stresses the interconnection between the EEC and the international levels.

Further underlining this inauspicious backdrop were some British, German, and Irish reflections indicating that monetary cooperation was not, in the present circumstances, their top priority. Three memorandums—a British secret diplomatic report, a German governmental foreign policy brainstorming, and an Irish food-for-thought pre-European Council paper—issued in the fall of 1975, all underlined revealing themes about their governments' European monetary policy preoccupations. The German memorandum about its European policy was not optimistic about European monetary cooperation. The German government had decided to examine its European policy in a seminar in Gymnich on 29 September 1975.[39] The result of this governmental brainstorming was a memorandum published on 3 November 1975.[40] It was a relatively long document, comprehensively addressing all European issues, from the CAP to the European Parliament. It started out with an unsurprising though significant confirmation that the European policy of the German government had priority in its overall policy, together with the Atlantic alliance and the policy of détente. In the long term, the German government announced that its goal was the creation of a European federation including an EMU. Yet while the German government affirmed its welcome to those currencies that returned to the snake, it rejected any change that might destabilize the current exchange rate system. In more concrete terms, the German government suggested some measures in order to intensify EEC economic cooperation, based on the current snake. Apart from this, it limited its suggestions to continuing and improving monetary cooperation in the Monetary Committee and the Committee of Central Banks Governors. On the British side, Michael Palliser, British permanent representative to the EEC, purported that although time was not ripe for EMU, the current state of disarray the EMU debate was in would not last long. The British government should hence already start thinking about an alternative approach. In the report on EMU issued on 26 September 1975, he even presciently wrote: "If we have nothing new to offer, the chances are that the next round of the debate, like the last, will focus solely on the monetary path to EMU. This will be far too soon for us, even if one may hope that in a year or two from now it may begin to seem more plausible."[41] He essentially suggested a "fiscal federalist approach," advocating for significant resource transfers from the richer to the poorer EEC regions (Ireland, Italy, and Britain), in phrasing that recalls the concurrent studies during the EMS negotiations. Palliser's proposal neglected the working of the exchange rate mechanism and centered instead on the redistributive function of the EEC budget. Callaghan did not follow up on this report. The Irish memorandum was, by contrast, fairly cursory about EMU.[42] It also focused more on the need for resource transfers than on the revision of the exchange rate system. This was a perennial Irish (as much as British and Italian) request, of which another good example could be found in the setting up of the Regional Fund, and later on, during the EMS negotiations, in the so-called concurrent studies. The Irish foreign minister Garret FitzGerald again suggested very similar ideas in January 1976.[43] Overall, although Palliser talked of a "distinctive British approach" mainly based on the assumption that Britain had a lower rate of growth per capita than the rest of the EEC member states, there was a distinctive British-Irish-Italian approach focusing on transfer of resources, as the EMS concurrent studies will later on confirm, contrasting with the German-French-Benelux focus on monetary mechanisms and their interpretation.

The Rome European Council came as the ultimate proof that EMU had by and large been forgotten for the moment. Though increased hopes of an economic recovery allowed the summit to take place in a relatively positive atmosphere, its concrete results were extremely small, especially concerning monetary affairs.[44] Four other topics dominated the agenda instead: the follow-up to the Rambouillet meeting, a short examination of the economic situation in the EEC, financial and budgetary questions, and preparation for the conference on international economic cooperation.[45] In contrast with the preceding session, the European leaders did not feel the need for a free exchange of views on the economic and monetary situation, probably simply because there was nothing substantially new on the monetary front, and because attention, as explained above, was very much focused on international discussions instead of traditional EEC bargaining. The European Council continued to rehearse its usual diplomatic statements, however, declaring, for instance, that it had "again stressed the need for close coordination to be maintained between the economic policies of the Member States."[46] Such a statement was extraordinary given the absence of *any* coordination between, for instance, the massive economic relaunch of the French government and the other, more limited measures taken by the Germans. Hence one may wonder what exactly was going to be "maintained."

The Rome European Council marked the beginning of some kind of uneasiness and resentment about German economic success and German economic intransigence. Schmidt indeed appeared surprisingly intimidating during the session. He was reported to have said that "so long as he was chancellor, German economic strength would not be used for selfish national ends, but it was always worth remembering that he could so use it. If everyone chose to paddle his own canoe, the Germans could do so too."[47] A British report of this episode is telling:

> At one point in the discussion Herr Schmidt said in effect that if anyone in the Community had to go it alone it was Germany, by far the richest Member State, which could afford to. This struck the Foreign and Commonwealth Secretary (he told us afterwards) as uncomfortably reminiscent of some of the attitudes of pre war Germany. But it was in fact a graphic illustration of the point many of us have often made in discussing the value of the Community; that if the elemental force which drove Germany half across the world thirty years ago and has led them to win the peace since is not safely anchored in a peaceable democratic Community, things could turn out badly for us all.[48]

It certainly appears, in many respects, an over-the-top comment, quite exaggerated in the context of December 1975. It is striking to note, however, that it was Schmidt who, during the secret Bundesbank meeting in November 1978, would use exactly the same argument about the need to anchor Germany in "the West"/ the EEC and to provide a "European mantle" able to cover German economic success and its (perceived) accompanying arrogance. This would indeed remain a central *problématique* of European monetary cooperation in the following years.

A Continuous Monetary Brainstorming

This unpropitious context did not discourage the extensive rethink of European monetary issues. The Tindemans report, made public in January 1976, was particularly interesting in that respect since it considered monetary issues to be one of the most fundamental aspects of a European Union. The European Council had commissioned the Belgian prime minister Leo Tindemans to produce a report in December 1974 at the Paris summit. It asked him "to define what was meant by the term 'European Union.'"[49] Observing that "in the present state of affairs, no real progress can be expected," Tindemans nevertheless suggested reviving discussions on EMU within European institutions on the basis of a "new approach."[50] A first feature of this new approach was to envisage an EMU not necessarily with all the member states of a would-be European Union from the start. Tindemans explained that those countries that were not yet ready to make progress on the road to EMU should not prevent other countries from doing so. This was different, however, from a Europe à la carte. According to Tindemans, even those countries that would not take the first "bus" should commit themselves to the achievement of the common objective. Only the timescale of achievement would be variable. The snake could become the starting point for action. To this end, Tindemans suggested a number of ways to improve the existing system. First, the snake ought to be reintroduced within the EEC system. Second, the snake participants should accept some new obligations regarding internal monetary policy (control of money supply, budgetary policy, some aspects of economic policy). Third, Tindemans asked for better coordination regarding alterations in pivotal exchange rates. Fourth, he proposed to strengthen and render automatic the short- and medium-term support between members of the snake. In parallel, the EMCF would be reinforced, so that it could become the embryo of a European Central Bank. Fifth, the free circulation of capital should gradually become totally effective. And last, "case by case" measures ought to be defined in order to help those countries not in the snake to join it. Tindemans did not give more details, however, arguing that it should be discussed and decided in European institutions. Looking to the future, the Tindemans Report was much more imprecise and open: imprecise in that it did not tackle concrete issues but rather mentioned methodological problems; and extremely open since it stated that future stages "must be discussed within the institutions."[51] It did not even make suggestions on the best way to proceed, failing to declare a preference, for instance, about one of the various options for monetary union, such as the debate over a common or a parallel currency.

While not revolutionary, it must be noted that the Tindemans Report made an interesting distinction between what could be achieved in the short term and the longer-term objective of EMU. So far, many plans or reports either refused to make new long-term proposals given the difficult situation—the case with the Marjolin Report, for instance—or pretended from the outset to design *the* comprehensive plan leading to EMU—such as the Werner Plan. Tindemans did a bit of both, with more concrete short-term measures and less grandiose long-term speculations. This approach was in itself something new, since it showed that advances on the road to EMU could perhaps occur simply by improving the existing system. Second, the Tindemans Report adopted a relatively classic monetarist approach, at least concerning the short-term proposals. After describing the modifications he suggested for the snake, Tindemans argued: "Thus consolidated and extended, the nucleus of monetary stability existing today becomes the basis for a real convergence of economic and monetary policies."[52] As regards the longer-term suggestions, Tindemans adopted an approach closer to the so-called parallel one, insisting on the need for "a balanced set of measures in the field of economic policy as well as monetary policy." A third observation concerns the content of the Tindemans proposals. Not only were at least three of them (reintroducing the snake in the EEC, increasing monetary support, and facilitating the return of those currencies not in the snake) quite close, at least in the hierarchy of preoccupations, to those put forward by the French government since 1974, but this was also true of the overall spirit of the report, which believed that concrete progress *could* be made at present. It was noticeable that the choice for incremental process in European monetary cooperation was thereby confirmed, and that the same set of issues would later appear on the EMS agenda.

Given the unpropitious context and the absence of revolutionary measures regarding EMU, the Tindemans Report did not attract considerable attention. The Italian government, which shortly considered recycling the Fourcade memorandum at the beginning of its EEC presidency, welcomed the idea of communautarizing the snake.[53] And logically, the French Treasury was satisfied to see the Tindemans Report adopting a strategy similar to its own.[54] De Larosière welcomed the proposal of Tindemans to accept a sort of "two-speed" EMU, more flexible and more realistic. Alongside such general thoughts there were also a variety of more technical reasons behind the French Treasury's renewed criticisms of the snake. De Larosière explained that the European exchange rate system had two main features that impeded the proper functioning of the system. First, fixed exchange rates between EEC currencies, understood as a preliminary to monetary union and as a precondition to economic union, were hardly sustainable in current circumstances. For a few years European economies had been facing inflation and disequilibrium of balances of payments, and maintaining fixed exchange rates in the EEC was, as a consequence, an unrealistic objective. A solution could be to introduce normal possibilities to modify the pivot rates for as long as inflation was not controlled and equilibrium of balances of payments unimproved. Instead of appearing as a failure of the system, and instead of being decided in a climate of tension, these modifications should be an integral part of the system's functioning. Second, defending this system against speculation was not based on sufficient solidarity, since the burden fell for the most part on the weakest currencies. Hence the two key words of any reform of the current snake according to the French government: flexibility and solidarity. Once more, one of the key ideas of the Fourcade memorandum—to spread the burden of adjustment more fairly—resurfaced. The Banque de France even went further than the Trésor by sketching out a reform of the snake.[55] While it did not mention the possibility of organizing the snake around the EUA, as the Fourcade memorandum had done, it recycled most of the themes contained in the French finance minister's ill-fated plan, namely, the request for symmetry and increase of the credit mechanisms. Even more interestingly, the Banque de France suggested carrying out intramarginal interventions once the fluctuations reached a certain limit. This was indeed, in spirit, the idea of the EMS divergence indicator, namely, to implement early and preventive interventions on the markets. This monetary brainstorming should not hide, however, the new difficulties encountered in early 1976.

Stepping Back?

Indeed the consistency of the criticisms against the functioning of the snake conceal that, by early 1976, the economic and monetary situation had again worsened. This section will analyze these developments. I will first examine what appeared to be a dangerous slippery slope for the EEC: following the economic U-turn of the French government, the French franc pulled out of the snake in March 1976, and, unable to make decisions at Luxembourg, the institution of the European Council started being called into question in April 1976. I will then delve into this fourth European Council, and the question of abandoning EMU. Finally, such evident failures should not hide the fact that expert groups, indirectly backed by the Commission, continued an interesting monetary brainstorming.

The EEC Structure Fissures

March 1976 was a gloomy period for European monetary cooperation. The Dutch government decided in that month to discontinue the monetary arrangement (the so-called worm) between the guilder and the Belgian franc.[56] Although the end of the worm was not, per se, an event of tremendous importance,[57] it symbolically underlines the lowest ebb of European monetary cooperation in early 1976. Of greater impact was the pulling out of the French franc from the snake, which changed the EEC exchange rate system into a mere DM-zone. The departure of the French franc from the European exchange rate agreement was a direct consequence of the Keynesian relaunch of late 1975. In increasing domestic demand, these expansionary measures augmented in parallel the demand for imports, and, in fine, aggravated the deficit of the French balance of payments. As a consequence, this exerted downward pressure on the French franc, which was forced to pull out of the snake.

The French government attempted, however, to remain in the snake. It sought a realignment of snake currencies, but the negotiations failed. Hans Apel, the German finance minister, and Fourcade met on 14 March in order to see how realignment could be brought about, so that the French franc could remain in the snake.[58] The question was how to share the burden of realignment, and Apel was opposed to a revaluation of the DM. Moreover, he thought that the French franc had reentered the snake a year earlier at an unrealistically high level. The French finance minister argued that the current franc weakness was due more to an appreciation of the DM than to the French government's economic policy. Yet no agreement could be found on how to share the burden, not least because the French franc's weakness seemed more structural—given the inconsistent French economic policy, the balance of payment was unlikely to return to equilibrium in the short run—than momentary. De Larosière's handwritten annotations explain further that the French delegation, under pressure from both Giscard and Chirac, gave up quickly, mainly for domestic political reasons. Indeed, both the negative election results (a stability-oriented economic policy was hence even less likely) and the fact that leaving the snake would be more popular in public opinion than a disguised devaluation, encouraged Giscard and Chirac to ask Fourcade over the phone to give up.[59] These failed negotiations contributed to the spread of the belief among some French monetary authorities that the French franc's departure from the snake was due more to speculation and a failed realignment than to French economic policy.[60]

Even more widespread was the idea that if the French franc left the snake once more, it was because the snake's mechanism itself was flawed. The French franc's new pulling out of course thus prompted new thinking about reforming the snake. Fourcade hence restated the main thrust of his ideas during a private lunch with journalists on 18 March 1976.[61] The idea was that he would put them forward again on the occasion of the joint meeting of EEC foreign and finance ministers on 5 April—which he ultimately did not do.[62] The rebuff suffered by the Fourcade proposals in 1974 and 1975 obviously limited the French enthusiasm for formally putting forward its ideas once more, which would again be along similar lines, and would thus very likely suffer the same fate. The Italian government also shared the French preoccupations, and noted that the snake no longer had a Community character: only five out of nine EEC countries belonged to it, and three external countries were associated![63]

This was also a tremendous personal defeat for the French president. Not only had he personally supported reentry of the French franc in the snake but he was also directly behind the economic relaunch in the fall of 1975 that led to the pullout of the French currency. Nevertheless, Giscard kept on arguing—and Schmidt confirmed—that the other EEC members would have refused to help maintaining the French franc in the snake.[64] Yet such help would certainly not have prevented for long the longer-term trends to exert pressure on the French franc. Giscard explained the decision of the French government to pull out of the snake at the opening of the European Council in Luxembourg in April 1976.[65] Giscard then presented a document to his counterparts, "of a political nature," in which he wrote that "the economic and monetary union of Europe is not the work of a day or even a year. It is the task of a generation: ours."[66] For the first time at the level of the heads of state and government, he clearly stated the long-standing French complaints against the snake: the asymmetry of interventions and the lack of flexibility in the overall system, in particular the pivot rates.[67] This time the thinking of the French Treasury, analyzed above, was echoed at the EEC level. However, he refused to make any immediate proposals for reform, arguing that to do so would encourage speculative movements.

Schmidt immediately reacted by saying that he was stunned that "some may believe that one can correct budgetary or wage mistakes by monetary mechanisms."[68] If this immediate reaction of the German chancellor was predicable—Schmidt often said that exchange rates were a consequence of economic policy—such a statement was also surprising in that it sounded like an incredibly sharp criticism against both the policy of the French government (in particular the *relance*) and even Giscard himself. This was rather surprising for someone who was meant to be close to the French president, both in personal terms and, more importantly, in intellectual terms. Coming right after Giscard's short speech, in which the French president had criticized the malfunctioning of the snake and partly blamed this for the franc's departure, Schmidt's remark seemed directly aimed at the French president. The German chancellor added that he was not able to discuss the Commission papers because they were in French, a language he did not read (!). He then explained that he would now talk "as an economist and not as a German chancellor."[69] Schmidt went on in the same vein as in Rome in December 1975: "Monetary acrobatics would not enable one to get around the overriding need to tell one's own parliament, one's own trades unions, or one's own industry the truth."

The French franc's second departure from the snake instilled, however, a new idea in the European monetary cooperation debate. It indeed made clear that the European exchange rate arrangement in its present form would not be able to carry on for long, and in order to further European monetary cooperation, something new, or at least *seemingly* new, would have to be created—a point retrospectively made by Emminger.[70] Overall, this important episode not only showed the failure of French European monetary policy but it also underlined the growing divergence of economic priorities, especially between the French and the German governments. Indeed, in deciding to leave the snake, the French government showed that it preferred abandoning a monetary mechanism to imposing a more restrictive economic policy—German style—in order to stay on board. But at the same time, it indirectly reinforced the need for a new initiative.

Given this gloomy context, it soon became clear, at an early stage in its preparations, that the European Council of Luxembourg would not bring many rewards.[71] And indeed, the Luxembourg European Council mainly limited itself
to this revealing exchange of views on economic and monetary issues analyzed
above. To make matters worse, the apparent failure of the summit meeting triggered the reappearance of traditional criticisms on the functioning of the European Council and even of the institution itself.[72] Most, if not all, EEC member
states of course deplored the lack of consensus in the EEC and the failure to make
decisions. But some criticisms, directed at the institution of the European Council itself, actually showed that the consensus on its functioning was somewhat
fragile.[73] This particularly worried the French government.[74] Started as a press
campaign, it would have been nurtured, Robin explained, by an official declaration of Gaston Thorn criticizing the last session in Luxembourg.

The overall judgment was slightly dramatized, however. Though the European Council was sharply criticized after its April 1976 session, many member
states also felt that such reactions against the institution itself were unjustified
and exaggerated.[75] The expectations before each summit meeting were often
extremely high. Yet, as Patrick Nairne (cabinet office) had written to Palliser
after the 1975 Brussels European Council, "We should not look to the European
Council for more than it can give."[76] A British steering brief for the July 1976
European Council shrewdly described the last session in Luxembourg as a mere
"failure in public relations terms."[77] It must indeed be noted that these expectations were constantly nurtured by the nature of the meetings themselves—new,
and involving the highest, most powerful European leaders—hence the extensive
media coverage and, in fine, the public's higher expectations. But paradoxically,
it was widely recognized among the heads of government that not much could
come out of each of these meetings. Therefore, while the lack of decisions between the EEC heads of government was not a drama in itself—and was not
interpreted as such by the principals themselves—it became one in retrospect
because they appeared powerless, and because this powerlessness was echoed
and dramatically increased by the press. This was of course something that had
not often happened with the Council of Ministers meetings, for instance. All in
all, the European Council needed to make more trailblazing decisions in order to
affirm itself. This was especially true with the prospect of a potentially stronger
European Parliament after its first direct elections.[78]

Another issue linked to the question of EEC governance was that of the *directoire*.[79] In early February 1976, Giscard told a number of French journalists—
normally "off the record"—that a "*directoire européen*," presumably a triumvirate
(Britain, France, and Germany), would be needed in order to help the EEC move
forward.[80] The revival of this idea showed that the EEC was indeed in such a state

of disarray that institutional tricks (as much as monetary ones) were hoped to provide an appropriate answer to deeper-rooted problems. An institutional innovation, like the creation of the European Council, or like a *directoire*, could not by itself improve the situation. It is a mere *tool* to be used, not an end in itself. Arguing that the *directoire* idea underlined the European Council's failure, as some commentators did, would be, to paraphrase Nairne, asking the institution created in 1974 more than it can give. But the very discussion about the *directoire* also proved by example that the European Council had not become such an institution. This was quite remarkable, since for a long time, the smaller member states, in arguing against the institutionalization of summitry, said that it would turn out to be a *directoire*—which it precisely did not. A letter written by Tindemans to Schmidt, in which he outlined his fears about the *directoire* idea, was a case in point. The Belgian prime minister, in order to criticize the *directoire* idea, ironically became an ardent supporter of the European Council, an institution that he proposed to strengthen in his report.[81]

The criticisms against the European Council in particular, but also the EEC institutional setup in general, did contain some more constructive aspects, however. At a rhetorical level, it should first be noted that the remarks usually pointed out that the European Council had *yet* to find its equilibrium. They did not reject the institution as such but rather observed its organizational difficulties. Actually it was relatively clear, even from member states that had never strongly supported the creation of the European Council, that summitry had (logically) lost some of its spontaneity through its institutionalization.[82] Hence the constant will of the French government both to avoid bureaucratizing the preparation of the summits and to keep some informality in the course of the summit itself. In more concrete terms, the German memorandum analyzed above recognized and welcomed the new role taken by the European Council.[83] Schmidt, in particular, took it for the most important element of the EEC's institutional setup.[84] According to him, it had a coordination role similar to the one of the Federal Chancellery in Germany. Although the EEC now had a better source of leadership and a stronger agenda-setting body, many institutional problems remained to be solved. Hence, for instance, the German government suggested the issuing of a "*relevé de conclusions*" after each European Council, to avoid diverging interpretations of the discussions and to make them easier for the other EEC institutions to use.

Abandoning EMU?

In spite of a gloomy context, Giscard insisted on the inclusion of economic and especially monetary issues at the top of the agenda of the Luxembourg European Council. In a letter to Thorn on 23 March 1976, he argued that priority should be given to this topic in light of the international context.[85] Though the French president was willing to tackle the issue, his European counterparts were certainly not willing to make any new decisions. Already during the preparation of the summit, in late March, Hans Lautenschlager, head of the European economic integration division of the Auswärtiges Amt, made clear to his French counterpart, Henri Froment-Meurice, that the German government would not agree to any softening of the snake, and that in any event no further progress could be made concerning monetary cooperation as long as economic convergence had not improved.[86] Hence, while Giscard wanted to prioritize monetary issues at the European Council, Lautenschlager doubted that heads of government would go further than a simple exchange of views. And indeed, during the European Council itself, Schmidt intervened in order to sink Giscard's initiative regarding the adoption of a text by the European Council reaffirming the goal of EMU.[87]

To crown this diplomatic imbroglio, the Commission tried to (re)take the initiative on monetary cooperation at this very unpromising moment. To do so, the Commission presented a communication titled "Economic and Monetary Action" to the heads of government on the occasion of the summit in Luxembourg. Probably taking into consideration the fact that the European Council had now acquired the leading role in the EEC, the Commission took care to present its suggestions directly to the European Council, certainly in order to be more efficient and to obtain more quickly an exchange of views on them. The European Council reacted only by inviting the Council of Ministers to examine the communication of the Commission. This was very much akin to a rapid burial, since it was clear that the finance ministers would not strike an agreement. It was also an easy exit strategy for those who disliked the objective, such as the British government.[88]

This communication deserves closer attention, however. Showing once more that it was trying to regain leadership on economic and monetary issues, the Commission stressed the importance of providing a Community response to current challenges.[89] More surprising, after reaffirming that EMU remained a "fundamental objective," it stated that "for the time being, the Commission proposed to reinforce the coordination of economic policies and the monetary organisation of the Community." For an institution that was reputedly monetarist, this was a discreet but not insignificant turn. This statement was actually quite close to the "parallel approach" defended by the Werner Plan and, more recently (and to a lesser extent), by the Tindemans Report. Economic and monetary affairs tended no longer to be seen as opposed, or evolving in separate worlds, but instead as being very much interconnected. The Commission proposed to give a binding character to the coordination of economic policies. The Commission first remarked that the application of the decision of February 1974 regarding the coordination of economic policies would, of itself, bring significant progress. But the communication of the Commission aimed at going further. Instead of "orientations," for instance, the Commission was now speaking of "norms." In addition, the Commission stressed that those new measures had to be binding, and that financial penalties (like the suppression of EEC aids) could be taken against those member states not complying with the norms. As for monetary policy, the Commission was less clear, proposing the development of the exchange rate mechanism (without specifying a means of development, but interestingly mentioning the snake *and* the currencies out of the snake), the reinforcement of the role of the EMCF, and the integration of the snake into an EEC framework.

Although this communication was presented at the European Council, the new European institution did not discuss it properly. Ortoli introduced it at the start of the session, and the initiative was then forgotten. It was thrown into the usual EEC pipeline and was due to be examined by the Finance Council later in the month. Contrary to what the Commission expected, and contrary to what could have been the role of the European Council, the Luxembourg meeting did not pronounce any guidance concerning the communication of the Commission, and actually asked for a technical examination in the Council before any political agreement was reached. In other words, the European Council had buried the initiative without even organizing a decent funeral.

In addition to the partial abandonment of EMU, Franco-German relations encountered some tensions in early 1976. It has already been noted that since early 1975, French and German governmental opinions regarding economic policies had progressively diverged. This became very clear with the September 1975 *relance*. It must be noted that beyond the official stance of the French and German governments, according to which the economic plans should have been decided in close mutual consultation, French economic policy was actually far more expansionary than that of Germany.[90] There was in fact absolutely no parallelism between the two series of measures, except for the fact that they were both expansionary. But Berlin took measures amounting to 0.5 percent of its GNP, while Paris injected the equivalent of 2 percent of its GNP into the economy.

The situation did not improve in early 1976. Franco-German disagreements took shape in two different contexts: the traditional bilateral consultations and the EEC framework. This atmosphere of disharmony was first made palpable on 15 April 1976, with a relatively unimportant remark made by Schmidt. During a television interview, Schmidt suggested that the strength of the Communist Party in France was partly due to Gaullism.[91] Chirac curtly reacted on 6 May at the National Assembly, declaring that the German chancellor did not have to make such "thoughtless remarks." This story was published on the first page of *Le Monde*.[92] The French newspaper commented that Franco-German relations were going through "a sudden deterioration." Sigismund von Braun, the German ambassador in Paris, correspondingly reported that "the harmony between Bonn and Paris is .. somewhat disturbed at the moment."[93] Though the incident apparently attracted much attention, the disharmony did not seem genuinely deep-rooted. This was certainly why Braun simply suggested, to put an end to the episode, "The less said or written now, the better." The much better atmosphere of the Franco-German foreign ministers consultation of June 1976 proved that everything had been rapidly put back in order.[94]

This little dispute, which would normally have gone unnoticed, actually acquired additional significance because of the more general EEC difficulties. Indeed, after the Luxembourg European Council, Schmidt appeared to the French government (and to some extent in public opinion) as *l'homme fort*, inflexible, refusing any compromise while the French situation was difficult. As mentioned above, he personally rejected, for instance, the French suggestion to write up a declaration on economic and monetary affairs. Furthermore, as had already been the case in July 1975 during the Brussels European Council, Schmidt and Giscard once more showed in Luxembourg their slightly divergent understanding of the situation. While Giscard insisted on the shortcomings of the European exchange rate mechanism, Schmidt put the emphasis on economic divergences. While Giscard suggested an effort to improve the snake, Schmidt reacted abruptly, saying that "it is useless to rig the thermometer!"[95] In spite of their diplomatic facade of unity, the French and German economic philosophies seemed to be drifting apart. As Joop den Uyl put it in summing up the Luxembourg European Council discussion, the perennial central question still was "could common monetary policies precede economic convergence?"[96] The economist versus monetarist opposition was more clear-cut than ever.

Experts to the Rescue? The Academic Debate about a European Parallel Currency

The nearly permanent debate about European monetary cooperation among policymakers should not be allowed to obscure the bold ideas launched by the academic debate in the mid-1970s. If they were certainly not likely to be immediately translated into European texts, they do, however, attest to the particular climate surrounding the EEC's (lack of) discussions and (non) decisions in economic and monetary affairs. These academic reflections came from two channels: one independent (the All Saints' Day Manifesto) and one indirectly backed by the Commission (the Optica Report).

The so-called All Saints' Day Manifesto was an article signed by nine economists and published in *The Economist* of 1 November 1975.[97] Many of these economists had been involved with other reports mentioned earlier: the Kiel Report (Giersch), the Marjolin Report (Giersch, Peeters and Thygesen), and the Mac-Dougall Report (Peeters). As usual with such initiatives, its authors claimed to be concerned with the current "lack of progress" of EMU. The Manifesto proposed three radical methodological shifts. First, contrary to previous initiatives (like the Fourcade memorandum and the Tindemans Report), the signatories asserted that their "proposal offer[ed] the best ways of achieving a monetary system which will be not only European-wide in scope but stable as well." This constituted a significant methodological shift. Since 1974, all suggestions to improve the European monetary situation had been at pains to avoid comprehensive plans with far-reaching consequences. As a result, the Manifesto broke new ground by being written from the perspective of the creation of a full monetary union. Of still greater importance was the second methodological shift proposed in this Manifesto. The signatories asserted that it was difficult to envisage a monetary union created through legalistic structures. Instead, the Manifesto suggested that monetary unification had to evolve in the marketplace. This would of course imply a radical U-turn in the strategy for European monetary integration, which, from the very outset, had always envisaged monetary cooperation through legal agreements and intergovernmental bargaining. Third, instead of concentrating on exchange rate unification, the signatories of the Manifesto argued that monetary unification was the key. In other words, they suggested abandoning the traditional goal of coordinating policies, and rather focus on monetary reform "based on the free interplay of market forces."[98] Monetary reform meant the progressive replacement of all national currencies by a new common one. Pascal Salin, one of the signatories of the Manifesto, had explained this point a few years earlier. Getting closer to a single currency did not necessarily imply narrowing exchange rate fluctuation margins, as much as pooling reserves was not the same as creating a common central bank. This "progressivity thesis," commonly accepted, according to which monetary union will come from the gradual narrowing and then definitive fixing of exchange rate margins, was very debatable, Salin explained.[99] The Manifesto accordingly called for the launch of a new common parallel European currency, dubbed the "Europa." A common and parallel currency—as opposed to a *single* currency—meant that the Europa would coexist and circulate with the existing national currencies. The Europa would thus be in competition with other currencies, and the market would determine its fate.

This debate about the introduction of a European parallel currency was not an isolated initiative, however. The *Optica Report 1975* advocated a similar solution.[100] This report was written by a group of independent experts set up by the Commission, composed of Giorgio Basevi (chairman), Emil Claassen, Pascal Salin, and Niels Thygesen. The usual disclaimer—"the opinions expressed therein are the responsibility of the group alone and not of the Commission or its staff"—applied, although the sympathy of the Commission for the parallel currency approach was publicly known, at least since its *Report on European Union*, published in June 1975. It is noticeable that the Commission again provided a secretariat. An alert reader could also not miss the fact that all the authors, except for Emil Claassen, had signed the All Saints' Day Manifesto and that Thygesen had been a member of both the Marjolin and the Optica groups. It is also particularly amusing to see that the authors of the *Optica Report 1975* (among whom were Basevi, Salin, and Thygesen) wrote in a seemingly detached fashion that "from a purely economic viewpoint, the group considers the proposals set out in the [All Saints' Day] Manifesto to be perfectly sound," since the same three were themselves signatories of this Manifesto![101] Unsurprisingly therefore, the *Optica Report 1975* was very much in the same vein as the Manifesto. It was obviously in favor of European monetary integration. The central idea was the same, namely, the introduction of a new second legal currency in each member state. This new European parallel currency was meant to be the vehicle for the achievement of two targets. The first was "the progressive harmonization and reduction of national inflation rates," and the second was "the realization of the benefits of a fixed exchange rate system or, in its extreme formulation, of a single European currency."[102] This revived interest of some authors of the All Saints' Day Manifesto for exchange rates was certainly derived from the fact that their analysis started from the theories of OPTImum Currency Area—hence OPTICA—and that for this reason they were particularly interested in the economic equilibrium in the EEC.[103] But why did the analysis and proposals of three former authors of the All Saints' Day Manifesto change over a few months? The main reason was that they included an additional factor in the *Optica Report 1975*, namely, the political viewpoint. As a consequence, the Optica group preferred suggesting "gradual' solutions" instead of the more "radical" suggestions contained in the Manifesto.[104]

The idea of creating a parallel European currency was far from new, however. At the theoretical level, Giovanni Magnifico had already suggested the creation of a European parallel currency in 1973–1974.[105] Jacques Riboud proposed the creation of a *Eurostable* in early 1975.[106] Robert Mundell established a *Plan pour une monnaie européenne* at various stages in the early 1970s.[107] At the practical level, various financial instruments had already introduced (European, composite) units of account in international capital markets. The Eurco was one such early endeavor at creating a composite unit of account.[108] This "Euro-cocktail" was, as the nickname suggests, based on a basket of the currencies of the nine members of the EEC. It had first been issued in 1973 by the EIB. It must be said that it was in principle the same as the EUA adopted by the EEC in March 1975.[109]

As recalled in chapter 2, the Kredietbank of Luxembourg had already created an EUA in 1961 and 1973. The Italian company ENEL had even issued European Currency Units as a multiple currency bond in June 1971.

If it underlined a strong interest in European monetary cooperation, this academic debate about the creation of a European parallel currency had, so far at least, an extremely limited impact on the discussions of the heads of government of the EEC. The debates of the latter concentrated for the moment on exchange rate fluctuations, both internationally (reform of the international monetary system) and in the EEC (the snake). The parallel currency approach was hence limited to the academic debate and the Commission itself (in its *Report on European Union*). An exception to this rule was the Fourcade proposal, which gave a significant role to the EUA, although it was not really meant to become a parallel currency. Given the difficult economic situation of most EEC member states, the time was certainly not yet ripe to evoke such a big new step as a European currency—be it parallel or not.

Conclusions

Although anecdotal, it is, however, quite revealing to find in the archives of the Council of Ministers a few letters from an unknown Belgian "poet," Marcel Florestan Vanlathem.[110] Struck by the European sclerosis, he proposed at various times in early 1976 several plans—usually written in the form of poems—to create "a new society" in which, among others, unemployment would be banned and citizens would determine their state's and region's borders in direct elections. The situation in the EEC was indeed so worrying as to arouse such desperate initiatives. Increased economic divergence had as a logical consequence ruled monetary integration out of the agenda of the EEC. In spite of these indisputable setbacks, some positive elements did remain. In this concluding section I will identify what the deadlock and setbacks over the issue of monetary cooperation revealed about the overall process of monetary cooperation in the EEC, and then will pick out some more positive elements that showed that monetary cooperation in the EEC had not totally been buried in mid-1976.

Dark Background, Dark Perspectives

The first of these worrying elements concerned the methodological disagreements over monetary cooperation. This involved a series of yet unanswered questions about monetary cooperation, concerning, to simplify, its nature, its scope, and the strategy to reach it. Was the EEC the best framework in which action should be taken? This question constantly resurfaced in late 1975 and early 1976. The Commission was acutely aware of the problem. In its *Report on European Union*, it stated, for instance: "To start with, the Member States must recognize that the Community is the framework in which the battle against inflation and recession has to be fought, and at the same time is the essential means for international cooperation."[111] Late 1975 and early 1976 were a period of international agreements: in Helsinki, Rambouillet, and Jamaica. If agreement at one level (international) did not prevent agreement at another (European), it did give the impression of a different hierarchy of priorities. It was not a complete coincidence that the lowest ebb of European monetary cooperation corresponded with one of the highest points of international monetary cooperation.

Was monetary cooperation an economic or a political question? This issue had still not been clarified. Even more than before, the stance of the French government, and of Giscard in particular, was always to try to move the issue away from experts and to bring it back into the political forum. He made this point clear at the Brussels European Council in July 1975.[112] He confirmed it in Helsinki a few days later: "It is a fundamental topic [monetary issues] about which political leaders have not talked until now, leaving the question to the experts."[113] Logically, Giscard had also described the return of the French franc into the snake in May 1975 as "a decision of political character."[114] As a consequence, Giscard constantly talked about the need for the creation of *a* political forum, both in the EEC (the European Council) and at the international level (G6/7). There was a fundamental parallelism in both initiatives.[115] He thus stated at the opening of the Rambouillet conference: "What is most important is that this meeting took place."[116] Giscard was not alone in insisting on the political dimension of monetary problems. Not only did the Commission stress this aspect but Tindemans also. He maintained, for instance, that the number one reason for the lack of progress toward EMU was a "failure of political will."[117] It must be noted, however, that the Commission, in its communication from March 1976, and Tindemans, in his report, showed little sign of change. As discussed before, both of them were keen on saying that economic convergence and monetary cooperation were linked. In doing so, they tended to return to consensus around the "parallel approach" of the Werner Plan. Not all EEC members shared the opinion of the French president or the Commission, however. The German government in particular continued to affirm the primacy of economic convergence. Indeed, still worse for the EMU project, the economist versus monetarist dichotomy was getting stronger. As seen above, on the occasion of two European Councils—in Brussels in July 1975 and in Luxembourg in April 1976—the opposition between a monetarist French government (backed by the Commission) and an economist German government (supported by the snake members) was at its starkest. As long as the division between the two options could not be overcome, European monetary cooperation would remain at a permanent standstill, and would only be able to produce an impressive theoretical brainstorming. Most important, the strongest economic power of the EEC—Germany—constantly affirmed the primacy of economic issues. Following its economist thinking, Germany continually affirmed that monetary divergence was a consequence of economic divergence—not the opposite.[118] The dark side of this German economic force was naturally that it could sometimes be perceived as a show of arrogance.

Finally, should monetary integration be implemented through a qualitative leap forward or rather through an incremental process? This was certainly the only question for which a clear answer emerged. Given the difficult context, a wide consensus materialized in favor of an incremental process. Hence, for instance, after the Marjolin Report, the Tindemans Report also privileged a pragmatic approach.[119] By contrast, the academic debate over monetary unification was much more in favor of a qualitative leap forward. This was particularly the case with the approaches encouraging the creation of a parallel currency. The extent to which such discussions could influence policymakers remained very limited, however.

Still more worrying for the advancement of monetary cooperation in Europe, the two main supporters of EMU seemed powerless. The French situation was paradoxical. Indeed, the significance of the September 1975 decision of the French government should not conceal the fact that, since June 1974, the French position concerning European monetary cooperation had on the whole been quite inconsistent.[120] Fourcade recognized without difficulty that the 1975 plan of relaunch was "in absolute contradiction with the hope aroused by the return of the franc in the European monetary 'snake.'"[121] Indeed, the new economic equilibrium that permitted the reintroduction of the French franc in the snake in early 1975—a diminution of the inflation rate, an improvement of the external trade balance—was actually known by the *rue de Rivoli* to be precarious.[122]

In that respect, it is striking that the attachment of the French president to European (monetary) cooperation did not lead him to employ the traditional strategy of using foreign pressure to achieve a domestic decision. In other words, he did not choose to carry on the 1974 "cooling-off plan" in order to preserve a fragile but improving economic situation, thereby improving European monetary cooperation. Quite the contrary, Giscard apparently did not even try to reject the option of a Keynesian relaunch to maintain the European monetary commitments of the French government. And he did so while constantly affirming, at least up until late July 1975, that the French and German economic analysis was similar, and that economic measures would be coordinated and adopted at the same time in France and Germany.[123] Since the genuineness of Giscard's commitment to European (monetary) cooperation usually goes unquestioned, it must be concluded that he simply misinterpreted the economic situation. As a consequence, while being so far the greatest advocate for reform of the European exchange rate mechanism with the Commission, the French government never followed the economic policy that would have allowed monetary improvements. If this behavior was not necessarily in conflict with a strict monetarist position—efforts needed to be concentrated at the European level that in turn would lead to the evolution of national economic policies—it was, however, so evidently incompatible with German policy that it rendered any closer European cooperation unlikely. Of the two strategies for EMU—monetarist and economist—it was quite clear that the economists, and in particular the Bundesbank, would not be ready to accept any modification of the snake as long as individual economic situations continued to be so divergent. Even though limited and appropriate, the French proposals, made without the adequate backing of a consistent economic policy, were always likely to be rejected by the German government.

Equally unpromising was the apparent impotence of the European Commission. At various times between mid-1975 and mid-1976, the Commission tried to take the initiative regarding monetary affairs. Interestingly, this period witnessed a protracted and continuous pattern of the Commission directing its attention to the European Council. For instance, it considered putting forward a paper to the European Council in Rome in December 1975 but only did so in Luxembourg in April 1976. This was a noticeable change, since this type of communication—as had been the case with the Commission's "urgent measures" of June 1974—used to be addressed to the Council of Ministers. Admittedly, though, it did not accomplish much, since the European Council transmitted it back to the Council of Ministers, hence going round in circles. Yet the crucial point was that the Commission, in so doing, had acknowledged the new centrality progressively taken by the European Council. The Commission confirmed the European Council in its function of agenda setter and position taker. But the European Council revealed itself also to be on this occasion an excellent initiative burier since it did not want to make any decision. It was noticeable, however, that the Commission did try, throughout this period, to provide some leadership on this issue. But its twofold strategy, based on an attempt at controlling the agenda and its expertise, failed. Indeed, two types of factors constantly complicated the Commission's situation. First, institutionally, the affirmation of the European Council as an important agenda-setting body somewhat undermined the Commission's ability to take the lead in, among other issues, monetary affairs. Hence, while the Commission was willing to reintroduce this topic in Luxembourg in April 1976, the European Council indirectly rejected this initiative. Second, and in parallel, the sensitivity of monetary issues—arguably the most sensitive issue after defense for the

European nation-state—and the peculiarities of the institutional systems of each member state—the independence of the Bundesbank, for instance—did not give the Commission much room for action. Its expertise was not necessarily recognized by the national authorities of each member state. It therefore had to stick to the role of pathfinder, but with a limited ability to actually influence domestic French economic policy, say, or the policy of the Bundesbank.

The transnational informal network of academic economists behind the various parallel currency proposals was another strong source of support for the cause of European monetary cooperation, but an even more powerless one. The personal interconnections between the authors of the various reports mentioned above and in the preceding chapter have shown that the same persons were very often behind these various similar proposals. Yet they were utterly unable to enter the EEC decision-making system. They were indirectly supported by the Commission that in many cases appointed them and provided them a secretariat. Nevertheless, the reports merely remained on the desk of monetary officials and made their way into the historical archives—but never came to be discussed in EEC forums (such as the Committee of Governors or the Monetary Committee) nor even mentioned in the notes produced by national finance ministries. The transnational (monetary) learning process was thus happening among an elite group of monetary officials (central bankers, heads of treasuries, finance ministers, economic advisers) of which this transnational informal network of academics seemed de facto largely excluded. In stark contrast to these powerless actors—chiefly the Commission, the French government, and a transnational informal network of academics—the German government's (op)position was even stronger.[124] The next chapter will particularly highlight this point.

The European Council: "A Workmanlike Affair without Dramatics"

Alongside these negative signs—Tsoukalis, writing his introduction in 1976, called it "A Post-Mortem?"[125]—some more positive hints of improvement could be detected. For a start, initiatives did continue being produced. They came from various sources, from the EEC (Commission), from reports about a European Union (Tindemans, Commission), and from academia and civil society (All Saints' Day Manifesto, *Optica Report 1975*). Hence, in one form or another, EMU remained on the European agenda. But more important, there were two longer-term trends—two learning processes—under the surface: one institutional-intergovernmental (the emergence of the European Council), one transnational (monetary policy learning), so far evolving in a very compartmentalized fashion.

Before turning to these more technical aspects, it is important to note that the long-standing institutional problems of the EEC seemed to be improving slightly. In 1975–1976, they were still considered to be a significant issue. The Commission recognized, for instance, that "the inadequacy of the Community's decision-making process" was one of the causes of the slow pace of progress in economic and monetary matters.[126] The European Council was meant to be, as we saw in the last chapter, one answer to this problem. After four sessions, it could be said that the new institution had experienced, in practice, a relatively smooth, discreet, and efficient installation. In short, it had become, as Wilson put it, "a workmanlike affair without dramatics."[127] From the records of the meetings themselves, and according to the diplomatic milieu, the European Council had, by early 1976, clearly been accepted as a permanent feature of the European institutional landscape.[128] This did not mean, however, that its organization was perfect, or that every member state had yet understood how best to use it. If there was an ongoing learning process among a transnational monetary elite, there was also an ongoing learning process about how to make effective use of the European Council, in a fashion similar to other EEC institutions in the late 1950s and early 1960s.

The critiques surrounding the April 1976 Luxembourg session clearly showed this. But in spite of critiques and mixed results, the European Council affirmed its role in the EEC's institutional structure as a potential source of strong leadership and, first and foremost, as the EEC's main agenda-setting body. This was clearly articulated by Giscard, Schmidt, and Wilson in July 1975, when they argued that for the foreseeable future any important decision related to European integration would not originate from the European Commission but the European Council.[129] From the perspective of a future European Union—and in addition to a positive general evaluation of the European Council—the Italian government noted that the European Council could be included in the institutional system as the institution gathering economic and political competences at the highest level.[130] In a similar vein, according to Nairne, Giscard saw the European Council "as giving direction to the Community, ordering priorities, taking stock, laying down the lines of advance, and seeking common positions on the major world problems. He does not want issues to be referred to it by the rest of the Community machinery or prepared by officials: the channel of impetus and influence leads down from it, not up to it."[131] Equally revealing were the positive remarks found in official reports. For example, the Tindemans Report stated that the European Council was a step forward for the EEC as such, but also, crucially, as a tool for future progress regarding EMU.[132] That the European Council was now accepted was one thing, but that it had to be maintained or improved was another. It was noticeable, for instance, that the French government—and also to some extent the German one—continued to try to avoid a bureaucratic preparation of the sessions of the European Council, and hence preserve the scope for informal discussions between the heads of government.[133] Smaller member states were also keen on protecting the informal nature of the European Council. In a meeting with Callaghan, Max van der Stoel thus underlined that he was in favor of the "fireside chat" model for future European Councils.[134]

Even more crucial with regard to monetary cooperation, it had now become customary for the European Council to examine the economic, monetary, and social situation of the EEC. Again, the question was not necessarily whether to take bold decisions ex nihilo. The heads of government themselves were aware of this. During the Rome European Council in December 1975, after Aldo Moro, who acted as chair, had suggested an agenda, the immediate response of Schmidt and Giscard was to ask to talk about economic and monetary problems first. And they revealingly commented that "the members of the European Council were not in Brussels solely to agree on documents."[135] The point of the European Council, in such a period of disarray, was rather to have free (and retrospectively, for a historian, very revealing) exchanges of views. Hence Schmidt, at some point in the same meeting in Rome, asked foreign ministers, interpreters, and others to leave the session so that heads of government could have a completely confidential discussion.[136] Keeping the European Council's sessions informal was thus a perennial challenge facing the new EEC institution.

The British civil service gave an excellent example of this institutional learning process. In mid-1975, Nairne (cabinet office) and Palliser (British permanent representative in Brussels) exchanged their views about the role and place of the European Council in the EEC's institutional setup. A first feature emerging from this exchange was Palliser's awareness of both the importance and the limits of informal top-level regular meetings:

> The fact of the matter is that only Prime Ministers can when necessary over-ride the particular interests of specialist Ministers such as Finance or Agriculture Ministers—and not even they can always do so. . . . However slow the pace may seem, there is a continuing *approfondissement* of Community policies and with it an increasing domestic sensitivity in the issues involved. I believe that this will prove to be particularly the case in the institutional field as and when decisions are needed to transfer further political and e.g. Parliamentary powers to Community institutions. Progress of this kind will inevitably involve Prime Ministers more and more in the work of the Community.[137]

Michael Butler, undersecretary in charge of the Community, made a very similar point in his memoirs, hence showing that this view was quite widely shared.[138]

More to the point of monetary cooperation, it must be noted that beyond diplomatic statements, EMU genuinely remained on the agenda of most of the EEC member states. For instance, if the salience of the economist versus monetarist debate was worrying in itself, it must also be noted that it was actually a disagreement about the strategy to use in order to reach EMU, not a disagreement concerning the eventual goal of monetary integration. Some of the issues initially brought to the fore at the initiative of the French government in 1974 were now echoed within the EEC machinery. Hence the Commission initiatives as well as the Tindemans Report mentioned the problem of the reintegration of non-snake members into the exchange rate mechanism, or, in one form or another, the policy vis-à-vis the dollar. As a British official put it, there was in the Commission "no shortage of old ideas on this subject [setting up some form of association between the snake and non-snake currencies] which could be brushed up if and when the staff were asked to produce proposals."[139] The same was also true for the issue of the repartition of the burden of interventions. In addition, concrete smaller steps were still being implemented, such as the expansion of the use of the new EUA. As of December 1975, it was indeed used for the ECSC budget.[140] Even more important, and in more general terms, the learning process was also about understanding the new significance gained by monetary issues following the breakdown of Bretton Woods and the oil crisis. This was true at various levels. At an administrative level, Bernard Donoughue, senior policy adviser to Wilson, explained to the British prime minister that "the one thing that is certain is that with a floating exchange rate and the integration of international financial markets in recent years, monetary policy is now much more central to strategy than it used to be. Moreover, its implications for counter-inflation policy, industrial policy and housing policy suggest that it would be very dangerous to leave it to unilateral decision by the Chancellor."[141] At a heads-of-government level, Schmidt similarly stressed that since 1973, world monetary policy had become a decisive factor not only in international relations but also in the domestic situation of individual states— and that governments had not yet all grasped this point.[142] Beyond economic divergences, and beyond the little *refroidissement* of Franco-German relations in early 1976, it was also noticeable that there remained a genuine Giscard-Schmidt political agreement on the need for further European integration. Much has already been written on the amity between Schmidt and Giscard. Of course this friendship could not by itself bring progress in European integration as long as concrete issues were not settled. But its existence, especially at a time when difficulties could have seriously undermined the cooperation between their two countries, helped keep some coherence and left some hope of future close and concrete cooperation.

Of still greater importance, there was, beyond the governmental divergences between France and Germany, a genuine convergence in the thinking of the French and German monetary authorities. It has already been noted in chapter 2 that the French Treasury, though strongly supporting the technical improvement of the snake, had an economist vision of European monetary issues. De Larosière thus wrote in February 1976: "Operators support their reactions less with facts than with the sentiment that they draw from the policies carried out in different countries. If they have the impression that the fundamental options in Paris and in Bonn are not the same, speculation can begin at any moment."[143] French monetary authorities were therefore well aware that progress in the European monetary field was linked to an alignment of French and German economic options. Even more tellingly, Clappier, in a speech during the *conseil général de la Banque de France* on 4 December 1975, praised the functioning of the snake: "When some currencies are linked between them by the start of a stabilization agreement, things go in a much more harmonious manner than when no agreement exists."[144] This was, in other words, a plea for having some kind of *EEC-wide* exchange rate system—a plea progressively shared by other member states, as the next chapter will show.

ECONOMIC RAPPROCHEMENT, MONETARY STANDSTILL, JULY 1976–JUNE 1977

We no longer live in a Keynesian world.

—Raymond Barre

Keynes's methods worked in the 1930s; they don't today, and there is no Keynes.

—Helmut Schmidt

In this chapter I analyze the paradoxical double turnaround in mid-1976: the improvement of economic convergence among EEC member states but the relative standstill in European monetary cooperation. I cover the period starting with the decision of the newly appointed French government to follow a strong anti-inflationary program until just before the Commission's decision to prioritize monetary union in mid-1977. First, I analyze the "Duisenberg proposals" (named after the Dutch finance minister Wim Duisenberg) put forward in mid-1976 and the emergence of an essentially Franco-German consensus about the need to prioritize the fight against inflation. Second, I scrutinize the reactions to the Duisenberg proposals over the winter 1976–1977, and examine in parallel how the heads of government reacted to the sudden worsening of economic prospects. Third, I examine the planned revival of discussions about EMU among heads of government and the final rejection of most of the propositions contained in the Duisenberg initiative. Taken together, the three parts of this chapter should show, as chapter 2 did with the Fourcade memorandum, that although they failed, the Duisenberg proposals introduced in the EEC a number of ideas that would remain on the European monetary agenda in the following years. In addition, I will argue that the revival of monetary discussions at the highest political level started much earlier than is usually portrayed, namely, as early as in January–February 1977, and initially among the heads of government, not the Commission. I will further argue that the nomination of Raymond Barre as French prime minister considerably changed the situation, by putting French economic policy on a clear stability-oriented course. This was a noticeable change since it must be said that up to this point, it was mainly the failure to converge economically that had prompted the failure of monetary initiatives. The foundations of a would-be monetary proposal thus appeared slightly healthier.

A Sense of Déjà Vu

The Dutch presidency in the second half of 1976 was the first since the French presidency in the second half of 1974 to officially prioritize economic and monetary issues. The Irish and Italian presidencies had only contemplated the option of taking the initiative again, and eventually opted for concentrating on the proposals already under discussion. Almost at the same time, the French government, under the leadership of its new prime minister Raymond Barre, decided to adopt stability-oriented economic policies, thus getting closer to the German approach. In this section I examine the impact of these decisions, clearly distinct but potentially interconnected, on the course of European monetary cooperation.

The Duisenberg Proposals: Target Zones and Economic Coordination

"They might be seen as converting the snake into an autoroute with exits and entrances along its path enabling countries to drop out when they really had to, but without too much freedom to do so."[1] While this summary of the Duisenberg proposals given by the Commission president Roy Jenkins certainly oversimplified the content of the Dutch initiative, it did hint, however, at one of its central features: that it aimed to bring all EEC currencies back into one single and flexible structure. The so-called Duisenberg proposals were in fact largely designed by Conrad Oort, Treasurer-General in the Dutch Ministry of Finance. Oort first outlined his ideas in a speech at the University of Edinburgh and at Chatham House, and then formally in a letter to the president of the Monetary Committee.[2] The official Dutch EEC initiative hence started off in early June 1976, when Oort, former chairman of the Monetary Committee (January 1974–January 1976), wrote to Karl-Otto Pöhl, the president of the Monetary Committee. In his letter, Oort stressed his growing preoccupation with the exchange rate developments in the EEC. He raised two issues: first, "the lack of any serious discussion on these matters among governments of *all* member countries"; and second, "the growing division between countries that do and those that do not adhere to the 'snake arrangement.'"[3] Given that the French proposals of 1974 had not met the approval of the snake countries, Oort proposed to use a different starting point, namely, the concept of "rules for floating" of the IMF. These rules could be made operational in the EEC without, according to him, weakening the snake arrangement. Overall, then, this was a further example of the strong ideational influence of international monetary rules over European discussions.

Following the cancellation of the Finance Council initially planned for 5 July, Wim Duisenberg, the Dutch finance minister (whose name would afterward remain attached to these proposals), wrote on 6 July 1976 to his EEC colleagues in order to express his regret about that cancellation and to set out his economic and monetary ideas in more detail.[4] Regarding the coordination of economic policies, Duisenberg wrote that "the medium-term economic policy programme of the Community should be made to play a central role in a periodic review of national programmes." He also proposed the use of the EEC credit mechanisms, on an increasingly conditional basis, to support the economic convergence of the EEC member states. Concerning monetary cooperation, the starting point of the Dutch initiative was identical to that of the French memorandum in 1974 and the various propositions of the Commission: the current exchange rate instability was excessive and thereby harmful for the common market. The Dutch government added to this a further observation. The currencies that were independently floating—the non-snake members, in other words—had in fact no obligations vis-à-vis their EEC partners in the snake. Duisenberg hence proposed the creation of "a general Community framework for consultation and surveillance of exchange rate policies," linking both snake and non-snake currencies, based on the "guidelines for floating" of the IMF outlined in June 1974. These guidelines centered on the concept of "target zones" for exchange rates—hence the other name of the Duisenberg proposals. The Dutch finance minister was careful to emphasize that the guidelines did not impose any obligation of intervention, but instead that there was a presumption that the member state would act with the objective in mind and thereby bring its economic and monetary policies into accordance. They would thus provide a trigger and a guideline for consultation and mutual discussion.

Another note for discussion, outlined during the same period by the Bank of England (also referred to as the McMahon/Balfour note), was originally conceived as a contribution to the wider stocktaking discussion of the Committee of Governors about the snake, which will be analyzed in more detail below. On 6 September 1976, Kit McMahon and Richard Balfour thus presented a long note first analyzing the pitfalls of the snake, and then reviewing some possibilities for improvement.[5] Of all the points made one in particular deserves attention, that about asymmetry. Indeed it stressed the issue that the onus for intervention fell on deficit countries, thereby making a point traditionally backed by the French government but of which the British officials, together with Irish and Italians, were becoming the strongest defenders. The second part, concerning the ways in which the snake mechanism could be improved, interestingly underlined the ongoing learning process. It thus not only reviewed the two main proposals made in the last European discussions—the French discussions in 1974, the Dutch in 1976, but as usual not mentioning the parallel currency academic debate—but it also compared and contrasted them, explaining why, from experience, the Dutch proposal would be easier to implement than the French one. Hence the most important feature of the McMahon/Balfour note was not what it said—it actually concluded by leaving all options open—but instead the way in which it said it, testifying to an ongoing learning process among European monetary elites.

In terms of monetary thinking the Oort/Duisenberg ideas were, however, the most significant proposals emanating from an EEC government since the Fourcade memorandum presented first in September 1974 and in a revised version in May 1975. The Dutch government itself clearly saw it as a major initiative.[6] Interestingly, these proposals came from a snake member (this was not the case of France in 1974) and from a country faring rather less badly than other EEC member states (this was also not the case of France two years before). In contrast to the French proposals therefore, the Dutch suggestions could not be seen from the start as a way to dissimulate the wrongdoings of its own domestic economic policy. The Banque de France suggested that one of the motivations behind the Dutch initiative was perhaps the Dutch weariness of their "tête-à-tête," in company with a few other small countries with a much more powerful partner, Germany. The Dutch government would have been willing to dilute this tête-à-tête by enlarging the snake.[7] Indeed the basic aim of these proposals—namely, to bring back EEC member states into a single broad exchange rate system, thus putting an end to the division between the snake currencies (essentially a DM zone) and the independently floating currencies—was also that of Fourcade in 1974 and 1975. It ran, however, contrary to the Tindemans Report, which had suggested a two-tier EEC structure in the economic and monetary field. Yet the Dutch initiative, in contrast to the French one, did not envisage any weakening of the snake mechanism. A merger of the Duisenberg proposals with the Fourcade memorandum was therefore very unlikely, even according to the Trésor itself.[8]

In formally presenting his ideas to the Finance Council of 26 July 1976, Duisenberg set out the framework in which his initiative was to be understood: a return to fixed parities was clearly out of the question (but there was a built-in bias pointing in that direction); the proposal for target zones was not meant to weaken the snake (but to bring the snake and non-snake members closer together); and there was a strong element of economic discipline, since member states ought to pursue economic policies that would prevent their exchange rate from moving out of their target zone.[9] While the Commission welcomed and shared the ideas of the Duisenberg proposals, the member states were more cautious in their reception.[10] Indeed the proposals were by then still rather vague, and the main issue to be decided was whether discussion on the topic should be carried out—this was certainly not the most problematic issue. But once more detailed work started in the Monetary Committee and in the Committee of Governors, a number of points of divergence came out into the open.

Given the significant economic differences between European states, the first most common reaction was calling the initiative premature, and this even among non-snake members. "There is no point in putting the monetary cart before the economic horse," observed a British official.[11] In the first Monetary Committee meeting to examine the Dutch proposals, Jacques de Larosière warned that a target zone could only become a weapon used by speculators.[12] Predictably, Pöhl affirmed that "rather than always examining unrealistic proposals, it is better to fight against inflation and reinforce the coherence of economic policies." Formally, however, a longer and more detailed discussion on the Dutch proposals was postponed to a later meeting, and most members were keen on carrying on this discussion, even if it was quite clear early on that it would remain at a purely theoretical level, regarding both the economic and the monetary leg of the Dutch initiative.[13]

At a more technical level, the Dutch proposals were welcomed in theory but rejected in practice. The suggestions in the field of economic coordination provoked virtually the same reaction as that of the Commission in its communication to the European Council in April 1976: disapproval. For instance, according to the Trésor, the question was not how to create new mechanisms but instead how to properly use the existing ones, like those contained in the 14 February 1974 directive on economic convergence.[14] Similar reasoning prevailed in the German Finance Ministry.[15] Another significant objection was the issue of secrecy. Clearly the target zones would have to be kept secret, even if intervention was not obligatory, in order to avoid speculation. But the French members were very reserved about this aspect of the proposal, arguing that keeping these target zones secret for more than a short while was quite unfeasible.[16]

On the whole, due to the initial vagueness of the proposals, there was an impressive number of misunderstandings about the Dutch initiative. The proposition of establishing "target zones" for the fluctuation of currencies, while clearly supported in Duisenberg's mind by a strong coordination of economic policies, aroused almost Pavlovian antimonetarist reactions from some member states. Although Duisenberg insisted that there were two aspects to his approach—economic coordination and target zones—the latter attracted more attention. This initial misunderstanding would leave its mark on later discussions of the proposal.

The Emergence of a New Economic Consensus

The priority given by the Dutch government to monetary cooperation was not the only significant event of mid-1976. The other important aspect was the timid emergence of a European economic consensus aimed at prioritizing stability and in particular the (re)burgeoning of a Franco-German economic rapprochement along this anti-inflationary line. This section will first analyze the results of the Brussels European Council of July 1976 and then turn to the economic policies of the three biggest member states: France, Germany, and Britain.

The meeting of the European Council in Brussels on 12 and 13 July 1976 offered a new opportunity for the heads of government to freely exchange views. In spite of the relative failure of its preceding session in Luxembourg in April 1976, the European Council now seemed like a useful exercise. This session marked a sharp contrast with the one of April 1976: the economic climate was better, and if there had been no notable improvement in terms of employment, the signs of economic recovery seen in the past few months had been confirmed.[17] The conclusions of the European Council even stated that Europe's leaders were "confident that this recovery will persist in 1977."[18] Another element contrasting with the Luxembourg session was that this meeting of the European Council was overall seen as a success. Agreement was reached on the question of the distribution of seats in the new, directly elected European Parliament. The heads of government also announced that they would support the nomination of Roy Jenkins, proposed by the British government, as Commission president. A British official could even conclude that "Europe . . . is now moving out of the doldrums."[19] The conclusions also showed for the first time that the debate between economist and monetarist strategies about EMU had seemed to cease among EEC heads of government: "The European Council agrees on the necessity of increased convergence of economic and monetary policies, while recognizing that agreements concerning exchange rates are meaningful only if they are supported by a co-ordinated policy."[20] Yet if this was a clear "economist" statement, it did not necessarily imply that all EEC member states would be strictly on the same page. The ongoing discussions about the Duisenberg proposals were the best example of this. Some governments still attached importance to monetary mechanisms (such as the French government), while others remained focused on economic discipline (as did the Germans). Schmidt once more recalled that "it was not possible to correct divergences in budgetary or income policy . . . by using monetary policy alone."[21] Joop den Uyl, the Dutch prime minister, rightfully noticed that "there was a need for greater convergence. This was so far only a matter of pious words. What was needed now was action. Finance Ministers should make proposals for the European Council to consider."[22] Nevertheless, this "pious" declaration of the European Council was an important step, since it had been made this time by the new EEC institution in charge of directing the future endeavors of the EEC as a whole.

Together with the Duisenberg proposals, the appointment of Raymond Barre as French prime minister was the other significant event of mid-1976. Jacques Chirac's resignation did not come completely as a surprise. Indeed, even though Giscard had apparently planned to keep Chirac as prime minister until the March 1978 general elections,[23] their relationship was troubled, to say the least. The possibility of a prime minister's resignation—a completely unusual event under the Fifth Republic, since it is normally the president who dismisses his prime minister—was becoming more and more likely in early 1976.[24] Chirac eventually resigned on 25 August 1976. The choice of his successor was not obvious. Knowing that he wanted to adopt stability-oriented economic policies and that Barre was discreet and respected, Giscard decided to appoint the then relatively unknown minister of trade.[25]

Giscard described his new prime minister as "the best economist in France."[26] The new French prime minister had started out as a civil servant and university lecturer. He was the author of a two-volume textbook on political economy that had become the standard work for the study of economics in French universities in the 1960s.[27] He decided to pursue an economic policy that could bear fruit only in the long term—the long term being a notion usually foreign to most politicians, according to Barre.[28] It was also likely to help him have better relations with a number of parts (*Directions*) of the French administration, and the Trésor in particular, which usually kept its distance from traditional politicians.[29] Barre thus established weekly consultations with the most important parts of the civil service, among them the Banque de France (represented by its governor, Bernard Clappier) and the Trésor (represented by its director, Jacques de Larosière).[30] Barre was a former commissioner in Brussels in charge of the Economic and Financial Affairs portfolio (July 1967–January 1973), and French minister of trade (January–August 1976). He claimed to have gained from these experiences the conviction that "a country that matters is a country whose currency is strong and stable."[31] Although in a less systematic fashion than Giscard, Barre also was a supporter of fixed exchange rates.[32] The British ambassador to France described Barre as "a new phenomenon in French politics," "imperturbable and portly."[33] He was therefore in many ways the exact opposite of his predecessor.[34]

"Fighting inflation" immediately became the single-minded motto of the new French prime minister. In his very first speech, his fourth sentence, after three formal declarations of gratitude for the new appointment, was "The main objective of the policy of the new government will be to fight inflation and to maintain the stability of our currency."[35] In his *déclaration de politique générale* before the

French National Assembly—the vital first public statement of a prime minister in the Fifth Republic—he used the word "inflation" more than twenty times.[36] The fight against inflation was a way to improve the French economic situation, to catch up with Germany economically, but also to make progress in European integration: "I am personally convinced that progress in the construction of Europe will become easier the more economic policies of the EEC member countries can be brought in line with one another."[37] Yet if for Barre "monetary stability was an absolute necessity," he had to choose, when he took power, from among three options: to carry on the same policy as before he arrived, to pursue a policy of deflation, or to pursue a policy of disinflation.[38] The first option was quickly ruled out since it contradicted the goal of monetary stability, although it would have been supported by the UDR (the Union des démocrates pour la République) and the Union de la gauche. Deflation would have been, according to Barre, too sharp a choice for a country that had been used to a high inflation rate for quite a while. By contrast, the last option, disinflation, could help rebalance the French economy more smoothly by simultaneously acting on the money supply, the budget, salaries, and the exchange rate. Barre thus opted for the last option. His anti-inflation program essentially involved a strict credit and budgetary policy and a reduction in the rate of overall wage increases.[39] In the framework of the anti-inflation Barre plan, it was the first time that targets for the money supply were set out in France.[40] The use of such targets was a good example of the progressive (but partial) dissemination among European governments and monetary authorities of monetarist thinking (in the sense of Friedman's monetarism).

Interestingly, the French move toward the adoption of stability-oriented economic policies was happening virtually in parallel with the same trend in Britain, and the confirmation of it in Germany. Indeed the German general elections of October 1976 saw the reelection of the SPD-FDP coalition, and thereby the confirmation of its economic policy.[41] More important, in Britain, following the agreement reached with the IMF in 1976, the Callaghan government started prioritizing the fight against inflation.[42] Indeed, because of the IMF loan, the government had to reduce public expenditures in order to restore confidence in the sterling. The chancellor thus took a series of measures in July 1976.[43] Even more interesting, the British Treasury began thinking that inflation was primarily monetary in origin.[44] There was, therefore, a growing consensus in the EEC to prioritize the fight against inflation. The reactions to the adoption of the Barre plan marked a sharp contrast, not only with the June 1974 anti-inflation plan of Fourcade but also with the numerous anti-inflation plans of the different French governments since the mid-1960s. The new economic policy of the French government appeared this time much more credible and likely to last. In particular, Barre made clear from the very beginning that he would carry on with his stability-oriented program even though local elections were approaching in March 1977.[45] Unsurprisingly, the German government welcomed the appointment of a new French prime minister whose economic views were close to its own.[46]

All this is certainly not to suggest that a single man could change the course of European economic and monetary cooperation, however. For a start, the French domestic political scene remained particularly complex in mid-1976. Although Giscard had appointed a trusted prime minister, the French president still found himself in an uneasy situation with an opponent in his own majority (Chirac) and parliamentary opposition in a position to win the next local and general elections in 1977 and 1978.[47] Moreover, as much as the EMS did not appear ex nihilo in 1978, the thrust of the Barre plan—fighting inflation—was in the French administration's pipeline for already a few weeks and months. Already in June, the *Commissariat général au Plan* encouraged giving first priority to the fight against inflation.[48] Similarly, Jean-Pierre Ruault, one of Giscard's economic advisers, argued that a new anti-inflationary plan "should take on a very spectacular character."[49] Naturally, the success of the Barre plan was not a given. Françoise Giroud, a former member of the Chirac government and a famous columnist, concluded in her 1977 book, for instance, that Barre was "an engine without fuel."[50] What it does indicate, however, is that the *perception* of the French government's economic policies by the other EEC member states, and particularly Germany, after Barre's appointment to office, markedly changed. This psychological dimension was crucial in many ways. Indeed, the fight against inflation has a lot to do with the often irrational anticipation of inflation by economic agents. The reputation and credibility of an anti-inflationary program, and of the one who launches it, therefore really did matter, and was likely to make a difference in the future, in political, diplomatic, economic, and monetary terms.

Political Anemia, Technical Brainstorming

As in 1974, the year 1976 witnessed the combination of a monetary proposal (Fourcade in 1974, Duisenberg in 1976) and the holding of a summit of heads of government in the country issuing the proposal (France in 1974, the Netherlands in 1976). And as in 1974, this theoretically promising combination did not bear fruit. Indeed, if the last meeting of the European Council in Brussels in July had been rather encouraging, the atmosphere of the session in The Hague on 29 and 30 November 1976 was considerably less positive. The unexpectedly bad economic forecasts of late 1976 quickly wiped out the more positive climate that had emerged in the EEC over the summer. If this time the proposals had been mentioned during the meeting (this had not been the case in 1974), the discussion did not prove successful given German opposition and the lack of support from other member states. Even though Den Uyl proposed that the Nine should declare their readiness to make progress in the direction shown by the Duisenberg initiative, his call was ultimately not followed.[51] The French president suffered a similar blow. In a long statement Giscard analyzed the current economic and monetary state of the EEC.[52] After a rather traditional analysis of the current causes of anxiety in the EEC (level of activity lower than expected, monetary relations in utter disarray, energy problem), Giscard proposed "a three-point program of preserving, reestablishing, and developing: preserving the Community's attainments; reestablishing the balance of our economies; affirming our intention of resuming the construction of the Economic and Monetary Union as soon as circumstances permit." In setting out these points in more detail, Giscard merely made some declarations of principles instead of giving a detailed program of action. He vaguely proposed that "a special meeting of the European Council should be held at the end of 1977 in order to review progress in restoring balance to our economies, and to determine the procedures for resuming the indispensable construction of an Economic and Monetary Union." The conclusions of the meeting did not record his proposal.

More surprising was, again, an apparent divergence of views between Giscard and Schmidt. Indeed, while Giscard was keen on proposing a new program for action, Schmidt limited his talk to the current problems of the EEC. He came back to the focus of German economic policy: "The root of all current evils was the failure to get a grip on inflation. . . . To the German people inflation was still the biggest enemy."[53] As a consequence, he criticized expansionary policies: "We are no longer in the times of Keynes."[54] To fully nail his point, Schmidt declared later that "EMU in a situation of such disparities is only a dream of diplomats." Anthony Crosland, British secretary of state for foreign and Commonwealth affairs, unsurprisingly described Schmidt's tone as "apocalyptic" and "a little hectoring."[55] As had been the case in the April 1976 meeting of the European Council in Luxembourg, there was thus again an apparent opposition between what Giscard and Schmidt had said. While the French president looked to the future and proposed to take stock of the economic and monetary projects in about a year, Schmidt was simply observing that EMU was so far merely a diplomat's dream. If their two positions were not completely contradictory, they were based on a different hierarchy of priorities, the French president being keen on the reaffirmation of a long-term objective and the German chancellor being much more reserved if not pessimistic.

This session of the European Council therefore witnessed inconclusive but revealing discussions. No concrete decision on first-rank issues like economic and monetary cooperation was reached, and the meeting hence tended to appear as a "flop."[56] Giscard even declared during the meeting that "if the public knew the nature of the descriptive and passive exchanges of views we have just witnessed, it would have very serious doubts as to the capacity of the European Council members to carry out their responsibilities."[57] Admittedly, the conclusions of the meeting stated that "the achievement of Economic and Monetary Union is basic to the consolidation of Community solidarity and the establishment of European Union."[58] This sentence was, however, merely a tribute to the Tindemans Report. Moreover, Tindemans's own insistence on having his report analyzed as a coherent whole instead of having it "chopped into pieces" did not necessarily help.[59] Tindemans indeed feared the so-called salami process, whereby his report would be examined in separate chapters, with, for example, the economic and financial chapter examined by the Finance Council. In the end none was ever really examined. In spite of the usual diplomatic declarations affirming the heads of government's interest in the Tindemans Report, discussions about it in the various EEC committees seemed to be endless and brought no actual results, and the heads of government were simply willing to bury it.[60] This observation was therefore a platitude constantly repeated while talking about the prospect of the European Union rather than a consciously thought-out statement about EMU, what it implied, and the way forward. One of the consequences of such hollow statements in European Councils' communiqués was to prompt Giscard, among others, to suggest a number of ways in which the functioning of European Councils could be improved in the future.[61]

Political anemia should indeed not hide ongoing trends happening under the surface. Late 1976 and early 1977 was indeed a period of brainstorming about the working method of the European Council. After now two years of operation, a number of heads of government indeed thought that time was ripe to take stock of the evolution of the recently created institution. There is, however, neither need nor space here to delve into the details of this reform. The importance of these discussions lay in the fact that heads of government, in order to render the European Council more efficient, wanted to clarify the distinction between the discussions that aimed at making decisions and those that did not. A lengthy exchange of opinions between heads of government underscored this institutional learning process.[62] As early as in late December 1976, van der Stoel, the Dutch foreign minister, outlined some ideas for reforming the European Council's functioning.[63] The Dutch memorandum distinguished between the two above-mentioned types of discussions held in a European Council: those that aimed at reaching a conclusion (formalized in a final communiqué), and those that did not. It concluded very sensibly that the general exchange of views should be based on a common document (such as the Commission's analysis of the economic situation) and did not need to produce written conclusions (unless needed for dealing with public opinion). "Discussions aimed at reaching concrete agreements," by contrast, ought to be more thoroughly prepared. In a letter to his European counterparts sent in late January 1977, Giscard raised the issue of the mutual influence between the media and the European Council: "The interest inevitably aroused by our meetings in the media lead them to search and judge the substance of our decisions, even if the real interest of some of our discussions consists more in informing each other and exchanging our reflections rather than reaching conclusions."[64] This remark underscored two points: first and foremost, the main task of the European Council was not necessarily to make decisions but to allow a free exchange of views; and second, that this free exchange of views, because of extensive media attention, did not completely remove the need for some secrecy. The Schulmann-Clappier-Couzens group, which would secretly outline the Bremen Annex, would be a case in point. On the whole, this brainstorming about the European Council's functioning thus summed up well the crux of the European Council's dilemma. It had to strike a good balance between free exchange of views (without concrete results), proper decisions and arbitrations (thoroughly prepared and leading to a formal communiqué), and good public relations with the media. By exchanging their views on why they regularly gathered, EEC heads of government had therefore managed to relegitimize the European Council and to improve its working procedures. The next sessions would be obvious testing cases.

The new Commission presided over by Roy Jenkins thus took office on 1 January 1977 in rather difficult conditions. First and most obviously, the general economic and monetary context was still worrying. As had been the case since the collapse of the Bretton Woods system and the first oil shock, the Commission was in an uneasy situation, as the one institution meant to safeguard the *acquis communautaire* at the very moment when the EEC member states were most tempted not to think in a *communautaire* fashion. It must also be remembered that Giscard was not a great supporter of the EEC Commission and that Schmidt was famous for his recurrent tirades against "the Brussels bureaucracy."[65] Added to this was the fact that, following a decision taken at the meeting of the European Council in Brussels in July 1976, the new presidency of the Commission was meant to review its staffing and its overall structure.[66] As a consequence, the first task of the new Commission president would actually be to reduce his own staff.[67] Whether the Commission's apparent decline was a direct consequence of the emergence of the European Council is not a question that can be dealt with fully here. It seems, however, that the two evolutions were largely coincidental, particularly with regard to monetary affairs. Indeed, if the Commission did try to reassert its leadership on monetary issues, but had so far failed to reach concrete results, it was due to scarcely reconcilable differences of opinion between member states rather than the emergence of the European Council as such. After such an unpromising start, the first basic challenge the new Commission faced was thus to find way to reassert itself.

The Relaunch of the Franco-German Tandem

Encouragingly, the Committee of Governors, in its session of 8 February 1977, observed that in the past few months, economic convergence outweighed divergence in the Community.[68] Not only were inflation rates converging but also, as a consequence, the gaps between exchange rates were narrowing. This was a direct consequence of a more restrictive monetary policy. François-Xavier Ortoli, now vice president of the Commission in charge of the economic and monetary portfolio, present for the first time at a session of the Committee of Governors, similarly noticed a trend toward a better convergence of monetary policies.

Concomitantly, the French and German governments made the same observations as their central banks and tried to find a consolidation of this trend on a bilateral basis.[69] The Franco-German economic rapprochement, discerned in late 1976, came to be confirmed in early 1977. The economic atmosphere had clearly changed. After a period of considerable pessimism, the German government had been encouraged by the latest upturn in the French economy.[70] The progress of the Barre plan would have thus impressed Schmidt.[71] As a consequence, the two governments aimed at improving their bilateral economic coordination. In the framework of the bilateral cooperation enshrined in the 1963 Élysée Treaty, a Franco-German summit meeting took place in Paris on 4 and 5 February 1977. The French government seemed to put much hope in the collaboration. The two governments announced that they would from now on specifically undertake economic coordination, involving finance ministries, foreign affairs ministries, and central banks, all of whom would meet four times a year.[72] This economic coordination was not meant to be a closed Franco-German circle with political afterthoughts.[73] Jean-Pierre Dutet, one of Giscard's economic advisers, thus declared to a diplomat of the British Embassy that "there would be genuine economic content in the Franco-German rapprochement; it was not simply a political gesture."[74]

Why was cooperation more interesting at this bilateral level? Indeed, the type of discussion envisaged was much the same as in other EEC structures. There were, however, two significant differences. First, the French and German governments already had quite a long history of working together bilaterally and had in-depth knowledge of each other's economies since they were significant trading partners. The French government was fundamentally interested in moving toward Germany and the Benelux countries rather than Britain or Italy.[75] As a consequence, the discussion could go much deeper and potentially be more productive than in any other multilateral framework. Second, this type of bilateral situation could leave much more time for discussion than in the EEC structures. And, crucially, the discussions were taking place between a snake and non-snake member.

The content and actual results of this cooperation were of course still quite vague in early 1977. Nothing concrete—apart from the inception of this much closer bilateral cooperation—had really happened. It could thus be quickly concluded that this consultation had been a superficial diplomatic gesture. This endeavor deserves closer attention, however, for at least four reasons. First, although it could be ruled out as a mere diplomatic statement, it should be noted that the joint final declaration declared that "the Federal German government and the French government wish to see the Community resume in 1978 its progress toward economic and monetary union, which is essential stage on the road to European Union. . . . They declare their intention of putting to the European Council, before the end of 1977, proposals aimed at an effective harmonization of the economic policies of the member states."[76] While this declaration logically fit with Giscard's previous statements, it was also an ambition of the German government.[77] Given the traditional reluctance of the latter, and in particular of its Federal chancellor, for that kind of call for EMU, this was quite remarkable. It should indeed be remembered from earlier in this chapter that Schmidt declared at The Hague meeting of the European Council in November 1976 that given the present circumstances, EMU was merely "a dream of diplomats." Quite strikingly, however, this Franco-German declaration disregarded the ongoing discussions of the Duisenberg proposals, whose central aim was, precisely, economic coordination. Many initiatives in the EEC were therefore simultaneously pointing in the same direction, but patently lacked political coordination. It was hence not a coincidence that the declaration pointed to the European Council, the new EEC structure able to orient and give some coherence to future endeavors of the entire Community.

Second, this meeting confirmed that the terms of the EMU equation had changed for the French government. Although EMU remained the ultimate aim of the French government, the most immediate question was no longer whether to rejoin the snake but how to create stable and lasting conditions for an economic convergence with Germany, one that would lead in the end to an improvement of monetary cooperation.[78] The hierarchy of priorities had thus been reversed. This was a considerable gain from the German point of view: the French had at last accepted that monetary integration could take place only on the basis of prior economic coordination.[79] And as a consequence, the French government would not seek to reenter the snake prematurely—"prematurely" meaning before the actual success of the Barre plan—as it had in early 1975.[80] This was no less than the end—or just a cease-fire?—of the long-standing quarrel between economists and monetarists. As a consequence, there was from now on a clear link between this miniconvergence and the future revival of EMU discussions, as set out in the final joint declaration. Preparing the Finance Council of 14 March, Jacques de Larosière thus clearly said that any further discussion regarding EMU had now to wait until the first results of the Franco-German bilateral experiment.[81]

A third reason gives more significance to the Franco-German experiment, namely, that it was a strictly bilateral initiative. It was designed outside of—but not against—the EEC, and without much consultation with the other EEC members. The French and German governments, under Giscard's and Schmidt's leadership, were naturally more inclined to work closely together, but this was the first time since 1974 that they were taking an initiative necessarily excluding any other government, at least at the beginning. Indeed, the French and German governments were careful to make plain that what they had in mind was simply "a pilot project," which could be extended, if successful, to the rest of the EEC.[82] It was therefore an attempt, in a sense, at the bilateral rescue of the EEC.

The corollary to this point was that the Franco-German "miniconvergence" experiment crucially implied the de facto exclusion of the British government. This was certainly not a Franco-German gesture purposely directed at excluding the British, nor a British self-exclusion (the British government showed signs that it was quite willing to keep in close touch with the Franco-German bilateral experiment).[83] Yet the British government was well aware that this nascent collaboration left it in a particularly uneasy situation. Indeed, an extension of the Franco-German experiment to Britain seemed highly unlikely given that it would certainly arouse the opposition of the "smaller" EEC member states: "A triangular arrangement with the Germans might look too much like a 'directorate.'"[84]

The Examination of the Duisenberg Proposals

Although it would be considerably delayed, detailed analysis of the Duisenberg proposals was carried out in the fall, involving a number of revealing discussions. Given the divergent opinions on the topic, the Finance Council of 8 November 1976 simply stated that it "was convinced that both the development of the Community and the greater stability of intra-Community exchange relations require the convergence of the economic policies of the Member States and the alignment of their economic situations."[85] The Council then asked the specialized committees to undertake further study of the proposals and to detail how they could be made operational by the end of the year. All the members except the Commission had misgivings, to various degrees, about the Dutch text.[86] The call for further study thus resembled no more than a polite burial. It was even observed, during the meeting of the Committee of Governors of 9 November, that given the report of the Monetary Committee, it would be difficult to tell how the Duisenberg proposals could be made operational before the end of the year.[87] Equally problematic was the recurrent use of the word "convergence." The term was overworked and ambiguous: it was used both in the context of a limited but genuine economic coordination (like the Franco-German bilateral initiative) and to mean simply that some people would regularly come together to discuss their economic problems. As for the Monetary Committee and the Committee of Governors, they were still busy with earlier initiatives, and particularly the communication of the Commission of April 1976.[88] Following the Commission's communication to the European Council of April 1976 and the Dutch proposals of July 1976, the Monetary Committee decided to present in November 1976 a number of suggestions relating to the EEC exchange rate system, the fixation of quantitative monetary targets, and control of the Euromarkets.[89] The Monetary Committee included the Duisenberg initiative in its study and recognized that the proposals had a number of advantages, in particular their flexibility and the fact that they would allow building on existing mechanisms instead of devising a new one. It advised, however, against implementation given the still strong economic divergences.

Providing a good example of the monetary learning process, the Committee of Governors, on 11 May 1976, had requested the alternates to present some propositions on how to ensure a greater stability of exchange rates in the EEC, taking into account the experience gained in 1976.[90] The alternates presented this report, titled "Possible Arrangements for Contributing to Greater Exchange Rate Stability among All Community Currencies," to the Committee during the session of 9 November 1976.[91] It also logically incorporated the Duisenberg proposals in its study. This report was in two parts. The first analyzed the exchange rate problems of the EEC. The second part took stock of the various proposals advanced in the past few years, namely, the Fourcade memorandum (1974 and 1975), the Duisenberg proposals (July 1976), and the note of the Bank of England (September 1976). They unsurprisingly concluded that these proposals were impossible to implement given the current situation, and that the EEC should instead be looking for more limited arrangements. The alternates proposed only a number of very technical suggestions related to intervention techniques in the snake.[92] The concluding remark of the alternates was typically economist in spirit: "In the last resort, however refined the exchange rate mechanisms used, real progress towards greater stability in European exchange rate relationships can only be achieved through greater convergence of the individual economies."[93]

The examination of the Duisenberg proposals gave birth to an interesting discussion between the governors about the nature of the snake. At the outset of the debate on the alternates' report, Gordon Richardson, president of the Committee of Governors and governor of the Bank of England, observed that although it had a number of merits, the snake was not, at present, an instrument for EEC integration.[94] Richardson explained that the current system was such that non-snake members could not join the mechanism. Klasen, president of the Bundesbank, and other members of the snake of course rejected this opinion, underlining the fact that non-snake members had first to balance their economies. They would then be able to join the snake without any need to modify the exchange rate mechanism. Clappier nuanced this: "Originally, the 'snake' has been conceived as a Community mechanism aimed at facilitating economic and monetary integration. Over the years, it has rather become a monetary mechanism." This small disagreement illustrates well the fact that one of the central issues of monetary cooperation in Europe was to bring all the *EEC* member states into a single *EEC* mechanism. The discussion was closed on an economist line, supported by all members, even those with a floating currency. In its session of 11 January 1977, the Committee of Governors announced that the alternates would not be able to submit a report about the Duisenberg proposals before March.[95] They contended that it did not really matter given that the work of the Monetary Committee was not much advanced either. It is quite striking to observe that neither committee seemed very disturbed by this delay. Not only was the final conclusion—a rejection of the Duisenberg proposals—no great secret but given the lack of political pressure and the existence of other more urgent important issues, the EEC committees were not in a hurry to submit their reports.

An exchange of letters between Duisenberg and Schmidt underlined this last point about the foreseeable failure of the Duisenberg proposal. Writing as "one professional economist to another," the Dutch finance minister exposed in some detail his thoughts to the Federal chancellor, following the meeting of the European Council in The Hague.[96] Duisenberg was under the impression that his initiative had been misunderstood. He therefore reformulated his main points: that "target zones would *not* oblige a country to intervene"; that they would by contrast oblige a country to direct its economic and monetary policies to preventing a movement of its exchange rate *below* the target zone (hence a strong element of discipline); that the main intention of the proposal was to strengthen the element of policy coordination in the EEC (the target zone would trigger consultation); that "the main political motivation . . . was to reintegrate the 'weaker' countries with a floating currency into some kind of Community exchange rate mechanism"; and finally, that he did not intend an immediate application of this system (the situation in Italy and Britain was too uncertain for that), but that he was willing "to prepare the ground on the technical and the political level, so that we can move ahead as soon as conditions permit."[97]

In late January 1977, Schmidt replied to Duisenberg.[98] Although he affirmed sharing the same basic concerns as the Dutch minister, he explained that he still had doubts about the ability of target zones to really encourage governments to improve their economic policy coordination. And even more problematic than that, the German chancellor feared that the Dutch proposals would nurture the illusion that a monetary mechanism would help get under control a problem that can ultimately be solved only by economic policy measures supported by a strong political will. This reaction was of course consistent with what he had said so far, and notably recalled his acerbic comment during the Luxembourg European Council of April 1976 against those "[who can] believe that one may correct budgetary mistakes . . . by monetary mechanisms."[99] But while Schmidt's thinking was consistent, it was noticeable that he did not really answer to Duisenberg's letter. The Dutch minister made a full argument, in five clear points, not exclusively monetarist, while Schmidt simply replied that he did not believe—without giving much support for his point of view—that target zones would work.

Monetary Cooperation Back at the Top of the EEC Agenda

After a promising summer in 1976, and then a rather depressing autumn and winter, monetary cooperation progressively regained prominence in the spring of 1977. While seasonal variations certainly cannot help explain this pattern, the dynamism of the Franco-German tandem and the existence the European Council do, and will be analyzed in turn in this section. Before turning to these matters, however, it is first necessary to recall that because of the coming elections, a relatively high political instability characterized the domestic situation in a number of countries of Western Europe in early 1977. France was probably in the most difficult position. The government had suffered a setback in the municipal elections of 13 and 20 March 1977, and this in turn increased speculation that the Union de la gauche might win a majority at the legislative elections of March 1978.[100] The last municipal elections had been marked in particular by a personal humiliation for Giscard with the election of Chirac as mayor of Paris. This was likely to have an impact on French European policy: a revitalized right would press for a less pro-European/more Gaullist line regarding European cooperation. The uncertainty about the 1978 elections was thus "casting a long shadow."[101] A number of other elections were to take place soon, including in Belgium (17 April) and the Netherlands (25 May).[102] And although the German general election had already taken place in October 1976, the SPD-FDP coalition in power also had to face a number of domestic difficulties.[103] Finally, since March 1977, Callaghan was heading a minority government in Britain. There was thus a general sense of political uncertainty in the EEC over the spring of 1977. Virtually all governments noticed this while preparing the meeting of the European Council in Rome.[104] They all expected that this would in one way or another have an impact on the meeting. It must finally be noted that these political uncertainties were also influenced by the United States. As early as March 1977, Robin—Giscard's diplomatic advisor—wrote to the French president that "the coming to power of Mr. Carter introduces a considerable factor of uncertainty and destabilization."[105] This factor would grow in importance over the next few months.

"The Power of German Veto"

The more in-depth discussions of the Duisenberg proposals revealed considerable differences of opinion among the EEC member states, and above all their reluctance to take any risk with a new scheme given the uncertainty and fragility of the economic context. More than their final reports, it was the discussions within the Monetary Committee and the Committee of Governors that were the most revealing. The first extensive discussion of the Dutch ideas took place in the Monetary Committee, on the basis of a draft report written by the alternates.[106] The debate saw the opposition of two camps, a "majority" and a "minority" that was essentially composed of the German members.[107] The majority thought that a system of target zones for all currencies (snake included) was feasible. A procedure of consultation (regarding exchange rate and economic policies) would be put in place once a currency had reached its limit of fluctuation. The overall system was meant to become more and more strict. It would start only once relative stability in exchange rates had been observed and once the divergences in the economic and monetary situations of the member states had been reduced. The minority was strongly against this. Pöhl thus rejected the proposition of any kind of new scheme that could be used as an alternative to the snake. This refusal of mechanistic arrangements—described as "chasing the symptoms"—was a constant feature of German economic and monetary policy, recalled once more on the occasion of the January 1977 Anglo-German summit.[108]

Yet misunderstandings about the Duisenberg proposals remained another constant feature of the debate. Oort thus rejected the description of the Duisenberg proposals given by the majority. He argued that the system proposed was not meant to imply intervention, and was certainly not meant as an alternative to the snake. It was designed merely to serve as a bridge between the snake and non-snake currencies. The German members eventually opposed any reference in the final report to the possibility of implementing target zones. Pöhl suggested that the Monetary Committee should propose the establishment of closer consultations about exchange rate developments and the continuation of further studies about the Dutch ideas. This vague and less ambitious proposal won the agreement of most other members. The next meeting of the Monetary Committee would eventually officialize these points as its definite conclusions to be submitted to the Finance Council of 14 March.[109] As a consequence of the divergences within the Monetary Committee, it even decided not to submit a written report, but instead asked its president, Pöhl, to make an oral presentation during the next session of the Finance Council on 14 March.[110] Given that both committees had failed to reach an agreement about the implementation of target zones, the main outcome of the Finance Council of 14 March was a basic agreement that periodic consultation on exchange rate developments within both committees should immediately be implemented. The results of these consultations should be reported to the Council. They would—of course—have no constraining character. Although this new measure was not extremely innovative, it had the merit of improving and intensifying consultation among *all* the EEC member states about exchange rates. In other words, it was a step forward in the attempt to bring monetary cooperation clearly back under EEC jurisdiction. Duisenberg welcomed the outcome of the Council but repeated once more that contrary to what was implied in the reports of both committees, his initial proposal about target zones was not based on an obligation to intervene in the market.[111] This was further proof of widespread misunderstandings about his ideas. The first attempt to apply this principle was the Monetary Committee session on 9 June.[112] Discussion started on the basis of a general document from the Commission. This allowed the Commission to discreetly underline the fact that given the stability of the past few months, the institution of target zones would certainly not have had disastrous effects. In an even more detailed fashion, the Banca d'Italia had interestingly done a simulation of the effects an implementation of the Duisenberg proposals would have had from 1972 onward.[113] Taking all due qualitative and quantitative methodological caution that such data must be interpreted with, the Banca d'Italia drew positive conclusions: however complex it was, the system, perhaps because it was less ambitious, would have had a greater degree of flexibility—and thereby would have had more "vitality"—than the snake.

In spite of the fact that target zones were not meant to trigger automatic interventions, a misunderstanding on that point somewhat polluted part of the debates. In particular, the German outright opposition and lack of constructive criticism threatened to spoil the atmosphere of the EEC debates. Another letter written by Oort to Pöhl, about half a year after his first one outlining the Dutch proposal, gave a striking example of this. Upset by the way in which his proposals were portrayed, Oort employed an unusually undiplomatic tone in remarks that are worth quoting in full:

> I was surprised and even shocked by the reaction of some of my col-leagues when I gave my comments on the draft report of our alternates on the "target zone proposal." The qualification of disloyalty on our part I find unacceptable. What are the facts? In the original letter of Mr. Duisenberg to his colleagues, and in every single note we have submitted to the Monetary Committee and to the alternates, we have emphasized time and time again that our proposal does not imply in-tervention obligations at any stage. . . . I only wish to make it very clear that any allegation of a disloyal change in our position is completely un-founded. I would appreciate it if you would communicate the content of this letter to the other members of the Committee.[114]

In the end, therefore, the overall discussion was altered by this misconception—which was apparently not deliberate, but which revealed, however, a certain state of general misunderstanding even among snake members. This should not hide the fact that the proposal under discussion bore a striking resemblance to the EMS divergence indicator—in spirit especially, since the aim, once the deviant currency was identified, was also to trigger consultations. A section title in the Committee of Governors' report of 3 February 1977 analyzing the objectives of the Dutch proposals was in that respect explicit: "Target zones as a mechanism to trigger Community consultations."[115] Moreover, the very point raised in the above-mentioned argument between the Dutch officials and some other EEC members would also be at the center of discussions about the EMS divergence indicator. Indeed, in 1978 the question would be whether the identification of the diverging currency should lead to intramarginal automatic interventions or mere consultations. The discussion would be more diplomatic, but bring a similar out-come, namely, unbinding measures.[116]

The thirtieth round of Franco-German consultations in the framework of the 1963 Élysée Treaty, but only the second round of the "miniconvergence" experi-ment between the two countries, took place in Bonn on 16 and 17 June 1977.[117] In writing to Otto Schlecht, German secretary of state for the economy, de La Genière outlined the way in which the French and German government may concretely further their cooperation. The first aspect was a comprehensive and quick mutual information about economic policies, the second was to explain the mutual policies, so as to better coordinate them. Meetings, quite informal, would take place once a term, and would include five or six representatives of Finance/Economics Ministries and central banks.[118] The first of these meetings took place on 8 June 1977 in the *rue de Rivoli*. In a note to Barre, de La Genière described the rationale of the reinforced Franco-German cooperation, based on a modest but thorough consultation. The phrasing employed, in particular with respect to the learning process, was particularly revealing. He stressed the need to improve the sharing of information about ongoing trends, perspectives, and possible actions to be taken, in a very informal fashion.[119] This second round confirmed two important trends that had emerged earlier in February. First, as can be deduced from de La Genière's description, it verified the constructive spirit of the consultations and the satisfaction from both parts of the new scheme.[120] The greater economic convergence witnessed in the EEC in early 1977 was also corroborated by the latest analysis of the economic and monetary situation.[121] And, as in February, the talks were described as "more than a simple exchange of views."[122] They were indeed meant to help achieve convergence of economic objectives (on money supply targets and interest rates) and to coordinate new and improved economic measures by consulting each other in advance. Yet monetary cooperation, slated for reexamination later in the year, was not mentioned, not even superficially. The image of a Franco-German tandem that was as close as ever was then reported to the press: Giscard declared that France and Germany "had beaten the world record for meetings between major partners," and Schmidt added that in "no part of the world were the discussions as frank and as open as those between the FRG and France."[123] Second, the bilateral character of the situation was still raising questions. Ortoli, in a discussion during a session of the Committee of Governors on 8 March, thus worried that "actions in monetary affairs [were] currently deliberated and implemented at the bilateral and international level rather than at the Community level."[124] Although he did not explicitly mention the Franco-German "miniconvergence," this kind of experiment clearly fit in the category he described. The next meeting of the European Council in Rome would provide, however, a good counterexample to Ortoli's point.

The Resurgence of EMU Discussions at the Political Level: The Rome European Council

A few pious words apart, EMU had largely been forgotten at the top diplomatic level in 1976. Interestingly, the topic reemerged in early 1977 with more enthusiasm. Giscard first made a few remarks about EMU in public speeches in January, then the Franco-German tandem endorsed the call for taking stock of the EMU debate in February; and finally, the March 1977 European Council agreed to do the same by the end of the year. This section will explore the reasons and analyze the limits of this renewed call for EMU.

Although it was obviously difficult to have a ceremony at a time when the economic context was visibly darkening, the European Council meeting held in Rome, on 25 and 26 March 1977, celebrated the twentieth anniversary of the treaties signed in the Italian capital. In addition to this, the heads of government could not really afford a third fiasco in less than a year after the Luxembourg (April 1976) and The Hague (November 1976) sessions that were poorly regarded. This would surely not be a good point for the European Council as such, which was after all still in its infancy, or for the British presidency, which was in charge of organizing the session for the first time and which was held partly responsible for the disarray in which the EEC found itself.[125]

The meeting took place, however, in quite a good atmosphere.[126] Admittedly, a number of contentious issues were on the table, such as the question of representation of the EEC at the London summit and the reform of the European Council itself.[127] Monetary cooperation stayed in the background as a relatively low-key issue but saw a more positive outcome than usual. To be sure, Giscard's call for a revival of the EMU objective at the meeting of the European Council in The Hague in November 1976 had gone relatively unnoticed, or at least aroused no particular reaction. By contrast, the beginning of 1977 saw more calls for action from various groups, not officially coordinated, but all directed toward the same aim set by Giscard in late 1976. He himself repeated in Strasbourg on 28 January that "we must restore to the attainment in full of economic and monetary union its central place in our own efforts. . . . Economic and monetary union is the essential stepping-stone to European Union."[128] Henri Froment-Meurice writes in his memoirs that Giscard told his government in January 1977 that "the next step of European integration would be Economic and Monetary Union and that it would require a great effort."[129] The Trésor pointed out the risk that the EMU objective would increasingly appear an ideal but abstract objective, the realization of which was out of reach.[130] This did not mean, however, that the French government would soon be able to reenter the snake or any similar exchange rate mechanism. It was still too early, as the Banque de France explained in mid-January 1977, and as French monetary authorities would actually carry on saying even during EMS negotiations.[131] Added to this was the February 1977 Franco-German declaration about European monetary cooperation mentioned above. Noël could thus write to Jenkins in February 1977 that "the need to reactivate economic and monetary union is starting to be understood better."[132] The fact that the conclusions of the meeting of the European Council in Rome stated that "the European Council agreed to conduct at its meeting at the end of the year an examination of the results obtained in the fields of growth, employment, and the fight against inflation, and to assess the Community's prospect of making progress toward Economic and Monetary Union" came therefore as the logical result of this trend toward a reactivation of the EMU objective discernible since late 1976, and crucially early 1977.[133] The widespread view in the literature, according to which the revival of EMU discussions is credited exclusively to Jenkins, is therefore an oversimplification.[134]

The scrutiny of the discussions held during the meeting of the European Council help verify this upturn. Giscard, for instance, declared that "confidence must be restored, and to this end we should revive the target of Economic and Monetary Union. This could not be the immediate target but should be taken up again at a suitable moment in the not too distant future."[135] Yet, paradoxically, Den Uyl, the Dutch prime minister, weakly supported the only proposition currently under study regarding economic and monetary cooperation designed by his own government. At the end of his talk, he discreetly "commended Mr. Duisenberg's ideas on closer economic and monetary cooperation," without daring to say anything else. Den Uyl's remark was therefore akin to a more decent funeral than the Finance Council of 14 March had offered the Dutch initiative.

Should this reappearance of EMU in the conclusions of a European Council be interpreted as mere ritual or as a genuine call for EMU? Though monetary issues had been absent for quite a while from European Council conclusions, their sudden reintroduction was by itself not necessarily promising. EEC heads of government had made very similar declarations of intention before without putting words into deeds. This call was slightly different, however, and for two interrelated reasons. First, as suggested above, this one came as the peak of a trend discernible at various levels (members states, Commission) and backed by a nascent economic consensus, instead of as a ritual similar to earlier appeals, made at a time when economic policies were increasingly diverging, both in thinking and in actual terms. Second, it was much more cautious than before, thereby underlining that the EEC member states wanted first and foremost to economically converge before thinking about monetary cooperation any further.

The following meeting of the European Council in London on 29 and 30 June 1977 did not logically study monetary issues in depth. It was dominated by issues related to political cooperation and also the reform of the working of the European Council. Above all, this meeting came "a little too soon," as Callaghan stated during the press conference, after the March meeting, to be able to witness any profound difference.[136] Time was ripe for a review of the functioning of the European Council created three years earlier, but not yet for a review of prospects for EMU.

As I have observed in previous chapters, intergovernmental discussions should not hide the fact that significant developments were also taking place under the surface. The spring of 1977 thus also witnessed the publication of an important report, that of the study group on the role of public finance in European integration chaired by Donald MacDougall.[137] As the report rightly notes, it focuses on one aspect of EMU so far largely neglected, that of public finance: "not only taxation and public expenditures," that is, "but also the many regulatory, co-ordinating and non-budgetary activities in the economic field in existing economic unions."[138] Even more explicitly than the Marjolin Report, therefore, the MacDougall Report introduced in the EEC economic and monetary discussions the theme of the convergence of economic development. In order to fulfill this last point, the report notably suggested a considerable increase of the redistributive dimension of the EEC budget, "from 0.7% to around 2–2.5%."[139] This theme would be recycled by the British, Irish, and Italian governments in the EMS concurrent studies, whereby they would similarly ask for transfer of resources from richer to poorer regions also notably through the EEC budget.

It is also noticeable that the MacDougall group—as much as Marjolin or the so-called *Optica 1976* report, released on 10 February 1977,[140] a follow-up to the preceding Optica report—had the privilege of being assisted by the secretariat of the Commission (most often the secretariat from the directorate-general for economic and financial affairs, and in particular Michael Emerson, who would later be involved in the drafting of Jenkins's Florence speech). And although the usual disclaimer applied—"the opinions expressed therein are the responsibility of the group alone and not of the Commission or its staff"—the very first page of the report often bore only the name of the Commission as its author, instead of the name of the group as such.[141] All this was not fully innocent, and at least alluded to a consistent way of thinking that always gravitated, not coincidentally, toward the Commission. It should hence come as no surprise that the Commission chose to prioritize monetary affairs in late 1977—as the next chapter will show.

Conclusions

As far as European monetary cooperation was concerned, the period from July 1976 until June 1977 was a slightly mixed bag. If the overall economic, social, political, and monetary climate was certainly not the most promising, a number of smaller yet crucial elements gave some interesting signals. There had thus been unspectacular progress and debates over the past few months, but they had at least taken place, and had shown where each member state of the EEC stood, which suggested more optimistic prospects. In this last section I assess these ambiguous developments of monetary cooperation in the EEC from mid-1976 until mid-1977. I will do so in three steps. First, I will assess the reasons for the lack of tangible results in the field of economic and monetary affairs in the EEC.

Second, I will analyze the emergence of an economist consensus about European monetary cooperation following the second U-turn in French economic policy. Finally, I will analyze the state of the EEC monetary learning process and its likely implications for future developments.

Four main factors explain why little had yet been achieved in terms of monetary cooperation in the EEC from mid-1976 until mid-1977. First, as we saw in previous chapters, a number of problems regarding the objectives of monetary cooperation in the EEC still remained. Crucially, the problem of defining what monetary cooperation was all about was still salient. The search for more monetary stability was the common objective of all member states. As a means to obtain this stability, however, talking about the EMU objective was not the same as devising plans for an improved exchange rate mechanism. Admittedly, the latter might well be a first step leading to the former. Yet they implied measures of very different dimensions, and, as a consequence, a number of misunderstandings among EEC partners. Closely linked with the above issue was a second point: the lack of actual convergence of the European economies. As shown before, there were convincing signs of an emerging economic consensus in the EEC. This consensus simply had not yet borne fruit. Third, and more worrying, was the apparition of a new factor in the EEC institutional equation: the apparent weakness of the Commission. Indeed, as noticed earlier, Jenkins's first six months in office had been highly difficult. Given that the Commission was traditionally defending its expertise in the monetary field,[142] and that it had (and still has) a right of initiative, it clearly needed to reassert itself after such a bad start. Finally, in more general political terms, any new move in European integration was suspended until the next French general elections due in early 1978. As early as in March 1977, a British diplomat in Paris rightly summed up the situation: "The French were realistic and knew very well that they could take no decisive action until after next year's legislative elections. Meanwhile they wanted to start talking to the Germans by way of preparation, though the modalities had not yet been fixed."[143]

A Cease-Fire on the Economist versus Monetarist Front

In order to make a fair and balanced assessment of the period from mid-1976 until mid-1977, it must be noted that although little had been achieved regarding monetary cooperation, a number of important themes emerged from the EEC monetary discussions. For a start, two main features became apparent on the occasion of the discussions of the Dutch initiative: the strong German opposition to any new European monetary scheme and the emergence and necessity of having an indicator for intervention in a European exchange rate system. As de Larosière put it, the Duisenberg proposals revealed "the power of German veto."[144] The key member state for there to be any type of progress in the monetary field was indeed, more clearly than ever, Germany. Not only was the German government faring better than other EEC members and hence was the only one able to take on the clear economic leadership of Europe (although it refused to do so) but it was also the most conservative in terms of monetary arrangements over the past few years. The Duisenberg initiative thus underlined the inflexibility of the German government, and particularly that of Schmidt, at a time when many other member states were at least willing to have an open-minded discussion. As a Bank of England official observed, "The Community should be able to speak freely about this sort of subject, even if the chances of influencing the Germans in any way are very slim."[145] But during the examination of the Duisenberg proposals, even a fair discussion involving the German government seemed out of reach. By contrast, even though the British government carefully maintained an "uncommitted, agnostic position," it was seen as a fair player.[146] De Larosière thus took note of the British open-mindedness during the discussion of the Duisenberg proposals, in spite of their skepticism.[147] The key to any European monetary change therefore clearly lay in convincing the German authorities, and in particular Schmidt. In order to convince the German government, a new scheme would first and foremost need to be at least as strict as the snake. The German opposition was this time more surprising than it had been to the Fourcade memorandum, since the Dutch initiative was, by contrast to the French one, much more balanced between its monetarist and economist dimensions. The problem lay in the fact that the most contentious issue—the creation of target zones—was in essence a monetary arrangement, the economic foundations of which were, in the debates, totally overlooked.

Although the Duisenberg proposals had fewer actual results than the Fourcade proposals, they were seemingly more widely discussed. This certainly sprang from the fact that the French scheme appeared overambitious and was ill timed. The Fourcade proposals were indeed proposed by a country that was not a snake member, during one of the peaks of the economic crisis, and their examination became tangled up with many other, more urgent issues, like British renegotiation in the EEC and the reform of the international monetary system. By contrast, the Dutch initiative was put forward in a slightly improved economic and political context, and had much less far-reaching implications.[148]

Finally, and perhaps most important, the Dutch initiative introduced a new set of ideas in the EEC monetary debates. It further contributed toward breaking the rigid demarcation between snake and non-snake members (which would be central to the EMS negotiations) and underlined a genuine flow of debate between the two, in a transnationally connected monetary elite. And, as explained above, it introduced the idea that some kind of indicator of divergence was needed in the European exchange rate regime. This indicator would serve as a trigger for action for the EEC member states. This concept would resurface in 1978 on the occasion of the EMS negotiations.

By mid-1977, stability-oriented economic policies were more widespread than ever among the governments of the EEC member states. It is noticeable, however, that the four main turning points identified during this period—namely, the Dutch initiative, the appointment of Barre, the Franco-German "miniconvergence" experiment, and the reassertion of the goal of EMU—originated from individual national measures and bilateral cooperation (particularly Franco-German) and not from an EEC, supranational framework. The ambition was to generalize individual and bilateral initiatives, not to implement a supranational program agreed on in EEC institutions. In short, this was a tentative bottom-up process rather than a top-down one. Thanks to the appointment of Barre, the French administration had now somewhat reached a consensus on European monetary affairs. It must be recalled that this had been the main obstacle to any coherent French position at the European level so far.[149] It was now recognized and accepted at various levels of the French administration that economic convergence needed to precede the devising of any new monetary mechanism. A British diplomat could thus, for instance, describe the position of the French Ministry of Finance as "EMU by all means but with the precondition of convergence."[150] It had been noticed in previous chapters that there was quite close thinking between the French and German monetary authorities (Trésor and Bundesbank). With the appointment of Barre, this consensus reached a new level and was extended to the heads of government. The French premier thus said to Jenkins that "the Federal Republic and the other members of the snake should constitute the 'terms of reference' for the French government."[151] The increased cooperation between the French and German governments was another significant feature of the past few months. Both governments now favored a strong currency, balanced budgets, and a strict control over the money supply. As noticed earlier, it is possible to take this growing consensus more seriously simply because the German government took the French efforts more seriously. This had not been the case in 1974, with the last French anti-inflation plan. The birth of this new consensus was therefore a good illustration of how a purely domestic issue (the resignation of Jacques Chirac and his replacement by Raymond Barre) could have tremendous consequences for European economic and monetary developments. Barre's coming to power, and the success of his plan, were, in this sense, necessary preconditions to any new initiative in the field of monetary cooperation.

It must finally be noted that these developments happened outside of the EEC structures. For a start, the existing EEC mechanisms proved largely useless. The

Council decision of 18 February 1974 on "the attainment of a high degree of convergence of the economic policies of the Member States of the EEC" played no role (either in public discourse and in actual terms), for instance, in the birth of the Franco-German economic consensus. The existing supranational procedures were much too weak anyway. On the occasion of the launching of the Barre plan, the SGCI thus explained that there was no real EEC binding measure constraining the French government to formally seek the EEC's approval of its economic plan.[152] Another factor allowed such bilateral cooperation to develop outside the EEC framework. The good degree of trust from which both Schmidt and Giscard benefited did a lot to reduce the fear of a Franco-German directorate. This had already been seen during the creation of the European Council in 1974: Giscard was not de Gaulle, and the other EEC member states did not fear a resurrection of the Fouchet Plan. In the case of Franco-German bilateral economic cooperation, the situation was comparable. The move was initially not necessarily welcomed, but given that Giscard and Schmidt were trusted, and showed their willingness to extend the procedure to the EEC at a later stage were it to be successful, the fears of a Franco-German directorate faded away. Yet, as Jenkins put it, "Giscard and Schmidt . . . were firmly in control of Europe, but for the moment they had no direction in which they wished to take it."[153] The past few months gave a few hints, however, at the directions in which the European monetary learning process was heading.

A Transnational Learning Process

The discussions about the Duisenberg proposals clearly underlined the existence of a learning process regarding monetary cooperation in the EEC. While discussing the Dutch initiative, constant references were indeed made to the various proposals outlined in previous years. This underlined the fact that debates about monetary cooperation in the EEC were a *continuous* feature, slowly building up experience on previous initiatives. In the first Finance Council that examined the Dutch initiative, on 26 July 1976, Duisenberg himself declared that "the earlier Fourcade proposals were still on the table and should be discussed."[154] He also recalled a number of previous initiatives, such as the Tindemans Report, and the various calls for improving the EEC economic and monetary situation made in the past few years, such as those of the European Councils.[155] The German Finance Ministry produced a note restating in some detail the main points of the Fourcade memorandum, while the Irish Department of Foreign Affairs consciously took stock of the various monetary proposals since 1974.[156] The report of the Monetary Committee of November 1976 reflected the same preoccupation: "Account was also taken of proposals made by the French delegation in

1975. The Committee noted that the two sets of proposals are motivated by the same considerations."[157] Indeed, both considered the current situation unsatisfactory, were preoccupied with improving the cooperation of snake and non-snake currencies, and believed that the evolution of all the currencies of the EEC member states should be under some kind of EEC supervision. The Committee of Governors was no exception. In the second part of the report of its alternates of 2 November 1976, due reference was made to the various proposals advanced in the past few years: namely, the Fourcade memorandum (1974 and 1975), the Duisenberg proposals (July 1976), and the note of the Bank of England (September 1976).[158] Finally, during the Finance Council of 14 March, Pöhl revealingly described the start of closer consultation about exchange rates within the EEC committees as "a first step on the road that had been signposted by Duisenberg, the French, and Tindemans."[159] Hence, not only were older proposals unearthed when discussion of new ones began but they were given a new perspective, with the advantages and drawbacks of all again carefully weighed.[160]

Another interesting feature of this transnational learning process was that new monetary initiatives regularly stressed that they were themselves part of a wider monetary brainstorming rather than merely prepackaged formulas. In presenting his paper, Oort thus explained that "it was a working document aimed at provoking a discussion in the Committee."[161] Kit McMahon, in his letter to Marcel Théron introducing the Bank of England note, made very similar remarks.[162] The informality of the discussions was also stressed by the chairman of the Committee of Governors' Alternates, who hoped, at the opening of the session taking stock of the snake mechanism, for "a positive, personal, and uninhibited discussion (which need not commit their central banks or their Governors)."[163] All of these statements strikingly echoed de Larosière's declaration, mentioned in chapter 2, about the Fourcade memorandum, according to which "these proposals aimed at provoking a Community reflection." Pierre Werner, in taking stock of the monetary discussions since the failure of his plan, also paid careful attention to these various proposals.[164]

On a more technical note, at least five recurrent features regarding European monetary cooperation clearly emerged from this learning process. First, the French call for more symmetry in the EEC exchange rate system, which had appeared with the Fourcade memorandum, resurfaced on the occasion of the Duisenberg proposals' discussion. For example, de Larosière's main problem with the Duisenberg proposal for target zones was that they would completely exonerate the snake members of any obligation of intervention.[165] Second, another idea coming from the Fourcade memorandum had reemerged over the past few months, namely, the fact that the fluctuation of the exchange rate system should be determined with respect to the European Unit of Account. This idea was set out in the so-called Times Group Proposal published by a number of economists on 26 July 1976.[166] And, crucially, it was part of the Duisenberg initiative. Indeed the target zone was not meant to be denominated in terms of the dollar, nor in terms of bilateral exchange rates against other currencies, but instead of a basket of currencies derived from the trade-weighted average of rates (which was akin to the new European Unit of Account created in April 1975).[167] Incidentally, with regard to the idea of a transnational informal network of academic economists, the composition of the Times Group is particularly noticeable. Indeed, among them could be found, again, Alexandre Lamfalussy, Giovanni Magnifico, Conrad Oort, Andrew Shonfield, Robert Triffin, Pierre Uri, and Jacques van Ypersele. They all had had or would have their name associated with a monetary initiative (e.g., Lamfalussy and Uri with the Kiel Report, Shonfield with the Marjolin group).[168] Third, it emerged from the last discussions that any new monetary arrangement would make sense only if it were to include all the EEC member states. This was, of course, the Dutch point of view, but also that of the Trésor and arguably of all the EEC members states.[169] Fourth, it was clearly out of question that a new monetary scheme could be weaker than the snake. This had been one of the main drawbacks of the Duisenberg proposals: that is, that the German government believed that this new monetary arrangement could pose a threat to the discipline and unity of the snake. Fifth, the influence of monetarism was gradually acknowledged in the EEC. For a start, more and more governments and central banks were setting quantitative monetary targets.[170] Although most central bankers described themselves as not dogmatically monetarists, Jelle Zijlstra, head of the Dutch Central Bank, stated that "if monetary policy cannot solve everything, one must recognize that monetarists have played a useful role in recalling the importance of monetary realities and the harmful effects that a negligence in that domain may have on the external and internal equilibrium."[171] In more general terms, this period also once more underlined the influence of international (monetary) discussions on European developments. Not only was the Duisenberg proposal much influenced by the IMF discussions, so was the European Commission. In a note dating from August 1976—after having retold the story of the failure of the Fourcade memorandum—the Commission detailed at length the system of target zones of the IMF (created in June 1974) and how it could be implemented.[172] The improved consultation between central banks decided at the Finance Council of March 1977 was also very consciously in the spirit of Rambouillet.[173]

At a political level, three elements must be remembered. First, in terms of public discourse, the French government, and in particular the French president, was definitely the most ardent supporter of EMU. Giscard defended the EMU objective at the European Council meeting in The Hague in November 1976, once more in a public speech in January 1977 in Strasbourg, insisted on making reference to it in the conclusions of the Franco-German bilateral consultations of February 1977, and certainly did the same in Rome a month later during the European Council. If the actual economic results were not (yet?) there, the political will for improving European monetary cooperation was already present. And the political dimension of economic and monetary cooperation should not be downplayed. As Barre explained before the National Assembly in September 1976: "The fight against inflation is fundamentally of a political nature."[174]

Second, the leading role of the European Council was confirmed. This was the main outcome of a more institutional learning process. The June 1977 reform of the way the institutionalized meetings of the heads of government functioned marked the end of a trial period for the new EEC institution.[175] Giscard could thus think that "with the European Council we have more at our disposal the adequate instrument to have an appropriate overview, to give to the existing institutions, to our ministers, . . . in conjunction and in harmony with the Commission from which we expect much, the necessary impulse. . . . We must more and more act together as a government, the government of Europe."[176] Nevertheless, if the European Council was now adopted into the EEC structure, it seemed more like a useful yet unused tool rather than an overused one, at least as far as monetary cooperation was concerned. To paraphrase Jenkins's remark about the Franco-German tandem, it could be argued that the European Council was firmly in control of steering future European monetary cooperation, but for the moment it had no direction in which it wished to take it.

The situation of the EEC monetary debate in mid-1977 was thus rather paradoxical. The new Dutch monetary proposal was advanced just at the time when a firm national commitment, particularly coming from the French government, toward stability-oriented economic policies was being devised and implemented. And when the Duisenberg proposals reached the final stage of examination within the Community institutions, economic convergence was only slowly beginning to bear fruits. A Franco-German bilateral élan and the reapparition of the topic of monetary affairs at the heads of government level had by then replaced the Duisenberg momentum.

Almost three years after the unofficial abandonment of the Werner Plan it was therefore surely not a lack of proposals that hindered progress in European monetary affairs. There was a profusion of technically interesting projects but they were ill timed, economically or politically or both. The Fourcade memorandum had failed in 1974 and 1975 because of the absence of a strong economic and political consensus able to support it. The Duisenberg proposals suffered, mutatis mutandis, the same fate. All in all, two interlinked problems hindered progress on monetary cooperation: the lack of actual economic convergence and the obstinate refusal of the German government to accede to any new monetary scheme. So far the only incentives for action came from within the EEC, in the form of new monetary proposals (from Fourcade to Duisenberg), and all had failed. Perhaps it was not a brand-new idea that was needed, but rather a strong political impetus or an external trigger for action. The new French anti-inflation program, much more credible than previous ones (in 1974, for example), the new monetary ideas brought forth by Duisenberg in the EEC monetary debate, and the burgeoning of a bilateral Franco-German economic cooperation inspired thoughts of a possible change of fortune.

CONFLICTING OPTIONS, JULY 1977–MARCH 1978

> What has actually changed? What's changed essentially is (a) the newly emerged stability-consciousness in Rome, above all things in Paris, and the will. One of the most important preconditions. And another thing (b) has naturally changed, that the American benign neglect, concerning the dollar balance of payments, in the meantime became a malign neglect under Messrs. Carter and Blumenthal. And it was urgently necessary that the Europeans say to the Americans: That's not going to carry on.
>
> —Helmut Schmidt

In this chapter I analyze the reappearance of the EMU debate at the very top of the EEC's political agenda, from the decision of the Commission to prioritize monetary cooperation in mid-1977, until before preparation of the European Council's meeting of April 1978 in Copenhagen. I will do so in three steps. I will first examine why and how the Commission decided to prioritize monetary cooperation in the EEC in mid- to late 1977. Second, I will scrutinize events before, during, and after the Brussels European Council in 1977, at which the EEC heads of government had planned to take stock of perspectives on EMU. Finally, I will examine Schmidt's turnaround—the German chancellor became convinced around January–February 1978 that a new European monetary scheme was needed—and the reelection of the French government in March 1978, which allowed the French president to participate in a new European initiative. The three parts of this chapter will therefore highlight the conditions in which the revival of European monetary cooperation took place, and how and to what extent the failed initiatives, analyzed in the previous chapters, resurfaced on the occasion of this *relance*.

The Multiple Origins of European Monetary Cooperation's Revival

It was certainly not for lack of proposals that progress regarding economic and monetary cooperation in the EEC had stalled since 1974. The summer of 1977 confirmed this trend, with the proposals of the Belgian government, most importantly the initiatives of the Commission, and the ongoing Franco-German bilateral discussions. And much like their predecessors, they all highlighted in advance some central themes of the EMS negotiations. In this section I analyze these three points in turn.

Reinforcing Economic Coordination: The Geens Initiative

As had been the case with the French government in 1974 and the Dutch in 1976, the Belgian government clearly intended to give prominence to economic and monetary questions on the occasion of its EEC presidency. This intention was made plain by a number of proposals set out in detail in a memorandum on 23 June 1977, and then more formally on the occasion of the Finance Ministers Council of 18 July 1977 chaired by the Belgian finance minister Gaston Geens.[1] Geens announced a rather traditional goal: "I think we are all in agreement on the most important objective. We must reduce in practical terms the differences in economic and monetary conditions between the Member States and at the same time reduce the structural differences between our economies."[2] He asked for a continuation of the Duisenberg Plan—thereby stressing once more the continuity of monetary discussions among the European monetary elite—through reinforcement of the coordination of monetary and budgetary policies. In addition to this, he called for more coordination in other various areas (budget, setting of monetary targets, etc.). He also suggested that Ortoli, commissioner in charge of the economics and finance portfolio, could take part in the meetings of the snake so as to render the exchange rate mechanism more *communautaire*.[3]

The Belgian memorandum contained a coherent albeit rather vague list of suggestions. It did tackle most of the interconnected issues linked to economic and monetary affairs, namely, economic and monetary coordination, credit mechanisms, transfer of resources, and fiscal policy. But it did so in a particularly vague fashion, listing mostly self-evident truths.[4] No specific statement was made about exchange rate arrangements or the possible extension of the use of the EUA. The most revealing point of the Geens proposals was that, regarding credit mechanisms, they manifested concerns that were similar to those expressed during the EMS negotiations. They first showed that the issue of improving EEC credit mechanisms was constant and shared by many EEC member states. Fourcade had already tackled the problem in 1974 and 1975. He had proposed an increase of short-term monetary support (STMS) as well as medium-term financial assistance (MTFA). Geens asked for some more specific technical adjustments—essentially the introduction of an element of conditionality in order to improve the coordination of economic and monetary policies—and an increase of both the STMS and MTFA facilities.

This memorandum also reflected the continuing Belgian—if not Benelux—enthusiasm for economic and monetary union, which later crucially reappeared in the EMS negotiations with the so-called Belgian compromise that helped avoid a deadlock in negotiations. It kept some focus on the EMU debate within the EEC. On the whole, it looked more like a ritual—yet surely genuine and apropos—plea for closer economic and monetary coordination in the EEC than a truly new and original plan. It was arguably not originality that mattered most, however, given that previous, more innovative proposals (like the Fourcade memorandum and the Duisenberg initiative) had failed, partly because they were seen as too unconventional or far-reaching. The lack of originality stemmed from the fact that much—if not all—had already been said about monetary cooperation through the various proposals aimed at improving the snake since 1974, if not earlier. More than originality, therefore, what was needed was a major political impulse, likely to lead to a recycling of these ideas into a new scheme. The German monetary authorities, in particular, were not likely to be more enthusiastic about the Geens plan than they had been about the Duisenberg proposals. Indeed, added to the traditional German monetary conservatism was a new factor in late 1977, namely, that for much of the autumn, Schmidt was principally preoccupied with terrorism. The *Deutscher Herbst*, together with the SPD conference and the weakness of the dollar, as will be seen later, understandably left little time for the Federal chancellor to focus on EEC questions in late 1977.[5] According to Jenkins, Schmidt was hence full of "Teutonic gloom" by mid-November 1977.[6] It was against this rather bleak and unpropitious backdrop that the president of the Commission decided to revive the Commission's leadership on monetary issues.

A Split Commission

I will analyze the Commission's decision to prioritize monetary cooperation in three steps. First I will review Jenkins's decision to opt for monetary affairs as the topic for a new initiative and the subsequent special meeting of the Commission at La Roche en Ardennes in September 1977, where the modalities of this new initiative were discussed. I will then successively analyze the implementation of the two options that emerged from the La Roche meeting, namely, the more "economist," Ortoli-inspired approach and then the more "monetarist," Jenkins-inspired approach.

In mid-1977, Jenkins was well aware that his first six months in office had been disappointing. As mentioned in chapter 4, his Commission was initially perceived as weak, and the integration process seemed to be stagnant: "A new initiative was therefore manifestly necessary."[7] Looking for a new theme able to revitalize the Commission, Jenkins eventually opted to reassert the goal of monetary union "in the last two weeks of July."[8] From archival sources it is unfortunately difficult to trace the exact origins of Jenkins's decision. While it is possible to identify the competing options during the La Roche en Ardennes meeting, it is more complicated to see exactly where Jenkins's ideas came from. A meeting between Jenkins and Callaghan on 21 July—fitting in with Jenkins's own chronology—does provide, however, some archival background for the Commission president's change of mind. He was indeed reported to have said that "the Commission's ideas involved the co-ordination of monetary targets at the Finance Ministers' Council and some discussion of the exchange rate movements which might take place."[9] He then "regretted that Duisenberg had not been given more serious consideration," and affirmed that "what was needed was better co-ordination leading to greater exchange rate stability. He [Jenkins] favoured a phased programme over a period of 10 years towards monetary union." Although he did not give any further details as to what this program would concretely entail, he indicated that he hoped to get things moving in the fall, and that this "would be done by means of a paper to Finance Ministers." Jenkins's ideas were hence logically still very vague.

Jenkins's decision came as a relative surprise. The short briefs prepared for Callaghan's meeting with the Commission president thus stated: "We do not know why the Commission have been discussing this [EMU] or what Mr Jenkins may want to raise."[10] Yet if this move came as a relative surprise, it did fit within the timetable set by the European Council in March 1977. Indeed, the Rome declaration had announced that the heads of government would take stock of the EMU debate by the end of the year. Furthermore, as discussed above, it happened at a time when the Belgian presidency had announced that it would prioritize economic and monetary cooperation. Finally, a revealing internal note of the Commission, produced in mid-1976 for the new Commission that was due to take office on 1 January 1977 (hence the Jenkins Commission), had already presciently set the priorities for the next administration: "It must be a top priority for the new Commission to try to make progress in the economic and monetary field. . . . Both coordination of economic policies, and development of monetary instruments, need to be placed in the longer-term perspective of achieving *economic convergence and eventually of economic and monetary union*."[11] In that light, Jenkins's decision represented a logical follow-up to this older trend.

The Commission met in La Roche en Ardennes from 16 to 18 September in order to devise its strategy with respect to monetary cooperation. During this meeting, two papers circulated, one written by Ortoli, in charge of the economics and finance portfolio, and the other by Jenkins. Ortoli advocated a gradual and cautious approach to economic and monetary cooperation.[12] He noted that even if the European Council, in March 1977, planned to take stock of the EMU perspectives during its last meeting of 1977, nothing had been specifically asked of the Commission. He thereby underlined that if one were to speak of an EMU revival in 1977, it would have to spring from the discussions between the heads of government in early 1977, not from the Commission's actions over the summer. Yet, as the Commission had already shown in the past few years, it did not want to be left out of the reflections on EMU and was willing to assert its expertise in this field.

With regard to its structure, Ortoli's paper first described what a European Union would exactly entail, then listed a number of new elements that had emerged in the past few years, and finally set out in some detail his five-year program. Although Ortoli did not make explicit reference to the Marjolin or Tindemans reports, his presentation of a European Union was very much along the same lines. A European Union meant, according to him, the existence of a common market, a harmonized fiscal policy, a centralized economic policy, increased budgetary means, and last but not least, a common currency. By starting with a definition of "European Union," Ortoli certainly wanted to follow Tindemans and Marjolin in their warnings that the far-reaching implications of monetary integration had been underestimated and dangerously neglected. According to Ortoli, the changing international economic and monetary context and the prospect of further EEC enlargement, elements that had emerged in the past few years, should be included in the wider picture. The two main rationales behind monetary stability thus resurfaced, in the traditional order: the need to protect the *acquis communautaire* and the ambition to make some progress toward a European Union. In short, a "defensive" rationale combined with an "offensive" one.

As an immediate measure, Ortoli advocated the completion of a five-year program, focused on five points. The first point was certainly not revolutionary, yet it had never been put into practice: this was a new call to reinforce and render more constraining the measures adopted in 1974 regarding economic convergence in the EEC. To use and improve already existing EEC mechanisms for economic coordination was also a long-standing call of the French and German monetary authorities. Second, and much more pathbreaking, Ortoli proposed the completion of the single market by 1982. This meant the elimination of the remaining obstacles to the four fundamental freedoms in the EEC (namely, the circulation of goods, capital, services, and people). In particular, Ortoli explicitly spoke about the need to "eliminate trade barriers" as one of the actions that should be in a 1978 program to be adopted at the December European Council.[13] This point foreshadowed Arthur Cockfield's June 1985 white paper listing nearly three hundred trade barriers and, more generally, the mid-1980s *relance*.[14] The third point was devoted to monetary action but was very vague. Ortoli gave only a few hints at possible measures, without clearly determining what was really needed.

He thus mentioned the development of the EUA, the concept and limits of a parallel currency (without stating whether a parallel currency was a desirable strategy), the safeguard and improvement of the snake mechanism, and finally the reinforcement of EMCF. Fourth, Ortoli sketched out a few proposals aimed at improving economic growth in the EEC. Ortoli's final point was an open question. He wondered whether the financing of international trade development and aid to Third World countries was really a good means of improving EEC economic growth. These five points were thus the bare bones of Ortoli's five-year program. The European Council would retain an overview of the overall process through a periodic review. Each year, the European Council would set a detailed program for the following year, based on a Commission proposal.[15] Interestingly, this confirmed the leadership role of the European Council. And, crucially, this confirmation came from within the Commission itself, which could potentially have been its strongest opponent.

Although it was ostensibly a complement to Ortoli's paper, the Jenkins paper strikingly contrasted with it.[16] It was more than double in length (twenty-three pages against nine for Ortoli). It gave the impression of a well-thought-out analysis, perhaps more academic than political and practical, since it even included a bibliography. The contrast was not limited to these purely formal aspects. Virtually every single conceptual point made by Ortoli in his paper was called into question in Jenkins's. In response to Ortoli's gradual and cautious approach to economic and monetary cooperation, which, according to Jenkins, would permit "a centipede's advance towards EMU,"[17] the Commission president said that "the bull ha[d] to be taken by the horns."[18] Three important features of Jenkins's paper must be borne in mind.

First, Jenkins's approach was clearly monetarist in thinking. Revealingly, the Commission president systematically talked about "monetary union" instead of "economic and monetary union." His paper was hence a case in favor of monetary union in the EEC, not about EMU. Second, Jenkins rejected from the outset the more gradual approach advocated by Ortoli. He gave a number of reasons explaining the failure of the Werner Plan, underscoring the overall inefficacy of this approach as a means to reach monetary union. The Duisenberg proposals, which, according to Jenkins, were in the same gradualist spirit, thus logically suffered the same fate. The tone of Jenkins's paper was overall much less cautious than Ortoli's. In the concluding section, the rationale of Jenkins's paper was all the clearer: "We need to reduce our present embarrassing reliance on rather dated, gradualistic doctrines, which are not taken seriously by the press and are maintained by member states as cover for their lack of political will, and as intellectual imprisonment for the Commission."[19] Third, Jenkins's paper focused less on the practical implication of a monetary union than on its theoretical advantages. According to Jenkins, at all levels ("smaller" member states, "big" member states, and the EEC itself) and in various domains (including inflation, employment, growth, and regional issues), the advantages of a monetary union were tremendous. Overall, Jenkins's analysis was much more academic than political. If the benefits of a monetary union were clear, therefore, the way in which it could practically be implemented was much less obvious.

There was therefore little common ground between the two papers discussed at La Roche. Admittedly, both Jenkins and Ortoli were heading in approximately the same direction, toward increased EEC economic and monetary cooperation. Both were well aware of the difficulties ahead, and both rightfully underlined the fact that the implications of an EMU were largely underestimated. Jenkins and Ortoli were thus very careful to define what an EMU would consist of and what it would entail. Yet Jenkins and Ortoli were clearly in favor of different strategies. Of particular importance is the fact that the La Roche weekend revived the long-standing methodological debate between the "qualitative leap forward" and the "incremental process" approaches to reach EMU. There was much more, however, than simply a question of method at stake. Jenkins and Ortoli simply did not have the same objective in mind. Jenkins talked of monetary union, while Ortoli defended *economic and* monetary union. Jenkins was strictly monetarist in his thinking, while Ortoli's approach was much more comprehensive. Hence, at a time when the economist versus monetarist dichotomy was fading away among the member states of the EEC, and especially between the French and German governments, and had been replaced by a rather economist consensus, this very dichotomy now appeared within the Commission itself. If Jenkins wrote that the "gradualistic approach" was now dated, it could be said in echo that his own monetarist approach looked relatively outmoded and surely unrealistic by late 1977.

Parallel Implementations

These differences of opinion became quickly familiar to most European governments.[20] Both papers, which were not supposed to be circulated outside of the Commission's circles, soon arrived in London, Paris, and Bonn.[21] The implications of this will be analyzed at a later stage, together with the reactions of these governments. Although he conceded "some internal Commission difficulty," Jenkins said that the internal debate in the Commission was settled relatively easily.[22] This should be nuanced, however. Deane Hinton, US ambassador to the EEC, for instance, depicted to the State Department a strong Jenkins-Ortoli split within the Commission in October.[23] The follow-up to the presentation of the two memorandums would clearly show the persistence of two schools of thought in the Commission.

The Commission presented a paper titled "Improving Co-Ordination of the National Economic Policies" to the Finance Council of 17 October 1977.[24] This paper was essentially a formal transcription of the ideas Ortoli had presented at La Roche. Ortoli had already made it clear, both at La Roche and through bilateral consultations, that no spectacular move was to be expected.[25] This communication stressed from the outset that it would build on existing mechanisms. The document was thus in line with both the 18 February 1974 directive and the decision of the Council of 14 March 1977. One of the most important suggestions made by the Commission was "to set objectives for domestic monetary policy in quantitative terms."[26] This was an interesting example of a bottom-up process: quantitative targets had progressively been adopted in France, Germany, and Britain, and the EEC as such was now willing to harmonize the procedure. Yet this method had been rejected earlier in 1977, and was unlikely to be accepted six months later.[27] The discussion essentially focused on setting a target rate of economic growth that was meant to be at least 4 percent.[28] This interestingly underlined another difference of focus between Ortoli and Jenkins: Ortoli placed economic and monetary stability in a more complex framework of causalities, while Jenkins tended to present monetary union as an all-encompassing solution.

Why did Ortoli put forward such a paper so rapidly after the La Roche informal weekend? Admittedly, the economic and monetary situation in which the EEC found itself required some rapid action. Yet it has also been suggested that Ortoli put forward this document "in order to forestall Jenkins' own ideas on EMU."[29] This was not unlikely given that the internal debate within the Commission had apparently not yet been settled, and given that, according to Michael Emerson himself (the member of Jenkins's cabinet in charge of economic and monetary affairs who largely drafted Jenkins's paper), Jenkins "had no firm views yet."[30] Furthermore, Ortoli and his cabinet were visibly careful to distance themselves from the Commission president's ideas. In preparing for Ortoli's visit to Healey, Denis Gautier-Sauvagnac, Ortoli's chef de cabinet, thus dissociated the former president of the Commission from the more radical proposals made by Jenkins.[31] Presenting a paper at the Finance Council was thus presumably a way to translate these words into deeds.

In contrast to Ortoli, Jenkins did not immediately set out his ideas in more concrete form. Throughout the fall, Jenkins tried instead to do some "monetary proselytising" in the EEC, mostly through public speeches and bilateral meetings.[32] The most important and most famous speech given by Jenkins on this topic was the first Jean Monnet Lecture, which he delivered at the European University Institute in Florence on 27 October 1977.[33] He devoted his speech to a single issue: "the case for monetary union." Jenkins first rejected the apparent antithesis between the gradual approach (advocated by Ortoli) and the dramatic advance (his own view): "Evolution is a process which once begun goes both gradually and in jumps. . . . The process had to be seen as one." While this reasoning was certainly logical, Jenkins also surely wanted to avoid giving an impression in public of inconsistency within the Commission. In the core of his speech, Jenkins set out in detail seven arguments for monetary union: a monetary union, he said, would provide the EEC with "a more efficient and developed rationalisation of industry and commerce than is possible under a Customs Union alone"; "a major new international currency backed by the economic spread and strength of the Community"; "a common rate of price movement"; and "the regional distribution of employment and economic welfare in Europe." It would have "a beneficial effect upon employment" and had major institutional and political implications. Finally, he said, it could be "a vehicle for European political integration."

Two qualifications need to be made here. First, as mentioned above, it is again important to note a semantic yet crucial point. As during the La Roche meeting, in the Jean Monnet Lecture Jenkins was talking about monetary union, not *economic and* monetary union. To be sure, he also mentioned a number of economic structural policies, such as regional redistribution, but overall his call concerned monetary affairs strictly speaking. Interestingly, this point underlines once more the recurrent issue of the problem of defining what "economic and monetary co-operation" exactly entailed. Second, Jenkins's overall objectives were perhaps less far-reaching than they might at first appear. He thus declared on this occasion— and repeated later in his memoirs—that "my belief is that we should use the period immediately prior to the first direct elections of the European Parliament to re-launch a major public debate on what monetary union has to offer. . . . The debate must be re-opened and subsequently sustained." In short, Jenkins wanted above all an immediate public debate about monetary integration more than monetary union itself, at least in the short run. Third, and perhaps most important, Jenkins did not outline a proposal for a European monetary system, contrary to what is sometimes said in the literature.[34] Not only did he talk about monetary union but his talk had also very little, if anything, in common with the EMS as it came into force in March 1979.

Unsurprisingly, reactions to Jenkins's speech were generally skeptical. To the "qualitative leap forward" suggested by Jenkins, *The Economist* famously replied, "Look before you leap."[35] Jenkins's speech was not taken too seriously, in the sense that it seemed quite obvious that his suggestions would not be implemented any time soon. A common reaction was simply to mention that Jenkins had made a far-reaching proposal, without going any further—as Karl-Otto Pöhl did at the Bundesbank on 3 November 1977.[36] Second, though they were tackled in more detail, discussion of Jenkins's ideas remained, however, at a fairly philosophical level. Doing justice to all of his arguments would have been quite a massive task for what was, after all, only a speech made by the president of the Commission at a time when the institution over which he was presiding was clearly not united on the matter. A brief of the British Treasury reflected this point.[37] Ironically enough, and still at the level of general principles, it can be noted that Jenkins was described by a French official as "hyper 'monétariste'"—a description that was revealing when made by a government that tended to be itself quite "monetarist."[38] An alternative (and logical) reaction was that Jenkins's speech prompted the production of various notes about the history of European monetary cooperation since the 1960s.[39] The exception that proved the rule was at a technical level, and concerned only one particular aspect of Jenkins's ideas. Indeed, thanks to the Jenkins proposals, the issue of the "parallel currency approach" to European monetary cooperation, about which discussion had so far been confined to academic circles, reached, at last, another level and came to be (inconclusively) discussed in the Committee of Governors in December 1977.[40] Still, most of the debate remained confined to the Commission or to academic economists. An academic study of the DG II on the case for a parallel currency (drawing an explicit parallel with the *Times* proposal) was written as a contribution to the EMU debate relaunched by Jenkins.[41] Similarly, Giovanni Magnifico restated his support for the parallel currency approach, and suggested the "upgrading of the European Unit of Account to the role of official reserve and settlement asset, i.e., currency for official use."[42] This remained confined, however, to the internal workings of the Banca d'Italia.

At the level of ministers and heads of government, the basic reaction was that the time was not yet ripe for such a great leap forward. An informal meeting of EEC foreign ministers in Villiers-le-Temple on 8 and 9 October confirmed this trend.[43] Jenkins presented his ideas again, and the ensuing discussion was, predictably, inconclusive. Needless to say, Schmidt also commented along these lines.[44] Other reactions amounted to a polite—and perhaps genuine—approval of Jenkins's goals, of the sort expressed by Raymond Barre and Giuliano Andreotti, the Italian prime minister, in two conversations they had with the president of the Commission.[45] Though the eventual goal was shared, it was, however, considered too early to take action. As Henri Froment-Meurice, director of the Economic and Financial Division in the Quai d'Orsay, put it in his memoirs, "This acceleration toward the monetary wrong-footed the 'economists,' Ortoli in Brussels, La Genière and Larosière in Paris."[46] For the French "economists," the focus was so far much more on the Franco-German miniconvergence experiment.

Of particular significance was the British attitude to the renewed debate. This particular importance stems from the fact that, of the nine EEC members, Britain was quite obviously the least inclined to accept further monetary cooperation, if not even the goal of monetary union in itself. Yet, as had been the case during the discussions of the Duisenberg proposals, the British government was very keen to appear open-minded. Crucially, the British government did not want to appear to be "the first to pour cold water."[47] Of course, this was clearly a strategy to help allay doubts about its European stance, severely damaged by the 1974–1975 renegotiation and the subsequent referendum. But the British government also did not want to be left out or even perhaps to again "miss the bus" of a new project related to European integration. Indeed, as to the substance of the discussions, the British government did not want to (or did not see how, in the present circumstances, it could) rejoin the snake. As a consequence, any scheme—such as the Duisenberg proposals and their Belgian follow-up, which displaced attention from the snake and thus showed that the snake was not the only way to improve European monetary cooperation—had some attraction for London.[48] By contrast, it believed that "any exclusively theoretical approach to EMU [was] misguided."[49] The next important step would be the translation of Jenkins's ideas into concrete proposals before the Finance Council of 21 November and, crucially, the European Council in Brussels.

The Ongoing Franco-German Bilateral Discussions

The Franco-German miniconvergence experiment carried on, with a new meeting in early October and a visit to Bonn by Barre on 20 and 21 October. As noted by a British official, the closer Franco-German bilateral collaboration had not (yet?) provided any extra impetus for closer cooperation at the EEC level.[50] Matters at that level were instead following their own timetable. EEC matters and bilateral cooperation were indeed two separate though interconnected issues.[51] Despite the difficulties, "the aim [was] still for the two countries to present the results of their experience to their partners in the Community before the end of 1977, and EMU [was] still the lodestar."[52] The French Finance Ministry still considered Franco-German bilateral cooperation the most appropriate scheme in the present circumstances.[53] Reporting to the Monetary Committee about the French economic and monetary situation, the French members stated that the economic and monetary policy that had been pursued for eighteen months was now bearing fruit.[54] The question was posed whether it was appropriate to communicate to the December European Council the results of the ongoing Franco-German experiment. Since it had really started in June 1977, and a new meeting was due to be held on 13 January 1978, the French judged that it was still premature to try to gauge the results of this miniconvergence.[55]

The fall of 1977 confirmed a number of trends that had appeared on the occasion of the first meetings of the new Franco-German scheme. It was now becoming even clearer that much of the emphasis put on Franco-German co-operation as a foundation of the EEC derived from the facts that Italy appeared relatively weak and that Britain found itself in a rather uneasy position. The British government indeed liked to appear constructive in EEC debates but at best was simply neutral. Giscard and Schmidt, by contrast, were in a relatively stronger position, benefited from their mutual entente, and were seen more or less as "pro-Europe." The way was therefore clear for increased bilateral coopera-tion between the French and German governments. The French government in particular was certainly willing to exploit the new foreign policy situation. With the relative coolness of the Washington-Moscow relationship, with the perceived decline and detachment of Britain and the German readiness to question its link to the United States, which will be examined later, Giscard felt that there was an opportunity for France to appear as an arbiter in Europe. The Franco-German experiment was thus still carried out, de facto at the expense of the British (and also Italian) governments. As the British ambassador in Paris acknowledged: "I think it fair to say that the Franco/German side of the European triangle is being strengthened compared with the other two."[56] The British government thus found itself in an uneasy position. It did not want to be left out of the main source of political impetus, but did not want to cooperate as closely as France and Ger-many either—let alone "trilateralize" the meetings. Callaghan hence wrote in the margin of a note from February 1978: "Too many meetings between everyone. I would not want to get into Franco/German routine."[57]

Taking Stock of EMU Perspectives

Having opted for monetary cooperation as his new flagship policy, Jenkins had now to convince the nine EEC member states. In order to do so, his most impor-tant target was the meeting of the European Council due to be held in Brussels in December 1977. In this section I will look at how monetary issues were discussed in the EEC institutions in late 1977, focusing on the preparation for the Brussels summit, the summit itself, and the period that followed.

The Transatlantic Facet of European Monetary Cooperation

Before moving to the Brussels meeting, however, it is first necessary to stress the growing importance of the transatlantic factor in European monetary coopera-tion. Indeed, as of mid-1977, a central feature of the debates among both experts and heads of government was the decline of the dollar.[58] The first signs came in July 1977. The issue was first tackled during a meeting of the Committee of

Governors in that same month. Emminger, who had replaced Klasen as Bundesbank president on 1 June,[59] attributed the dollar's fluctuation to the dollar's fall rather than the DM's strength.[60] He thus concluded that occasional operations could be needed, but that for the moment nothing more was envisaged. The interpretation changed over the autumn. In November 1977, a document presented by the Commission to the Monetary Committee underlined the fact that the current deficit of the US balance of payments was now a structural phenomenon that could essentially be corrected through a depreciation of the dollar.[61] The German members complained about this situation and noted, as had been the case a few months earlier, that it was not the responsibility of European countries alone (and certainly Germany even less) to bear the consequences of this. Generally speaking, it was felt that the Germans were progressively abandoning their rather phlegmatic attitude to express their exasperation a bit more openly: "One of his [Emminger's] colleagues, recalling the Connolly policy of 'benign neglect,' had unkindly described the Carter policy as the same without the 'benign.' . . . In public he, Dr Emminger, naturally felt compelled to reflect relaxation and optimism, but if pressed to speak sincerely, he would be worried."[62] In early December, the interpretation changed radically. For a start, the German members of the Monetary Committee (as well as the Danish and Dutch members), who had so far been relatively passive and fatalistic regarding the decline of the dollar, now changed their discourse and suggested a more active policy.[63] The French members, although they too shared the same basic concerns, stressed more the absence of EEC monetary unity. In describing the situation on the exchange market in November and early December before the Committee of Governors, François Heyvaert, president of the group of experts working for the Committee of Governors, painted a dramatic picture of the situation: "The vulnerability of the dollar . . . has exploded in what has been, at certain moments, true chaos."[64] A multiplicity of causes could be advanced in order to explain the dollar's weakness. The Committee of Governors thus identified a wide variety of sources for the ongoing decline of the dollar: the US balance of payments deficit, the energy crisis, the prolonged miners' strike, inflationist trends, widespread distrust of the US administration, and so forth.[65] Yet the "dollar problem" did not remain confined to experts' circles. Since mid-1977, the dollar's decline (and the DM's appreciation) had been a source of concern among heads of government. Rumors that the US-German relationship was worsening spread quickly, notably in the press. Both Carter and Schmidt were well aware of this and quite early on agreed to try to counter this speculation.[66] In a conversation with Barre in February 1978, Schmidt "expressed doubts as to whether the American leadership knew what they were doing: the enormous, increasing trade balance deficit and the fall of the dollar had extraordinarily negative consequences not only in economic terms but also in terms of world politics."[67] Carter began to think of the external effects of the dollar only in early 1978, after his visit to Europe.[68]

A series of public declarations and technical arrangements, by governments and monetary authorities, attempted to improve the situation. On 21 December, Carter made an unexpected speech in which he promised that some market intervention would be carried out.[69] A few weeks later, during Carter's trip to Europe, on 4 January, the US Treasury announced that it had activated the exchange stabilization fund and the swap agreements in order to reestablish order in the foreign exchange markets.[70] Finally, on 13 March, the United States and Germany issued a joint communiqué. In this declaration, both governments agreed that some recent exchange rate movements had been "disorderly" and "excessively rapid," and that they were determined to cooperate closely so as to avoid the recurrence of such an event. A number of limited technical arrangements were announced.[71] In commenting on the 13 March declaration, Emminger explained that one of its principal objectives was to dissipate the impression that a disagreement existed between the two countries.[72] Yet, overall, the improvement of the international monetary situation arguably was more dependent on the will of US authorities than on a bilateral accord, as some members of the Committee of Governors remarked in March 1978.

The weakening of the dollar became an additional motivation for further EEC monetary cooperation. Jenkins could thus say to Margaret Thatcher, leader of the British opposition, in early December 1977 that "one of the many reasons for wishing to move to a common European currency was the disarray of the present world monetary system and the declining fortunes of the dollar."[73] The decision of the German chancellor to prioritize European monetary cooperation in early 1978 is thus also often portrayed, with some reason, as an answer to the "dollar problem." Nevertheless, one important alternative being considered at the time—the creation of a so-called substitution account—should not be overlooked.[74] The idea was to absorb surplus dollars into an account managed by the IMF, the dollars being exchanged against SDRs. The overall objective was to replace reserve currencies (essentially the dollar) with an international asset (the SDR), and thereby stabilize the international monetary (non-) system. The creation of such a substitution account was briefly discussed, for instance, in a meeting of the Monetary Committee on 4 April 1978. It was partly thought of as a response to the dollar's decline, and partly also conceived as a way to create additional liquidities—hence the German opposition.[75] The proposal was under discussion at the international level from the early 1970s until its abandonment in 1980, which was mainly due to the inability of leading states and the IMF to agree on way of distributing the potential costs.[76] Another initiative that was thought of as a partial answer to the weakening of the dollar was the promotion of an economic stimulus by surplus countries. This was also known as the "locomotive theory," according to which increased economic growth in surplus countries (essentially Germany) would nurture international consumption and thereby rebalance international economic development. Economic growth targets would thus become a constant underlying theme in 1977 and 1978 not only in the EEC but also at the international level, through, respectively, the Ortoli proposals and the G7 Bonn summit, which will be examined in the next chapter.

"About EMU, one is harbouring illusions in Brussels": The Reception of the Commission's Proposals

EEC monetary discussions over the fall of 1977 differed slightly from those that had been taking place since 1974. Instead of focusing on one proposal, like a reform of the unit of account or the creation of target zones, the debate was, in more general terms, about whether to once again proclaim the goal of monetary union and subsequently how to reach it. Hence these discussions were more about personal contacts between heads of government or members of the Commission rather than strictly technical discussions in the specialized committees.

Following his speech in Florence, Jenkins toured European capitals to do some "monetary proselytising."[77] He had thus had talks with Barre and Andreotti. Most important, the president of the Commission went to Bonn on 10 November 1977. His visit did not prove to be very promising.[78] Schmidt was not won over by Jenkins's ideas, and he only "half agreed" that he would not "throw cold water on monetary union when he could not see an alternative way forward himself." The US attitude, the issue of economic leadership, and obviously terrorism were the main issues occupying Schmidt's mind by mid-November 1977. The basic German attitude had therefore not changed since the beginning of Jenkins's efforts to revive the EMU public debate.[79] The French position was less clear-cut. The French government favored the goal of monetary union in principle but found it, given present circumstances, highly utopian.[80] Furthermore, as we noted in chapter 4, the French government was now slightly more "economist" than it used to be, and, to be sure, Jenkins was more "monetarist" than the French government had ever been. But most important, the March general elections were approaching. The prospects for Giscard and Barre were not promising, and they thus constituted "a certain deterrent to French initiatives."[81] The French government was therefore likely to remain on the defensive until after the March vote.

Following an initiative of the Commission, a fairly technical though significant topic of debate throughout the fall was the issue of fixing quantitative targets for monetary policy. This debate had been a constant theme of all the Committee of Governors meetings in late 1977–early 1978.[82] Ortoli, in starting a discussion about this topic, observed a progressive convergence of views regarding the mechanisms of economic policy.[83] Ortoli attached great significance to the setting of general objectives (regarding growth, the fight against inflation, etc.) in order to have greater complementarity between the final objectives and the means employed by the member states to reach these ends. According to Alexandre Lamfalussy, the fixing of quantitative monetary targets had three origins and motivations: the wish to avoid the mistakes made by monetary authorities around 1971–1973; the wish to slow down inflation; and the influence of monetarist (in the sense of Milton Friedman) theory.[84] Yet, as was often the case with monetary discussions, the most—if not the only—skeptical members were the Germans. This was particularly true in the session of 26 January of the Monetary Committee, when "the discussion virtually split the meeting between the Germans on the one side and the rest of the Community on the other."[85] The Monetary Committee thus proposed a half-baked conclusion regarding the improvement of monetary coordination, whereby it suggested to the Council that member states should present, as far as possible, their quantitative monetary objectives or orientations.[86] A similar half-baked conclusion was reached at the Committee of Governors, much to the regret of Ortoli.[87]

In order to carry on the debate about EMU at the Finance Council to be held on 21 November 1977, the Commission published its proposals on 17 November.[88] This document looked like the eventual compromise between the two papers presented at La Roche. Yet it had had quite a complicated gestation. Naturally, the merger of the Jenkins and Ortoli approaches, which roughly shared the same long-term goal but differed in substance, was not accomplished without difficulty. As Jenkins put it in his memoirs, the difficulty of reaching a Commission consensus was more a problem for him than for Ortoli since he was the one anxious to make a new, more ambitious move.[89] Jenkins eventually adopted a conciliatory attitude, and downplayed his monetarist ambitions. Nevertheless, this episode did not improve the internal cohesion (or, arguably, the later chance of success) of the Commission. Jenkins referred to this episode as "the one low point of my monetary union campaign of that autumn."[90]

Even though the Ortoli and Jenkins approaches were formally reconciled, Ortoli's clearly predominated. In a nutshell, the document revealed that the Commission from then on disregarded the option of a "qualitative leap forward" and disregarded the Werner-style approach of establishing a very strict timetable leading to EMU. Instead, it analyzed the current state of monetary cooperation, identified the reasons for the failure of previous initiatives, and listed the advantages of a monetary union. It then sketched out the two approaches to monetary union—a qualitative leap forward and a step-by-step advance—and immediately stated that while both strategies were indeed complementary, in the short run it would be impossible to implement the former. This was, crudely put, the victory of Ortoli over Jenkins. The Commission's communication then proposed a banal program of action: reaffirm the objective of EMU and ask EEC member states to take concrete action and learn the lessons of the past.

Ortoli's general line, which was actually very similar to Giscard's position, was to argue that just because EMU could clearly not be achieved in the near future, one should not refrain from trying to make any progress toward it. Ortoli was thus reported to have explained to Otto Graf Lambsdorff, the German economics minister, that if one could not expect big changes in the short term, one should not renounce taking smaller, more concrete steps in the meantime.[91] Before the Finance Council, Ortoli defended a plan of action that included an "agreement on the need for greater convergence of economic policies," "a strengthening of the 'snake,'" and a program of financial aid.[92] Given that the paper had arrived just a few days before the Council in the European capitals, the ministers gave only very preliminary opinions, dominated by little enthusiasm—Lambsdorff unsurprisingly being the most skeptical.[93] The paper still had to be examined by the various EEC committees.

On the eve of the Brussels European Council, the discussion of monetary issues therefore originated from three distinct sources: the follow-up to the Franco-German initiative of February 1977 regarding the coordination of economic policies, the decision of heads of government at the Rome European Council of March 1977 to take stock of EMU discussion by the end of the year, and the follow-up to the initiative of the Commission in the fall. That Giscard attached great importance to the Brussels Council debate about EMU is in little doubt. In a preparatory meeting before the heads of government meeting, Giscard thus asked what of significance could come from it, and his own answer referred only to EMU.[94] Thus, in spite of the prospect of a difficult general election, Giscard wanted to make full use of the Brussels European Council. If the elections were likely to prevent him from making any new initiative, they would not restrain him from keeping the debate alive. Yet, as evoked above, Giscard was one of the very few in the French government and civil service to be so enthusiastic about the EMU debate. Admittedly, reaffirming the long-term objective of an EMU did not pose a problem. Henri Froment-Meurice, head of the Direction des Affaires économiques et financières of the French Foreign Ministry, thus thought it justified to reaffirm the EMU objective.[95] The problem was that it was felt that the Commission—and particularly its president in his public speeches—-was going too far, too early. It was also too early to do anything following the Franco-German experiment, and one needed to wait at least until the spring of 1978 to do anything about the Commission's proposals. Similarly, on the occasion of a discussion about the Commission proposals, Jacques de Larosière (and also, in a similar fashion, Renaud de La Genière) advised against any proposal in monetary affairs or a return in the snake "so long as the inflation differentials were of about six points."[96] The Banque de France similarly explained, in December 1977, that it was too early to rejoin the snake, but presciently stated: "It remains, however, that the future of the 'snake' . . . will be above all ordered by factors of a political nature."[97] The reactions of the other EEC member states seemed, by contrast to the French case, much more uniform. The British government was not enthusiastic. Nevertheless, Callaghan said to Jenkins that he would examine his ideas about EMU "constructively."[98] He had "no 'ideological' objections, only practical doubts." His own approach would be to say "Show me."[99] Jenkins replied that what he wanted above all was to launch a substantive debate on EMU over the next six months or so. Unsurprisingly, the German reaction was that time was not ripe for EMU.[100] Schmidt's own current "generally pessimistic frame of mind" certainly did not help.[101] Emminger was similarly reported to have expressed "great skepticism" about the Commission's plans.[102] The Banca d'Italia was even more openly critical of the monetarist approach adopted by the Commission in its communication to the Brussels December 1977 European Council: "One must avoid repeating the implicit fundamental mistake in the Werner approach according to which the establishment of monetary constraints in the states of the Community would suffice, *by itself*, to obtain an effective coordination of economic policies and a reciprocal compatibility of objectives in the transition period."[103] The Italian Foreign Ministry argued, for instance, that a reinforcement of regional policy would render the call for EMU more credible.[104] This was a position of course shared by the Irish government, which consistently supported parallel progress in economic and monetary integration.[105] Yet, although the German chancellor declared, during a conversation with Andreotti, that "about EMU, one is harboring illusions in Brussels," Schmidt seemed apparently well aware that he should not appear too negative. He thus added, in his conversation with the Italian prime minister, that he would restrain himself in Brussels, to avoid giving the impression that he was pessimistic.[106] The discussions during the European Council would confirm this trend.

Tout ça pour ça?

Jenkins opened discussion on the economic situation in the EEC by declaring: "I see no medium way forward except by giving a new, non-utopian but more urgent and contemporary impulse to the old idea of economic and monetary union, particularly its monetary aspect."[107] The November 1977 Commission paper, recommending a five-year program to be reviewed annually, constituted the basis of the EMU discussion. After explaining that each and every member state of the EEC (be it "strong," "weak," or "in-between") would benefit from further monetary cooperation, Jenkins put forward two points: first, that monetary union needed a "major act of political will," and second, that "it is not the case that an equality of performance is a pre-requisite for EMU." Jenkins finally carefully stressed that his project was not utopian, thereby trying to counter the main criticism he had been facing for a few months. The overall analysis was, in that sense, not very different from what the Marjolin Report or the Tindemans Report had said.

Given the high ambitions aroused in the preceding months, the inconclusive discussion between heads of government was of course disappointing. It paradoxically seemed to have left quite a positive impression on Jenkins: "I spoke for just over half an hour, which was longer than I had intended but it seemed to hold people's attention. . . . Only Schmidt looked as though he was asleep, which he mostly does when anyone other than himself or Giscard is speaking."[108] And admittedly, a number of heads of government, such as the Italian prime minister Giulio Andreotti, remarked that, given the economic context, "it was easier to talk about EMU than it had been a few years ago."[109] Most of them could even agree on the long-term goal of EMU—it would not constrain them very much anyway to say so—while carefully adding to it, as Schmidt did, an all-too familiar list of preconditions: reform of the CAP, budget, credit policy, and so on. The overall atmosphere was also quite good. Schmidt thus surprisingly described himself as "not unduly depressed" by the economic situation. When portrayed as an "optimist" by Callaghan, however, he curtly replied that "he had not expressed optimism but the absence of pessimism."[110] The only clear negative sign came from Callaghan, who openly recognized that he was pessimistic about EMU, although he argued that his frame of mind was "show me that it would have advantages."[111] But the heads of government found themselves utterly unable to go beyond this very general discussion. The vagueness of the EMU project certainly helped reach this low-key consensus. Schmidt, Giscard, and Callaghan could easily agree on the need to undertake further in-depth studies about monetary cooperation, without committing themselves to anything concrete.

The European Council hence called for the implementation of the "strategy for economic growth" approved by the Finance Council on 17 October 1977, adding that this should be accompanied by progress on the road to EMU.[112] While the EEC heads of government not only reaffirmed their commitment to EMU but also showed a willingness to take further and more concrete steps forward, they seemed nevertheless to unofficially abandon the project. The diplomatic phrasing and the introduction of the Commission's proposal into the tortuous EEC monetary decision-making pipeline looked very much like "a first-class burial," as a German European MP put it, similar to that of the Tindemans Report, for instance.[113] The heads of government had perhaps not poured "cold water" on EMU, but the ambition had not clearly been regained either. As Jenkins put it in his memoirs, "While my monetary union initiative had not been offered anything like a safe passage, it had not been shot down in flames."[114] In early 1978, the Commission started implementing its action plan. This took the form of the first annual report of the Commission in the framework of the five-year plan, published on 10 February 1978.[115] Ortoli presented this twenty-six-page document, organized under four major headings (economic convergence, single market, structural policies, and social policy), to the Finance Council of 20 February 1978, which sent back the various parts to the EEC specialized committees.[116] This project would, however, soon be superseded by another initiative, surprisingly coming from the German chancellor.

A Double Turnaround

Two relatively unexpected events occurred within a few weeks in early 1978: Schmidt's sudden conviction that a new European monetary plan was necessary and Giscard's victory in the French general election. Before turning to these two events, however, it is first necessary to examine one monetary scheme that chronologically preceded them, the van Ypersele proposal.

The van Ypersele Proposal and the Transnational Monetary Learning Process

Following the conclusions of the European Council, Jacques Van Ypersele, Belgian chairman of the Monetary Committee, proposed a plan titled *Rapprocher les monnaies européennes*. He presented a first sketch of his ideas in early February 1978, and gave a more detailed version in mid-March.[117] This van Ypersele Plan matters in that it gave the clearest hint at the existence of a transnational monetary learning process, building on previous experiences: "This new debate [the van Ypersele proposals] is in line with the impulsions given in the past by the prime minister, Mr. Tindemans, then by the Dutch minister, Mr. Duisenberg, and recently by Mr. Jenkins and Ortoli."[118] The overall structure of the first sketch of his proposals, presented in early February, already was a perfect example of this learning process. He indeed first analyzed the "four options" that existed, he said, in order to improve European monetary cooperation; the first three were the return to the snake, the Fourcade approach, and the Duisenberg approach. After analyzing the shortcomings of each of these, he presented his own approach—the fourth option—which he said had a number of advantages over the other three. In short, he wanted to show that he had learned the lessons of the previous failures.

The crux of van Ypersele's proposals can be summarized as follows. He suggested maintaining the snake as it was, without weakening or strengthening its structure, and creating a single common target zone for the other non-snake currencies. This target zone would be the average of the movements of the snake and the dollar. At the start the weighting would be fifty-fifty, but the objective would be to gradually diminish the dollar's proportion and respectively increase that of the snake. The proposal of the then president of the Monetary Committee continued the preoccupation of the last few years regarding policy vis-à-vis the dollar. It reappeared on the EEC agenda in September 1974 thanks to the Fourcade memorandum, and an attempt at having a coordinated policy had been carried out for six months following the agreement reached at the Committee of Governors in March 1975.[119] As of late 1977, the dollar decline rendered the problem of the dollar–European currencies (and particularly DM) fluctuations particularly acute. Interestingly, the Bundesbank did not seem unsympathetic to the proposals of van Ypersele.[120] Even more important, van Ypersele suggested the idea that intervention debts could at least partly be settled in a European monetary unit (instead of in dollars).[121] This European monetary unit would be equal to the EUA basket. It would be issued by the EMCF, partly against deposit of gold reserves. As the next two chapters will make clear, this suggestion was strikingly close to Schmidt's as well as that contained in the Bremen Annex.

Schmidt's Change of Mind and the French General Election

Schmidt's sudden conversion to the idea that increased monetary cooperation in the EEC was urgently needed is one of the puzzles of the EMS story. How could someone described by Jenkins as "asleep" in early December 1977 during a vibrant plea for EMU suddenly become an ardent supporter of the same issue about a month later? The first basic answer to that question is simply that, contrary to what is sometimes suggested in the literature, it was indeed *not* the same issue. Jenkins had talked about full-fledged monetary union. What Schmidt had in mind—as we will see more clearly in the next chapter—was a pooling of reserves in order to reinforce the snake and protect the DM against the dollar's decline.

The key trigger for action explaining why Schmidt became interested in the emergence of a European currency bloc was the weakening of the dollar, and even more than this, Schmidt's distrust of the US administration's economic and monetary policy. Schmidt was particularly concerned with the growth of the German money supply and the effects it would soon have in terms of inflation.[122]

As the German chancellor made plain before the Bundesbank's central council in November 1978, "In my view, the decisive risk for our currency is . . . not what happens in Europe, but the decisive risk for us is the United States of America, its balance of payments, its inflation policy, its exchange-rate policy."[123]

If the trigger for action was the dollar's weakness coupled with Schmidt's distrust of the US administration, it would be, however, certainly a bit simplistic to suggest a strict and straightforward causal relationship between the two. For a start, the dollar's weakness did not immediately prompt Schmidt to search for a new European monetary plan. For a while, the German chancellor appeared to be hesitant. Though in mid-July 1977, in an answer to a question from Giscard about the fall of the dollar, Schmidt said that "the Federal Republic would not remain passive," the Federal Republic indeed remained passive for about seven months more.[124] Describing Schmidt's passivity toward the dollar's decline, Callaghan even said to his German counterpart in early 1978, "You remind me of the band playing 'Abide with Me' while the *Titanic* went down."[125] Yet after a while, Schmidt's conduct evolved. Jenkins, who met with the German chancellor on 28 February, reported that "he [Schmidt] wasn't very friendly across the Atlantic. . . . And as a result was looking for rather more drastic solutions than I have found him at any time in the past year."[126] This last remark showed that Jenkins was well aware of the importance of Schmidt's change and of the existence, therefore, of an opportunity that ought not to be missed. It also highlighted that this change had not really been expected, and that he was unsure whether it would last. Since the window of opportunity may not remain open for long, the president of the Commission was asking to act fast.

Second, Schmidt's quest for a European solution cropped up on fertile ground, composed of a new institutional tool (the European Council), the monetary ideas analyzed in previous sections and chapters, and, in more general terms, a long-standing German disquiet about the economic situation in general: "He [Schmidt] had a well-kept garden, free of weeds, but with a brick wall around it, and the German people were getting tired of walking round and round it. They were satisfied materially but dissatisfied psychologically."[127] Being able to count on his French ally was the last element missing in order to make the context fully propitious, as will be further explained below.

The exact timing of Schmidt's change of mind is slightly imprecise in the literature. Most accounts situate it around the beginning of 1978, but the documentation able to support it is patchy.[128] The most recent research on this topic is unfortunately unable to provide further information. Neither David Marsh nor Guido Thiemeyer supply more detail.[129] More surprising, Hartmut Soell and Matthias Waechter, both of whom had access to the German chancellor's private papers in Hamburg, fail to provide new insights.[130] The traditional landmark is the visit by Jenkins to Bonn on 28 February, when the German chancellor shared his plans with the president of the Commission.[131] He then informed Callaghan on 12 March of his "exotic idea" on the occasion of a visit by the British prime minister to Bonn.[132] Schmidt also informed Giscard, but the German chancellor was aware that it was probably best not to mention any kind of European monetary reform before the French general elections had taken place. Otherwise, the communists or Gaullists were likely to revive the old argument that Giscard was abandoning France to Germany's economic might.[133]

Schmidt had seemingly made up his mind earlier to act. He openly elicited this option as early as 15 February 1978. During a cabinet meeting, following discussion of foreign and economic policy and a number of remarks made by the economics, finance, and foreign ministers, Schmidt made a long and revealing comment on monetary policy. Although the author of the note—Klaus von Dohnanyi, secretary of state in the Auswärtiges Amt—explained that it was not verbatim ("but definitely a precise description of contents"), it is worth giving in full the comment he attributed to Schmidt:

> However unpleasant this may be to monetary policy experts, we have to figure that the question of a gradual standardization of European monetary policy will come to the fore in the next few months. When I read the newspapers, in particular foreign newspapers, it appears to me that the constantly repeated demands of Mr. Jenkins are having an effect. I believe that already at the European summit in April, the Federal government should take initiatives based on concrete proposals. With this it is important to make clear that we, without openly announcing it, are ready to aid our partners in the stabilization of their currencies. I also consider it important that the political and administrative leadership in France know they can count on the full support of the Federal Republic of Germany in the event that the franc needs support. I do not consider it sufficient that these assurances are given between presidents of central banks. The political and administrative leadership must get in touch in a cautious and unpresumptuous manner.[134]

This shows that Schmidt had changed his mind much earlier than usually thought. If he openly shared his thoughts with his cabinet on 15 February, this certainly means he had made up his mind earlier. It also contradicts the usual belief that his volte-face and his plans were devised in great secrecy.[135] His declaration was admittedly quite vague. But however vague it was, he had made it in front of his entire cabinet, explicitly saying that the Federal government should make "concrete proposals" at the European Council in April 1978. After this cabinet meeting, significant portions of the German administration could therefore potentially have been aware of the German chancellor's willingness to move forward on European monetary issues. Yet they seemingly (and surprisingly) did not attach much importance to it, since Genscher, commenting on the note of von Dohnanyi, advised adhering to previous actions as defined before.[136] Schmidt had indeed to give still more concrete ideas.

Any such move forward was, however, dependent on the outcome of the French general elections of March 1978.[137] Once more—and this is even more striking in the case of France—a purely domestic political event had significant consequences for the European policy of a member state. The French general elections took place on 12 and 19 March 1978. Almost until the day of the elections, the Left was ahead in the opinion polls.[138] A victory by the Left would have had tremendous consequences for French economic policy. The stability-oriented economic program pursued by the Barre government since mid-1976 would have been abandoned in favor of a return to expansionary policies. The French and German economies would have again set out on different courses and thereby rendered tighter monetary cooperation even more complex. The German government hence wanted, almost openly, the reelection of the right-wing majority in France.[139] In the end, the majority was reelected, and Schmidt, who had clearly made the continuation of his scheme conditional on Giscard's electoral victory, could further outline his plan, details of which will be one of the subjects of the next chapter.

Conclusions

In this section I will provide some further reflections on the new trends that appeared during the period from July 1977 to March 1978, and survey where exactly the "learning process" about European monetary cooperation stood in early 1978. I will also scrutinize the new triggers for further monetary cooperation that emerged over the past few months, namely, the dollar's decline and the prospect of enlargement. Finally, I will try to assess the role played by the Commission.

The Continuity of Monetary Reflections

Although monetary affairs were more actively discussed in the EEC in mid-1977, no real new technical proposal—in contrast to what had happened between 1974 and 1977—emerged from these discussions. As has been shown above, earlier ideas—target zones, an exchange rate mechanism centered on a unit of account, a parallel currency—resurfaced from time to time. There were, however, a number of new elements or clarifications regarding the method to reach EMU and the importance of personalities.

Before we turn to these points it is necessary to note that the EEC monetary discussions from mid-1977 until early 1978 witnessed again multiple cross-references to earlier proposals, thereby stressing the *continuity* of the reflection about monetary issues. One could distinguish two types of reference. One was a sort of "self-reference," such as that of a French official mentioning the Fourcade memorandum in a note analyzing the Commission's proposals, or of a Dutch official supporting the Commission's plan since it was in a similar vein to Dui-senberg's.[140] In a similar fashion, Geens made reference to the Tindemans Report in his speech at the Finance Council outlining his proposals for economic and monetary cooperation.[141] If this was not very astonishing, such allusions still highlighted a continuous brainstorming about monetary issues. More interesting was a second trend: multiple cross-references made, in various documents, to these earlier proposals. Hence, in the same speech, and in a less nationally biased fashion, Geens described his proposals as continuous with parts of the Duisen-berg Plan. The Irish Department of Finance noted that the van Ypersele propos-als were "in the same mould" as the Fourcade and Duisenberg ones.[142] Another case in point was the multiple references openly made by Ortoli to Duisenberg's "target zones."[143]

Three main lessons emerged from the monetary discussions since mid-1977. The first major lesson of the past few months had certainly been the eventual abandonment of the "qualitative leap forward" strategy to reach EMU. While a number of people had supported it in the past few years, Jenkins had certainly been its strongest advocate in 1977. Yet Jenkins put forward his ideas at a time when they clearly were not possible to implement. Seen as improbable both in theory and in practical terms given the economic circumstances, his option clearly did not convince the EEC member states—not even the vice president of the Commission himself. Jenkins's call therefore had the unintended effect of a reductio ad absurdum, and ended up discrediting the "qualitative leap" as an option for further monetary cooperation.

By contrast, the economist versus monetarist debate, which seemed to have been fading away in chapter 4, resurfaced on the occasion of the EMU debate of late 1977. The Franco-German economic rapprochement had therefore not marked the end of this debate but merely a cease-fire. If this debate did resurface, however, it did so in a slightly different incarnation. Indeed, so far, since the early 1970s and especially since the oil shock, many debates about EMU recalled the necessity of economic convergence prior to monetary union. "Economic convergence" and "economic coordination" were the mottoes. But nobody re-ally said what degree of convergence or what degree of coordination was pre-cisely needed for the achievement of EMU. There was hence an impression that "economic convergence" was the catchall expression for any monetary reform in the EEC. Jenkins refined the analysis by arguing that convergence of policy and common disciplines were required but not *equality* of economic performance. The contrary would postpone economic and monetary union forever.[144] This was a constant argument of Jenkins, and even of Ortoli. It was a crucial nuance, since it allowed some to push for increased monetary cooperation at a time when economic convergence had not yet been fully reached. To offset the uneven economic development of the EEC member states, it is also noticeable that the Jenkins/Ortoli proposals of late 1977 gave more centrality in the EEC monetary debate to the idea of resource transfers, from "richer" to "poorer" EEC member states. This theme would come back during the EMS negotiations.

A third element appeared to become crucial in monetary discussions, namely, the importance of personalities. So far EEC monetary discussions had been mainly focusing on technical issues (unit of account, exchange rate mechanism) and were carried out in specialized committees holding secret discussions. Admittedly, the two most important proposals made since 1974 bore the names of their initiators, Fourcade and Duisenberg. Yet these ministers did not bear the whole burden of the initiative. In the case of Fourcade, the Finance Ministry and particularly the Trésor were largely involved in the proposal. The same was true for the Dutch initiative, the first sign of which was actually a speech made by Oort not Duisenberg. By contrast, the two most important turning points described in this chapter were the result of personal decisions made by individuals: Jenkins's decision to prioritize EMU in mid-1977, and Schmidt's commitment to the reform of the snake. It is hence no coincidence that we cannot date with precision the moment they changed their minds; though influenced by several factors, their decisions seem to have been very personal and not concerted. On a more methodological note, this last point also underlines the limits of archival sources.

New Triggers of Further Monetary Cooperation

To be sure, older triggers of European monetary cooperation still existed. The protection of the functioning of the CAP and the common market, as well as political and symbolic goals, were still significant arguments for increasing EEC monetary cooperation. More specifically, however, during the period examined in this chapter, two new factors clearly emerged as triggers for action: the dollar's decline and the prospect of enlargement. In fact, these were the only two factors mentioned by Jenkins in a conversation with Giscard in February 1978.[145]

The issue of the dollar's decline has been largely developed above and probably need not be further discussed. What is worth noting, however, is that the rationale behind the claim for further European monetary cooperation clearly shifted, within less than a year, from the exclusively trade- and CAP-based argument to the problem posed by the weakness of the American currency. The instability of the dollar came as an additional disequilibrating factor accentuating the fragility of intra-European exchange rate relationships. And in a sense, it also provided the long-awaited external trigger for action in the EEC. "The apparent readiness of Schmidt and the Federal government to question for the first time the absolute nature of their link with Washington"[146] was also a direct consequence of the German distrust of US economic and monetary policy, as well as of the neutron bomb episode, as will be shown in the next chapter. Schmidt's "apparent readiness" had some important consequences, at various foreign policy levels. Bilaterally, it further reinforced the Franco-German link, arguably at the expense of Britain. And it also led Schmidt to envisage the possibility of closer European (monetary) cooperation.

A second significant feature was the appearance of the argument about future enlargement in the EEC monetary debates. Admittedly, the prospect of a further enlargement of the EEC was not new in late 1977 and early 1978. For the first time, however, at various levels (Commission, member states), the possibility of an enlargement of the EEC was mentioned in combination with monetary discussions.[147] The rationale for this was quite obvious. Indeed, because it was feared that enlargement would cause further economic and monetary divergence in the EEC, a number of officials in the Commission and in the EEC member states started to think that if economic and monetary cooperation was ever going to be improved, it would have to be done before any enlargement.[148] As Ortoli put it: "Enlargement could jeopardize the cohesion of the Community unless there were greater economic convergence and faster progress toward economic and monetary union."[149] The candidates for EEC membership—Greece, Spain, and Portugal—were indeed all three rather poor European countries and would further augment the uneven economic development of the EEC as a whole. But as usual, the issue of what "EMU" exactly meant could also slightly modify this analysis. If a monetary union between, say, Spain and Denmark seemed indeed unlikely in the late 1970s, the immediate implementation of a new exchange rate system and its progressive extension to newcomers was a different matter. In any case, the old theme of "widening, deepening, and accelerating" thus somehow reappeared on the EEC agenda.

Assessing the Role of the Commission

Finally, the revival of the EMU debate was also the revival of the Commission's leadership on monetary issues. In the past few years, the Commission had, notably through two communications (in June 1974 and in April 1976),[150] tried to uphold its initiative in the field. Yet both attempts were limited and ultimately unproductive. By contrast, its fresh attempts in mid-1977 gained more attention, to such an extent that it is today most commonly (though inaccurately) seen as marking the revival of the EMU debate. A number of important themes emerged from this episode.

Jenkins's call for EMU was certainly the most personally engaged since that of Pierre Werner in the early 1970s. Although it is perhaps the most complex, the first basic feature that comes to mind thus concerns the assessment of Jenkins's personal role in the revival of the EMU debate. If his main goal was to revive the debate in the EEC about EMU, he clearly succeeded. His offensive launched over the summer of 1977 did manage to attract some attention both from heads of government and, quite remarkably for a topic that was most often confined to specialized circles, the media. Yet to suggest that Jenkins spontaneously, and free from any external influence, opted to revive the debate about EMU in mid-1977 would be quite misleading. First, the presence of EMU at the top of the EEC's agenda was not due to Jenkins but to a decision made by the European Council in Rome in March 1977, and, before that, to the Franco-German bilateral summit meeting of February 1977. Jenkins's initiative thus clearly fitted within a longer-term framework, to which he himself incidentally never made reference. Yet Ortoli did, and many other European actors interpreted Jenkins's move the same way. In informing the Bundesbank Council of the two Commission proposals, Pöhl made clear that they had been prompted by a suggestion of the EEC heads of government earlier in March.[151] Second, Jenkins's initiative was very much linked to the need for *a* new initiative, of any kind, and not for monetary union per se. From the US perspective, for instance, the Commission's initiative was closely connected to the relative decline of the institution of the Commission even more than to the weakening of the dollar.[152] It is hence a good illustration of the need to go beyond an interpretation focusing merely on "material interests." Jenkins's decision to call for EMU was indeed a good way to reassert the Commission's leadership. In that sense, therefore, it was more about power politics than monetary stability per se. Third, his personal preference—a qualitative leap forward—was both dismissed within the Commission (this culminated with the 17 November Commission's paper) and largely disregarded at the heads of government level. In the end, he substantially pruned his proposals and eventually set them in the perspective of what could reasonably be achieved over the next five years. Finally, the consequence of the internal debate within the Commission was that for a few weeks, member states simply did not know what line the Commission would take.[153] This was ultimately unfortunate, since it certainly limited the visibility and credibility of the Commission's initiative. Overall, therefore, the focus of our attention should shift from Jenkins back to other actors (such as Ortoli) and wider trends (such as the reappearance of monetary issues at the top of the EEC agenda over the winter and spring of 1976–1977 analyzed in chapter 4).

Was Jenkins successful in his initiative? As far as the implementation of his ideas is concerned, he surely was not. As of mid-November, Jenkins's option for a "qualitative leap forward" had already virtually faded away. Indeed, it was Ortoli's ideas, not Jenkins's, that eventually prevailed in the Commission's paper of 17 November. And this was all the more remarkable since it was Ortoli who, by contrast, appeared to have "lost" at the Commission meeting at La Roche.[154] Yet should all this be considered a personal defeat for Jenkins? Maybe not, given that Jenkins's aim was not to press exclusively for early decisions but to reopen and set in motion a serious public debate about EMU, one that could contribute, in a better climate, later on, toward the formulation of specific proposals.[155] As a Commission official noted, "If monetary union is not presented in terms of current problems, politicians and public opinion will consider the subject as an obscure theological dispute, of interest to scholars but not to ordinary sinners."[156] The goal was to stimulate a wide public debate—which it succeeded in doing. Furthermore, Jenkins gave essentially a political impulse rather than a technical one. This was a significant element since political will (plus, of course, economic convergence) had been severely lacking so far in the EEC. And, crucially, political will was one of the most important factors in overcoming the remaining economic differences between member states.

This last observation leads logically to the second major feature underlined by the revival of the EMU debate, namely, the centrality of the European Council. The European Council's centrality in the EEC decision-making process was first accentuated by the presence of a president of the Commission, Jenkins, who was fully aware of the significance and usefulness of the new tool in the EEC's diplomatic arsenal. Admittedly, Ortoli had already, on various occasions, underlined that he supported the institution created in 1974. This time, however, Jenkins was even more aware of the need to make full use of it. Jenkins clearly conceived of EEC institutionalized summitry as giving rhythm to the political life of the Community, and presented it as "an intimate and on the whole useful occasion."[157] Jenkins aimed for a decision of principle at the Brussels European Council, instead of any kind of pledge from the Council of Ministers.[158] And even before this meeting actually took place, his next target was already the following European Council, slated to take place over the spring 1978.[159] Another case in point was the communication of the Commission of 17 November. Although it was first presented to the Council of Ministers, it did not make the usual explicit reference to the Council on its front page (namely, "Communication de la Commission au Conseil") but instead wrote only "Conseil européen, les 5 et 6 décembre, à Bruxelles," hence highlighting the importance of the institution created in 1974.[160]

And indeed, the Commission plan itself reinforced the centrality of the European Council in the EEC's decision-making process. The Commission's scheme planned that progress made by the five-year plan would be monitored at summit level. The Commission thereby interestingly acknowledged the European Council's role as the main agenda-setting body of the EEC. Hence in his opening speech at the December 1977 European Council in Brussels, Jenkins asked the European Council to "encourage the Commission to elaborate in more detail what . . . would be the conditions and merits of an accelerated move to economic and monetary union."[161] In a sense, he killed two birds with one stone: he recognized that the European Council could provide leadership and orientation to the future endeavors of the EEC and he reaffirmed the primacy of the Commission on technical issues. Later Jenkins explained: "In conclusion, I believe the European Council should deliberate in such a way as to reawaken interest outside the Community institutions in this project—in political, academic, business and trade union circles." The president of the Commission was thus aware of the potentially far-reaching implications of any statement by the heads of government. It is interesting to notice that he left out one sector on which the heads of government meetings had influence: public opinion. This was in a sense revealing, given that if the goal of monetary union in itself could well attract some interest in civil society, the technicalities of narrower margins of exchange rate could hardly have the same impact.

Finally, the importance of secret deliberations, particularly regarding monetary affairs, also reinforced the centrality of the European Council. Two levels of secret deliberations could be identified: those among experts (as in the Committee of Governors) and those between heads of government (as between Giscard and Schmidt). As de Larosière underlined, political discussions of financial issues were risky, particularly at a time when foreign markets were very sensitive. By contrast, secret discussions among experts who would refer back to their national authorities were, given the circumstances, more appropriate.[162] The importance of the confidentiality and intimacy of the European Council's debates hence resurfaced. The strongest and most constant defender of the informal and intimate nature of the European Council's debate was the German chancellor. Schmidt often stressed that the European Council ought not to become the Council of Minister's court of appeal. Virtually every new preparation or holding of such a summit was an opportunity for him to insist on this point. He thus told Andreotti, before the Brussels European Council, that he "would be very happy, if Andreotti together with himself and Giscard would emphasize that the European Council had been created to conduct a political exchange of views and not to solve the 'remaining homework' of the Ministers."[163] During the meeting itself, Schmidt abandoned the homework metaphor for a more classic remark: "The

European Council must not be an instance of appeal for the questions not resolved in the usual mechanics of the Treaty."[164] All heads of government were
apparently worried by the current trend of European Council meetings: "All the
heads of government had agreed that the present mode of European Council
Meetings was intolerable. The heads of government should not meet in capitals,
but in secluded venues, with no teams of officials present. The Prime Minister
commented that this after-dinner discussion had nevertheless been the best of
the day—precisely because the heads of government were alone."[165] The next European Council in Copenhagen would probably be a good occasion to put these
ideas into practice (except for the question of the capital!) and to stress further
the importance of such informal contacts.

A SEMISECRET NEGOTIATION, LATE MARCH–MID-JULY 1978

[Ken] Couzens looked rather pole-axed and kept on repeating, "But it is very bold, Prime Minister. Did the Chancellor [Schmidt] really go as far as that? It is very bold. It leaves the dollar on one side. I don't know what the Americans will say about it. It's very bold, Prime Minister." After about twenty-five minutes of this, we went back to the Royal Hotel where I talked to Crispin [Tickell] before going to bed, in a state of some excitement, for it had been a remarkable day, at 2 o'clock.

—Roy Jenkins

In this chapter I analyze the quest for a new philosophy of the EEC exchange rate system, from Schmidt's "exotic idea"[1] of late March to publication of the Bremen Annex in mid-July 1978. One of the characteristics of the negotiations leading up to the Bremen European Council was that they were conducted at various levels (heads of government, specialized committees, ad hoc committee) but also in a semisecret fashion. In addition to the usual chronological analysis of the period, I will therefore have the additional task of giving a clear picture of this multilayered negotiation. The actors themselves saw each of the two summits (Copenhagen and Bremen) as "part of a pattern for the summer," the success of which could be gauged when they got to the Bremen summit.[2] This chapter examines this period in three steps. First, I delve into the monetary initiatives taken in March 1978, and culminating at the European Council in Copenhagen in early April 1978. Second, I scrutinize the parallel attempts at sketching a new plan for European monetary cooperation, following the Copenhagen summit, until the presentation of the Schulmann-Clappier draft that would form the basis of discussion at the Bremen European Council. Third, I explore the road to the production of the Bremen final communiqué that outlined the final guidelines of the EMS. Although these three phases could be summarized as the outlining, working out, and presentation of the Schmidt Plan, careful attention will be paid to other options that existed at the time. These three phases indeed also corresponded to James Callaghan's plan for economic reflation, the continuous work of specialized committees, and the G7 Bonn summit—which were all, in one form or another, geared toward a similar goal, namely, monetary stability.

Taken together, the three parts of this chapter will show that, over this period, the main technical and "philosophical" features of monetary discussions in the years 1974 to 1977, highlighted in previous chapters, largely resurfaced following the initiative of the German chancellor. Furthermore, in this chapter I shed new light on the work (semi)secretly carried out by the so-called Group of Three, which devised what would become the Bremen Annex, attached to the conclusions of the Bremen European Council.

An "Exotic Idea"

Schmidt's change of mind and the French government's victory in the general election cleared the way for new initiatives in the field of European monetary cooperation. In this section I will successively analyze the period of gestation of these proposals during the month of March and then turn to the Copenhagen European Council in early April where these proposals were put forward.

The First Discussions of the Schmidt Plan

Although a fair image can be given of the Schmidt Plan, the German chancellor's ideas remain surrounded by much vagueness. In his memoirs, Giscard explains only that the inception of the EMS has been prepared by "successive meetings," without naming them, apart from an undated dinner at the Élysée Palace.[3] It is known, for example, that Schmidt and Giscard met on 2 April in Rambouillet, and that the chancellor set out in some detail his ideas about "some kind of new European monetary structure" to the French president.[4] Nothing concrete leaked out of this meeting, however, since no one else was present during the discussions. Even after the Copenhagen summit, Jean-Pierre Dutet, Giscard's economic adviser, was able to report only that this meeting had been "very important."[5] Schmidt himself explains in his memoirs that he does not recall that he, alone, took the initiative for a new European monetary plan that is usually attributed to him, but that he did so in close cooperation with Giscard.[6]

A number of shared details do emerge, however, from the cross-analysis of various European archives. The best source of information is a record of the Callaghan-Schmidt meeting on 12 March, when Schmidt outlined his ideas to the British prime minister. This description of his plan deserves to be quoted in full:

> The Prime Minister told me [Kenneth Stowe, principal private secretary], when alone, that Chancellor Schmidt had explained to him "an exotic idea" that he was pursuing. . . . The idea was to create another European snake, but of a different kind. He would not be going as far

as Roy Jenkins wished to in terms of EMU, but what he would propose was that the FRG and certain other members of the Community should each put half of their reserves into a new currency pool, the currencies of which would be fixed against a European Unit of Account. This Unit of Account would be the currency which operated vis-à-vis the dollar, and would be the sole unit of intervention. The pool would be managed by Finance Ministers. Countries in difficulties could borrow from this pool, and repay in one of three periods: over eight weeks; over six to twelve months; or over two years. He would not want this pool to be tied to the dollar because the US economy was too large and uncontrollable: the captain was not in charge, even though he was well meaning. On this basis, the FRG will put in $20 billion and the United Kingdom $10 billion, with the French making a comparable contribution. . . . Chancellor Schmidt said that he could tell the Prime Minister that one effect would certainly be to weaken the German mark.[7]

The suggestion to give a greater role to the EUA admittedly was not new. The most original aspect of Schmidt's proposal was in fact the pooling of reserves. It quite strikingly recalls the various plans for EMU sketched out in 1957–1961 by Monnet, Uri, Marjolin, and Triffin, and, in particular, the idea of a Fonds euro-péen de réserves (FER).[8] Schmidt, however, seemed to suggest a pool that would be intergovernmentally managed. Nevertheless, it remained quite a bold project, since it did not appear to be thought of as a mere swap arrangement. It should further be noted that Schmidt's turnaround was only geographic not intellectual: he did not suddenly turn monetarist with regard to European monetary coopera-tion. Quite the contrary, he remained an economist in thinking, fundamentally attached to the convergence of European economies prior to monetary unifica-tion.[9] What changed was his sense of the urgent need to do something in Europe, not his idea about how to do it.

The reactions to and interpretations of Schmidt's vague but exotic idea were revealing in that they uncovered the fundamental thinking of some European leaders. At first, however, Callaghan, quite understandably, did not react to the ideas suggested by Schmidt. On 31 March, during a conversation with the British prime minister, Jenkins gave, by contrast, rather patchy insight into Schmidt's overall philosophy. Jenkins said to Callaghan that Schmidt was planning to do "something pretty substantial pretty quick in order to deal with the international currency aspect of it [Jenkins's scheme for monetary reform]."[10] He added that Schmidt had discussed his plans only with two people, his finance minister and the head of the Bundesbank.[11] A couple of weeks after he had first heard of the plan, Callaghan's position seemed to be unfavorable toward it. For a start, he did not want any move that might threaten the transatlantic link: "I would be very much against us moving on the European front on currency because it might give the impression to the Americans that we weren't really interested in them." Second, Callaghan did not follow Jenkins's argument that a more united European monetary position would improve world monetary stability:

> CALLAGHAN: I think there comes a clear question—do we try to build a world monetary system or are we going to have a European one.
>
> JENKINS: I don't think the two are necessarily contradictory. I think we ought to play a larger part. I mean, we aren't going to create a European single currency.... But I think we might move to a substantially more coordinated European monetary position which could help to create a better world monetary position.
>
> CALLAGHAN: Well it might or it might not.... I would want to make my point clear that I would prefer a world monetary system rather than a block system of this sort.[12]

Kenneth Couzens, second permanent secretary at the British Treasury, had a similar basic understanding of the content of the German chancellor's plan. Couzens reported that Schmidt had suggested the pooling of part of each EEC country's reserves, presumably with a view to influencing currency relationship by market intervention.[13] To be sure, Couzens listed a familiar list of pros and cons: the Schmidt proposal would offer greater exchange rate stability and thereby help in the fight against inflation; greater economic convergence was needed prior to devising new monetary arrangements; the change of parity within an arrangement such as the snake, even if possible, was never an easy one; membership in the snake (or any new similar arrangement) would artificially keep the sterling average exchange rate higher than if it stayed outside it—thereby losing a competitive advantage, as British industry often feared. Yet for Couzens the crux of the problem lay elsewhere. For a start, the German proposal—whether on purpose or not—"may have the effect of cutting across the 5 point plan." The so-called Five-Point Plan was a British government initiative aimed at the international level that focused on growth, long-term capital flows, energy, trade, and greater currency stability.[14] The British government particularly stressed that the plan should be considered as a coherent whole, and consequently that singling out individual elements—like currency stability—should be avoided.[15] The British international economic initiative and the Schmidt currency plan truly clashed. They had both been outlined in March 1978, with a view to both being most substantially discussed in July 1978 (the British plan at the Bonn G7, the Schmidt Plan at the Bremen European Council). The regularity and frequency of the European Council gave a decisive advantage to the European initiative. The Copenhagen European Council indeed provided, as I will show in the following pages, a decisive early political impetus to the European currency scheme. Second, the German proposal treated the dollar, according to Couzens, as "a lost cause": "The German emotional reaction to the state of the dollar is to turn away from it and withdraw into Europe; the British reaction is to go and see our American friends." The British concern that the European monetary debates were perhaps a way to show distrust in the dollar was not a cosmetic way to hide the British government's own reluctance to embark on a European scheme. The British government's obsession with doing no harm to the dollar was perennial. For example, in the framework of the IMF substitution account debate—which ran roughly parallel to the EMS negotiations—the British government used similar arguments. The British Treasury, for example, stated that although it found Johan Witteveen's proposal "very attractive," "we must be careful not to activate this proposal in a way which suggests lack of confidence in the dollar."[16] By contrast, Giscard was certainly happy to see, at last, Schmidt's change of mind regarding European monetary cooperation, regardless of its origin (the dollar's decline, the new Franco-German economic consensus) and its implications (moving away from the issue of growth). Admittedly, Giscard's basic preference was for a (near) fixed exchange rate regime. And although he mentioned the possibility of a return of the French franc in the snake in 1978, he was not really keen on returning to the *existing* snake. Indeed, it should not be forgotten that the French franc opted out twice, and that although it could certainly largely be attributed to the wrongdoings of French economic policy, it had been partly attributed at the time to the limitations of the snake itself. Furthermore, the last time the French franc left the snake, it constituted a severe blow to Giscard's personal prestige.[17] The French president therefore needed to be able, to some extent, to blame the exchange rate system itself, and show that he would not let France join a rehash of the same flawed mechanism. Crucially, therefore, Giscard needed a new scheme—or at least, as we will see in the next chapters, a scheme that *seemed* new.[18]

Devising bold monetary plans was not, however, an exclusive prerogative of the German chancellor. It is again noticeable that monetary initiatives continued to flourish, and precisely at the time of the Schmidt Plan. Jenkins thus distributed some "proposals for a possible immediate advance" in early April, before the Copenhagen European Council, drafted, as before, by Michael Emerson.[19] Jenkins's proposals strikingly recalled the ill-fated Fourcade memorandum, in that he suggested "grouping the other currencies round the Snake, but keeping the Snake, using the European unit of account as a reference point and envisaging interventions in this way between Community currencies and, indeed, in dealings between Community currencies and the dollar."[20] Similarly, Jenkins reveals in his memoirs that the Belgian Finance Ministry had been devising plans for monetary advance to be presented during the European Council. These couple of initiatives therefore emphasized the political rather than the technical originality of the German chancellor's gesture. That Western Europe and the EEC needed more monetary stability was widely acknowledged, and many people were ready to suggest ideas about how to reach greater intra-European currency stability. Yet these ideas usually did not reach the appropriate decision-making channels, and this is why the Schmidt Plan stands out. It also shows that, although the Franco-German semisecret working of a plan for currency advance may have aroused the suspicions of the other EEC heads of government, the general climate was so propitious that such suspicion could be quickly overcome.

The Copenhagen European Council

Preparations for Copenhagen highlighted the general EEC governments' frame of mind. Three important features emerged: the reluctance, if not outright opposition, of the Bundesbank; the skepticism of large parts of the French government and civil service; and the consistency of the Irish and Italian positions. As for the latter, the Italian Treasury, when assessing the various monetary proposals under discussion, recalled the Italian position (which was largely similar to the Irish) based on two key words: parallelism and symmetry. Parallelism in the monetary *and* economic advances; symmetry in the obligations between the economically strong countries and those "in convalescence."[21] An exchange between Pöhl and Schmidt described well the German position. Following his new interest in closer European monetary cooperation, Schmidt had asked Pöhl, vice president of the Bundesbank, to provide him with an overview of the monetary plans currently under discussion in the EEC. On 21 March, Pöhl replied that his colleagues were "consistently critical and skeptical" about the possibility of a European political initiative being a contribution to solving the dollar problem.[22] By contrast, the reluctance of some parts of the French government and civil service was slightly more surprising. Admittedly, as we saw in the preceding chapter, a number of French departments, and in particular the Trésor, had voiced their skepticism. In examining the likelihood of the reintegration of the French franc in the snake in February 1978, the Banque de France concluded that "it would take time."[23] In January 1978, it had even dubbed the DM's domination of the snake as *la tyrannie du mark*.[24] On 6 April, Jean-Pierre Ruault, one of Giscard's economic and monetary advisers, told Giscard he was skeptical about the viability of a new fixed or quasi-fixed European exchange rate system: "I am convinced that [the rigidity of exchange rate relations] could only be 'doable'—and still with a great risk of failure—only if we were resolved to carry on a policy more rigorous than the 'Barre Plan' . . . , a policy that would imply the acceptance of an almost nonexistent phase of growth. Is that conceivable?"[25] Ruault's note ended with this rhetorical question, to which the answer seemed quite obviously negative to him. This reflection highlighted an argument constantly employed by those who doubted the possibility of a new exchange rate system: that the economic differences, notably between France and Germany, were still too big. All these reactions—the reluctance of the French and German monetary elites as well as the Irish and Italian focus on parallelism and symmetry—therefore confirmed that for a plan to be devised, it would need to be worked out in detail outside these official channels.

A notable exception to the rule was Bernard Clappier, governor of the Banque de France. On 30 March 1978, Emminger wrote to Schmidt to inform the German chancellor of his telephone conversation with Clappier the day before.[26] During this telephone conversation, Clappier had evoked a range of possibilities for improving the present European exchange rate arrangement. He logically first ruled out the option of the franc's return to the present snake, which he considered too risky, as did his colleagues of the Trésor and the Élysée. But he then set out three options for a new system: a progressive narrowing of the fluctuation margins, a weakening of the snake along the lines of the Fourcade Plan,[27] and the association of the non-snake currencies to the snake through target zones along the lines of the Duisenberg Plan. Both governors showed "great skepticism" about the last two options. Clappier then mentioned two more far-reaching options: the partial pooling of European reserves and the development of the role of the EUA (a parallel currency was even suggested). These two options interestingly were very similar to what Schmidt was thinking about (the parallel currency apart, at least at that stage). Clappier's relative exception in the French economic and monetary landscape would quite soon be exploited by Giscard after the Copenhagen summit.

As a way of better preparing for the meeting of the European Council on 7 and 8 April in Copenhagen, the Commission president sent a memorandum to the EEC heads of government on 3 April.[28] Since he was well aware that "Commission papers [were] slightly jargonish and [that not] everybody reads them by any means," Jenkins wished to circulate a more personal paper, which he intended as a "sort of analytical letter," to the heads of government.[29] This memorandum set out five points Jenkins thought EEC action should focus on: the sluggish growth in the European economies, the (lack of an) international monetary system, the international division of labor, the dependence on overseas energy, and the prospect of enlargement. Jenkins had thus quite strikingly downplayed the monetary issue, in favor of a wider, more complex, and somehow Ortoli-inspired analysis of the problems faced by the EEC. Yet the heads of government would not really discuss it, and would instead discover the ideas of the German chancellor.

On the morning of 8 April, Giscard, Callaghan, and Schmidt shared an early, private, and discreet breakfast before the formal session in order to discuss Schmidt's plans.[30] The initial plan was that Schmidt and Giscard would talk privately with Callaghan about monetary affairs prior to the formal discussion with all heads of government present in the European Council later in the evening. Yet, for whatever reason, Schmidt had completely changed his mind and started talking about monetary issues already on 7 April, thereby preempting the breakfast planned for the following day.[31] This had a twofold consequence. First, it completely (although apparently involuntarily) short-circuited Tindemans's own plans. Jenkins indeed reports in his diary that Tindemans had planned "to present some proposals for currency advance" at the Copenhagen European Council.[32] He eventually did not present his plan, because Schmidt's plan apparently, according to Jenkins, went further than what he had in mind.[33] This episode once more emphasizes that advancing European monetary cooperation was not a strictly Franco-German preoccupation. Even more interestingly, it further stresses the centrality of the European Council. The Belgian prime minister had decided to present his plan, prepared by the Belgian Finance Ministry, to the EEC heads of government and not to the other EEC institutions. It also explains why the potential bitterness created by a Franco-German currency proposal, prepared bilaterally and in secret, was so swiftly overcome: even a small country, scarcely supporting intergovernmental cooperation, was willing to take a move in the same direction, and by using the same institution. The second important consequence of Schmidt's departure from the initial plan was that it would considerably reduce the significance of the private trilateral breakfast scheduled for the next day. As Jenkins put it, Schmidt had decided to "spill the whole beans," and thereby took aback even those who were in his confidence.[34] Callaghan also noted, in reporting on the 8 April trilateral breakfast, that because Schmidt had "talked in some detail about his plans on the Friday night of the Copenhagen Council, . . . there was very little else to talk about at the next morning's breakfast."[35]

What Schmidt said was, in essence, close to the ideas he had put forward earlier to Callaghan and Jenkins. He declared that he wanted "to achieve a much greater role for the European Unit of Account (EUA) in a European bloc"; that he wanted the stabilization of European currencies through the creation of a pool of reserves; that he envisaged a contribution to a pooled reserve of 15 or 20 percent of FRG dollar reserves, with comparable contributions from other countries; that each country would make available indefinite amounts of their own currencies; that credit in the intervention scheme would be for one month or, if need be, longer term for up to six to eight years; that the EUA would be used in settlements between central banks; that a "central European Fund" would exist, and be a sort of European IMF; and finally, "he appeared to envisage that ultimately the Community countries would be related to the European unit of account and would not be directly quoted against the dollar; it would be the EUA which would be quoted against the dollar."[36] In conclusion, he stated that this scheme was not meant to replace the snake, but to swallow it.

Unfortunately, there is no detailed record of the discussion that followed between the heads of government in Copenhagen.[37] This certainly is a pity, since it would have been interesting to see the reaction of the "six" who were not in the confidence of the Jenkins-Schmidt-Giscard-Callaghan quartet.[38] One alternative archival source is the notes used by Schmidt for the meeting that confirms what was already known.[39] Yet there is little to learn since it seems quite clear that the other six heads of government, apart from having a basically positive reaction, did not in fact register any detailed immediate reactions. The surprise and the technicality of the topic certainly prevented them from taking the floor. Andreotti and Callaghan made only general, noncommittal remarks.[40]

The last important step in the Copenhagen episode was the private breakfast of Callaghan, Giscard, and Schmidt on 8 April.[41] The British prime minister gave an account of this meeting to Couzens on the return journey from Copenhagen. This breakfast helped clarify some technical, political, and practical points. In technical terms, the substance of Schmidt's plan was confirmed: "The proposal *was* basically for a new European snake; the intention *was* that the European unit of account should be used for settlements between central banks only. It was, however, intended that the EUA should develop into a new currency in the longer term."[42] The planned amount of the pooled reserve was diminished (compared to the amount mentioned by Schmidt to Callaghan in March) and totaled US$10 billion—a change that just underlines that the scheme had still to be set out in more detail. A number of motivations and conditions became clearer. The first referred to the membership of the scheme. While Schmidt stressed that it was imperative to have the Italians on board, Giscard made it absolutely clear that if the British government did not join, the French government would nevertheless reenter the snake as of July, thereby showing the French president's determination to go along with the initiative.[43] Second, Callaghan believed that Schmidt's scheme "reflected a turning away from the dollar and from US financial policy." This interpretation of Schmidt's move, in purely transatlantic terms, would remain at the center of Callaghan's thinking for the remainder of the negotiations, together with the issue of growth.[44] Third, Giscard apparently accepted "that the final result of the evolution being discussed would be a deutsche mark zone, just as there had formerly been a sterling area." Fourth, the British prime minister confirmed his skepticism for a scheme of this kind and announced that he would not hide it in public. But in spite of its skepticism, the British government would never try to be an obstacle to the EMS initiative, nor at any moment during the whole negotiations.[45]

Finally, in practical terms, the method and timetable of the negotiations were agreed on. Schmidt suggested that each of the three countries should propose one paper to the three heads of government. Indeed, clearly aware that, although much depended on Germany, his country could not be openly seen to take the lead, Schmidt said that he did not like the idea of a single paper proposed by Germany. They finally agreed that Germany and France would each produce one paper, and that Britain would adopt a "neutrally critical" stance. Papers were meant to be available within one week. Only three people would then consider the two papers. These three people would be a nominee of each head of government. The choice was apparently already made at the time of the breakfast, since the German chancellor immediately said that he had chosen Horst Schulmann, his senior economic adviser, and Giscard announced that Clappier would be his nominee. Callaghan then opted for Couzens. They envisaged a timetable that would allow six weeks to complete the examination and a possible meeting on the evening before Bremen to discuss the results. If a decision could not be reached by midyear, France would presumably reenter the European snake.

Admittedly, some of the details of this strategy were not respected. The papers were not provided within a week, but were instead devised, later on, by the ad hoc group itself. The importance of this discussion lies elsewhere, however. First, the identity of the three experts chosen in a sense preempted the final outcome that the three heads of government wanted. Clappier was one of the most "pro-Europe" civil servants in the French administration. Giscard had clearly chosen him in order to bypass the misgivings within his own administration (particularly Raymond Barre, prime minister; René Monory, economics and finance minister; and Renaud de La Genière, *sous-gouverneur* in the Banque de France) regarding the immediate advancement of monetary cooperation.[46] Schulmann was one of Schmidt's trusted aides, and he had worked in the European Commission.[47] Moreover, the German chancellor was well aware of the opposition of his own administration.[48]

By contrast, Couzens was not very well versed in international monetary arrangements, and, more revealingly, Callaghan clearly avoided nominating those people (Harold Lever, Michael Butler) who were likely to "coax him forward" into the EMS.[49] Callaghan thus clearly showed where he did not want to go, in spite of Schmidt's and Giscard's willingness to have Britain on board. The most important aspect of this breakfast certainly was that it created a tentative directorate of three, thereby keeping the British government on board even if it had been openly reticent about the scheme from the very beginning. The same reasoning equally applies to the very existence of the Schulmann-Clappier-Couzens group.[50] Moreover, it was also perfectly consistent with a constant preference of Schmidt and Giscard for informal cooperation, illustrated by their attachment to the so-called Library Group or to the European Council.[51] The negotiations leading to the Bremen European Council showed to what extent this strategy would be effective.

Sketching a Plan for European Monetary Reform

The story of European monetary cooperation following the initiative of the German chancellor is one of parallel initiatives influenced by important, wider interconnected issues. These initiatives—namely, the work of the EEC specialized committees and of the Schulmann-Clappier-Couzens ad hoc group—indeed occurred at the same time but had no point of contact.[52] Yet these initiatives were influenced by two significant factors: the ongoing debate concerning economic reflation and the transatlantic link.

Maintaining and Opening Up the Snake: The Work of the Specialized Committees

The importance of the specialized committees' work rests in their good illustration of a learning process among a transnationally connected monetary elite. In the absence of information about what had been discussed in Copenhagen, the specialized committees could only do some general thinking about exchange rate systems. But precisely because of this vagueness, they offered insights into not only the technical aspects of monetary cooperation but also the more general philosophy behind it. Even more significant, the work of the committees showed on what basis an EEC-wide consensus might be formed. A first case of this learning process came from the so-called van Ypersele and Janson questionnaires, outlined, respectively, by the Monetary Committee and the Committee of Governors. These indeed showed the extent to which monetary authorities needed to simply exchange information and learn to understand what the other was doing, as well as the "Socratic dimension" of the quest for monetary stability.[53] In late April 1978, the alternates of the Committee of Governors thus issued the so-called Janson questionnaire outlining very basic questions about monetary cooperation:

> What exchange rate objectives are currently being pursued by your country and what position do they occupy in overall economic policy? . . . Towards which exchange rate system do you consider the member countries of the Community should steer on the assumption that the

conditions for greater stability are fulfilled: the "snake" system, with a large degree of independence vis-à-vis the dollar? The "snake" system with a more clear-cut Community policy vis-à-vis the dollar? A new system?[54]

Similarly, in May 1978, Jacques van Ypersele, Belgian chairman of the Monetary Committee, set out a list of questions to EEC member states regarding monetary cooperation. This list of questions was meant to provide a reading grid for future discussions. Interestingly, it represented a sort of analytical summary of the monetary discussions since 1974. The four questions listed under the heading "exchange rate arrangements" were thus:

1. Are we of the opinion that it would not be realistic to expect all non-snake currencies to join the snake in the near future?
2. If the answer is positive, do we think that it would be useful to help convergence of movements of snake and non-snake currencies? To this end, would it be useful to develop a nonrigid intra-EEC exchange rate arrangement in the near future?
3. If the answers to the question under 2 are positive, which type of arrangement would members find more adequate in the near future for non-snake currencies?
   - E.g., Target zones approach for effective (trade-weighted) exchange rates
   - Target zones formulated in terms of the European unit of account (EUA), i.e., a fixed-weight basket
   - Target zones formulated in terms of an average of the snake and the dollar, with the weight of the snake being gradually increased (cf. my article dated 30 January 1978, which was circulated to the members)
4. What are the possibilities of applying some nonrigid guidelines for the movements of the snake vis-à-vis the dollar?[55]

Patently, the three options inventoried by van Ypersele were the same as those he had set out in his communication a few weeks earlier, namely, the Duisenberg approach, the Fourcade approach, and finally, his own.[56]

When these questions were answered, the lines of division emerged more clearly. Georges Janson (National Bank of Belgium) identified, in general terms,[57] two groups of thought (but did not formally single out which country belonged to which group). The first was in favor of the status quo, thought that member states ought first to improve their economic situation, and believed that a more dynamic dollar policy than the one established in 1975 was not possible. The second group favored the implementation of a number of improvements to the current system, among them the creation of a new exchange rate system based on the EUA and the establishment of target zones[58] for the non-snake members. Hence, not only were the two proposals for improvement quite obviously recalling the Fourcade and Duisenberg plans (as had been the case during the last session of the Committee of Governors) but the two general categories (status quo versus improvements) corresponded, mutatis mutandis, to the economist and monetarist approaches.

The fundamental question was hence whether the snake had to be maintained as such (with a few limited changes to help the non-snake members rejoin the exchange rate system) or whether a new system should be devised (such as the one based on the EUA).[59] Zijlstra, head of the Dutch Central Bank, remarked that such a choice did not belong to the Committee given that it was highly political.[60] A number of members stressed their skepticism. Emminger unsurprisingly did not favor the creation of a new system, especially given that the current proposals ("a new system based on the EUA") were still very vague. Ortoli supported Emminger and proposed a very incremental method. He suggested asking the non-snake members what new system they would be ready to accept, and seeing then what implications it would have for the existing snake. Clappier was one of the few to be slightly more ready to call into question the snake mechanism. Talking about the relationship between domestic economic policies and exchange rates, Clappier remarked that "one could say that the countries outside of the snake should just pursue a general economic policy more comparable to that of the countries that are members of the snake, but this is easier said than done." He thus favored a more in-depth analysis of the shortcomings of the snake, in order to find a system able "to gather, as soon as possible, the greatest number possible of Community currencies." A couple of days after the meeting of the Committee of Governors, the Monetary Committee meeting also ended in a deadlock.[61] The German position remained unchanged: the member states whose currencies were not in the snake had to improve their economic situation in order to be able to join the snake again.[62] The German members were prepared to make only one concession: that the candidates for snake participation could have, for a probationary period, wider fluctuation margins. Overall, therefore, this early position taking largely corresponded to that of the post-Bremen EMS negotiations, as the next chapter will show.

The next sessions of both committees managed to outline the major options regarding the search for greater monetary stability. The Monetary Committee on 5 and 6 June identified three options: to defend a nominal exchange rate vis-à-vis each currency; to defend weighted exchange rates; or to create a system of concerted floating made of reference zones, which would not oblige a country to intervene but would automatically start consultations were a currency to reach its limit.[63] Although no open reference was made, it is quite striking that, at least in spirit, these three options were respectively akin to the existing snake, the Fourcade memorandum, and the Duisenberg proposals. The discussions following the presentation of these three options strikingly highlighted this point. The Dutch members thus expressed their attachment to the principle of target zones, while the French members criticized it and then encouraged wider use of the EUA in a new system. This was, in virtually identical terms, the same French (Dutch) argumentation since the Fourcade (Duisenberg) memorandum. The report by the Monetary Committee on the possibilities of bringing about greater exchange rate stability in the Community, published on 9 June, interestingly noted at the outset:

> As a point of departure of its report, the Committee has assumed that the Council wishes to see progress toward exchange rate stability even before Member States have entirely solved the problem of differences in inflation rates and balance of payments performance; such progress on exchange rates could politically, psychologically, and technically contribute to improving the convergence of economic trends and policies of the Member States.[64]

This point was crucial, since it was more than a mere concession offered to the "monetarist" strategy. It elaborated on the idea that the narrowing of exchange rates (if not their locking) would in itself bring about economic convergence, even though the report later stated that "they all [all the options studied] presuppose a satisfactory consistency between the economic policies of the Member States and the exchange rate objectives they jointly pursue." This was all the more important since the salience of the economist versus monetarist debate had often been the main reason for failure of earlier monetary proposals.

The work of the Committee of Governors also underscored the circulation of monetary ideas in the EEC as well as the strength of the German position. Published on 12 June, the governors' report took into systematic consideration the latest monetary proposals.[65] The governors had used a similar methodology in their report of 2 November 1976.[66] This time, however, it did not include the Fourcade and Duisenberg plans, but instead the two Commission proposals (of 17 November 1977 and of 10 February 1978) as well as the conclusions of the Copenhagen European Council. Instead of listing three different options like the Monetary Committee, the governors came back to some more basic questions, such as the exact meaning of "stable exchange rate relationships." The governors noted that this expression was slightly ambiguous. Indeed, characterizing an exchange rate as "stable" very much depended on the parameter used to measure it. Overall, however, the governors recognized that European monetary stability could be improved in order to prevent the dislocation of the EEC and to make progress toward EMU. Yet, like the Monetary Committee, the Committee of Governors then surprisingly endorsed a nearly "monetarist" phrasing: "Without having to wait for an ideal convergence of economic performances, some progress in reducing short-term exchange rate fluctuations should be sustainable through the adoption of rules of exchange rate conduct acceptable to all Community member countries." Admittedly, the report later on described economic convergence as a basic precondition to a return to exchange rate stability. Yet the governors had rarely, if ever, recognized that the monetarist strategy could make sense, even if only in a limited application in the short run. More important, the Committee of Governors, like the Monetary Committee, stressed the importance of a political impulse. Charles Murray, governor of the Central Bank of Ireland, even suggested (and was backed on this by Gordon Richardson) they not wait for the political impulse to come but immediately carry out the "further studies" mentioned.[67] The Committee endorsed the suggestion in spite of an unsurprising slight reserve on the part of Emminger, who insisted that the governors not prejudge the *implementation* of one proposal or the other. This misgiving should not be overlooked, however. Indeed, as the next chapter will show, since the Bundesbank was the most independent central bank in the EEC, Emminger alone could virtually block any reform of the snake.

Outlining a Brand-New Scheme? The Work of the Schulmann-Clappier-Couzens Group

The work of the ad hoc group composed of Horst Schulmann, Bernard Clappier, and Kenneth Couzens certainly remains one of the most unclear parts of the EMS story. Information about when and where they met and what was said by the "Gang of Three," as Ludlow calls them, remains uncertain.[68] According to the British archival record, the Group of Three met three times (on 12 May at the Banque de France in Paris; on 26 May in Washington; and again in Paris on 14 June). Couzens and Schulmann (no one else was present) met separately a first time after the Copenhagen summit on 20 April, while Clappier and Schulmann met a last time in Hamburg, together with Giscard and Schmidt, but without Couzens, just before the issuing of the Schulmann/Clappier draft.[69] Since a study of their meetings is absent from the literature, in this section I will analyze their work through a strict chronological reconstruction. The idea that guided their work from the very beginning was to eventually provide a paper that would be "a semi-secret Franco-German statement of methods and objectives."[70]

The first Schulmann-Couzens meeting took place a few days before another important meeting between Schmidt and Callaghan, on 23 April. The reasons for such a separate meeting, in the absence of Clappier, are slightly obscure. A possible answer lies in the fact that the German side was well aware that the British government would be harder to convince than the French. This could explain why Schulmann did not regard the need for a proper trilateral meeting as urgent. It was recorded that at the end of the meeting he simply said that he envisaged a joint meeting with Clappier would be necessary "at some stage."[71]

Since there was still no paper setting out Schmidt's plan in more detail, this meeting of Couzens and Schulmann was only about "philosophy, not specifics" of monetary cooperation: "What seemed to be in his [Schulmann's] mind (and perhaps therefore in the mind of Herr Schmidt) was to seek a philosophical (if not emotional) commitment to a broad concept of linked European currencies and a Europe more self-reliant in monetary matters."[72] Apart from a timid positive remark by Schulmann, who stressed that the three main European countries had moved closer economically in 1976–1977, the rest of this first exchange of views was hardly positive, particularly on the British side. Couzens first openly doubted the rationale behind Schmidt's Europe-centered, monetary-exclusive endeavor.[73] He then discussed how difficult it would be for the British government to take a new step in European integration during a potential election year. Callaghan made a similar point on the afternoon of that same day.[74] If both had domestic political considerations in mind, it must also be noted that, in more general terms, it could be economically risky to enter a near-fixed exchange rate system of the EMS type in an electoral period, since this could well nurture speculation and currency pressure. It was, in a sense, ironic to see that European monetary discussions greatly benefited from the French elections (they were even precondition), but that general elections could also be one of the reasons why the British government would eventually opt out of the EMS. This point highlighted, once more, the strong impact of domestic politics on European integration. Third, Couzens stressed the importance of the sensitive issue of resource transfers. He insisted that in a monetary union, or indeed in any scheme aimed at a tighter monetary cooperation, there had to be some transfer of wealth from the "richer" to the "poorer" countries. He thus argued for the establishment of a "major resource transfer system"—which Schulmann unsurprisingly rejected.[75]

The substance of the discussions of this very first meeting of what was then still a "group of two" did not remain confined to Couzens and Callaghan. On the contrary, these issues were discussed at a meeting on the same day in the cabinet room, attended by Denis Healey, chancellor of the exchequer, and Gordon Richardson, governor of the Bank of England.[76] It thereby confirms the mere *semi*secret nature of the Schulmann-Clappier-Couzens group.[77] A rather clear

British reading grid of the would-be negotiation for a new monetary arrangement emerged from this discussion.[78] The first obvious obstacle, as mentioned above, was the general elections. In a possible election year, the British government could not afford to join a European monetary scheme seemingly created "against the dollar." In addition, were it certain that the new European monetary scheme was not a danger for the dollar, the next element to which the British government attached great importance was that the German government should agree to reflate. As the following developments will show, this analysis would remain the basic British position virtually up until the Bremen summit.

Because Schulmann had again not provided a formal document setting out in detail the Schmidt Plan, the very first discussions of the Group of Three, on 12 May in Paris, remained at the level of very vague principles.[79] The only basis of discussion was, therefore, what Schmidt had said at Copenhagen.[80] The discussion covered a vast array of possibilities, and most of the themes discussed at the level of experts and ministers since 1974 resurfaced during this discussion (and indeed in virtually all the discussions) of the Group of Three. Five important themes deserve to be more closely analyzed. A first feature was that any new European monetary arrangement should regroup *all* EEC currencies. "Although a two-tier 'snake' is technically feasible," Schulmann wrote to Couzens, "it is politically not very attractive."[81] This point further confirmed a constant feature of European monetary discussions since 1974. A second feature could regroup the array of technical issues envisaged by the three experts. The margins of fluctuation envisaged ranged from the 1 percent of the Bretton Woods agreement to as much as 5 percent. Couzens even suggested setting no fixed rate at all for an initial period![82] Interventions in the system would be made in EEC currencies, and the EUA would be used as a means of settlement. The possibility was mentioned that the EMCF could issue EUAs against the deposit of national currencies. Yet this would have the effect of increasing the total volume of international liquidity.[83] This last feature logically leads to a third theme, namely, the flexibility of the German proposals. Schulmann's proposal, for instance, was careful to mention only "possible elements" of a new exchange rate system. He insisted that the general principle was that the new arrangement would not try to oppose fundamental long-term trends but rather to coordinate intervention in the face of erratic fluctuations. An elaboration on the theme of flexibility was the constant German emphasis on the evolutionary nature of the future exchange rate arrangement. Schulmann talked of a "certain amount of '*tâtonnement*'" that would be necessary in the initial start-up phase, before the progressive narrowing of the exchange rate margins. A fourth feature, arguably linked both to the vagueness and the flexibility of the plans under scrutiny, was that a number of potentially contentious issues had been carefully left aside. This was the case with the question as to whether the EEC should seek the EUA to become in the future an international reserve asset. A last important feature was the little ambiguity left by the British position, conditioned by the dollar question and the possible general election: "For what it was worth, my personal opinion was that anything which appeared as a simple decision to enter the European Snake could be politically divisive and therefore possibly difficult before an election," Couzens wrote. "It might be different if the agreement were one which they could present as unambiguously in the interest of the UK: which also included the action on European growth, e.g., under the plan now being worked out by M. Ortoli and the European Commission."[84] Schulmann evoked the possibility of reaching an agreement on these proposals for the Bremen European Council. Clappier and Couzens thought this was too short a timetable. Schulmann finally said that he would prepare a paper to be discussed during their next meeting, which was planned for late May in Washington.

The three experts met again in Washington on 26 May. Instead of a Schulmann paper—he again failed to provide one—it was Clappier's ideas that were under scrutiny. The governor of the Banque de France put forward his ideas for a "European monetary system"—the new system was henceforth called "EMS" for the first time. His ideas centered on the creation of a European Central Monetary Authority that would act as a European IMF. Clappier definitively ruled out the idea that the EUA could be issued against national currencies, since, he said, it would create too much additional liquidity. For the rest, his ideas were close to Schulmann's. Clappier favored small fluctuation margins. "It would be an object of the exercise to make the new system as unlike the Snake as possible," he said. "This would have important political advantages both in France and in the United Kingdom, as well as dissociating the new system from earlier failures with the Snake."[85] This remark underlined a central preoccupation of the negotiations: namely, that it ought not to look like the snake. This system had a number of built-in flaws that could be corrected, and it might also well be a way to make the new system politically more attractive (akin to a question of political marketing). This time it was Clappier, not Schulmann, who asked Couzens whether he thought the British government would be able to make progress in this field before an election. Couzens merely recalled the "election obstacle" but confirmed the British government's willingness to remain associated with the elaboration of the scheme.

The new meeting of the Group of Three at the Banque de France on 14 June was the first one where discussion was based on two papers. Clappier submitted a paper outlining a far-reaching scheme, while Schulmann put forward a draft announcement that could be made after the Bremen summit.[86] Clappier's ideas clearly bore some resemblance to the Fourcade memorandum, while pushing it even a bit further. It envisaged that exchange parities would be defined by reference to the European Monetary Unit (identical with the European Unit of Account). Margins of fluctuation for currencies would be 1% in each direction. Some currencies could, however, have wider margins of fluctuation on a temporary basis.

European Monetary Units would be issued by the European Monetary Fund (EMF) to central banks of member countries in return for:

- American dollars or gold (for example, 20% of reserves) ...
- national currencies in an amount equal to 25 billion European Monetary Units.

Clappier's scheme was therefore going further than not only the Fourcade memorandum but also the Schmidt Plan.

By contrast, Schulmann's draft of an agreement at Bremen was much vaguer than Clappier's outline. This was partly because it was clearly intended to be more about the philosophy of the system than about its technical features, as Schulmann constantly remarked since the first meetings à trois. Schulmann's most important aim evidently was to formulate sentences in such a way that they could form the basis of an EEC-wide consensus. The titles of the two papers were revealing: Clappier "outlined a scheme," while Schulmann "drafted an agreement." Hence, Schulmann's piece would necessarily be vaguer than Clappier's. For instance, unlike the governor of the Banque de France, Schulmann did not give a figure for the width of the fluctuation margins. Incidentally, Schulmann wrote rather vaguely that "the EUA will be given a greater role in the new system. First, it will serve as its pivot. Second, it is also envisaged that the EUA will become the principal instrument of settlement between participating monetary authorities."[87] Focused more on the philosophy of the system, Schulmann suggested the following:

A system of closer monetary cooperation will be established in the Community. In terms of exchange rate management it will be at least as strict as the so-called snake. In the initial stages of its operation, however, member countries currently not participating in the snake may opt for somewhat wider margins around central rates. Changes in central rates will be subject to mutual consent. The European Unit of Account will be the *numéraire* of the system.

The simultaneous reference to the strictness of the new arrangement and to the possible wider margins underlined Schulmann's quest for a consensus by carefully paying attention to the two extremes of the European monetary situation: it reassured the snake members that a new scheme would not weaken the current one, and it showed its flexibility for newcomers. The very last sentence of the draft paid the traditional lip service to closer economic convergence.

Couzens's reaction was hardly promising for the Franco-German project. He first regretted the lack of reference to the question of the resource transfers.[88] Even more important and even less promising was his second point, which deserves to be quoted in full:

> There was no possibility that the UK could subscribe at Bremen to a statement that: "A system of closer monetary co-operation will be established in the Community . . . at least as strict as the so-called snake." . . . The most conceivable was that the heads of government might give directions, without commitment, for the preparation for their further consideration of a more detailed scheme having certain specified characteristics. The characteristics would be in very broad terms, e.g., relationship to a basket of currencies rather than a single currency; greatly increased credit on a scale capable of impressing markets and matching the extent of intervention experienced in recent months; greater use of the EUA. I could not guarantee that even this would be acceptable but would consider whether I could outline such a remit in writing.

On the surface, the British counterproposal indeed looked unpromising. It was much more general and much less committal than the French or German draft proposals.[89] It was also slightly ambiguous. Couzens's suggestions were not very far from the ambitious scheme outlined by Clappier (reference to the basket of currencies, greater role of the EUA). Another draft counterproposal even explicitly said that the government was "building on M. Clappier's ideas."[90] The counterproposal even envisaged a substantial role for a "European Monetary Fund" in the new system, notably in that it could issue EUAs against the deposit of member states currencies.[91] Couzens's negative reaction thus seemed to be based on the "integrationist" phrasing of Schulmann's draft more than its very substance. It also further stresses that the lack of political commitment at the top level of the British government hindered a full discussion à trois of the technical issues. As Michael Butler put it in his memoirs, "On this occasion we might have done well to join in with some zeal. Unfortunately we hung back in so clear a way that the French and Germans went ahead and produced proposals for Bremen on their own."[92] Nevertheless, at the very least, Couzens had not completely closed the door to a later agreement.

But when Giscard and Schmidt met in Hamburg on 23 June in order to discuss the Schulmann/Clappier draft, only the two authors of the draft were present, not Couzens. Clappier kept him informed, however, of what had been decided during this meeting.[93] The reason for Couzens's absence is slightly unclear. It could quite logically be that Schmidt and Giscard already doubted the British government would join the scheme under review.[94] A more straightforward explanation might be that, given that Couzens did not make any sort of concrete contribution to the discussions of the Group of Three—the British government eventually did not put forward its counterproposal—he was unlikely to suddenly make a constructive suggestion. The "neutrally critical stance" he had adopted from the beginning was certainly not the best way to get an invitation to the Hanseatic city, and therefore it prevented the British government from having a say on the final wording of the Schulmann/Clappier draft. The Hamburg meeting was principally an occasion for Schmidt and Giscard to agree on a timetable and a procedure for the negotiations, and, paradoxically, they did not really consider the Schulmann/Clappier draft.[95] The basic idea was to make a proposal at Bremen that would first be endorsed by the European Council and then would give a mandate to the specialized committees for working out the specifics of the scheme by 31 October. A month would then remain for the EEC governments to consider the proposals to be submitted to the meeting of the European Council in December. An entry into force of the new scheme could thus follow in early 1979.

The Schulmann/Clappier draft dating from 28 June was very much in line with the agreement drafted by Schulmann and discussed in the Group of Three a couple of weeks earlier. For the first time, however, two expressions—"zone of monetary stability" and the name "European Monetary System (EMS)"—appeared in this common, Franco-German document and would from now on permanently be used.[96] In more detail, this draft made six points. First, it confirmed "this system will be at least as strict as the so-called snake," and stated "the European Currency Unit (ECU) will be at the centre of the system." The second point concerned the initial supply of ECUs. The third point regarded the coordination of exchange rate policy vis-à-vis third-party countries. The fourth point announced the consolidation of the planned arrangements through the creation of a European Monetary Fund. The fifth point recalled that the system would "only be successful if participating countries pursue policies conducive to greater stability at home and abroad." The sixth last point set a definite timetable according to which the competent EEC bodies were required to conclude their work no later than 31 October 1978. The overall result of the work of the Group of Three had therefore been the production of a draft (already) very much along German lines.

Quantitative Economic Growth Targets

Two important issues were interlinked with these negotiations: the debate about the fixing of quantitative economic growth targets and the influence of the

United States on the EEC monetary debates. In early 1978, virtually all (EEC) governments identified similar problems, namely, slow economic growth and exchange rate instability. Yet partly because of the dollar's decline, but also partly because it rejected the "locomotive theory," the German government focused more on European monetary affairs. Even the Bundesbank, famously conservative in the past few years regarding the conception of new European monetary arrangements, seemed to find some rationale for this new focus. A session of the Bundesbank's Zentralbankrat on 20 April witnessed a surprisingly positive comment regarding European monetary cooperation:

> Some members are of the opinion that the Federal Republic cannot always act as a "brake," [to European monetary integration] but instead . . . should make a constructive and positive contribution to monetary integration in Europe. . . . Some members believe an examination of the proposals for monetary integration in Europe to be sensible and possible only in conjunction with the European political intentions of the Federal government, as ultimately the willingness to make concessions is dependent on it.[97]

By contrast, the British government was more preoccupied with the necessity of providing an economic stimulus: "We were not sure that monetary instability within Europe was the cause of low economic growth. We rather thought that this instability was a symptom of unequal performance of the economies of Member States."[98] A clash of ideas came into the open in early 1978, when Schmidt pressed for European monetary reform, while Callaghan attached the highest importance to his Five-Point Plan for collective action at the world level.

The debate about the setting of quantitative growth targets was a case in point. Almost constantly since mid-1977, the German government had been pressured by most Western European governments and the United States to reflate its economy. The German government did not want to. For instance, during the Finance Council of 22 May, Schlecht, though isolated among the other eight members who were all willing to endorse the objective of a 4.5 percent growth target, expressed doubts about the political and economic feasibility of such an objective.[99] In a draft letter for Schmidt to Giscard, Schulmann insisted that the German government could not, for domestic political reasons, afford to reflate under international pressure, particularly since Germany's partners were themselves not contributing enough to the improvement of the international economic situation in other areas (energy, trade, the fight against inflation).[100] Conversely, Healey interpreted Schmidt's monetary initiative as a way to distract "public attention from the real problem of growth."[101] The EMS "concurrent studies" would represent another example of this dispute.

The Transatlantic Dimension

A further problem was the German government's distrust in US economic and monetary policy. The concern about the US administration's policies had been a constant feature of the monetary discussions within the closed circles of the EEC specialized committees since mid-1977. Early 1978 was no different. But the dollar's weakness was not the only reason for the German government's distrust in US economic and monetary policy, nor was it the only incentive for further EEC monetary cooperation. It was also, paradoxically, a potential obstacle to it, as I will explain below. Defense—or, more precisely, the neutron bomb—was the other contentious issue between the US and German governments in 1977–1978. The neutron bomb episode can be summed up briefly as follows. President Carter had announced that he would provide US forces in Europe with neutron bombs, but he needed German consent for the deployment of this new arsenal. Schmidt was reluctant but managed, with difficulty, to convince his government.[102] On 4 April 1978, the *New York Times* revealed that the US president had abandoned his project, without having warned Schmidt in advance.[103] Giscard argues in his memoirs that "the loss of trust of Helmut Schmidt in the Carter administration has been definitive."[104] Some commentators or actors at the time linked Schmidt's resentment following the neutron bomb fiasco to his new European monetary ambitions. Jonathan Story quotes Bernard Clappier stating, "I consider that Schmidt's launch of the EMS was his response to Carter's shelving of the neutron bomb."[105] But there is little archival evidence or chronological logic to support this view. The fiasco occurred in April–May, while Schmidt's change of mind, following the weakening of the dollar, happened earlier in January–February. What it did reflect, however, was the general climate of distrust in the US administration, but also the growing self-confidence of the FRG. Giscard thus quotes Schmidt saying to him: "Americans must stop believing that they just have to whistle for us to obey!"[106]

The weakness of the dollar could in fact, as suggested above, render EEC monetary cooperation even more complex. First, it was one of the most important reasons why the British government was reluctant to support the current EEC monetary schemes. This was not only true among many British politicians but many British civil servants too. Kit McMahon, of the Bank of England, underlined a constant British point: namely, the need to put European monetary issues in a wider transatlantic context.[107] Second—and here was the paradox—European monetary stability was rendered more complicated due to the depreciation of the dollar, which had originally been the trigger for action. This point mirrored the monetary discussions in Europe in the early 1970s, when they were both triggered by currency instability and eventually wrecked by the collapse of the Bretton Woods system. Lamfalussy, in presenting his note about the "US balance of payments and Europe," was quite pessimistic on this point.[108] Given that the weakness of the dollar played a destructive role during previous attempts at European monetary integration, he openly wondered whether it was at all possible to devise a new European plan before having solved the dollar problem. Clappier concurred with Lamfalussy. Ortoli commented that the Commission was in agreement, and that for this reason it did not propose the creation of a new mechanism but instead the establishment of a more flexible option, that of target zones without the strict obligation of intervention. Ugo Mosca, director-general of the DG II, insightfully concluded that "it is right that the problem of the dollar complicates the task of establishing a better cohesion among Community currencies, but at the same time it renders still more necessary the realization of this objective." In addition to the convergence of economies, the EEC had now an additional obstacle on its road to further monetary cooperation: a weakening dollar.

The transatlantic factor in the sketching of a common EEC monetary strategy should not be limited, however, to these negative aspects. A more constructive dimension—namely, the US attitude to the European monetary schemes—should indeed be taken into account. The US reaction to the early plans for European monetary cooperation in the first half of 1978 was at best benevolent, at worst ambivalent, and most often merely silent. The Carter administration in general had a rather positive a priori attitude toward European integration. More precisely, on 28 April 1978, the State Department issued a "guidance" affirming the support of the US government for European efforts aimed at improving monetary stability.[109] By contrast, the US Treasury was more reserved on the European initiative.[110] Its fears predictably centered on the evocation, in the European monetary discussions, of a "dollar policy."[111] These fears would be revealed to be groundless, and Carter gave "his political agreement in principle."[112] As Peter Ludlow makes clear, one of the consequences of the US attitude was to undermine the British position according to which further European monetary cooperation might damage transatlantic relations—a point confirmed by Jenkins, who noted in his diary as early as mid-June that even Michael Blumenthal, US Treasury secretary, was happy with the European initiative.[113]

Getting EEC Legitimacy: The Bremen European Council

The discussion of the Finance Council on 19 June came as the logical conclusion of a nearly three-month-long intense brainstorming about EEC monetary cooperation. Healey formally set out the British preconditions for a closer EEC monetary arrangement.[114] The chancellor of the exchequer stated that closer cooperation should not be damaging to the dollar; that it should be seen as durable; that it should "reduce the constraints on growth which are imposed by excessive fluctuations in exchange rates"; that it should lead to greater economic convergence and imply a transfer of resources from "the strong to the weak"; and finally, that substantial resources must be made available for interventions. Yet still, in spite of this long list of preconditions, he recognized that closer EEC monetary cooperation could help resolve the current economic problems.

The finance ministers, having digested the reports of the Monetary Committee and of the Committee of Governors, broadly agreed on a number of features that a new system should follow. A new system should (1) include all EEC currencies (possibly with a transition period for the non-snake currencies) and be open to other currencies; (2) respect a symmetry of responsibilities between surplus and deficit countries; (3) not be damaging to third currencies; (4) permit the continuance of the snake for its members; and (5) involve intervention obligations and firm economic policy commitments. The Council "expressed interest" in giving a more active role to the EMCF and crucially stated: "The Council wishes to see progress toward exchange rate stability even before Member States have entirely solved the problem of differences in inflation rates and balance of payments."[115] In short, the finance ministers merely agreed that the snake should be maintained and opened up.[116] Tellingly, however, this would indeed be the eventual result of the EMS negotiations. It is finally worth noting a stark difference between the French and the British records of the meeting regarding Ortoli's conclusions. According to the British record, Ortoli commented that "nothing could be decided today. It was for the European Council to take decisions, but the Finance Council should give a clear lead."[117] According to the French, Ortoli said that "real progress has been achieved and an agreement could happen in Bremen."[118] Though not necessarily contradictory, the two ways of summarizing the conclusions reflected very well the basic attitude of both administrations as well as their general approach to the Bremen European Council.

As had been the case in Copenhagen in April, and as would be the case in Brussels in December, the European Council of 6 and 7 July in Bremen was tense and witnessed a rather spectacular volte-face. A brief discussion between Giscard, Schmidt, and Callaghan on 6 July preceded the evening session of the European Council.[119] It sealed the "neutrally critical" position adopted by the British government since the opening of the semisecret negotiations, which it would maintain until the end of the year. The record of the conversation does not record a proper *conversation*—that is to say, it was not an exchange of ideas. Schmidt first said that he accepted the principle of concurrent monetary and economic studies; Callaghan then gave his comment on the Schulmann/Clappier paper and said that he would be prepared to participate in the working out of the details of the proposals, but he refused to give an agreement, in principle, to the whole scheme under discussion. There was never a conversation about the substance of the proposal but merely its principle. Little surprise, therefore, that Jenkins describes in gloomy terms the arrival of the "Big Three" at the evening session.[120]

The most important aspect of the official evening session of the European Council, à neuf, was thus the reaction of the other six EEC members. Although the ideas contained in the Clappier-Schulmann draft had apparently quite widely circulated prior to the European Council—the two authors had indeed toured EEC capitals (with the notable exception of Dublin), and Jenkins had informed Ortoli of the main thrust of the paper[121]—the discussion began with Giscard's presentation of the Schulmann/Clappier draft. Anker Jorgensen, the Danish prime minister, reacted that this was "a very exciting prospect," to which Callaghan curtly replied that "it was equally exciting if you drove over a cliff except that you hurt yourself at the bottom."[122] Schmidt briefly came back on the motivations of the proposal and stressed that "there was a twofold political purpose [to the monetary scheme]: it was not antidollar, but the yen might suffer, and it would mean progress in the Community." Many heads of government then asked for mere confirmations of what was anyway clearly written down in the Franco-German draft. This was particularly true with the issue of the strictness of the new scheme, for instance.

The issue of the participation of non-snake members then occupied the rest of the discussion. Giscard, replying to a question from Jack Lynch, Irish prime minister, said that wider margins for non-snake members should be limited (since, as Schmidt noted, they would encourage markets to speculate) but that they could be negotiated. Lynch and Andreotti further argued that since they had only recently been informed of the scheme, and since neither of their economies had yet converged enough with those of Germany or France, they could not at such short notice accept the substance of the measures proposed. A consequence of the still salient economic differences in the EEC was that the British, Irish, and Italian prime ministers insisted on the undertaking of concurrent studies on economic policy. Callaghan had decided to raise this issue of "resource transfers" in the plenary session, where he could benefit from the support of the other participants, rather than in the tripartite private session, and his strategy eventually yielded good results.[123] Indeed, Schmidt, willing to obtain an immediate agreement on the general philosophy of the Schulmann/Clappier draft so that his negotiating timetable could be respected, swiftly accepted the undertaking of concurrent studies, but "on that timescale with decisions in December."[124] But the German chancellor's swift agreement sprang from the fact that he did not attach great importance to these concurrent studies, as the next two chapters will show. It was thus agreed that the conclusions (as proposed by Schmidt, and then modified by Callaghan and Lynch) would be "without any commitment in principle but with a clear commitment to studies of both the economic and monetary aspects." Once this agreement had been reached, Jenkins, Schulmann, and Lynch stayed behind in the room and drafted the Annex.[125] Rather unexpectedly, therefore, a general consensus had been reached on the Schulmann/Clappier paper.

The second session, on the morning of 7 July, showed that this was a short-lived and superficial agreement, however.[126] The session opened with a new discussion of monetary matters.[127] The discussion centered on the question of the publication of the Schulmann/Clappier draft as an annex to the European Council's conclusions, and again in a slightly tedious manner. Callaghan's continuing doubts about the Franco-German scheme led him to wonder about the wisdom of publishing the draft and, most important, about the status it would have. More worrying for the Franco-German project, however, was that the Italian prime minister shared the British point of view. Andreotti supported Callaghan, stressing that the Schulmann/Clappier draft "read as though everyone agreed." The other participants, however, did not see the text in that way, nor did they interpret it as a Franco-German document.[128] Obviously, the preoccupations of the two critics of the Annex were different: while Andreotti politically supported the scheme (his doubts here were more about Italy's economic capacity to join), Callaghan did not. The French and German leaders then explained that the idea was to show what the heads of government intended to do, not to make binding decisions. The draft in annex was meant to be a basis for discussion but certainly did not prevent counterproposals from being made. After long and tense exchanges, the European Council agreed along these lines, with the Franco-German tandem happy to have the Schulmann/Clappier draft annexed to the presidency's conclusions, and the British prime minister content that this implied no commitment. What Callaghan probably failed to perceive was the strong legitimacy it gave to the Franco-German initiative, the impact of which will be the focus of the next chapter.

Another important step was the G7 summit held in Bonn on 16 and 17 July 1978. The Bonn summit does not deserve, in itself, to be extensively dealt with when examining the EMS negotiations.[129] What is important to know is that it was instrumental in two respects. First, it underlined that the tone of the EMS was not anti-American. Though the EMS had been arguably born as "an act of self-defence," as Ludlow puts it, Schmidt managed to downplay this dimension, not least because it would further nurture the British skepticism.[130] Second, the G7 summit showed the conciliatory attitude of the German government in accepting reflation. Schmidt thus agreed to a stimulus that would amount to

1 percent of GNP.[131] Therefore, while the Bonn summit did not prove to be a seminal moment in the history of the EMS, "it rounded off the political strategy that Mr Schmidt had pursued since the Copenhagen summit and left him in a position of incomparably greater strength and authority."[132] Schmidt was indeed relieved of the outside pressure for budgetary reflation and had also mitigated the antidollar dimension of the European plan for currency advance—thereby clearing the way for a European solution.

Conclusions

Four important features emerged from the EEC monetary discussions in the first half of 1978. A first, quite familiar one was the reluctance, if not outright opposition, of national monetary authorities (both in national and transnational settings). As had been the case since 1974, the Trésor and the Bundesbank in particular, were, at varying degrees, quite skeptical about any new EEC monetary scheme. A second important feature, new this time, was the decisive roles played by a few European heads of government. As I mentioned in the concluding section of the preceding chapter, some important changes had mainly depended on the decisions of a few people, Jenkins or Schmidt, for instance. The first half of 1978 clearly confirmed this trend. A third feature was the stark difference that existed between the initial Schmidt Plan and the final Schulmann/Clappier draft annexed to the Bremen communiqué—as strong a difference as there would be between the Bremen Annex and the eventual EMS. The Bremen Annex was indeed strikingly different from the plan that Schmidt had described to Callaghan on 12 March. At that time, he had outlined an extension of the snake, a rather grandiose scheme for a pooling of reserves that would have put German reserves at the disposal of the EEC, and even mentioned the possible development of the EUA into a currency in the longer term! This plan quickly evaporated, however.[133] If the Clappier/Schulmann draft did mention some of these possibilities, it gave the impression that it was much less ambitious than the initial Schmidt Plan. An obvious last feature of these negotiations was the multiplicity of levels involved in the discussions. There were at least five: heads of government (European Council), Group of Three (Schulmann-Clappier-Couzens), the European Commission, Finance Ministers (Finance Council), and specialized committees. It could even be argued that there was a sixth, the bilateral level (essentially Franco-German), which handled most of the negotiations. Admittedly, any kind of EEC negotiation was, and still is, bound to be multilayered. Yet in the case of monetary discussions in general, and these EMS negotiations in particular, the number of levels involved was much higher. Indeed, two EEC committees dealt with monetary issues (the Monetary Committee and the Committee of Governors), the European Council was still a relatively new institution in the EEC machinery, and the Schulmann-Clappier-Couzens trio was a mere ad hoc group. One of the keys to success was thus Schmidt's (and Giscard's) excellent command of this complex machinery. The European Council, the secret negotiations of the Group of Three, the bilateral meetings, but also the bypassing of the Finance Council, and, most importantly, the bypassing of the specialized EEC committees, were all necessary ingredients to the success of the Franco-German initiative.

A number of important factors contributed to the emergence of a (partial) consensus leading to the Bremen final communiqué. The emergence of the European Council as a central actor in the EEC decision-making process has regularly been underlined in previous chapters. The negotiations over a new EEC monetary arrangement further confirmed this trend, and arguably provided the best example of this since the creation of the European Council in 1974. The European Council indeed represented a useful tool that had the positive aspects of a top-level dining club and—in spite of its members' high profile—managed to keep a high level of secrecy if needed. Although heads of government met regularly, they managed to avoid leaks about their plans and kept them as strictly confidential as possible so as not to affect the currency markets. As we learned in the preceding chapter, Jenkins was well aware of the importance of EEC institutionalized summitry. The memorandum he sent out to the heads of government prior to the Copenhagen meeting patently underscored this point. At the opening of this document, Jenkins wrote: "We have two European Councils [Copenhagen and Bremen] falling unusually close together. . . . The authority of this European Council should be used to set the Community institutions—relevant Councils and the Commission—to work with a new intensity of practical purpose to prepare firm and detailed proposals for endorsement at the Bremen European Council."[134] The fact that the European Council was able to guide the work of EEC institutions was already bearing fruit. With the overall change of climate—monetary affairs seemed to be much more fashionable in the EEC than it had been three years before—the specialized committees were now much quicker in their reactions. It did not take them (more or less) half a year to produce a report on specific proposals, as it had been the case with, for instance, the Fourcade and Duisenberg proposals. They worked with "a new intensity of practical purpose," as Jenkins put it in his memorandum to the Copenhagen European Council. If this was partly due to a more important political impulse, it was also to some extent a consequence of the learning process. Indeed, the options considered by the Monetary Committee in its report were now very familiar ones, and the opinions given were indeed merely the reappearance of analysis already produced a few months or years before. This was most obviously the case in the reference made to the Duisenberg memorandum, recycled by the Commission. The regularity of meetings of the heads of government also helped in the sense that it "accelerated" the timetable, putting extra pressure on leaders in attendance to make decisions. Schmidt thus clearly pressed for an agreement at Bremen because he wanted to make the final decision six months later at the Brussels European Council.

The existence of the Group of Three was an original feature and a second important factor in these early negotiations. One of the main characteristics of these monetary discussions was that they were this time à trois between monetary experts nominated by heads of government rather than confined to the EEC specialized committees or to the Council of Ministers. In contrast to the specialized committees, they were now happening at a level (in very close connection with the heads of government, that is) where decisions could quickly be made. The Group of Three, together with the European Council, allowed the bypassing of other EEC institutions (the Finance Council, specialized committees) that would have otherwise very possibly killed Schmidt's initiative. Yet the European Council also crucially permitted the reintegration into the EEC machinery an initiative that had been developed externally. Simultaneously, the Group of Three allowed the ironing out of a number of differences between the French and German governments, so that the proposal would not immediately get stuck in the EEC committees. Admittedly, the increased importance of this type of secret deliberations nurtured what would become, from the late 1970s and arguably up to the present day, a recurrent criticism against European integration: namely, the lack of democratic process.

Britain's self-exclusion was also, in an ironic way, a factor in the success of the Franco-German initiative. Giscard and Schmidt did not fail to try to keep Britain on board until the last minute.[135] In a letter to Giscard on 1 June, Schmidt reiterated his support for British participation, although he was clearly well aware of the obstacles to it.[136] He wrote that in any case, the door should be left open for later participation of the British government. Yet, as it was reported from the meeting in Hamburg of Giscard and Schmidt on 23 June, "President Giscard was prepared to wait for us [Britain], but not for very long."[137] The strength of the Franco-German tandem was such that they were ready to go ahead, even without Britain.

One of the main reasons why the British government was reluctant to join a new EEC monetary scheme was the prospect of an early general election. According to Jenkins's diary, Healey on 16 July, and then Owen on 4 September, told the Commission president that they were certain that a general election would take place in October of that same year.[138] Incidentally, the British government clearly seemed to be focused on international cooperation, not European, and particularly on its Five-Point Plan for collective action. This point was quite clear in a conversation between Jenkins and Callaghan on 31 March: when Jenkins said that the Bremen summit would take place about ten days before the Bonn summit, Callaghan was seemingly surprised—or at least he clearly had not realized that a European Council was taking place right before the G7.[139]

Saying that the British government was opposed from the very beginning to the Schmidt Plan would be an overstatement, since it actually did not appear to have ever seriously considered joining a new, closer EEC monetary arrangement. The strategy adopted by the British government, of a "neutrally critical stance," remained constant throughout these early negotiations. While the British government had carefully tried, in the monetary discussions of 1976 and 1977, not to appear too pessimistic, it no longer hid its pessimism in 1978. Couzens was a mere spectator in the debates of the Group of Three, asking questions and taking notes, but never really trying to find out how the scheme could be adapted to fit with the British government's political and economic agenda. Admittedly, the prospect of an early general election, coupled with a Franco-German endeavor that appeared from the very beginning as part of a European integrationist ambition, and added to the British government's own focus on the Five-Point Plan, left little hope that it would be willing to embark on such an EEC project. Yet contrary to what the British attitude had been for a number of years, the British government this time did not even try to properly discuss or influence the course of negotiations. Though the British entered the discussions at an early and formative stage, they never really tried to steer these discussions in a direction that might better suit them. Couzens, Callaghan, and Healey used to observe that they did not like a number of proposals contained in the Franco-German scheme, but they never really attempted to make counterproposals, if only very general ones. It is striking, for instance, that the only counterproposal that existed, the "UK possible counter-draft," apparently was not put forward at any stage of the negotiations, nor even discussed or mentioned at any stage by Couzens, Healey, or Callaghan.[140] Surprisingly, Couzens wrote that he had outlined this to Schulmann and Clappier during their meeting on 14 June. Even more surprising, it is impossible to find a trace of this in Couzens's own record of this meeting, and logically even less of Schulmann's or Clappier's reactions. The British draft paper merely summed up the main monetary suggestions discussed since 1974 to provide guidelines for discussion to the Finance Council and the specialized committees. In Couzens's words, it was intended as a "more general, less committal and more politically realistic" paper. In any case, this counterdraft was apparently a stillborn initiative.

As we have seen in the preceding sections of this chapter, a number of themes and ideas that had emerged since 1974 resurfaced during discussions of monetary issues in the first half of 1978. These ideas centered especially on the Fourcade and Duisenberg plans. The technical monetary brainstorming that followed the strong political impetus provided by the Copenhagen European Council again clearly drew on the technical studies that had been carried out a few years earlier. The members of the Commission present at the Monetary Committee of 11 and 12 May, as well as Mosca at the Committee of Governors on 11 April, thus openly recognized that their ideas were largely inspired by the Duisenberg proposals.[141] Henri Baquiast, a senior official of the Trésor, stated that "the Fourcade proposals . . . should be looked at again."[142] Even more striking, the way in which Couzens presented the Schmidt Plan to Callaghan reflected very well the learning process and the continuity of the thinking about currency reform. Couzens thus started his note by saying: "We now have before us at least 4 European currency schemes or sets of schemes of recent origin, in addition to the more long standing schemes, elements of which sometimes reappear in newer versions."[143] The four schemes he referred to were the "Schulmann proposals," the "Clappier proposals," the "Ortoli proposals," and the "van Ypersele proposals" (noticeably themselves the outcome of a learning process between the Fourcade and Duisenberg ideas). Therefore, contrary to what is usually portrayed in the literature, the Schmidt Plan was not the only one under scrutiny in the EEC in early 1978, but instead was one out of many other proposals. A DG II note and the report of the Monetary Committee of 9 June emerged as arguably the best examples of this learning process.[144] In setting out an exhaustive list of the monetary options offered to the EEC, they actually provided a synthesis of the most salient features of the monetary discussions since 1974. Finally, and perhaps most obviously, the Bremen final communiqué and the Schulmann/Clappier draft bore some resemblance to previous failed proposals. The working out of the specifics of the new EEC scheme, which will be the subject of the next chapter, will further highlight the recycling of these older monetary ideas. Besides this, a technical learning process was ongoing. In taking stock of his chairmanship of the Monetary Committee, Pöhl developed the case of monetary targets.[145] He explained that since 1976, monetary targets, which were so far examined internally in each member state, were now also discussed, compared, and evaluated in the Monetary Committee. This is one further example of a slow, tortuous, but continuous monetary cooperation over the 1974–1979 period. To be sure, there was not yet a common European monetary policy—this was perhaps not even the aim. But we were clearly moving from monetary policies run virtually independently to a proper EEC-wide monetary cooperation.

Finally, it is noticeable that the mythology surrounding the EMS negotiations was under way. The appearance of the ECU acronym was a case in point. Giscard claims in his memoirs that he invented the name during the Bremen European

Council. Not only is this not confirmed by the archival record of the session (and the ECU acronym had already appeared in the Schulmann/Clappier draft of 28 June) but Froment-Meurice writes in his memoirs that Giscard had planned to suggest this name before the summit.[146] As the next two chapters will argue, this mythology was needed, particularly on the French side, to compensate for the difference between the bold advance described in public statements and the technical reality of the scheme under discussion.

CHASING THE GHOSTS OF FAILED NEGOTIATIONS, MID-JULY–LATE SEPTEMBER 1978

For a happy few Eurofanatics and Europhobes this [the EMS] is a clear-cut issue on which we can and must stand up and be counted. For most of those who are neither Eurofanatic nor Europhobe, however, and who have taken the trouble to study the matter, it is a hideously complex and awkward issue, both economically and (more important) politically—and the interaction of the economic and political considerations serves only to make it worse.

—Nigel Lawson

The immediate post-Bremen atmosphere was well captured by *The Economist*, which wondered, in August, whether EMU would "lay an egg."[1] This snappy catchphrase showed the extent to which the new monetary negotiations, which had (officially)[2] commenced after the Bremen European Council, had a historical record of inefficiency to contend with. As I have shown in the previous chapters, European monetary cooperation since 1974 had witnessed a circulation of fascinating monetary ideas that were often, however, ill timed and ill suited, and always suffering from a lack of political support. In many respects, the EMS negotiations thus looked like an umpteenth rehearsal of many of the debates that went on during the previous monetary discussions (at least since 1974), and the prospects of these debates therefore seemed quite uncertain.

Technically, the story of the negotiations about the contours of the new exchange rate system was the story of coming to grips with one voluntarily fuzzy phrase of the Bremen Annex: "The ECU will be at the centre of the system." The old discussion linked to the Fourcade memorandum about introducing a new exchange rate system that was based on a basket-weighted unit of account (instead of the parity-grid system) would thus come back to the center of the debate. Interestingly, the old economist versus monetarist wrangle would thereby, after a short-lived cease-fire, resurface in this more sophisticated form. The vagueness of the Bremen Annex admittedly helped give a strong political impulse to the technical negotiations. Once these started, however, obvious differences of interpretation came out into the open—and these will be the focus of this chapter.

In chapter 7 I analyze the EMS negotiations from the Bremen European Council until late September 1978, when the debate over the role of the ECU in the new exchange rate system had been largely settled. This is again the rendering of a complex multilevel negotiation, from its domestic political aspects to its international implications. It should be noted that for these negotiations, the subgroups (the Heyvaert Group for the Committee of Governors and the alternates of the Monetary Committee), even more than in previous monetary discussions, played a substantive role in the debates and deserve careful examination. In the first section below I analyze the early technical discussions leading up to the first post-Bremen Finance Council of 24 July. In the second section I delve into the second phase of discussions in August, during which the EEC member states made their official positions known. In the third section I examine the progressive evolution of the negotiations along a Bundesbank-inspired line over the month of September. In the last section I break somewhat from the chronological order of the chapter, delving into a theme that is better analyzed separately over the whole three months: the "concurrent studies."

The main goal of the chapter is to stress how the EMS negotiations relate to monetary debates of the previous years. This will shed new light on their outcome, and their wider, longer-term implications. Instead of suggesting, as is often purported, the novelty of the monetary ideas discussed, I highlight instead their resemblance with previous proposals. This has three consequences: it downplays the originality of the EMS, stresses the political dimension of the initiative, and, even more important, helps us better understand the EMS negotiations. In particular, I argue that it became clear very early on that the new exchange rate system would have much smaller ambitions than expected. In both the concurrent studies and the technical negotiations, the main task was indeed to progressively whittle down the range of issues on the negotiating table until there remained only the already existing snake. In this chapter I demonstrate that by September 1978, an irreversible polarization of opinions on the most important points was already discernible.

Coming to Grips with a Fuzzy Sentence

The general reaction in the EEC after the Bremen European Council was quite positive. The overall objective—monetary stability—was extremely consensual: it could hardly be imagined that someone would argue in favor of monetary instability. Added to this, the claim that the new system needed be "durable and effective" was equally so obvious that it did not bring much new weight to the idea. A case in point was that even the actors who were most reluctant about a new European monetary scheme (the British government and the Bundesbank in particular) agreed to the principle of having a zone of monetary stability in the EEC. All EEC governments had, however, continuously reaffirmed their hope for greater monetary stability since the collapse of the Bretton Woods system, yet they had achieved little. It is therefore the working out of the more technical features that would reveal the positions and real intentions of the EEC member states.

In this section I analyze the new conditions in which the EMS negotiations started, until the Finance Council of 25 July. The discussions immediately following the Bremen summit mainly centered around a sketching out of the central issues of the future debates and on organizational problems. This stemmed from the fact that a session of both the Committee of Governors (11 July)[3] and the Monetary Committee (18–19 July) preceded the Finance Council (24 July), which was meant to give detailed instructions to the EEC specialized committees. In the absence of detailed instructions, the specialized committees could not properly begin their work, and the Finance Council had no detailed report yet to examine. These three sessions gave, however, a number of interesting insights, precisely because the various delegations could quite freely exchange their views. There were three important elements in the post-Bremen discussions: the consequences of the political impulse given by the European Council; the outlining of the main issues at stake in the negotiations; and finally, the shift in the centrality of the actors involved in the negotiations.

The Political Consequences of the Bremen European Council

The original strong political impetus provided by the European Council to the EMS negotiations had two interlinked consequences. It injected into the EEC machinery strong political pressure to find an agreement, and it set up a strict timetable for negotiations. If the European Council was able to exert strong political pressure, it was primarily because it avoided presenting the Franco-German agreement as a fait accompli. The European Council was instrumental in providing EEC legitimacy to a set of guidelines that had been designed not only in a bilateral fashion (Franco-German) but also completely outside any traditional administrative channels (the Clappier-Schulmann-Couzens ad hoc group). If it had, admittedly, annoyed a number of actors in the negotiations, the Franco-German conception of the Bremen Annex did not cause profound or irreversible damage to the negotiations as a whole. Because it had been a missing element since 1974, the strong political impulse given by the European Council deserves closer inspection. Many acknowledged both the importance of the European

Council in the decision-making process and, even more significant, the momentum that had appeared in the EEC since the Bremen summit. This momentum was not very far from the "air of adventure" whose loss was one of the reasons for the EEC's "stagnation," according to Tindemans in his 1976 report.[4] It manifested itself in various forms. In spite of all the disagreements that appeared during the discussions, all the reports issued (and not least the Bremen Annex) referred to "*the* EMS," not "*an* EMS" (and this was equally true in languages other than English). It seemed that the creation of a new system was already agreed on without any of its technical aspects being defined. A second clue can be found in the discussions between experts in July. For example, during the Committee of Governors meeting on 11 July, Clappier (and, tellingly, Ortoli) ended his speech by calling on his counterparts to avoid easy criticism and instead join the discussion of this new attempt in a constructive spirit.[5] This was a remark he had already formulated during discussions of the Fourcade memorandum, yet this time it was better received.[6] And it is indeed striking to see that there was much more willingness to analyze the Bremen Annex because of the initial strong political impulse from the European Council than had been the case four years earlier following the isolated initiative of an obscure French finance minister.

Our earlier examination of the ill-fated Fourcade and Duisenberg proposals showed that when the Finance Council alone set a timetable for the EEC committees, this timetable was scarcely respected. The timetable set by the European Council was here instrumental in providing extra authority to the Bremen Annex.[7] During the first post-Bremen session of the Committee of Governors, for instance, Ortoli stressed that every member state had until early December to ask for modifications to the scheme as set out in the Bremen Annex, and said that member states had until this same period to say whether they would take part in the scheme.[8] The main consequence of the impulse—and, crucially, the reaction of the EEC institutional machinery to it—was therefore that it starkly reaffirmed the chief functions of the European Council that had been emerging, as we saw in earlier chapters, for about four years: it was an increasingly important agenda setter and a creator of political guidelines. It is also once more interesting and revealing to note that the president of the Commission fully supported the European Council. He claimed, for instance, during the Finance Council of 16 October, that he had warned the finance ministers that "they were all drifting away from the objectives of the Bremen communiqué."[9] Similarly, during the Committee of Governors session of 11 July, it was vice-president Ortoli who, in order to dispel the fear expressed by some member states that the new system might not be durable given the economic differences remaining between the member states, recalled that the Bremen communiqué mentioned that some studies would be undertaken in order to see how these economic differences could be compensated for.[10] The president of the Commission, as well as the commissioner in charge of economic and monetary affairs, therefore acted as guardians of the political directives given by the European Council. This was no small evolution for an institution originally conceived as the guardian of the treaties. Of course, the actual outcome of the negotiations was not known. But there was a general sense that, given the political impulse given by the European Council, something had to be agreed on. The interpretation of the Bremen Annex in technical terms would show, however, that agreeing on a new system would be quite difficult.

The Technical Consequences of the Bremen Annex

Studies about the EMS generally depict the negotiations based on the Bremen Annex as "filling in the details." This is most obviously the title of a chapter by Peter Ludlow, but a similar idea is found in virtually all accounts of the EMS negotiations.[11] Andrew Moravcsik, for example, writes that "senior officials [in the specialized committees] were told to 'work out the details' of the plan rather than 'questioning the fundamentals.'"[12] It is true that the general political sequence was such that the EEC machinery had to "fill in" the broad guidelines given by the European Council in Bremen. It is also true that by "details," the above authors mean, in part, that the elements in question were of a technical nature. Their complexity rendered them allegedly less significant than the political impetus given by the Bremen European Council, for instance. And perhaps it is believed that the technical working out of the monetary system was less important than its politics.

Without downplaying the importance of the political dimension of the EMS negotiations, such an expression gives the deeply misleading impression that the most important matters had already been decided. A (perhaps unwelcome) side effect of this, however, is that it has a strong teleological force. It gives the impression that the mere existence of the Bremen Annex meant, in itself, that the birth of an EMS in the coming months was a given since only "the details" had to be filled in. It therefore completely overlooks the facts not only that the "details" may completely change the nature of the EMS, but that the entire initiative may fail. These "details" would crucially make the monetary system under discussion genuinely new—or not. It was the very discussion of these "details" that gradually transformed a bold political enterprise proclaimed to be a step toward EMU into a simple extended version of the snake. The debate between a parity grid or an ECU-based system was, in essence, a choice between a new system (whatever its technical feasibility or desirability) and the old snake.

The question of the novelty of the system not only matters in order to give an accurate comparison with the snake, but it was also fundamental to many actors of the time. The German chancellor indeed initially aimed at a bold enterprise.[13] The ambition to have a "new" system was even more important for the French president, who had suffered a personal blow when the franc had last left the snake in 1976.[14] Hence, both in technical and political terms, in the first half of 1978, the French president needed the EMS to be a *new* initiative, not simply an arrangement aimed at bringing the French franc back in the snake without saying it. It would indeed be much easier for the French president to present the EMS as a new system if it was genuinely new. More generally, the question of the novelty of the system under discussion was just as fundamental to the current non-snake members. Indeed, besides the economist versus monetarist debate, there was a very basic rhetorical question: If the non-snake members found themselves unable to join the snake, why would they miraculously be able to join a copied or disguised version of exactly the same mechanism?

The first reactions of the EEC members who were the most unsure of the new monetary scheme—Britain, Ireland, and Italy—broadly indicated their governments' positions. There was no mystery that the Italian government favored, in principle, almost any new step aimed at furthering European cooperation.[15] Similarly, on 20 July, the Irish finance minister, George Colley, strongly took position in favor of the EMS, going further than the equally positive (but more prudent) declaration made by Lynch after the Bremen European Council.[16] This initial position taking was grounded, however, in still very vague proposals and was, by definition, subject to change.

The first sessions of the EEC specialized committees—namely, the Committee of Governors on 11 July[17] and the Monetary Committee on 18 and 19 July[18]—mainly centered on setting the foundation for work on the new monetary system and outlining the basic issues at stake. The discussion focused on three main areas: the nature of the unit of reference and its implications for the system as a whole, the rules of intervention, and the European Monetary Fund (EMF). Regarding the meaning of the statement that "the ECU will be at the centre of the system," two broad interpretations existed that corresponded to (but, as I will show in the next section, should not exclusively be seen as) an opposition between snake and non-snake members (plus the Commission).[19] The arguments made were virtually (and logically) identical to those set out during the discussion of the Fourcade memorandum. They will therefore be only briefly summarized here. The snake members—and in particular the German government—wanted to use the ECU only as the basis for the sketching of a (snake-type) parity grid. By contrast, the non-snake members and the Commission supported the view that the ECU would be used as a proper *numéraire* in the new system. The pivot rates would thus be expressed in ECUs, and the margins of fluctuation would be based on these pivot rates. Such a mechanism would allow readier identification of the currency that would diverge vis-à-vis the rest. Of the snake members, the Germans (Manfred Lahnstein, secretary of state in the Finance Ministry, and Karl-Otto Pöhl, Bundesbank vice president) were unsurprisingly the most vocal. But Lahnstein did not completely close the door on a future possible compromise by saying in private to the French members that he was much more open to discussion than Pöhl. Of the non-snake members, it is also important to note that the Italian and British members had a slightly different vision of the ECU. They thought that it ought not to be composed as the current EUA. Indeed, since it was a weighted basket of currencies, the EUA was subject to change according to the currency fluctuations. In the case of a DM appreciation, for instance, its overall weight in the basket would accordingly be increased, thereby pushing the whole exchange rate system upward. In order to avoid this, the British and Italian governments—for quite obvious reasons since their currencies were among the weakest—suggested an ECU composed of one fixed part and another subject to variation.[20]

The Committee then tackled a series of other questions. Would the future EMS be able to tolerate that not all EEC currencies would participate? The answer obviously depended on the nature of the system. If it were akin to the snake (with a parity grid), the absence of one EEC currency would not matter more than it currently did. But if it were centered on the ECU, the situation would be more problematic, for which a number of solutions were suggested (allow a temporary leave or modify the ECU basket, for instance). Could the pivot rates be easily and frequently revised? The answer to this was positive, as far as any modification was preceded by mutual consultations. Would the future EMS be compatible with the snake? The answer was again positive: the principle would be that the snake would continue to exist as long as the EMS was not fully operational. In case of a conflict of rule, the strictest would apply. The issue of the choice of the currency of intervention clearly derived from the nature of the system. In a parity grid system (like the snake), the question did not really exist since only two currencies, at the bottom and at the top of the margin, were meant to intervene. In an ECU-based system, the question was trickier and a decision would have to be made in order to know which criteria to use (the currency that diverged the most, or the strongest one in the basket if this one were under its pivot rate, for instance). The issue of the width of the margin of fluctuation did not arouse much interest at this early stage of the negotiations. It was similarly too early to talk about the EMF, given that its contours were still particularly fuzzy.

The Finance Council of 24 July provided the first occasion to take stock of the negotiations since the Bremen European Council. The German presidency of the meeting set out a list of questions regarding the contours of the new monetary system.[21] A number of positions were surprisingly less clear-cut than at the specialized committees level. For instance, regarding the issue of the *numéraire* of the system, only the German (and to a lesser extent the Irish) government was reported as favoring a parity grid, while the British and Italian (but surprisingly not the French) governments and the Commission leaned toward an ECU-based system. On the other issues, the opinions were still at so early a stage that they need not be mentioned here in more detail.

The overall discussion was characterized by an almost unanimous reaction in favor of the Bremen communiqué—unanimity minus a few reservations voiced by Healey.[22] The chancellor of the exchequer was the only one to have discreetly and rather pettily tried to downplay the Community character of the Bremen Annex by recalling that it had "a Franco-German starting point," and then turned to his many misgivings concerning each and every point of the new system. If these misgivings were ostensibly meant to be "constructive,"[23] the reading of the German account of the meeting scarcely gives this impression. Healey identified the "Eight Principles" that were meant to be the British government's criteria for judging membership of a new European exchange rate system. These principles were as follows (quoted directly):

i. The EMS must be durable.

ii. It must be a system in which all Community Members can participate.

iii. It must favour higher growth in the EEC generally.

iv. It must be symmetrical in the obligations it imposes on countries with stronger and those with weaker currencies.

v. It must be backed by adequate credit facilities.

vi. The re-alignment of exchange rates must be possible by agreement.

vii. There must be no detrimental effects on the dollar, other major world currencies, or IMF obligations.

viii. The operations of the Community Budget must be made less perverse so that resource transfers no longer penalize the weaker economies.[24]

It is quite obvious, however, that behind the objective style of expression, these Eight Principles were highly subjective. To take but one example, determining whether and how the EMS would be a system "in which all Community members *can* participate" could be the subject of endless arguments. Following a declaration of the Irish finance minister Colley, the discussion then turned to the question of resource transfers.[25] He stressed that for the EMS to be viable, some measures needed to be taken in order to stabilize the situation of the financially weakest members. Following his suggestion, Matthöfer concluded that the COREPER would, on 27 September, formally issue a mandate to the EPC (which would exceptionally include, during the discussions, additional representatives from each member state). These negotiations will be analyzed in more detail later on.

A Shift in Power

A third important feature of the immediate post-Bremen period was the shift in power in the decision-making structures. While those responsible for the negotiations had been so far heads of government (Schmidt, Callaghan, Giscard) or their advisers (Schulmann, Couzens, Clappier), the discussions were now in the traditional decision-making channels, and particularly in the hands of the national monetary authorities, who were much less inclined to reform the snake. Since German monetary power effectively rested with the Bundesbank, it was this very institution that would become the single most central actor of the negotiations. In contrast, it is noticeable that the identity of the central French decision makers did not change. Giscard exerted considerable influence on the course of the negotiations, because of the great power of the French president in the Fifth Republic, and Clappier remained a central figure, since the French chief negotiator of the Bremen Annex was also the head of the Banque de France. A good illustration of this shift of power can be found in the list of participants in the Finance Council on 24 July. Indeed, not only did the president of the Commission himself take part in the meetings but Central Bank governors as well (they would do so also in later meetings).[26]

A number of meetings in Germany underlined this swift change. On 12 July, Emminger took part in a cabinet meeting in Bonn; on 13 July the first post-Bremen Zentralbankrat of the Bundesbank took place in Frankfurt, and on the same day a number of officials of the Bundesbank and the Finance Ministry met up to coordinate their position. Hence, in less than a couple of days, the actors who were the most opposed to the Bremen Annex entered the EMS negotiations stage. Although all these discussions constituted only a first exchange of views, they did give a number of crucial and detailed elements about the position of the various German actors. Most important, they showed that both institutions firmly rejected the ECU-based model. On 12 July, Emminger made his first declaration (still provisional, given that the Bundesbank Zentralbankrat was to be held the following day) on the Bremen Annex.[27] Emminger, however, gave the general negotiating line that the Bundesbank would follow in principle: that the new monetary system should "really bring more stability in Europe" and that it should be "durable," or, in other words, that it would not fall apart in just a few years' time. Emminger identified three risks regarding the Bremen Annex. The last two points were related to liquidity creation. He feared both the creation of too much international liquidity (which would in turn lessen monetary discipline) and the potential loss of control of D-mark creation. But first of all, Emminger pointed out the risk involved in having to stick, in the new system, to unrealistic parities. He particularly stressed the prestige issue, according to which a country would maintain an artificial exchange rate only to avoid having a potentially humiliating devaluation. The British pound and the French franc were quite obviously the two currencies most likely to fall into this category. Tellingly, it underlined how far the discussion was not so much about a new exchange rate system but the enlargement of the existing one. Schmidt's answers were (unsurprisingly) reassuring on all points.

Between the Committee of Governors meeting and a Monetary Committee's session, the Bundesbank held its first post-Bremen Council. Interestingly, Matthöfer, minister for finance, stressed once more that the German government took seriously the French government's efforts to fight inflation.[28] He insisted that the new system would have a disciplining effect and that, in any case, it was not meant to be less strict than the snake. Countering the argument according to which currencies would have to maintain an artificial exchange rate level, Matthöfer said that changes in parities should be unspectacular in the new system. Furthermore, he stressed that the new system should not lead to a creation of additional international liquidities—something the Bundesbank would nevertheless look at attentively during the negotiations. The first immediate reaction of many members of the ZBR was to complain that they had been poorly informed of the intentions of the German government; they were also profoundly skeptical. These members not only doubted that fixed exchange rates were the solution, they also queried the potential domestic disciplining effect such a system was meant to have. Pöhl then said that the exchange rate system first had to be compatible with the Bundesbank's commitment to stability. In particular, Pöhl frankly said that a system based on a unit of account raised complex questions, and that a system with bilaterally defined points of intervention had more advantages. He said that a fluctuation margin of 2.25 percent was, by experience, a good one, but he added that newcomers might be provisionally granted a wider fluctuation margin. He finally expressed a sensible position regarding changes in exchange rates, according to which such changes should be authorized but only with prior consultation so as not to make them too easy. Although he acknowledged the fact that the German government had its say in monetary affairs, and that Schmidt had so far not made any remarks that could lead anyone to think that his aims would contradict those of the Bundesbank, in concluding, Emminger did not fail to mention that the Bundesbank would do everything to preserve internal monetary stability.

Schmidt—and to a lesser extent, Giscard—was quite obviously worried about the reserves shown by the Bundesbank, as well as some EEC committees. By secretly working out the Bremen Annex, they managed to sterilize their opposition, which might otherwise have nipped the initiative in the bud. When the plan came out in the open, their opposition did not take long to form itself and become powerful—just as Schmidt had feared. These actors had been left out because their opposition was predictable; and once informed, it did not take long for these actors to voice their misgivings. As early as 14 July, a Bundesbank-Finance Ministry document confirmed the united line taken by the German monetary authorities.[29] They shared a common position on virtually all points left for discussion in the EMS negotiations: both supported a parity-grid system (and strongly rejected the ECU-based option), envisaged fluctuation margins of 1 percent (double for the newcomers in the transition phase), and considered that parity changes should be preceded by consultations and that the currencies of interventions would always (and not "in principle," as the Bremen Annex stated) be EEC currencies. In addition, they insisted, more generally, that any pooling of reserves should not lead to the creation of additional international liquidities. The addition of a monolithic position from the German monetary authorities to a shift in power at the EEC level in their favor foreshadowed the *rapports de force* in the negotiations that would follow.

The Resilience of the Economist versus Monetarist Debate

In this section I will delve into what was at the core of the negotiations in August: namely, the Franco-German disagreement over the Franco-German drafted Bremen Annex. This irony was indeed at the heart of the EMS negotiations. The situation naturally came from the fact that the men who drafted the Bremen Annex were not those who had to negotiate its adoption.[30] I will also focus on the emergence of a possible third way: the so-called Belgian compromise. I argue that the Franco-German technical dispute was a refined version of the economist versus monetarist debate that had been calming down in the past few years. The existing literature presents the EMS negotiations as a conflict between snake and non-snake members—or, put differently, the strong-currency countries versus the weak-currency countries.[31] While accurate, such a presentation fails to embed the EMS negotiations in the wider framework of monetary discussions of the 1970s. By contrast, as David Marsh rightly suggests (but does not elaborate on), the debate between the supporters of the ECU-based system and the defenders of the parity grid was "a new and more sophisticated version of the traditional

Economist versus Monetarist argument over the balance between technical measures and economic adjustment as the key to convergence."[32] Reference to this perennial dichotomy in European monetary cooperation provides a helpful reading grid of the negotiations and helps situate the EMS negotiations in the wider history of European monetary cooperation.

Parity Grid or Currency Basket

Although the positions of both the French and German governments were quite predictable, their first quasi-official *prise de position* occurred only in August. In what follows I will successively examine the French and German positions. Detailed archival research enables us to see, draft after draft, how deep-rooted their interpretations were. I will then look at how the other EEC member states positioned themselves with respect to this fundamental disagreement.

The successive drafts of the Banque de France's position highlight the strong continuity of the French monetarist thinking regarding the reform of the snake since the Fourcade memorandum.[33] As early as 24 July, the Banque de France was thus able to propose what it considered a first "coherent and operative conception" of the new EMS.[34] The first official position of the Banque de France—that which was sent out to the German government—is dated from 8 August, however.[35] It envisaged that, in the exchange rate system of the EMS, the ECU would be used to define the margins of fluctuations, serve as means of settlement, and be a reserve asset created by the new EMF. The ECU would be identical to the EUA; it would be based on a defined quantity of EEC currencies, following a weighting of GNP and intra-EEC trade of each member state. It mentioned a margin of fluctuation of 1 percent. This was considered strict enough in order to be credible, and flexible enough to avoid permanent interventions, particularly of smaller currencies. The rationale behind the French proposal for an ECU-based system was that it would directly pinpoint the divergent currency. Indeed, in a parity-grid system such as the snake, when one currency reaches its upper or lower band, at least one other currency is simultaneously reaching its own upper or lower limit. In the ECU-based system, one currency alone should be identified as the divergent one. The duty to intervene is a unilateral one: there is indeed little probability that when currency A has reached its margin from its ECU parity, currency B or C would also have reached its own opposite margin. Yet interestingly, the Banque de France did mention the potential new asymmetry that would appear in such an ECU-based system. Indeed, the currencies whose part in the ECU was large would be more "inert" vis-à-vis the ECU than those whose share in the unit of account was smaller. The note envisaged, as a solution, setting up a smaller margin of fluctuation for the "inert" currencies and a wider for the "mobile" ones.

A few days later, on 23 August, the German Finance Ministry set out its own position.[36] It did not take a monetary expert to observe that the two positions were quite different—the very first sentence of an introductory note presenting both papers did not fail to (politely) notice the difference.[37] The German Finance Ministry envisaged a much more limited role for the ECU than the one envisaged by the Banque de France. The ministry favored the option of a parity grid, which, in essence, meant that they wanted the snake to continue functioning as it was. As much as the Banque de France, the Bundesbank underscored the continuity of its own monetary thinking. A case in point was a letter from Pöhl to the members of the Zentralbankrat, which was a textual analysis of the Bremen Annex, sentence by sentence, in which skepticism or even opposition is easily perceived.[38] A meeting between representatives of the Finance Ministry, Economics Ministry, and Bundesbank that took place on 24 August in Frankfurt confirmed the German position, that the ECU-based model was once again rejected.[39]

Yet the most striking fact in the presentation of the French and German positions was that, beneath the discussion about technical issues of the EMS itself, there were revealing—though often cursory—remarks about perennial themes of European monetary cooperation. The EMS debate shed light again on the way in which the French and German monetary authorities thought about European monetary cooperation in general. It also showed that if both monetary authorities leaned slightly toward opposite interpretations, a third, consensual way emerged. While the Banque de France did not propose a strict monetarist vision—namely, that the narrowing or locking of exchange rate fluctuations would induce economic convergence—this thinking was still present. It indeed stressed that the constraints imposed by the EMS would act as a trigger for its members to better coordinate their economic policies, while the improved monetary mechanism would help currencies remain in the system.[40] In very similar terms, a note to Lahnstein interestingly envisaged that the EMS would bring discipline, thereby suggesting that a monetary mechanism would bring economic discipline (and thereby convergence), which was a typical "monetarist" point.[41] Yet on other occasions both the Finance Ministry and the Economics Ministry rejected such a typical monetarist interpretation: "A financial transfer to the economically weaker member states should not be provided through monetary mechanisms."[42] Here lies the paradox inherent in the discussions: while "economists" refused to accept that a monetary mechanism induced any resource transfer, they subscribed to one of the core "monetarist" theses—that the locking of exchange rates induces the convergence of economic policies, termed here the "disciplining effect." And it was indeed based on this disciplinary effect that a European consensus would slowly emerge. The French, Italian, and Irish governments, by joining the EMS in order to have an external anchor to their internal stability-oriented economic policies, subscribed to the disciplining effect thesis.

To conclude this section I will analyze the positions of the other EEC member states during the early EMS negotiations. The British position was characterized by a relatively divided administration.[43] Very early on, it was clear that, in addition to the reluctance of Callaghan and Healey, the disagreement between the Treasury and the Foreign Office over the EMS was irreconcilable—and this was of course to the benefit of the Treasury's position. Central to British Treasury fears was that if Britain were part of the EMS, the sterling rate might be higher than it would otherwise be. The Foreign Office—and particularly Butler—acknowledged that the pound exchange rate could indeed be higher than it would otherwise be because of a lower inflation rate. Yet what Butler stressed was that "it would be wrong to assume that membership of the EMS would prevent us from getting agreement to our having a reasonably competitive rate."[44] He further explained that France would presumably find itself eventually in a similar situation, and that Giscard would certainly try to defend a competitive rate for the French franc—as much as he did while he was finance minister. Hence, Butler argued, provided that the British government took measures that would be regarded by its EEC partners as directed at fighting inflation, they would not oppose an adjustment of the pound exchange rate. Couzens's long reply to Butler's letter showed that the positions of the Foreign Office and of the Treasury were diametrically opposed.[45] Couzens simply explained that he was not convinced that parity changes could easily be made. According to him, "We would surely come under pressure not to change our parity too soon but to make appropriate domestic policy changes and meanwhile to take advantage of the credit facilities which would be available." In other words, the main fear of the Treasury was the loss of the power to devalue. It is often (and in many ways rightly) said that EMS membership constituted, for the French government, a sort of external anchor or justification for pursuing its domestic economic policy.[46] Yet it was even clearer in the Italian case. On 31 August, the Italian finance minister Filippo Pandolfi presented his economic program, tellingly called "a program for development, a choice for Europe."[47] He very clearly seized this "heaven-sent" opportunity for the EMS debate to present the discussion of his economic strategy as a question of being for or against EMS membership.[48] It was thus not a coincidence that Jenkins stressed his support of the Pandolfi plan when meeting Andreotti on 8 September.[49] Finally, the remaining EEC members—the Dutch, Danish, and Luxembourgian governments—tended to follow an economist viewpoint.[50]

The Economist Option with a Pinch of Monetarism

Of the nine positions, the Belgian one deserves special attention, as it emerged as a way to reconcile the two main competing options: the ECU-based and parity-grid systems. Both systems had clear aims: the French-inspired one was designed in order to pinpoint the divergent currency, while the German-sponsored option was designed to conserve the solidity of the snake. What would become known as the "Belgian compromise" proposed a middle solution: a parity-grid system akin to the "solid" snake with an "indicator of divergence" able to pinpoint the divergent currency. The Belgian proposal raised the important question of the implications of the divergent currency's identification. Yet it is striking to observe that, in terms of monetary thinking, the idea of having a threshold to trigger interventions, which had been at the center of the discussion of the Duisenberg proposal in 1976–1977, resurfaced in the EMS discussions and progressively emerged as the basis for building a compromise between the French and German positions. The Belgian compromise, when mentioned at all, is said to have first appeared in the report of the Monetary Committee of 7 September.[51] It had actually already formally appeared in another report, that of the Heyvaert Group on 21 August, and was present in the EEC committees' discussions since early August. My analytical take in this section should therefore not lead us to downplay the chronological order of the suggestions made during the EMS negotiations: at their earliest, the French view dated from 8 August, the Belgian (the so-called compromise) from 10 August, and the German from 23 August. Naturally, these dates correspond to the official, detailed, written version of an opinion of which most participants in the negotiations were already aware. Yet they do underline one element: the Belgian compromise was on the table very early. If it is therefore true, as Peter Ludlow explains, that the Belgian idea was a "holding operation rather than a pre-packed formula to which both sides could give a final answer for or against," this should not lead us to think that the Belgian proposal appeared only once it had become obvious that without such a compromise, the negotiations would fail. On the contrary, the proposal appeared after the French and before the German one, in part presumably because the Belgian delegates felt more acutely the Franco-German divergence, and partly also because the idea had been in the air for quite some time. It would thus be highly misleading to believe that the Franco-German disagreement happened in an environment deprived of any alternatives or compromises.

The first mention of a possible Belgian compromise was made on the occasion of the meeting of the Monetary Committee's alternates on 10 and 11 August.[52] The British record mentions that "there will be a reference [in the report]—pressed by the Belgians—for what, perhaps looking ahead, they describe as a compromise proposal. This is the variant with a grid and a superimposed basket, so as still to identify the deviant." They could do this of course because the French and German governments' positions were predictable to a large extent. This further underlines the importance of the knowledge of each other's likely positions gained in the previous monetary discussions. And underscoring that this evocation was not a coincidence, it is also worth noticing that a similar reference to the Belgian compromise appeared on 21 August in the Interim Report on the EMS of the Heyvaert Group (the Group of Experts of the Committee of Governors).[53] Having "the ECU as the basis for a parity grid and an indicator of divergence" was described as a possible "compromise between the basket and parity grid variants." In both of the EEC committees central to the EMS negotiations, mention of the Belgian compromise had thus been made very early on.

The so-called Belgian compromise was, however, largely British (if not Dutch) in origin. Surprisingly never mentioned in the literature, another scheme indeed existed along very similar lines—the so-called Sangster Scheme, named after John Sangster, a Bank of England official. This scheme had indeed been evoked even earlier than the first hint of a possible Belgian compromise, as its first trace dates from 18 July.[54] The crux of the Sangster idea, or "composite scheme," was to use a parity grid equipped with a key to identify the deviant currency. Sangster explained that

> bearing in mind the difficulty that there will be in determining preannounced market intervention rates when working on the basis of a currency basket, [the objective was] to establish a system based on nominal exchange rates but preserving something of the basket approach in determining the intervention obligation.

Sangster also aimed "to incorporate a more articulated dollar policy into the new community system." Most important, Sangster's idea was in essence the same as that of the divergence indicator: "The key to intervention obligation would be determined by taking a simple average of each currency's deviation from its theoretical parity ... and determining which currency was furthest away from the average. The intervention obligation would then rest on this 'deviant.'"[55] Sangster interestingly mentioned interventions instead of mere consultations.

The only reference to this scheme in a multilateral European forum was made during a meeting of the Heyvaert Group in Basel, on 31 July–2 August—before the first mention of a possible "Belgian compromise," that is. It was reported that "Mr Sangster mentioned his suggestion that a parity grid system could be combined with the system for identifying the deviant (e.g. by the movement of the cross-rate against the dollar) and he received some support, for example from Rey of the Belgian Central Bank."[56] It is of course particularly revealing to see that the explicit support mentioned in this account of the meeting came from the Belgian Central Bank. The existence of this scheme primarily underlines that the preoccupations were more commonly shared in the EEC than is usually thought. In spite of its links with the Sangster Scheme, as well as its earlier intellectual links with the Duisenberg proposals, the compromise proposal suggested in August 1978 would nevertheless remain afterward exclusively associated with its Belgian origin.[57]

The Belgian compromise would from then on be present in successive reports of both EEC committees. The Interim Report of the Monetary Committee on the EMS thus evokes an option called the "reconciliation formula."[58] On 20 September, the Belgian members of the Monetary Committee set out in more detail their compromise formula.[59] The idea was to establish a new exchange rate system built on a parity grid and divergence indicator based on the ECU. In concrete terms, the system was supposed to function as follows. The bilateral limits of fluctuation, which determine when intervention obligation starts, would only be announced to the market. Once a certain width of fluctuation (the "divergence threshold"), measured in ECUs, had been reached, the stabilization of fluctuations would be preceded by consultations in order to adjust the fluctuation. The idea was that this early warning indicator would put some pressure on monetary authorities to consult before the intervention points were reached. The Belgian note suggested that the divergence threshold be 75 percent of each currency's maximum width of fluctuation. In short, the ECU would become the "barometer" of the system.[60] This proposal strikingly recalled the van Ypersele Plan presented earlier in the year—a plan that itself partly recycled some of the ideas contained in the Duisenberg memorandum—and reinforces the significance of the prehistory of the EMS.[61]

That there existed on the EMS negotiating table, quite early on, the possibility for a compromise between the two competing options was one thing; that the two supporters of the competing options were actually *willing* to find a compromise, along these lines or others, was another matter. As early as the first week of August, some signs of conciliation between the French and German position along the lines of the Belgian compromise were actually discernible.[62] Tellingly, during the meeting of the Committee of Governors on 12 September, Emminger seemed ready to move toward a compromise solution. If he maintained that he defended the parity-grid system, he immediately added that he did *not* think that "the new monetary system should be a mere enlargement of the 'snake,'" thereby getting closer to a point regularly made by Richardson, Paolo Baffi, and Clappier in particular. Even more important was the fact that he openly contemplated the possibility of using the ECU as indicator of divergence and then insisted that it be mentioned in the oral report made to the Finance Council.[63] Similarly, a detailed analysis of the successive drafts of the Banque de France's position helps see quite a striking readiness—or at least evocation—of a compromise. After a number of EEC meetings, the Banque de France issued on 23 August a new note on the EMS, in which it right away evoked the possibility of a compromise given the opposition to the French interpretation.[64] The Banque de France insisted that in principle, the real novelty of the exchange rate system under consideration would precisely be to use the ECU as the system's only reference. Yet it clearly stated that the French position was likely to be adapted in order to eventually find a consensus. The Banque de France's readiness for compromise partly stemmed from the fact that the French monetary experts were actually well aware of the technical complexity of an ECU-based system. Clappier himself was mindful of this technical complexity, both in theory and in practice.[65] In Clappier's own words, the parity-grid system would be a great deal simpler to operate than the ECU-based one.[66] Stressing the impression that the EMS was nothing more than a political gesture, Clappier did not seem to attach much importance to the fact that the EMS would not differ very much—if at all—from the snake. He did not even seem to be particularly convinced of the durability of the scheme. Since the idea to which the supporters of the ECU-based system were most attached was that of being able to identify the most deviant currency, the "divergence indicator" of the Belgian compromise offered quite an honorable exit strategy.

Negotiating along the Bundesbank's Line

The month of September witnessed a fundamental shift in the negotiations, which clearly moved in the direction of the Bundesbank. One of the landmarks of the period is the famous Aachen meeting, where Schmidt and Giscard are said to have taken a decisive step by agreeing on the adoption of a common line. The adoption of the Belgian compromise was, however, clearly the only possible option to overcome the Franco-German deadlock at the technical level much before the Aachen meeting, particularly given the strong initial political commitment. In order to show this, in the following section I will first scrutinize the relative standstill (if not deadlock) in negotiations prior to the Aachen meeting, then analyze the Aachen memorandum of understanding, and finally delve into the follow-up to the meeting and the EEC-wide consequences of this Franco-German agreement.

A Relative Standstill in Negotiations

The pre-Aachen period confirmed both the Irish and Italian governments' will to join the EMS and the British government's reluctance. The Irish government seemed very interested in taking part in the new European monetary scheme, and neither the economic differences nor the sterling link seemed insurmountable obstacles.[67] Colley declared in a radio interview on 10 September that he thought that Ireland would be able to join the EMS in January 1979.[68] Crucially, the Central Bank of Ireland concluded in a preliminary analysis of the EMS that membership was desirable, partly because it would imply a reorientation of domestic policies toward greater discipline.[69] In addition, the Irish government seemed perfectly ready, in the event of nonparticipation by the British in the EMS, to break the link with sterling.[70] Jenkins's tour of European capitals brought him to Rome on 7 and 8 September to talk about the EMS with the Italian government. The Italian government's favorable disposition, in principle, to join the EMS had apparently strengthened since the Bremen summit.[71] "He [Andreotti] is eager on economic grounds, and determined on political grounds, to come into the EMS," Jenkins wrote, "but he not unnaturally wants to get as much out of it as possible."[72] The position of the British government was in striking contrast with that of the Irish and the Italians. Ortoli's meeting with Healey in London on 5 September was a case in point.[73] Healey stressed once more that the British government prioritized economic growth, while the French and German governments attached overriding importance to the stability of exchange rates. Healey explained that, without adequate resource transfers, the sacrifices in terms of employment and output of such a semifixed monetary scheme would be too great for the British government. Couzens and Healey stressed that, regarding the question of the numéraire, they favored the "basket" solution and, more precisely, the "adjustable basket" option. This, as Ortoli noticed, somewhat rejoined the French position.

However preliminary (the basic organization of the system, parity grid or ECU-based, had not been firmly decided), the couple of meetings of the EEC specialized committees in early September gave interesting hints about the state of the negotiations.[74] For a start, the Monetary Committee stressed the importance of one topic that was absent from the report: measures aimed at improving economic convergence. "It [the EMS] cannot be durable and effective unless it is backed up by complementary policies."[75] The Monetary Committee agreed that the ECU would be used in the European Monetary Fund and in the settlement system; it also agreed that the central rates would be expressed in ECU. Where opinions differed, however, was on how the intervention limits should be defined: parity grid or ECU-based. A further problem was raised regarding the latter system—namely, that of the implications of a change in central rates. Indeed, under the ECU-based system, a change of parity in one currency would oblige all other participating currencies to change their parities vis-à-vis the basket. As mentioned earlier, the report then evoked a third option, namely the Belgian compromise. The objections against the ECU = EUA proposition were likely to be more easily solved. The first one was that were the EMS to be an ECU-based system, obvious problems would arise if a currency did not participate in the exchange rate system (or had to leave it at a later stage). The second, more fundamental objection was that since the ECU would be a weighted basket of EEC currencies, the stronger EEC currencies (and notably the DM) would naturally be less likely to reach their fluctuation margins than the smallest ones. Finally, since currencies' weights vary over time, a change of parity may have damaging effects on its counterparts. The parity change of one currency could push other currencies beyond their intervention points. A solution to all these problems, suggested by the Bank of England, was to adopt an ECU basket in which each currency had a constant weight.[76] A majority of governors, however, accepted the option of an ECU constituted as a revisable basket of EEC currencies.[77]

Yet arguably, the single most important event in the EMS negotiations in September was the formal *prise de position* of the Bundesbank, officially set out on 7 September.[78] Along familiar lines, Pöhl had declared in the Zentralbankrat meeting that he thought that the inflation rates of the EEC member states had not yet converged enough for a new monetary system to be created. The Bundesbank's official paper was in the same vein. True, it recalled in its first point that the Bundesbank, as much as the German government, found it desirable to have a zone of monetary stability in Europe and also supported European political unification. But the thrust of the Bundesbank's opinion quickly appeared in the second point, in which it uttered its "economist" doubts regarding the Bremen Annex, which it thought too "monetarist." Tellingly (and contrary to what the German Finance Ministry had done), the technical part of the Bundesbank document did not start by outlining the opinion of the German Central Bank, but rather by criticizing the French proposals. The ECU-based system had "considerable disadvantages" since it would constrain the Bundesbank to intervene on foreign exchange markets much more than in the current parity-grid system. The second important criticism was related to the value of the ECU. The Bundesbank indeed said that, according to the advocates of the new system, the basket definition would reflect the EEC's average inflation rate. The Bundesbank believed that this would, in the long term, reinforce inflation in the EEC, and that it would therefore be incompatible with German stability objectives. The Bundesbank logically concluded from the above perceived drawbacks that it favored the parity-grid option. The Bundesbank official *prise de position* thus clearly set the tone for the coming negotiations and, in the short run, clearly put strong pressure on the next meeting: that of Giscard and Schmidt the following week in Aachen.

Demythologizing Aachen

Since the contours of the Franco-German disagreements over the EMS were now clearly outlined, the objective of the Franco-German meeting in Aachen focused on reaching an "agreement in principle" over the issues on which both governments disagreed. It was in that context that a further meeting under the framework of Franco-German cooperation (strengthened since early 1977) was to be held on 14 and 15 September in Aachen. The Aachen meeting continues to carry disproportionate significance in the overall history of the EMS negotiations. It constituted, however, a mere ratification of an agreement (on the parity-grid system, with the possibility of setting a divergence indicator) that had largely become inevitable. As mentioned in the previous section, not only had the Belgian compromise been in the EEC committees' pipeline for quite a while, but both the German and French monetary authorities seemed ready to find a compromise that was just awaiting ratification by the heads of government. Although a good deal of demythologization of the Aachen meeting has already been accomplished, the Aachen meeting continues to be taken as an important step in the overall negotiations.[79] For Marsh, Aachen was "a seminal moment in the history of the EMS, which set the tone for twenty years of political debates about monetary union."[80] In this section, I will in contrast emphasize the importance of the formation of a transnational monetary consensus among monetary elites on the Bundesbank interpretation rather than on its merely inevitable ratification by the heads of government.

The Giscard-Schmidt talks that preceded the Aachen summit confirmed this interpretation. Giscard called Schmidt on 12 September, after the meeting of the Committee of Governors.[81] The French president said that he thought that the governors had been close to reaching an agreement, so that it should be possible to reach one during the Franco-German consultations. Schmidt, however, immediately dampened Giscard's enthusiasm by saying that he currently had difficulties with the Bundesbank and was unable to judge, as yet, what his position would be. He said that he would meet the Direktorium of the Bundesbank the following day. Giscard hoped that an agreement could be reached on the question of the numéraire and on the issue of the monetary fund. Schmidt said that the real problem for him lay in the first question, and that for this he had to wait to have a discussion with Bundesbank officials.

Yet in many ways, Giscard and Schmidt faced a nondecision. Indeed, failing to reach such an agreement would have damaging consequences on the overall project. The risk was clearly that the new monetary plan would remain stuck in the pipeline of the specialized committees, with the defenders of the EUA-based system on the one side and the supporters of the status-quo/parity-grid/snake option on the other side—as had been the case in 1974 and 1975 during the discussion of the Fourcade memorandum. With Giscard and Schmidt having assigned so much political importance to the EMS battle, it was scarcely imaginable that they would suddenly abandon the project. Both French and German officials were aware of this. Schulmann summed it up well: in the following Finance Council, the opposition between the snake and non-snake members would be reinforced; domestically, the opponents of the EMS project would be strengthened; and the entry into force of a putative new system would certainly not happen on 1 January 1979.[82] There was some sense of urgency to break the deadlock.

The outcome of the Aachen meeting was the (secret) redaction of the so-called memorandum of understanding.[83] The wording of the opening paragraph of this memorandum was telling: "In order to ensure a rapid conclusion of the work currently going on in various Community bodies, the French and German delegations will present a common position based on the following guidelines." The idea was hence to keep the momentum born in Copenhagen and Bremen in order to be able to reach an agreement, as planned, in December 1978. The rest of the memorandum is not presented in the literature and deserves to be outlined here. The first point was of clear "economist" inspiration. It stressed the importance of economic convergence of the EEC member states. The second point confirmed the adoption of the parity-grid method, while leaving open the door for the adoption of the "Belgian compromise": "The ECU might serve a useful purpose as an indicator of the need for intramarginal interventions, after consultation." The third point confirmed that changes in central rates would be possible, but with prior consultation. The fourth point stated that the ECU's composition may be revised after consultation, and that it should become the sole EEC unit of account. The fifth point stressed the importance of allowing sufficient credit facilities. The sixth point somewhat diminished the importance of the concurrent studies, by highlighting the Franco-German refusal to establish a bargaining link with the monetary negotiations and encouraging their autonomy: "The outcome of the 'concurrent studies' agreed upon at Bremen must not hinder progress on the solution of the monetary arrangements proper; they should be pursued on a timetable of their own but be available at the next European Council." The last point concerned the EMF. It strikingly postponed, until after the European Council of December, the definition of its exact final role; it suggested, however, that "it should be modeled after the International Monetary Fund"; and stated that in the interim period, the Bank for International Settlements could "serve as agent for the system." Two further points were made in a couple of paragraphs deleted from the final version but still present in the document. The first of these envisaged the possibility, "in extreme situation," of granting a leave of absence to a participating country. The second announced the creation of a Franco-German working group in charge of working out "the details for a common position on these matters in the Council meeting(s) before the next European Council." In addition, it would be responsible for devising "the ways which would enable Italy and the United Kingdom to participate in the EMS even if these countries chose not to become full members from the outset." Surprisingly, Ireland was not mentioned.

With this memorandum of understanding, the French and German delegations had therefore done what they were somewhat obliged to do: prepare themselves to present a common front at the next Finance Council on 18 September so as not to lose the élan they had managed to create in the first half of the year.[84] The expression of a Franco-German "compromise" reached at Aachen is therefore misleading. For a start, there was no real compromise, "middle way" solution agreed on in Aachen.[85] The system agreed on was, strictly speaking, that of a parity grid, supported by the Bundesbank, with a door left open for the use of the ECU as an indicator of divergence. The agreement was clearly devised along the position of the German Central Bank rather than any French monetary authority. Though, arguably, the Banque de France and the Trésor would have been keen to reform the snake in a more substantial way, the memorandum of understanding further stressed the importance of the growing comprehension that we've seen between the French and German monetary authorities. It should be noted, also, that there was no real alternative to the eventual outcome at Aachen. Put differently: an open disagreement in Aachen would have presumably meant the failure of the EMS negotiations, which Giscard and Schmidt could not afford. A covered and diplomatic nondecision on the important issues at stake would have let the entire EMS project sink in the EEC specialized committees—as had happened to the Fourcade memorandum and Duisenberg proposal before. In contrast to the European Council sessions in Copenhagen and Bremen, where the heads of government's political impulses were crucial and marked the beginning of a new phase, the French and German leaders' agreement in Aachen was the mere symptom of an evolution that neither the French president nor the German chancellor could really influence any longer. Yet in retrospect, it was presented as its defining moment in order to fit a certain European-integration mythology that the heads of government were keen on constructing. Giscard's famous remark about Charlemagne's spirit brooding over the Franco-German works is a case in point. However, as Amaury de Saint-Périer put it, if a spirit brooded over Aachen—if not over the EMS negotiations in September in general—it was certainly not that of Charlemagne but of the Bundesbank.[86]

The Parity-Grid Option Confirmed at EEC Level

Following the Aachen summit, the danger of presenting the other EEC members with a Franco-German fait accompli was much greater than it had been even at

Bremen. Since the Aachen meeting was a mixture of top-level summit (involving heads of government) and expert consultations (central bank governors and finance ministry representatives), the various EEC bodies could rightly feel they had been short-circuited. The Bremen European Council had been, by contrast, skillfully organized. By discussing the proposal in an EEC forum, Giscard and Schmidt had managed to appease those heads of government who were initially not involved in devising the scheme, which was, in spite of a number of technical insights, mainly a political guideline. Finally, the entire endeavor had been carried out under the auspices (and benediction) of the guardian of the treaties, the Commission.

With a Franco-German agreement ratified at Aachen and the preparatory work of the specialized committees completed on time, the Finance Council held on 18 September in Brussels was able to tackle the EMS features in some detail. Such punctuality had not been the case over the past few years, thereby further underlining how important had been the political impulse and pressure given by the European Council. The meeting opened with an oral report by the chairman of the Committee of Governors,[87] followed by a traditional "*tour de table.*"[88] Monory reiterated the traditional French criticism of the parity-grid system but paradoxically described the ECU-based option as "an original idea but technically complex to operate."[89] The only discordant voice came from Healey, who criticized the absence of any detailed report of the Aachen meeting and voiced his disappointment at the abandonment of the ECU-based option.[90] Even though the Finance Council as a whole did not officially opt for the parity-grid solution, it clearly regarded this option, as the diplomatic language put it, "with interest." This stemmed from the fact that it could not make any final decision yet about a proposal that was at the moment still very vague. Yet revealingly, no member had defended the only real alternative solution—the ECU-based system—during this meeting. If the official shift to the parity-grid system would therefore take a bit more time, mentally it had already been accomplished, even by the French officials—its original principal defenders.[91]

Achieving "Symmetry" by Other Means: The Concurrent Studies

Where the EMS negotiations took a genuinely original turn contrasting with earlier EEC debates was with regard to the so-called concurrent studies. Indeed, until 1978, it was assumed that the non-snake members willing to join the EEC exchange rate system but unable to do so because of their comparatively weaker economic situation would be simply left on their own. True, some discussions and reports about EMU (e.g., the MacDougall Report, the OCA debate) did take into account the issue of economic convergence, but the discussion remained largely stuck at a theoretical level.[92] Generally speaking, it was taken for granted that it was the responsibility of the "less prosperous" non-snake members to improve their economic situation so as to reach the economic and financial level of the snake members. The new momentum that had started in early 1978 and had led, so far, to the writing of the Bremen Annex, had such a strong political component that a transfer of resources was even envisaged to get the agreement of those weaker member states on the Bremen Annex—and, at a later stage, on the EMS. Whether they are looked at as an enticement or an incipient federalist mechanism,[93] the concurrent studies provide an interesting case study. The concurrent studies were indeed, in a sense, a sophisticated version of the issue of the symmetry of the monetary system. In other words, a monetary mechanism, however symmetrical, would not be sufficient to compensate for the economic differences between the poorer and the richer EEC member states. As much as the technical negotiations had focused on a fuzzy sentence referring to the role of the ECU in the exchange rate system, the concurrent studies would be, in many respects, a quest to clarify what "transfer of resources" exactly meant: What type of transfer? What kind of resources?

The concurrent studies were being handled in the Economic Policy Committee (EPC). The EPC had been mandated by the COREPER on 27 July to carry out the concurrent studies and to provide the Finance Council with a first report for its session of 18 September.[94] The participants in these meetings were representatives of the foreign and finance ministries and the central banks. The EPC first gathered on 11 August for an exchange of views on the concurrent studies, which gave a good indication of the future debates, and then again on 6 September.[95] It centered its discussions on two topics: the exact requests of the three potential beneficiaries and the reports presented by the Commission.[96] The discussions logically followed a pattern relatively similar to those about the exchange rate system, namely, that the first post-Bremen session remained limited to an initial exchange of views and to the instructions to other institutions (here only the Commission) to do some preparatory technical work in view of the following sessions. Another similarity was semantic. Indeed, in many ways, the expression "resource transfers" was to the concurrent studies what "the ECU will be at the center of the system" was to the monetary negotiations: the vagueness of the expression was both its strength and its weakness. It had been vague enough to satisfy the European Council, which thus adopted the Bremen Annex,[97] but it was also so vague that it could only provoke stark (and often irreconcilable) differences of interpretations once the detailed negotiations started.

Admittedly, the overall discussion was a caricature of a negotiation between "less prosperous countries" and their richer counterparts. Yet there was here an interesting insight into what a truly federative system could look like, with a central authority (the Commission) redistributing money, collected by taxes (contribution to the budget) from the richer countries, to the poorer parts of the (possible) federation. In that respect, a number of reactions were telling. For instance, a note of the Trésor clearly ruled out a federative interpretation of the Community budget.[98] The identity of the member states that were most interested in or most likely to be the beneficiaries of potential resource transfers was no mystery—these were Britain, Ireland, and Italy.[99] The interpretation of the extent of the concurrent studies accordingly varied. The potential beneficiaries (the British, Irish, and Italian governments) defended the idea that far-reaching studies should be carried out about how to even out economic development in the EEC. For example, the concurrent studies very explicitly prompted the British government to resurrect the Marjolin and MacDougall reports of 1975 and 1977.[100] The Marjolin Report had called for—among other things—the creation of a Community Unemployment Benefit Scheme, while the MacDougall Report had mentioned the need for developing the EEC budget in order to use it as a tool for proper resource transfers.[101] On the opposite side of the argument, the potential contributors (the Benelux, Danish, French, and German governments) of course stressed that the concurrent studies were taking place in the framework of the EMS negotiations, not in the framework of a full EMU. All three representatives (British, Irish, and Italian) underlined the constraining character of the new exchange rate system for their economies. The Italian delegation insisted that it wanted a wide-ranging scheme, the Irish stressed that it should start immediately, and the British repeated that for the EMS to be durable (and hence to avoid a snakelike experience), transfers of resources needed to take place. The trap of the concurrent studies was that some member states would try to use them in order to obtain what they had not been able to get during other negotiations. Colley, at a meeting with Jenkins in early September, thus mentioned the fact that there was a risk that some countries (chiefly Britain) would use the concurrent studies to obtain satisfaction on wider issues (its budget contribution).[102] The British government indeed somewhat reformulated the budget question that had been in discussion in 1974–1975.

A central issue, however, besides the exact measures that should be taken, regarded the definition of the expression "less prosperous countries" and the timetable. Which criteria would be used in order to define these less prosperous countries? The discussion was here particularly confused, not least because of the profusion of potential criteria: the balance of payments, unemployment rate, GNP, energy dependence, productivity, and infrastructure development were all mentioned. The Irish delegation even said that it did not really care about the criteria to be used, given how obvious it was that it was the least prosperous country of the entire EEC! The EPC finally asked the Commission to undertake three studies: an analysis of all the financial flows in the EEC, emanating from both inside and outside the EEC; a list of the different criteria ("structural indicators") that could be used in order to define the less prosperous countries; and an identification of the measures necessary so that the EMS could function. On the occasion of the second EPC meeting, regarding the criteria to determine the "less prosperous countries," three elements emerged: problems in external financing (balance of payments), standard of living (GDP per capita), and structural problems (no indicator was mentioned yet).[103] No final choice between these elements was made, however.

It would fall beyond the scope of this section to recount in extensive detail the Irish, Italian, and British demands—which are already very well-known.[104] To sum up briefly, Ireland and Italy argued for concrete resource transfers (other than loans). The Italian delegation even asked that the global amount of transfers operated by the EEC—credits and subventions—should reach 2 percent of GDP in the next few years (it was 0.76 percent of GDP in 1977).[105] The British delegation clearly was, from the start, in the uneasiest situation of all three potential beneficiaries.[106] The fundamental objective of the British government was to receive a share of EEC expenditure larger than its contribution to the EEC budget (excluding the CAP).[107] Unlike the Italian and Irish cases, the British request was not only linked to the EMS negotiations but more generally attached to the perennial British request to call into question its EEC budgetary contribution, as it had done since its entry into the EEC five years earlier, and indeed since its very first negotiations for entry.[108] While the Trésor, for example, admitted that the Irish and Italian requests were legitimate, it clearly stated that it should not follow the logic of the British demands.[109] In addition to the fact that the budgetary issue would arouse the hostility of the French and German delegations, the British case was also not necessarily the clearest one because on a purchasing-power parity basis, Britain was not so clearly among the "less prosperous countries." Another element working against British requests was that given the perceived weaknesses in the British case, and since at least the French and German delegations clearly wanted to avoid the formation of a Anglo-Irish-Italian axis in the EPC, it was obvious that politically and economically the weakest link was the British one—and hence the first one to criticize. Finally, it was particularly difficult for the British delegation to argue for resource transfer in order to compensate for the side effects induced by participation in an exchange rate mechanism in which they were, relatively clearly from the very beginning, not really inclined to take part.

The French and German delegations had also a subtle game to play. Indeed, as the Auswärtiges Amt emphasized, it would be difficult to sell a Franco-German initiative to the non-snake members without being ready to accept some resource transfers.[110] The monetary scheme would otherwise become a new snake, simply enlarged to France. The Irish, Italian, and British governments' inability, right from the beginning, to form a common front made the French and German governments' task of limiting the significance of the concurrent studies slightly easier. The French government clearly wanted to limit as much as possible the extent of these concurrent studies. The Trésor seemed also more inclined to help the Irish government (and Italian) than the British.[111] It stressed that the studies should deal with all financial flows (and not limit them to the EEC budget), thereby increasing its scope; and the notion of transfer of resources should not hide the importance of purely domestic economic measures that the member states had to take in order to improve the overall EEC economic convergence. The German government was of the same opinion. Even more to the point of the actual "resource transfers" that could take place, it was reported that Schmidt said during the cabinet meeting of 12 July that he only thought of measures taken by the European Investment Bank (EIB), namely, mere credits.[112] This remark was of crucial importance since it underlined the absence of strong political support at the top level, potentially able to overcome the differences of opinion. In that sense, the concurrent studies were the perfect counterexample to the ongoing monetary negotiations. In the German case, it could also be assumed that some reservations about the monetary project rubbed off on their opinion of the concurrent studies. On the whole, during these first two meetings the French and German governments adopted a rather low profile, avoiding direct confrontation—which sprang partly from the fact that they did not want to take the risk of wrecking an aspect of the EMS negotiations that may well prove vital in gaining the participation of Britain, Ireland, and Italy, and partly from the fact that clear ministerial guidelines had not yet arrived.

More important, the countries likely to bear the burden of the financial adjustment particularly stressed that the monetary negotiations would be carried out irrespective of decisions regarding concurrent studies.[113] That the French or German delegations defended such a position is not in itself very puzzling. Much more tellingly, this view was also particularly defended by Jenkins. In the president of the Commission's mind, creation of the EMS did not have to wait for the conclusion of the concurrent studies.[114] Hence, on the occasion of his visit both to Dublin (4 September) and to Rome (7–8 September), Jenkins said that "concurrent studies" should not be considered a precondition for the adhesion of Ireland and Italy to the EMS.[115] Jenkins stressed that the objective of the coming months was to reach an agreement on the EMS. The question of the transfer of resources would not be settled at the Brussels European Council—it would be too much for one Council. Yet what was possible was to state that there was a guarantee that within the EMS, the economies of the "less prosperous countries" would not be further constrained.[116] The crux of the problem was, for Jenkins as much as for Schmidt and Giscard, not to lose momentum as they went into the EMS negotiations.

Of course, this preparatory work could not prejudge the eventual outcome of the negotiations. The discussion over the actual resource transfer mechanisms would certainly offer more room for arguments. Yet as the presentation of the first EPC meetings has shown, it seemed quite clear that, very early on, the positions taken by each of the delegations in the EPC were definite. The French government stressed, for instance, both the high degree of Franco-German convergence in the approach to the EPC meetings and the fact that an agreement was unlikely. After the first EPC meeting on concurrent studies, a French official already wrote that no common conclusions were likely to ever be drawn from the Committee's work.[117] This, together with Schmidt's remark of 12 July, shows that the concurrent studies were a lost cause even earlier than Peter Ludlow argues (that is, in late September) if not even before they started at all.[118] The Finance Council on 18 September presented the first opportunity to assess the deadlock in the discussions on the concurrent studies. As planned, Hans Tietmeyer, chairman of the EPC, gave an oral report on the ongoing concurrent studies.[119] The following discussion witnessed a clear opposition between the Italian-Irish-British trio, who were disappointed, and the rest, who showed outright opposition to any move.[120] The meeting ended in a stalemate.

Conclusions

The various points made above—the leading role of the European Council, the swift and early overcoming of the Franco-German disagreement on the role of the ECU in the new system, the inclination of the Irish and Italian governments to join the EMS and the British reluctance to do so—all point in one common direction: the fundamental political nature of the EMS initiative.

The importance of the initial impulse given by the European Council was confirmed throughout the negotiations in July, August, and September. The Bremen European Council had set out a timetable, which the Finance Council endorsed, delegating the technical work to the specialized committees. Hence, all EEC institutions were set in motion following a *political* decision made by heads of government—a political decision to which none objected. Jenkins had again clearly perceived the importance of the European Council in the EEC institutional setup. As a consequence he repeatedly said, on various occasions, that one of the most important aspects of the negotiations in the second half of 1978 was not to lose the momentum of Bremen in order to reach an agreement on monetary issues in Brussels in December. To seek more than this would be too much for one European Council, Jenkins argued.[121] That was why, for instance, Jenkins himself ruled out any substantial reform of the CAP: "If such an attempt were made, with a high risk of souring the atmosphere, potential progress on both the CAP and the EMS would be destroyed."[122]

Another factor stressing the political nature of the EMS initiative is the absence of any real technical innovation, at least as of September 1978. The initial hopes at the outset of the EMS negotiations were high. The first official *prise de position* of the Banque de France thus clearly placed the new system in the perspective of "a serious step toward a future European Monetary Union."[123] In presenting the Bremen Annex to his counterparts, Clappier insisted that the objectives of the document were twofold: economic (to reach a higher level of economic stability) and political (to take this opportunity to (monetarily) organize Europe further).[124] Yet after the ratification of the parity-grid option at Aachen by Schmidt and Giscard, it became clear that the EMS, were it eventually to enter into force, would primarily be a political event instead of a technical one. The ECU, curiously presented as an "innovation" even in the specialized literature, by no means introduced a new method in something already established.[125] A careful reading of the Bremen Annex should help correct this mistaken impression: "The ECU has the same definition as the European Unit of Account." As far as the "acronym trick" is concerned, Ortoli had already suggested the name "ECU" for an EEC currency in late 1974.[126] In political terms, however, the non-snake members needed to be able to show that the EMS was something new—hence the perennial official, if not mythological, discourse saying so. It is particularly striking that virtually all the actors immediately adopted the two new acronyms, EMS and ECU, during the negotiations, and this *even before* their actual meaning and content had been agreed on. The novelty of the scheme had thus been politically decreed before the negotiations of its content had actually started. The absence of any real technical innovation was further underscored by the very early and swift abandonment of negotiations about the EMF. As early as on 18 September, Monory confirmed that, although the main features of the EMS had to be agreed on by December, not all the details of the EMF had to be settled by then—thereby leaving out the last, most potentially contentious issue.[127]

Giscard quickly forgot the absence of real technical innovation in the EMS since the primary aim of the French government was its economic and political rapprochement with Germany. As Schmidt put it: "Giscard and Barre were convinced that they absolutely needed the EMS for the realization of their own economic policy; I was also convinced of that."[128] This, together with the succession of a French and German presidency of the EEC, offered an opportunity to apply the regular consultation of both governments to European affairs, and thereby limited the risk of a failure of the initiative.[129] Such an extension of Franco-German cooperation to the European level had already been envisaged when the scheme for "miniconvergence" had been created in early 1977, but it also further confirmed the political, Franco-German dimension of the scheme, as well as Giscard's willingness to attach the French government's economic and monetary policy to that of the German government.[130] The Aachen agreement had significant consequences for the British position that will be analyzed in more detail in the next chapter. Indeed, until the Franco-German agreement, the French position was technically quite close to the British one, at least much more than to the German one. The British resentment following Aachen was caused not only by the fact that the British government had been bypassed by a bilateral agreement but also that London had lost its most important technical ally. The sudden reversal of the French technical position was hence badly resented by the British government.[131]

The political dimension, understood as a commitment to present an EEC answer to global problems, is further underlined by the fact that the attempts at setting up an alternative bargaining economic strategy completely failed. The link between concurrent studies and monetary negotiations existed but was so tenuous, and so strongly rejected by the French and German governments, that the British government's hope to be able to see the construction of a package deal including both quickly faded away. Moreover, the second option defended by the British government—namely, the preference for a global solution—also quickly failed. Alternative but limited options such as asking the surplus countries to reflate (at the Bonn summit) or creating a substitution account (as discussed in the IMF) had admittedly been envisaged, but they quickly faded away. The idea of a "world concerted relaunch" was in many ways linked to currency stability, since asking the surplus countries to reflate would augment the deficit countries' growth rate, and hopefully in turn limit the fluctuation of currencies (or at least bring down the DM). This point was acknowledged, for instance, by the Centre d'analyse et de prévision of the French Foreign Ministry.[132] Yet the growing consensus in Europe was on the snake model, which the French, Italian, and Irish governments were now politically ready to follow.

A last aspect underlining the political nature of the EMS negotiations was that the strongest defenders of the so-called symmetry were no longer the French but the British (and, to a lesser extent, Italian and Irish) decision makers. Quite ironically, during the 18 September Finance Council, Healey found himself alone against the other eight finance ministers defending what had been in essence the original French position. The concurrent studies were another case in point. Although the French would have certainly welcomed further resource transfers, they knew perfectly well that the German government would oppose this. And what was most important for the French government was to get a political agreement on the EMS, not an economic transfer of resources. By contrast, the British government, much less politically committed to the EMS initiative, did not fail to stress that it would economically need some transfer of resources. The British representative at the EPC meeting of 6 September hence declared that in order to function properly and to be durable (as the snake had not been), the new system needed to involve "symmetrical obligations."[133] Such reasoning was sensible, and would not have been rejected by some French, Italian, or Irish economic and monetary advisers, yet it underscored that the British government was not ready to commit itself politically to a scheme whose economic implications it found too costly. As Couzens put it in a letter to Butler: "In the EMS the decision to change the rate is a political one involving a specific admission of the failure of past policies."[134] This statement was revealing in two ways: it underlined that the EMS had a strong political dimension and that it was the fruit of a consensus on stability-oriented, anti-inflationary economic policies. The fact that the British government did not share this economic thinking, its euroskepticism, and crucially, the fact that all this happened while elections were approaching rendered joining the EMS an impossible task. In the midst of discussion about the nature of the EMS, on 4 September, Jenkins thus reported that Owen thought that "an election in early October was now definitely fixed."[135] Such timing undoubtedly led many British policymakers to think of the EMS in very abstract terms, given that proximity to the election was not propitious for such a decision—hence the permanent postponement of a final decision. Therefore, if not technically new, the novelty would have to be found elsewhere. The extending of membership (the inclusion of non-snake members), good political marketing (presenting the ECU as something new and pathbreaking), and a last-minute revival of the economist versus monetarist debate (the debate over the divergence indicator) would all help in this respect—and they are the focus of the next chapter.

A FALSE START, OCTOBER 1978–MARCH 1979

JENKINS: **If we had to drop this scheme, this would be very serious.**
SCHMIDT: **I would be a hero in my country.**
JENKINS: **Short-term hero at the expense of long-term reputation.**

—Brussels European Council, December 1978

The nature of the EMS, and singularly its originality in comparison with the current snake, will notably depend on the interpretation that will be given to the presumption of action resulting from the functioning of the indicator of divergence.

—Jean-Yves Haberer

In this chapter I analyze the end of the EMS negotiations and the launch of the new system. The chapter covers the second and last phase of the negotiations, from the decision to adopt a parity-grid system until the entry into force of the EMS in March 1979. By contrast to the previous chapter, this period was much more about "filling in the details," since the basics of the exchange rate mechanism had already been agreed on: by ruling out the ECU-based option as a basis for the new exchange rate system, the basic shape of the EMS had been laid out. The various negotiators involved had now to decide on the functioning of the "Belgian compromise," that is to say, how the divergence indicator would operate. The settlement of the credit system and the concurrent studies would also attract attention in late 1978. The agreement on the parity-grid system (or, put differently, the abandonment of the ECU-based option) had two interlinked consequences: the question of the novelty of the EMS, compared to the snake, was now directly addressed, and it broke the front of the "monetarists" in the negotiations. Indeed, the French government's adoption of the Bundesbank's approach at Aachen simultaneously meant that the British, Irish, and Italian governments had lost their best ally in the negotiations over the exchange rate system. I argue that these last negotiations would decide whether the EMS would become a truly new (that is, different from the snake) exchange rate system. In the first section below I delve into the last technical negotiations, dominated by the debate about the operation of the divergence indicator. In the second section I scrutinize the intensification of political contacts in order to win the participation in the EMS of the British, Irish, and Italian governments. In the third section I examine the end of the concurrent studies and the extent to which their deadlock had the potential to become an obstacle for the inception of the EMS as a whole. In the last section I concentrate on the Brussels European Council and the delayed launch of the EMS.

A New Case Study: The Divergence Indicator

The distance and even slight contempt shown by Schmidt in talking about the divergence indicator during the November 1978 meeting at the Bundesbank was very revealing about the overall likely outcome of this discussion: a divergence indicator deprived of any concrete implications. Discussing the functioning of the EMS, Schmidt had to ask Emminger the name of the "divergence indicator," which he surprisingly ignored. When Emminger had refreshed his memory, the German chancellor continued, saying that he would also learn this new expression![1] Given the Bundesbank's centrality (and reserve) in the EMS negotiations, and the memorandum of understanding agreed on at Aachen by the French and German governments, there was in fact very little room for maneuver. These last negotiations provide, however, a number of interesting insights. Four different but complementary features characterized the negotiations: the perennial economist versus monetarist debate, the confirmation of the centrality of the European Council in the EEC institutional setup, the significance of the quest for a genuinely new European monetary system, and, finally, the interplay between political and technical understandings. These four points will be analyzed here in turn, and will provide a new reading grid able to shed new light on these debates.

The Permanence of the Economist versus Monetarist Debate

The essence of the so-called Belgian compromise lies in the creation of a divergence indicator that would act as a warning system able to identify a deviant currency. The idea was that the movement of the EMS currencies against the ECU basket should be tracked so as to identify the potential "deviant" currency— which might, quite obviously, often turn out to be the DM. The continuity of the nature of the monetary debates in the EEC is again striking: the core of the discussion here was not a new preoccupation in the EEC monetary debates. Not only the identification of a deviant currency but also the nature of the measures to be taken once the deviant currency had been identified were exactly the debates that had been at the center of the discussions about the Duisenberg "target zones" proposal. The crux of the problem lies in defining what would be done once the deviant currency was identified. There existed three different interpretations: "consultation," "presumption of action," and "obligation of intervention." In practice, however, the presumption option differed very little from that of consultation, since the so-called presumption "would be open to discussion"(!).[2] The two extreme options were thus automatic intramarginal interventions and mere consultations. A further problem lay in the fact that the interval of time between triggering the warning system (and raising the question as to whether intramarginal interventions should be carried out) and reaching the limits of the parity grid (when the interventions were automatic) would often be extremely short. The operation of the divergence indicator had already largely been settled in Aachen between the French and German governments, however. The fact that the divergence indicator would not lead to automatic intramarginal interventions was a mere consequence of what had been stated in the Aachen memorandum of understanding: "The ECU might serve a useful purpose as an indicator of the need for intramarginal interventions, *after consultation*."[3] This wording was very careful and noncommittal.

Beyond the question of the predictability of their final outcome, these discussions underlined the continuing vividness of the economist versus monetarist debate. The position of the German government was economist, since it did not believe that problems related to internal economic weaknesses (if not mismanagement) could be solved by a monetary mechanism (the automaticity of intramarginal interventions). A side effect of this was that the German delegations always tended to stress their aim of protecting German economic and financial internal stability—*Modell Deutschland*—and thereby aroused some criticism, as has already been remarked in the previous chapters. This was again confirmed in late 1978. The British report of a session of the Monetary Committee Alternates thus points out the danger the German delegation faced by being so strict: "The Germans . . . especially when they get onto their persecution theme, 'You are sacrificing German internal stability on the altar of external monetary stability,' rightly get little sympathy."[4] Another criticism was that the German government's inflexibility obliged the other EEC member states willing to participate in a European monetary scheme to basically follow the German economic model. Healey thus noted that the German government's agreement on the concept of convergence existed "only if it meant that other Member States adapted to their policies and not vice-versa."[5] All these remarks, economic-technical as well as political-psychological, therefore contributed to widening the opposition in the negotiations between monetarists and economists.

Admittedly, however, the line between economists and monetarists was somewhat blurry. Those who supported automatic intramarginal interventions—who

were hence more monetarist—were also those who argued that transfers of resources were needed to help the convergence of economies, hence indirectly underlining a basic economist point. Healey made such an economist remark in the
cabinet: "It was impossible to have either a single European currency, or a fixed
exchange rate system, without similarity in economic performance which did
not prevail."[6] Yet the basic argument about the need for a *new* system—which
will be analyzed in more detail below—was in essence a monetarist one. Indeed,
stating—as Healey did in the 16 October Finance Council—that the snake was
not a system in which all members of the EEC could exist, was, in principle, a
monetarist point of view.[7] It purported that the EMS needed to be sufficiently
different from the snake to allow non-snake members to join, thereby meaning
that a monetary mechanism could be responsible for the (in)ability of a currency
to be part of it.

From the 18 September Finance Council, which adopted the parity-grid option, to the European Council in Brussels on 4 and 5 December, the technical
discussions carried on through the usual channels of the EEC specialized committees.[8] Besides the definition of the functioning of the divergence indicator,
the committees tackled the issue of the credit mechanisms and the width of the
fluctuation margins. The credit mechanisms of the EMS present a paradox. They
constitute one of the truly new features of the EMS compared to the snake (more
credit would be available), but gave birth to much less revealing (but more dauntingly complex) discussions, and can be much more easily summarized.[9] There
existed three types of credit: very short-term financing (unlimited credit available for thirty days, which the EMS augmented to forty-five days), short-term
monetary support (STMS), and medium-term financial assistance (MTFA). The
Bremen Annex stated that "an initial supply of ECUs (for use among Community central banks) will be created against deposit of US dollars and gold on the
one hand (e.g. 20% of the stock currently held by member central banks) and
member currencies on the other hand in an amount of comparable magnitude."
The German and Dutch governments argued that this amounted to a maximum
of 16 billion ECUs, while the other governments said it was 25 billion ECUs. The
reluctance naturally sprang from the fear that an increase in the size of credits
available would nurture inflation. A further question was how this credit should
be distributed between STMS and MTFA. The German officials rejected any increase in the MTFA, arguing that this would imply the devising of some new
piece of legislation. The ECOFIN meeting of 20 November settled in the main all
these issues, thanks to the eventual German acceptance of the 25 billion figure,
and managed to overcome the legal issue related to the MTFA.

The question of setting a wider fluctuation margin for the newcomers did not
really pose a problem. Such an option had actually been unequivocally set out

in the Bremen Annex. Paolo Baffi, the governor of the Banca d'Italia, could thus ask that, in concordance with the Bremen Annex, the lira would have a margin between 6 and 8 percent.[10] The only important aspect many governors stressed was that reference should not be made to the existence of two different fluctuation margins, but that the wider margins should be a temporary measure that should be narrowed down as soon as the economic situation permitted.[11] The 20 November Finance Council agreed that the width of the margin of fluctuation would be 2.25 percent, but that the current floaters could have a wider margin of up to 6 percent (but in effect concerned only Italy, which was the only country to request it).[12] This margin could be used from the outset, but could, in time, only be narrowed down (and not enlarged).

In contrast, the issue of the operation of the divergence indicator gave birth to much more problematic and lively discussions. Regarding the functioning of the divergence indicator, the idea was that the attainment of a minimum threshold of divergence would trigger intervention. As to the form these interventions would take, three options existed in the Monetary Committee. The "maximalist" one, supported by the British, Irish, and Italian delegations, envisaged automatic intramarginal interventions once the deviant currency was identified. The "minimalist" one, supported by the German, Dutch, and Danish delegations, was completely opposed to any form of automaticity of interventions. This stemmed from the fact that they considered the indicator insufficiently reliable, and hence refused any formal and binding obligation. The third, "compromise" option, defended by the Belgian, French, and Luxembourg delegations, suggested a mixture of consultations and automatic interventions, as well as the possibility to intervene in dollars. In that formula, the threshold could be fixed at 75 percent of its maximum fluctuation for each currency.

A central feature of the "symmetry of interventions" issue was that without such symmetry, the EMS currencies would basically be obliged to keep up with the DM. The EMS would hence be a DM-based more than ECU-based system. Imposing greater responsibility on the deviant currency—which had already been the basic rationale of the ECU-based system, although it might arguably have technically had the contrary effect—be it from strength or weakness, was the central idea of the divergence indicator. Yet the problem for the German government was quite obviously that the strength—and steady rise—of the DM was not due to the German economy only, but rather induced by the weakness of the dollar and the diversification of dollars into marks. The DM could thus often be identified as the deviant currency yet without being responsible for this deviance. While under the present scheme the burden of adjustment vis-à-vis the DM fell on the weaker currencies of the snake, similarly the German government did not want to take over the burden of adjustment in the EMS of the depreciation of the dollar. This was a sort of domino effect. And quite logically, no one wanted to bear the burden of an unwanted adjustment.

As much as during the debate about the choice between the ECU-based option and the parity grid, the position of the Bundesbank was strong and clear—and, as noticed in the previous chapter, arguably the single most important of all the actors involved in the EMS negotiations. On 5 October, the Zentralbankrat of the Bundesbank (and the representatives of the government, Matthöfer and Lahnstein) unanimously rejected the automaticity of intramarginal interventions.[13] The Zentralbankrat voted (eleven for, one against, four abstentions) the basis on which the EMS could be further discussed. Should this line of negotiation not be followed, then a new agreement between the government and the German central bank should be found again. Needless to say, this was hardly a welcome prospect for Schmidt. On 9 October, before the Committee of Governors, Emminger set out two important factors arguing against the automaticity of interventions: if the ECU was able to identify the deviant currency, it was not pointing at the real causes for this deviance; and early intramarginal interventions following erratic movements (due to speculation, for instance) would be useless.[14] Clappier and Richardson tried to defend the automaticity of interventions, principally by arguing that were the identification of a deviant currency only to lead to consultations, it was not necessary to build up such a barometer. Under the current system, any member already had the right, at any moment, to call for consultations. Lamfalussy suggested, as a compromise, introducing the "time factor" in the thinking on the divergence indicator. In other words, intramarginal interventions could be carried out only once a currency had diverged from its pivot rate for a "durable period." This would reduce the chance of overreacting to what might well be a simple erratic fluctuation. Yet the length of the "durable period" had yet to be determined.

The implications of setting a divergence indicator dominated the agenda of the Finance Council of 16 October in Brussels.[15] Strikingly, the two positions described as "extremes" during this Finance Council were the British and German ones. The French record, however, ironically noted that "the president of the Bundesbank, with his customary rigidity, claimed that he was not defending an extreme position."[16] Lautenschlager's account of the Finance Council was surprisingly positive in the sense that he stressed from the very beginning that the meeting took place "in a positive and open atmosphere."[17] Although the other accounts did not contradict this description, the sharp divergences of opinion between the participants hardly correspond to such a picture. Given the stark opposition of the different opinions, a number of participants logically called for a compromise. Monory claimed to defend a middle-way option, underlining the nonobligation of the interventions, but that if needed these interventions would be carried out as soon as possible. Ortoli and Geens also pleaded for a compromise, but the meeting ended in a deadlock.

Finding a way out of this deadlock before the Brussels European Council due to take place in early December was the task of the last Finance Council, on 20 November. An important but short meeting between Schmidt and Giscard (notably accompanied by Schulmann and Clappier), at the Élysée on 2 November, was sandwiched between the two Finance Councils.[18] Schmidt and Schulmann made it clear that they would not move on the divergence indicator, although the French delegation still seemed to hope to get through the "presumption of action."[19] The Schmidt-Giscard meeting on 2 November was thus in many respects a second "Aachen meeting," but without the mythology surrounding it. It indeed confirmed the trend discernible both in the technical discussion of the specialized committees and in the political discussions, and also confirmed that the EMS would be along the lines the Bundesbank wanted.

The sessions of the expert committees confirmed that the various positions were scarcely reconcilable. Discussion of the divergence indicator focused on the memorandum produced by the Belgian Central Bank. Emminger said that this memorandum "had even comforted him in his doubts about the usefulness and viability of such a system."[20] He then insisted that the ultimate decision could not be left to the finance ministers since it directly concerned central bank competencies. In addition, Emminger noted that the issue of the automaticity of intramarginal interventions resurfaced when discussing the width of the fluctuation margins: should the intramarginal interventions be made obligatory, an EMS with larger bands of fluctuations for the newcomers would become impossible. Such a problem would not arise if the crossing of the divergence threshold only implied consultations. Crucially (because he was the main ally of Emminger) Zijlstra also affirmed that he could accept the formula in its essentials. On 14 November, Clappier stressed the misgivings of the Banque de France on the five-working-days rule (the concrete consequence of Lamfalussy's remark about the "time factor"), according to which five working days of observation should occur between the alarm for the divergence indicator and the obligatory intervention.[21] Many simulations had shown, Clappier argued, that such a case would never happen, and that, as a consequence, intramarginal interventions would be even less frequent under the EMS than they were under the snake. The divergence indicator would thus not, in his view, fulfill its main objective of avoiding tensions with the monetary system. Clappier very much criticized the German note for not showing "any compromise effort."[22] Finally, the report of the Committee of Governors mentioned "an indicator of divergence based on the deviation of the daily value of the ECU expressed in each currency from the central rate."[23] The divergence threshold was to be fixed at 75 percent of the maximum theoretical spread for each currency, "for experimental purposes." Yet, as set out in more detail in the annex explaining the functioning of the divergence indicator, it seemed very likely to become a mere cosmetic arrangement: there was only "a presumption to act," and this presumption "would be open to discussion."[24]

The Finance Council meeting of 20 November in Brussels, unable to overcome the deadlock at which the expert committees had arrived, decided that the three options would be reported to the European Council.[25] The options remained the same, with the British and Italian governments defending the obligation of intervention, the German and Dutch the consultations only, and the four remaining EEC members the middle-way solution. The most striking event of this session actually did not directly concern the operation of the divergence indicator but rather Healey's criticism of the EMS negotiations, which will be analyzed in detail later in the chapter.

The Confirmation of the Centrality of the European Council

A second important aspect of the ongoing negotiations was that they further demonstrated the centrality of the European Council to the way in which the EEC work was organized. All the preparatory stages mentioned, relentlessly, that the preparatory work had to be ready before early December because the European Council had planned for a decision to be made at this session.[26] Accordingly, EEC committees, and crucially the Finance Council, often said that they ought to have ironed out divergences as much as possible so that the European Council could realistically make decisions on the remaining issues.[27] Not only was the agenda-setting dimension of the European Council respected but also the importance of *not* transforming it into a mere court of appeal for the other EEC institutions. It was hence particularly clear that the finance ministers and the various experts of the other committees were aware of the fact that they should, *during* the discussion, make real progress rather than simply passing on disagreements to the European Council. This stemmed from the fact that virtually all EEC governments (the British apart) genuinely wanted to reach an agreement in Brussels, and from the awareness that for the European Council to remain an efficient decision-making institution, it ought not to be overloaded with open questions that could have—and perhaps should have—been decided on earlier. The German presidency played a significant role in that it was consistently careful about narrowing down the options for consideration at the European Council.[28] The role of the European Council was to provide political leadership, a place for a free exchange of views between heads of state and government, and if need arose, an umpire, but certainly not a super Council of Ministers that, as Schmidt had put it, would do the homework left out by the ministers.

Narrowing down the technical options had the side effect of further revealing the political substance of the initiative. Confronted with a deadlock, many policymakers stressed the political dimension of the problem, and thereby indirectly the role of the European Council in making the final decisions. During the 16 October session of the Finance Council, Pandolfi and Colley both underlined that "the system must extend a welcome to all member states and this on a permanent basis. The problem is now political."[29] Even more telling was Monory's intervention, in which he "proposed to address himself principally to the political problem because, at a technical level, a reconciliation of the opposing views represented by Germany on the one hand and the United Kingdom on the other seemed unlikely. . . . An endless technical debate with no prospect of agreement was not what the heads of state had in mind at Bremen. . . . The Community must show itself capable of a political solution embracing all member states."[30] A couple of further points underlined the importance gained by the European Council and the questions raised by its role in EEC decision making. During the Brussels European Council, Callaghan (supported later by Thorn) started out his intervention by noting that, in order to respect the powers of the British Parliament, he would ask to replace the sentence "the European Council decided" by "agreed as follows."[31] An earlier cabinet meeting, on 26 October, had raised similar questions about the role of the European Council: "The procedure by which the EMS proposal had been developed also merited discussion. It had originated in a Franco/German initiative and there seemed to have been a commitment in principle at the European Council. This raised questions both of collective Cabinet responsibility and of the role of the European Council under the Rome Treaty. The constitutional implications of any limitation on the Government's freedom to decide its exchange rate policy would also need to be considered."[32] Discussion of the role of the European Council was not limited to Britain. A number of French MPs had argued that the EMS would have been instituted by a treaty signed without respecting the constitution of the French Fifth Republic. The French Conseil constitutionnel replied on 29 December that the European Council did not make decisions but reached political agreements. The Conseil constitutionnel explained that

> by a resolution on 5 December 1978, the European Council has planned for the creation of a European monetary system . . . and has outlined its broad orientations; this resolution constitutes a declaration of a political character and not . . . a treaty or an international agreement having by itself legal effect. . . . following this resolution it is the responsibility of the European Economic Community's authorities and, should the case arise, the national authorities to take the necessary measures to the

establishment of a new European monetary system within the framework of their respective competencies and according to the appropriate rules.[33]

Yet, if legally contentious, the European Council's impact was even more ambiguous with regard to public opinion, as I will show in the conclusions to this book.

The Lost Quest for a Genuinely New Exchange Rate Mechanism?

A third important way to see the discussions over the operation of the divergence indicator is by taking into account the issue of the novelty of the EMS. The question of the novelty of the system—or, the other way around, the absence of novelty in the system—was a perennial theme in the negotiations, considerably reinforced after the confirmation of the parity-grid system. The crucial point was that if the new system were indistinguishable from the snake, it would simply raise the question as to how Britain, France, Ireland, and Italy would now be able to join.[34] After arguing for years that the snake system was intrinsically flawed, the four non-snake members would indeed be in trouble explaining their sudden miraculous joining of the EMS. And it became particularly vivid as of late September–early October when the defenders of the ECU-based system (with the exception of two ambiguous cases, the French and Belgian governments) realized that the divergence indicator, and the way in which it would operate, was the last opportunity for them to truly bring an innovation into the exchange rate system.[35]

The issue of novelty could be observed at all levels. The report of the Committee of Governors on the EMS clearly stated that "the exchange rate system *would differ from that of the 'snake'* through the addition of an indicator of divergence."[36] The Banca d'Italia similarly stated, in its "Blueprint for the EMS," that were the alarm of the divergence indicator to be ineffective, "the new system would be no more than an extension of today's Snake."[37] Another case in point was that the debate during the 16 October Finance Council seemed much more lively than the discussion about parity-grid versus ECU-based systems in the previous Finance Council.[38] Very strikingly, a number of conflicts of interest and interpretation, hitherto latent, came out into the open, as it was the last chance to devise a system truly different from that of the snake.[39] Colley, for instance, explained that "it was quite clear that the Snake was incapable in its present form of containing all member states. . . . If the new system did not differ from the Snake, it had achieved nothing."[40] In a meeting with Schmidt in Bonn on 27 October, Jenkins similarly stressed that the EMS should be something more than merely an enlarged snake.[41] This would require some movement of the Germans notably on the question of the automaticity of intramarginal interventions. Yet Schmidt stated that he would not move one iota from his position. On another occasion, when directly asked by Callaghan whether the EMS was a snake in disguise, Jenkins's reply was characteristically unconvincing: "On any examination the EMS was very much more than the snake. It had great potentialities, in particular the use of large reserves."[42] He did not mention any other difference—there was actually no other real difference—and it was hardly a big one, at least certainly not one that should have implied such a long negotiation stretching over a whole year. And indeed, during the Schmidt-Jenkins meeting mentioned earlier, the German chancellor stressed the absence of originality of the technical discussions, as well as the fact that their outcome was largely predictable.[43] He thus remarked that the negotiations had lasted seven months and "that was seven months too long. In the past such issues had been settled in a couple of days."[44] Concerning the divergence indicator, Schmidt explained to the Bundesbank that it

> emerged first of all . . . as French-invented—now again I say something that may not be made public—*façon de parler*, swimming trunks, make-up, since the French are entering for the third time into a European monetary alliance that they have already twice left, and they very much wanted to demonstrate . . . that it is not the same as what they have already twice left. That is actually how this whole basket originally came about.[45]

Finally, during the Brussels European Council itself, Giscard stressed the novelty of the scheme under consideration. He insisted that the wording of the draft resolution's passage regarding the operation of the divergence indicator was not semantic but had a central character: "Shall we content ourselves with extending the snake system or do we want more? As it has already been understood that the EMS would be more than the snake, one must explicitly provide for interventions."[46] An option that would not be followed.

Schmidt's Technical Understanding with the Bundesbank, but Political Understanding with Giscard

Schmidt's and Giscard's differing interpretations of the role of the divergence indicator underline the fact that, beyond public affirmations of a common Franco-German vision, the French president and the German chancellor did not automatically share the same monetary thinking. As the Commission president said to Callaghan, "The extent of the agreement between Chancellor Schmidt and President Giscard was less than it might appear: the only thing on which they were wholly agreed was the necessity that they should agree."[47] Tellingly, Renato Ruggiero, the undersecretary for community affairs at the Farnesina, reported the following to the British ambassador: "As for the 'alarm bell concept,' he [Schmidt] described this as stupid and incomprehensible. He could not understand Giscard's idea of placing the ECU at the center of the system but had to include a reference in the Bremen communiqué to please the French."[48] A note of the SGCI similarly recognized that "from a technical viewpoint," French positions remained closer to the British ones than to the German ones.[49] What made the Franco-German initiative so strong was therefore certainly not its technical understanding but rather its political underpinnings, shared by the French and German leaders, and stressed at length by Schmidt during the Bundesbank's central council of 30 November.

The first visit of a German chancellor to the Bundesbank's central council since Adenauer in October 1950 constituted the only—secret—moment when the German chancellor had to provide a coherent analysis of the place of the EMS initiative in the overall framework of German foreign policy.[50] And thanks to the existence of a full verbatim of this meeting, it is possible to witness Schmidt's (and the Bundesbank's members') reasoning, in a frank, nondiplomatic fashion. For while it was both technically unimportant and symbolically and politically crucial, this meeting should be seen as the ultimate confirmation that the EMS was fundamentally an unoriginal technical step (marked by a strong Schmidt-Bundesbank understanding) but a tremendously important political one (marked by a strong Schmidt-Giscard understanding). The significance of Schmidt's appearance at the Bundesbank rests in the German chancellor's confirmation that the German central bank would not be bound by the EMS to carry out unlimited interventions in support of other EEC currencies. The very first topic of discussion concerned the possibility of parity changes and of leaving the system (and the legal enshrinement of this). The discussion was overall slightly specious, Schmidt sometimes even simply replying that it was "self-evident" that parity correction could occur. The fear of some members was even manifestly so exaggerated that Emminger himself intervened to say that "the changing of central rates is already expressly mentioned in the Bremen communiqué."[51] Schmidt gave the example of the DM floating in 1973 as a historical precedent. But even more telling was the other example he provided about the unimportance of not legally enshrining the possibility to leave the system: "The French too have not written out in the Treaty of Rome that, if we get violently annoyed with the EC all of a sudden, we won't take part in meetings of the Council of Ministers anymore, but they have done it." The empty chair crisis thus ironically became a convincing example for furthering European integration by joining the EMS! Schmidt notably took away absolutely any significance to the EEC scheme by saying not only that the DM could leave the EMS when it would have to but also—and even more strikingly—that the "when" would be decided at the discretion of the Bundesbank. On the more specific question of the operation of the divergence indicator Schmidt and Emminger manifestly shared their opposition to automatic interventions.

An even more significant feature of this Bundesbank's central council lay in Schmidt's presentation of the political dimension of the EMS. Schmidt is quite famous for his "monetary policy is foreign policy" saying, which he did not fail to repeat in Frankfurt. Schmidt began his speech by mentioning the reasons why a European initiative was necessary. The first reason he gave was the need to save the Common Market, the unraveling of which he said may endanger EEC political cohesion—a particularly unwelcome outcome in the course of the cold war. Another significant part of Schmidt's speech was an analysis of the consequences of *Modell Deutschland*, that is, the German example of (economic and monetary) stability. While he argued that the United States did not follow it, he stressed that the German model had now found some echo in France. Another consequence was the need for the German government to have "a European mantle" hiding its political and economic success:

> The more successful we are in the areas of foreign policy, economic policy, socioeconomic matters, and military matters, the longer it will be until Auschwitz sinks into history. . . . It is all the more necessary for us to clothe ourselves in this European mantle. We need this mantle not only to cover our foreign policy nakednesses, like Berlin or Auschwitz, but we need it also to cover these ever-increasing relative strengths, economic, political, military, of the German Federal Republic within the West.

Finally, the German chancellor once more raised the importance of trust, particularly salient since the coming to power of Giscard and Schmidt in 1974. He did so not only in a positive way (his trust of Giscard and Barre) but also in a negative one (his mistrust of Mitterrand).

Schmidt therefore did not really *convince* the Bundesbank. Admittedly, most points in the negotiations had already been agreed on, and, since the Bundesbank was independent, a speech by the German chancellor, however bright and convincing he might be, was unlikely to change the course of the story and win the support of the German central bank at the very last minute. Crucially, Schmidt was as convinced as the Bundesbank of the technical risks of the EMS (be it dubbed "Community of inflation" or "Community of deflation"). True, it could be said that Schmidt had to play the role, before Bundesbank's central council, of a strict anti-inflationary chancellor. But this was not an invented role. The

German chancellor who spoke before the Bundesbank's central council was the same German chancellor who had defended stability on various occasions from 1974 until the start of talks about European monetary reform. One just needs to recall Schmidt stressing at the 1976 Luxembourg European Council that exchange rates are a consequence of an economic policy, and that trying to correct budgetary mistakes by a monetary phenomenon was akin to working on a symptom rather than the cause,[52] to realize his deep understanding with Emminger, who declared in a public speech in Baden Baden on 21 October: "The most important thing is rather that in all participating countries an economic and monetary policy is followed that lets the existing exchange rate relations appear credible. All the rest is an attempt to cure the symptoms and to plaster over the real divergences with loans."[53] In his public discourse, Schmidt could not, however, for quite obvious political reasons, return to his earlier skeptical remarks about European monetary cooperation. Yet the technical content was the same: opposition to automatic interventions and stress put on economic convergence. The only—crucial—difference was the economic and political context that had changed and had made a new initiative, in his eyes, necessary.

I have, I hope, given a clear and coherent picture of the issues at stake. Yet it should not be overlooked that this debate, while as technical as the earlier one about the basics of the exchange rate mechanism, was this time scarcely intelligible if not, at times, specious. Indeed, although extremely technical, some of the issues involved can quickly be summarized (the credit mechanisms, for instance), and some discussions confined to the speciousness or the blurring of the references to such an extent that the overall debate progressively seemed to lose any coherence. For instance, both economists and monetarists were aware that each other's arguments were sound to some extent. A case in point was the discussions about the operation of the divergence indicator. Not only was the whole expert discussion between "obligation," "presumption of obligation," "presumption of action," and "obligation of consultation" in the end scarcely intelligible, but even more important was that how the wording differences between the various options could be translated into technical deeds was hardly identifiable. Another illustration of the complexity of the issues under examination came from the British Embassy in the Netherlands, which asked for a "child's guide" to the technical issues then being discussed.[54] If one cannot expect all the diplomatic staff to have a good grasp of the technical issues, it shows at least that these issues were difficult to understand, even for the people taking part in the negotiations. The meeting of the EEC heads of government in Brussels in December will be another case in point, yet this time much more problematic. A second important reason why the debate became scarcely intelligible in the final run-up to the Brussels European Council was more political. Indeed, in the background lay a myriad of interlinked questions. If Britain opted out, would Ireland join? If Ireland and Italy joined, would Britain also feel obliged to join? If Italy and Ireland could not participate, would France join at all? And if France were the only non-snake member to join, would it mean the failure from the start of the EMS? The sense of a potential domino effect was thus so strong that it seemed difficult to answer one question without having ten others immediately raised. Yet of all these parameters, only one seemed, as I have shown, unlikely to change, and that was the inflexibility of the German delegation. Its perennial work toward removing any practical consequences to the identification of a deviant currency under the operation of the divergence indicator manifestly worried the non-snake members, the French government apart. The technical discussions had therefore strong political consequences, which will now be examined in detail.

A Difficult Enlargement

In this section I will delve into the cases of three individual member states: Britain, Italy, and Ireland.

Aiming at a "Soft Landing": The British Case

The diplomatic and psychological dimensions of the Aachen agreement—the British government had been bypassed at the EEC level by a bilateral agreement—are presented in detail by Peter Ludlow.[55] Yet the crux of the problem was somewhat more technical: the British government had been "abandoned" by the main supporter (and best ally) in the defense of the ECU-based system.[56] Three options, supported by the British government, sought to achieve "symmetry." A first one was through the establishment of an ECU-based monetary system. Once this option had been ruled out, a second surfaced, in the form of the divergence indicator. A third option, discussed in parallel but without more success, was that of the concurrent studies. In October, two of the three options (ECU-based and concurrent studies) had already been ruled out in spirit if not formally. Hence, in technical terms, the hopes of the British government for a genuinely new EMS, different from the snake and more "symmetrical," were severely lessened by the French U-turn following the Franco-German agreement at Aachen. And this is the very reason why the discussion about the divergence indicator—although in a sense absolutely hopeless following the Aachen secret memorandum of understanding—revived such lively debates: it represented, for the British government in particular, the very last chance for devising a genuinely new, and, it was hoped, more symmetrical monetary system. At odds with German monetary thinking and having lost its best ally in the negotiations, the British government thus found itself completely isolated in the EEC.

The British government's isolation also corresponded to an uneasy domestic position. The EMS negotiations had not come at an opportune time, both for electoral reasons and for strategic economic reasons exposed in chapter 6. But even though the scrutiny of various types of discussions, both within the British government and at the EEC level, has shown that there was little mystery that the British government would not join the EMS, London remarkably managed to maintain an aura of ambiguity about its eventual decision. On many occasions, a not insignificant number of officials involved in the EMS negotiations seemed to have genuinely believed that the British government might well join the EMS. The British government was impressively consistent in claiming in public discourse, and even sometimes private, that it might enter the EMS if the terms were right.[57] As of late November, however, the British government's discourse changed when it became quite obvious that it would not participate in the EMS. Healey's last declaration during the 20 November Finance Council was thus particularly negative.[58] Healey's attitude contrasted greatly with that of the other eight ministers, and was obviously interpreted as preparing the way for the announcement of British nonparticipation in the EMS. In the main, he had spoken in the same terms in an early meeting prior to the Finance Council on 20 November with Pandolfi and Colley.[59] This early meeting revealed a spectacular difference in the approach to the negotiations between the three. There were still, quite obviously, considerable common interests between the three delegations. Yet while Healey stressed that "progress since Bremen had so far been inadequate," and at no point mentioned the importance of reaching an agreement at the European Council a few weeks later, the Italian and Irish finance ministers did. Both Colley and Pandolfi explained that they did not favor postponing the decision on the EMS, preferring instead to make compromises to get further progress. The green paper on the EMS, presented by Healey to the British Parliament three days later on 24 November, contained no surprises, and was mainly designed to inform MPs and public opinion.[60] It recalled that the British government approved the quest for European monetary stability, and that whatever its decision on the EMS, the British government would remain committed to it. Finally, on 30 November, the cabinet agreed on the so-called half-way house, namely, that Britain would not join the exchange rate mechanism but would maintain an "open door" for later participation, and would not obstruct the establishment and development of the scheme.[61] Callaghan then formally wrote to his European counterparts to inform them that he "was doubtful whether it will be possible for us to take part in an exchange rate mechanism on these lines."[62]

Peter Ludlow mentions an article in *The Guardian* by Peter Jenkins stating that Callaghan arrived at his decision not to participate in the EMS on the weekend of 8 October.[63] There is little reason to doubt this report, although it might be asked whether Callaghan had ever seriously considered participating in the EMS in the first place. As chapter 6 has shown, Callaghan, from very early on, did not seem genuinely interested in a European monetary scheme. Regarding the date itself, no archival source is able to confirm or contradict this timing. What British archival documents do show, however, is that Callaghan concluded a meeting on 10 October—thereby fitting Peter Jenkins's timeframe—by saying that participation in a scheme like the EMS, as it was then taking shape, was not in the British interests, but that for tactical reasons the British negotiators should continue to take part in the discussions.[64] Logically, as of mid-October, a so-called soft-landing approach started being devised in the Treasury—thereby confirming that the turning point in the British government's decision occurred during the first half of October. At the very moment of Callaghan's visit to Bonn, the idea emerged of an alternative British initiative imagined by Couzens.[65] On 23 October, a note from Couzens to Healey openly envisaged British nonparticipation in the EMS and examined how to operate a "soft landing."[66] The initiative was meant to be launched between mid-November and the Brussels European Council of 4 December.

The details of the proposal as well as the points made by Couzens to justify it further confirmed the probability of British nonparticipation in the EMS. The proposal, modest and largely procedural, was meant to encourage three types of action: action for economic growth, action to counter inflation, and action to make the Community budget contribute to convergence (i.e., a continuation of the concurrent studies). The aims behind Couzens's idea of a "soft landing" are quite self-explanatory. In the event of nonparticipation in the EMS, he wanted to minimize the risks to the pound exchange rate and to avoid British isolation in the EEC. It was also meant to counter the risk that British foreign policy would be described as reluctantly European by setting out a constructive policy, as well as prolonging the case for more economic convergence. Healey endorsed the idea for such an initiative, and minuted Callaghan on 25 October. Various internal notes showed that the British government did not think of this plan as a pathbreaking initiative, however. The most telling reaction was that of Owen, who commented, "No objection, but hardly a major initiative. I would not wish to become too enthusiastic."[67] It is hence not surprising to see that, during an informal discussion outside a meeting of the EEC foreign ministers in Gymnich on 28 and 29 October, when Jenkins asked Owen about British participation in the EMS, the British secretary of state replied that "although a participation from the beginning was not excluded, it seemed unlikely."[68]

The month of November confirmed that the trend discerned in October was a consistent one. In presenting a memorandum on the EMS to the cabinet on 2 November, Healey explained that "there was a growing feeling that unless there was a substantial shift in the rigid German position in the coming weeks, it would be a mistake for Britain to join the EMS."[69] In a note to Callaghan on 13 November, Healey directly addressed, for the first time, the problem of deciding on a plan "for dealing with a situation in which the Cabinet decides that we should not enter the proposed exchange rate mechanisms of the EMS when they first come into operation."[70] This document reused many points made by Butler (who had been among those more in favor of the Bremen endeavor) in an earlier note on 15 November.[71] It principally summed up the various tactical points that had been under discussion for a few months in the British administration. The only open question was that of the timing for the announcement: before or right after the European Council. More puzzling was the sentence "We should also pre-empt any leak about our decision," which gives the impression that Healey believed that the British government's claim that no decision had yet been reached was not questioned.[72] The puzzle lies in the fact that, from an outsider's perspective (the EEC member states and EEC institutions, that is), the British final decision had been in little doubt for quite a while.

As early as the very beginning of October, a rumor circulated that Owen had told French foreign minister Louis de Guiringaud that there was no prospect of Britain joining the EMS at the end of the year (which naturally Owen refuted).[73] While it is impossible to verify this rumor, it must be noted that it would make sense regarding the timing of Callaghan's own decision. A few days later, the French report of the Finance Council of 16 October did not seem to be very naive about the British stance either.[74] Similarly, in a meeting with Jenkins on 27 October, Schmidt said that if he had to make a guess, he thought that seven and a half EEC members would join the EMS (the half being Italy because of its wider margins!). His assumption was hence that the British government would not join,[75] an assumption widely shared in Brussels, according to Donald Maitland, British permanent representative to the EEC.[76] Although dated from 10 November, his letter used the example of his conversation with Jenkins on 3 November, during which the president of the Commission told him that he thought there was only a "30% chance" that the British government would join. Yet it is still fascinating that it was the consistent strategy of absolutely each and every British official, despite these rumors, to carry on saying that no decision had yet been made by the British government.[77] This pretense of ambivalence might have worked at the very least to keep everyone in a state of suspense. A case in point was Schulmann, who was surprisingly categorical in a note of mid-October to Schmidt where he stated that Callaghan and Healey had already made the political decision to join the EMS.[78] Yet Schulmann's remark arguably represented the exception proving a rule that can be summarized by two dates: February 1978, when Callaghan reacted with skepticism to Schmidt's proposal for furthering European monetary cooperation; and mid-October, when both the British prime minister and crucially the Treasury started sketching out plans for a "soft landing," thereby acknowledging that Britain would not join the EMS.

A Strong Political Commitment, but Many Economic Uncertainties: The Italian and Irish Cases

In contrast to the British case, there was little doubt about the Irish and Italian political eagerness to join the EMS. And that both the Italian and Irish governments were openly politically committed to the EMS made it naturally much easier for the French, and most important for the German government to be ready to make concessions to them rather than to the British government. In addition to this, both the Italian and Irish governments (as much as the French) seemed resigned to accept the DM dominance in the system.

The political interest of the Italian government in the EMS was clear. In his diary, Baffi wrote as early as 2 November that "Andreotti wants to enter in the EMS also without England" (an opinion he disagreed with).[79] If this could not certainly predict the final outcome of the negotiations, it still gives a clear indication of the Italian prime minister's intentions. In addition to this, the Italian government had undertaken, with the Pandolfi plan, a series of economic measures aimed at EMS membership, as I showed in the previous chapter. The Italian monetary interest in joining the EMS was to restore confidence in the lira and, even more than in the French case, to provide an external anchor to domestic stability-oriented economic policies. Belonging both to the EEC and to the most industrialized nations was also a political imperative. The negotiations up until the Brussels European Council confirmed these trends. Yet naturally the Italian government could not enter the EMS at any price. As a consequence, regarding the question of entry to the EMS from the start, the main issues were that of the width of the bands of fluctuations together with that of the transfer of resources to be obtained from the concurrent studies, and of the automaticity of intramarginal interventions in the operation of the divergence indicator. A series of bilateral contacts underlined these points. A meeting of Pandolfi, Baffi, Matthöfer, and Emminger on 16 and 17 October in Frankfurt underscored this,[80] as well a couple of crucial meetings of the Italian government with the French and German governments, respectively on 25–26 October in Rome,[81] and on 1–2 November in Siena.[82] All of these meetings helped in trying to convince the Italian government to join the EMS, in particular by showing the Franco-German attention to the Italian case.

The main consequence of these meetings was the progressive substitution of the request for "automatic intramarginal interventions" for that for wider fluctuation margins. After the 16–17 October meeting with the German monetary authorities, it must have become clear to the Italian side that there was not much to be hoped for from the divergence indicator. This is the reason why the option of wider fluctuation margins gained more centrality in the EMS negotiations from an Italian point of view, since it was the only possible option left to the Italian government to get the "special treatment" it needed. It was, moreover, an option enshrined without ambiguity in the Bremen Annex.[83] Hence, according to Schulmann, the main result of the Siena talks had been a "snake with two skins"—in other words, the current snake plus a new, more flexible, margin of fluctuation.[84] The most important demand made by Baffi was indeed for a fluctuation margin of 6 to 8 percent (and closer to 8 than to 6).[85] It must be noted, however, that the German government accepted this, although Schmidt himself clearly doubted that this measure was in the Italian interest.[86] The main reason for this doubt was the fear that it would arouse speculation against a currency—the lira—clearly labeled by this wider margin as the weakest one. "The dilemma for us," Baffi explained, "is between that which is politically unacceptable (special status) and that which is economically unacceptable (a too-narrow band)."[87] As a consequence, the wider band would be an integral part of the system. Interestingly, the *problématique* of setting wider fluctuation bands for newcomers was in a sense equivalent to the spirit of Fourcade's "waiting room" idea, Duisenberg's target zones, or van Ypersele's plan, and of course, most important, Rinaldo Ossola's idea for concerted floating discussed in chapter 2, further underlining that the 1978 discussions did not emerge ex nihilo, but were instead part of wider perennial issues.

The Irish case was slightly different in that the Irish government attached less importance to the exchange rate system than to the concurrent studies. The Irish government did not want wider fluctuation bands like the Italian government (it thought, like Schmidt for Italy, that it would designate the pound as a weak currency and therefore as a target for speculation) and seemed slightly fatalistic regarding the issue of the automaticity of intramarginal interventions. By contrast, it hoped to get some transfer of resources through the concurrent studies. Indeed, Ireland was the weakest of all EEC member states; about half of Irish exports went to the UK, and about a quarter to the other EEC members.[88] The Irish government asked for a transfer of 200 million UCE per year for five years (about 6% of the Irish GNP), in the form of budgetary transfers rather than interest rate subsidies. The EMS would therefore provide (as much as for the Italian and French governments) an economic anchor for the Irish government's effort directed at economic stability, as well as a political one. Charles Murray, the governor of the Central Bank of Ireland, supported EMS entry, regardless of the British decision: "The economic environment has altered greatly since the passing of the Currency Act of 1927 and the EMS would be more in accord than the sterling link with Ireland's present and prospective economic circumstances."[89] Where the Irish case was similar to the Italian one was in that it had a strong political commitment, in principle, to the EMS. Colley was, for instance, clearly seeing the EMS as an important step promoting European cooperation, and potentially leading to EMU. The visit by Monory to Dublin on 6 November,[90] and by Colley to Bonn on 9 November, underlined all these points very clearly.[91] There was particularly no doubt that were the British government to join, the Irish government would follow suit. In the case where the British government would decide against entry in the EMS, the problem for the Irish was not so much to make the decision of breaking with the pound, but rather to face the consequences of this break. The Brussels European Council would clarify these issues.

The Concurrent Studies: Deadlock and Ticking Time Bomb

The discussion about the concurrent studies before the Brussels European Council confirmed the trend, already discerned in late September, of an insurmountable deadlock. For while at their start the principle of such discussions was an interesting and genuinely new event, they considerably lost their relevance in the course of the following months.[92] The main feature of these discussions lay in the fact that their deadlock progressively transformed itself into a ticking bomb likely to explode during the Brussels European Council, since some countries directly linked their participation in the EMS to the granting of a transfer of resources.

The EPC meeting on 2 October rather unpromisingly opened with an introductory statement made by Tietmeyer, who said that the Council had not given really clear guidelines to the EPC, "except to keep slogging away."[93] The Irish and Italian delegations (supported by the British one) stressed that work on the concurrent studies should carry on so that they could genuinely be concurrent with the exchange rate system negotiations, and that a decision could be reached in Brussels at the European Council.[94] Tietmeyer agreed to this, but it is important to recall that Jenkins and some heads of government, Schmidt in particular, did not seem to think so. The British, Italian, and Irish requests—EIB loan subsidies and a transfer of resources, notably through the regional fund—remained similar to those set out in the preceding chapter. The position of the British government was, again, the most complex overall.[95] It had indeed three ambitions: it aimed at stressing the equal urgency of work on the concurrent studies and on the EMS; it wanted to be able to secure any transfer of resources even if it were not to participate in the EMS; and finally, it wanted to avoid suggesting that the implications of a new exchange rate system were the sole motivation for the British government to ask for a correction of EEC redistributive policies—when in fact, as in the case of the budget, this was instead a perennial theme. The British position on the concurrent studies also grew increasingly different from the Irish and Italian positions. The British delegation stressed even more its concern over the British net contribution to the budget as well as CAP reform. Ortoli expressed his concern to some British officials about their stance, and the fact that it tended to hinder progress in the EPC.[96] The rest of the meeting was a discussion of each and every paragraph of the EPC report, which confirmed the broad lines of division within the Committee, with, on the one hand, the Italian, Irish, and British delegations asking for substantial transfer of resources since, they argued, belonging to the EMS would pose certain economic difficulties; and on the other hand, EEC member states (led by the German delegation), who were reluctant about (if not outright opposed to) any transfer of resources.

The French and German governments maintained a minimalist interpretation of the help to be provided through the concurrent studies. The position of the French government was to exclude the British government from the additional measures and to limit those granted to the Irish and Italian governments to a simple mechanism of interest rate subsidy.[97] Schmidt similarly mentioned, during the 30 November meeting of the Bundesbank's central council, that the two ways to get Ireland on board the EMS would be, in small part, with help from the regional fund, and in large part, through EIB loans.[98] Similarly, in a call to Healey, Lahnstein expected that the outcome of the concurrent studies would be confined to interest rate subsidies for EIB bank loans to the Irish and Italian governments.[99] An important question linked to the concurrent studies was how to keep the potential non-EMS members from benefiting from the transfer of resources. While the French and German governments shared this opinion, Crispin Tickell, Jenkins's chef de cabinet, did not. He stressed that the mechanisms devised in the framework of the concurrent studies should have a Community character, especially because members who were not participants from the outset "might thereby find it easier to [join] later on."[100] Meanwhile, it should also be noted that Jenkins remained, as he had been in August and September, quite strikingly cynical and pessimistic about the concurrent studies. He thus openly doubted that the issues could be settled before the December European Council, and said to Frans Andriessen, Dutch minister of finance, that what was needed "was some measure of reassurance that their [the less prosperous countries'] problems would be dealt with in due course."[101] From the less prosperous countries' point of view, this was hardly a promising perspective.

The EPC met again on 26 and 27 October.[102] The British record of the meeting mentioned the deadlock reached in the discussion. It noted, for instance, that the only way to complete a final report would be to make open reference to the differences of opinion in the form of statements by "some members" and "other members." The final report of the EPC, issued on 13 November, accordingly set out in detail the deadlock of the discussions.[103] It thus stated that "some members regard an increased transfer of financial resources as absolutely essential if all Member States are to join and remain permanent members of the EMS," while "the majority of members is inclined to the view that no extensive additional budgetary transfers are necessary to underpin the stability and durability of the EMS." The eventual decision was left to the highest political level. The report concluded with, "If measures for the reinforcement of the economies of the less prosperous member countries are to become speedily effective . . . then, having regard to the time necessary to draw the measures up, quick political decisions will be necessary." The Finance Council on 20 November confirmed that any decision was left to the European Council.[104] Colley, Pandolfi, and Healey argued again for the need to strengthen weaker economies in the context of the inception of the EMS, while, by contrast, Monory and Andriessen rejected that resource transfers be linked with the EMS. Decisions and commitments were thus left for the Brussels European Council, the main task of which would thus be to try defusing this ticking time bomb.

The Brussels European Council and the Delayed Launching of the EMS, December 1978–March 1979

The prospects of the European Council were, as a consequence, quite uncertain. While the political will to reach an agreement was—Britain apart—clear, and while the preparatory work had been completed according to the timetable set out at Bremen, the technical issue at stake (the operation of the divergence indicator, and thereby the question of devising a truly new mechanism) and, even more crucially, the issue of the concurrent studies were not settled—and were likely to pose a problem in actually endangering the creation of the EMS. This session should be seen as the ultimate illustration that the EMS negotiations had started to evolve in two virtually separate circles. Some heads of government— Schmidt in particular—never meant to accept automatic interventions under the operation of the divergence indicator, and did not want to give much thought to

the concurrent studies—while all these topics were precisely still being negotiated (and causing trouble) in the specialized committees. The two most contentious topics were the CAP (and more precisely the MCAs) and the concurrent
studies. The couple of records that are available confirm Giscard's surprising
intransigence (but cannot, of course, verify whether his "bluntness bordered on
rudeness"),[105] but also underline that of Schmidt.[106]

The first topic of discussion of the 4 December session was of course the
EMS. Schmidt suggested a *tour de table* at which each head of government would
present his position. Andreotti insisted again on the political importance of the
EMS scheme, both for the EEC and in the view of his own government. Giscard's behavior was by contrast more puzzling. His very first contribution, on a
topic—monetary stability—he had been supporting for a number of years, and
which might at last allow some concrete result, was to stress that ECU, when written in French, and in the plural, would end in an *s*: *Ecus*.[107] He then elaborated
more generally on the symbolic importance of the ECU—particularly because
of the historical parallel with a former French currency—and the political dimension of an agreement on the EMS. After a few other technical remarks, he
then came to the relationship between the EMS and the CAP. He said that it was
abnormal for MCAs to continue being used in the exchanges of member states
participating to the EMS. They should progressively be eliminated. Then, after
Schmidt's presentation of the German position, Giscard came back again to the
same point about MCAs. Once this first *tour de table* ended, the discussion came
to an analysis, point by point, of the draft resolution. Andreotti raised the question of what would happen were a member state's parliament to decide against
entry into the EMS. Schmidt replied (and no one objected) that this would create
a serious crisis and that this would call for an emergency meeting of the European Council. This point not only confirmed that the European Council was a
central institution of the EEC but also stressed what would often be the case in
the future, namely, that dealing with a "no" was unplanned for. Discussion of the
operation of the divergence indicator did not provide many new insights, nor did
it bring about any change of attitude among participants. Schmidt, in the after-
dinner session, concluded that no delegation had asked for a modification of the
CAP, and deduced from this that the MCAs would not immediately be affected
by the implementation of the EMS. Giscard surprisingly did not react, and the
discussion finally ended on a new unproductive exchange about the operation of
the divergence indicator. This certainly sprang from the fact that everybody had
understood that Schmidt—and, to a lesser extent, the other snake members—
would not move one iota on this issue. Two other factors were that the session
lasted a long time, ending late at night (at one o'clock in the morning, according
to the *procès-verbal*, two o'clock according to Jenkins[108]), and that most of the

participants had, according to Tickell, "at best an uncertain grasp of the issues under discussion."[109] And it is noticeable that Schmidt voluntarily started off the meeting with complex technical issues—"a long, grinding niggle . . . dealing almost entirely with the internal mechanics of the EMS" according to Jenkins[110]—and probably managed to reach an agreement by intimidating his counterparts. As Tickell concluded: "The result, which was predictable and predicted, could have been reached in a third of the time."[111]

The session on 5 December turned to the concurrent studies. Although it may appear quite trivial, it should not be forgotten that the previous session had ended around one o'clock in the morning, and that this session started at ten, with, according to Tickell, "many of the participants sleepy and cross."[112] To this should be added, again, the complexity inherent in the topic under consideration, and that it was clear that the major point of difficulty would be the concurrent studies, which were the topic of discussion on this morning. In the morning session, Callaghan made his point about the need for a truly redistributive dimension of the EEC budget and criticized the current situation where two of the poorest member states—Italy and Britain—were net contributors to the EEC budget. Andreotti and then Lynch also summed up the already well-known position of their governments. The first reply to these requests came from Giscard. He explained that transfer of resources may only concern the members participating in the EMS, and that in this regard, the French government may benefit from them. He rejected the possibility of increasing aid from the regional fund. The only element he could accept was EIB interest rate subsidies. Schmidt followed suit and explained that he could not make any further concession. He even (curiously, considering what he had said earlier in the year) said that it would be easier if not more efficient for the German government to govern its currency alone rather than trying to make efforts in a Community context. Making further concessions, he argued, would deprive the German government of any interest in participating to the EMS. Hence, if Giscard's intransigence might have seemed surprising, or might have bordered even on rudeness, the most crucial element was, once more, Schmidt's change of mind. The German chancellor had been at the very source of the discussion about a new monetary scheme, and the voicing of his disappointment, up to declaring that his "interest in this whole operation [the EMS] will melt away very fast," was arguably the most severe blow to this debate.[113] Very strikingly, both Giscard and Schmidt also seemed no longer to attach much importance to having an EEC-wide scheme. Indeed, Giscard reportedly suggested to Andreotti, during an adjournment of the session, the adoption of a position similar to that of Britain, with Italy remaining outside of the mechanism at the beginning.[114] And in another adjournment, Schmidt similarly told Jenkins that "in his view the only thing to do now was to push the Italians out of the EMS."[115] Saying this should not, however, lead us to overlook that Andreotti's own attitude changed in early December, and that following the growing misgivings of the Banca d'Italia and the Communist Party, his position was much uneasier than it had been a few weeks earlier.[116] Schmidt then announced that, in these conditions, the European Council must recognize that it would not be able to find an agreement in the present session, in spite of all the efforts made: "We must prepare ourselves for failure."[117] It must be recalled here that Schmidt's and Giscard's intransigence, and the contrast it created with the hopes of Lynch, Callaghan, and Andreotti, was very much reflecting the gap mentioned earlier in this chapter between the EPC discussions about the concurrent studies and what Schmidt and Giscard really expected from them. As was noted earlier, Schmidt, from the very beginning, always thought that the aid to be granted to the less prosperous countries would never go beyond EIB interest subsidies. Yet these less prosperous countries dreamed of something more, and the two positions clashed in Brussels.

After the president of the session had advised the heads of government to prepare themselves for failure, the debates acquired a different, more pessimistic, tone, confirmed by Jenkins: "Andreotti and Lynch looked extremely depressed, Andreotti's head sank even further into his body, and poor Jack Lynch was almost on the verge of tears. Schmidt made a gloomy little speech saying that it all seemed absolutely hopeless and he wasn't sure that it was worthwhile going ahead with EMS at all, Germany would be better off without it in any case."[118] Andreotti, according to Tickell, looked "helpless."[119] The discussion centered on the requests of the "less prosperous countries" and was ended by Jenkins, who tried to resituate the ongoing debate in the wider context of the monetary discussions that had been going on since Florence and Copenhagen.[120] He also stressed the negative impact that a failure would have on the future development of the EEC (enlargement, direct elections of the European Parliament).

The session was then suspended so that all participants could talk over and refine their positions. After the suspension, however, the positions remained unchanged, and Lynch and Andreotti expressed their disappointment. Andreotti declared that he would ask for another suspension, so that he could think about his position regarding eventual participation in the EMS. Schmidt then wondered whether it would be better to postpone the decision to participate in the EMS, so that the hesitant delegations could go back to their capitals and think about it again; meanwhile, those who wished to participate could say it already. Jorgensen and Paul Vanden Boeynants then warned that a nondecision today by three member states to participate in the EMS would be regarded by public opinion as a failure. Schmidt then tried to show some willingness to agree on the granting of extra borrowing facilities. It was agreed that these would amount to

1 billion UA, that the interest rate subsidy would be 3 percent, and that the cost would be taken on the EEC budget. Sixty-six percent of these extra borrowing facilities would be devoted to Italy, 33 percent to Ireland, and these proportions would be revised if the British government were to join the EMS later on.[121] Giscard added that were Britain not to participate in the EMS, it should not ask to benefit from these loans, and France would not ask anything. But that if Britain participated and asked to benefit from these loans, France would ask to benefit from these loans on the same conditions. Andreotti, Lynch, and Callaghan then stated that they could not say that their countries would take part in the EMS. To clarify, regarding the exact impact of these measures, the sums discussed would not make any real difference to the ability of the Irish and Italian governments to join the EMS, and were indeed quite small from the point of view of the richer countries.[122] More generally, Murray himself had even already explained earlier in October that the outcome of discussions on the concurrent studies would not have an impact on the decision to enter the EMS. The new EMS would indeed call for a readjustment of domestic policies anyway, and the effects of potential transfer of resources would only be felt over the long term.[123] Hence a narrow dispute was having quite damaging consequences.

Another discussion on the MCAs soon resurfaced, and Giscard insisted again that the question was not to reduce them but to suppress them. The European Council eventually agreed that the inception of the EMS should not create new MCAs, and then that the existing MCAs would be suppressed. The discussion ended on a confirmation of the previous debates. Callaghan confirmed that Britain would not take part in the EMS on 1 January 1979, while Andreotti and Lynch voiced their misgivings and reserved their eventual decision for later on. Giscard confirmed French participation and stressed, as much as Schmidt, the (political) importance of the scheme. The French president naturally emphasized that it was different from the snake and particularly insisted, once again, on the importance of the new monetary unit.

Overall, in the course of the discussions, it is striking that Schmidt did not seem to press Giscard at all to make concessions.[124] He was certainly the only one who could make the French president shift, and he was not ready to do so. Schmidt explained to Jenkins that "he could not quarrel publicly with his French colleague. Too much depended on their relationship."[125] Giscard was described by Tickell as "notably insensitive," and as having made "a disagreeable impression."[126] Clappier seemed just as inexplicably menacing, particularly vis-à-vis Baffi.[127] The governor of the Banque de France appeared keen to put all the burden of a possible failure of negotiations on the Italians. "He is probably saddened to find himself only in the snake," ironically explained the governor of the Banca d'Italia.[128] The obvious question that arises is why did Giscard—and also, to a lesser extent, Schmidt—suddenly behave like this on the occasion of the decisive meeting about the EMS? One argument, advanced by Schmidt himself in reply to Jenkins's question, was that Giscard's internal position was difficult.[129] Nevertheless, Giscard, in contrast to his EEC counterparts, had fewer domestic difficulties, and the most difficult—namely, Chirac's *Appel de Cochin*, which will be dealt with below—was yet to come. Tickell's explanations were, by contrast, more convincing.[130] According to Jenkins's *chef de cabinet*, Giscard's attitude was explained by two factors: first, he feared that the inclusion of Italy and Ireland in the EMS would weaken the system; and second, and more fundamentally, he always thought of the EMS as an essentially Franco-German system. The gloomy atmosphere and the "limited success" of this European Council, as Jenkins put it, was not improved by Giscard's press conference, during which he thought it necessary to elaborate at length on the place of the ECU in the perspective of French history.[131]

As a whole, the Brussels European Council of December 1978 was therefore a mixed bag: it did manage to launch the EMS, but it launched an EMS with only six members out of nine EEC countries—one having definitely opted out, the other two having asked for "a pause for reflection." Yet it is surprising to note that despite the gloomy European Council that had taken place on 4 and 5 December, the Italian decision to join was announced on 12 December and the Irish decision on 15 December: Why and how was such an unpromising situation so swiftly overcome in only about ten days? A first reason explaining this sudden turnaround is that the Brussels European Council's apparent failure was largely due to Giscard's unexpected and inexplicable behavior. This point was summed up well in a British cabinet meeting on 7 December: "In discussion it was suggested that President Giscard had played a surprising role during the [European] Council. While the French had seemed to want Italy and Ireland to participate, he had brusquely rejected their demands for resource transfers and refused to agree to any increase in the Regional Development Fund. This probably reflected his domestic political difficulties and perhaps some disenchantment with the firm position which the Germans had maintained over the way EMS should operate."[132] Giscard's behavior was a momentary mistake rather than the expression of a long-term preference. It would not take long to bring the French president back to a more rational reaction.

Closely interlinked with the above issue was that the Irish and Italian governments' political will to join the EMS was still strong. It had been a constant feature throughout the negotiations. The unexpected obstacle in Brussels had been Giscard, not an Irish or Italian change of mind. Once the obstacle had been removed, negotiations over financial details could go quickly. This is indeed what happened in the Irish case. For a long time, many officials involved in the negotiations showed their readiness to help the Irish government. After the 20 November Finance Council, Jenkins, Ortoli, and Lahnstein came to reassure Colley;[133] about a week later, Schmidt shown much sympathy for the Irish situation, though he could not commit himself to specific figures;[134] and even after the Brussels European Council, a phone call between Lynch and Schmidt does not leave the impression that the German chancellor had to do much to convince the Irish prime minister to join.[135] Although Lynch made it plain that he had not made any final decision, Schmidt mentioned the possibility of delaying the entry to 15 January or 1 February, thereby showing some degree of optimism. In a series of bilateral and multilateral talks, the other EEC members (obviously with the exception of Italy) came to an agreement for a special financial package. A key meeting between Irish and German officials took place in Luxembourg on 12 December.[136] After seemingly intense but swift negotiations, and thanks to a strong German and French backing, a system of bilateral arrangements (hence *not* a Community-wide, supranational scheme), made up of loans and interest subsidy, was agreed on. On 15 December, Lynch informed his European counterparts that Ireland would join the EMS shortly before he announced it to the Dail.[137] The Italian case was even more striking. During the extra week of reflection asked for by Andreotti, no particular additional negotiation took place. During the bilateral negotiations with Ireland, German officials were even described as not concerned with the Italian case, since the Italian problem was about politics rather than resource transfer.[138] Andreotti mostly engaged in extensive domestic political consultations.[139] As early as 7 and 9 December, Baffi wrote in his diary that Andreotti had made the decision that Italy would join the EMS.[140] On 8 December the French ambassador in Rome, François Puaux, seemed to consider Italian participation in the EMS likely.[141] The decision was known on 11 December, and Andreotti announced it at the Camera dei Deputati on 12 December.[142]

The very last obstacle to the EMS entry into force was again French in origin, and of a dauntingly complex nature. On the occasion of the Finance Council of 18 December, Monory announced that the French government reserved its final decision on the EMS until agreement had been reached on the dismantlement of the MCAs.[143] The MCAs had been a perennial issue in EEC discussions. As its name suggests, the MCAs were a mechanism aimed at compensating farmers for sudden exchange rate changes affecting the price of their products. Its working, as much as the overall dispute over its limitation and dismantlement in early 1979, are virtually unintelligible and have scarcely any wider significance. In short, the disagreement mainly centered on the extent to which MCAs should be dismantled, and was based on different interpretations of one sentence of the Brussels European Council's communiqué.[144] An agreement ending the dispute was at last found at the Agriculture Council of 5 and 6 March 1979.[145] Where the

MCA dispute does have a wider significance, however, is in its origins, which was a fundamentally French domestic political situation. Indeed, if the French government suddenly attached so much importance to the dismantling of MCAs, to the extent that it put at risk the entire EMS enterprise, it was not because the MCAs had at once become intolerable. It was rather because Giscard, after the Brussels European Council, had had to face strong opposition from Chirac and the Gaullists (RPR) as well as the Communists. It was only one day after the Brussels European Council, on 6 December 1978, that Chirac made his so-called *Appel de Cochin*. In this speech he criticized in very strong terms the French president's European policy. With the prospect of the first direct elections of the European Parliament, this caused the French president concern. Defending the MCAs' dismantlement thus proved a good strategy to win the support both of agricultural lobbies and of their political supporters. Hence, once again, domestic politics proved to have a tremendous impact on European developments.

Conclusions

The false start of the EMS thus contradicts some of the mythology surrounding its creation. The whole EMS story was in fact full of paradoxes and ironies: the need for a seemingly new monetary system originated in the French franc's departure from the snake in 1976; the abstention of Britain eased the EMS negotiations; the reluctance of the Bundesbank rendered the outcome of negotiations less original, but arguably more coherent and solid; the failure of the Jenkins's Commission's first six months obliged the new Commission president to search for a new, bold, political enterprise; the international monetary nonsystem and the perceived US economic mismanagement encouraged the search for a European solution; the initial bypassing of the EEC institutional machinery precisely permitted the creation of an *EEC* monetary mechanism. This last point is very striking, and would probably need careful consideration by both "eurofanatics" and "europhobes." The EMS, one of the most important steps of European cooperation in the 1970s, was principally the outcome of actions taken on the margins of, if not outside, the Treaty of Rome. The snake was an intergovernmental animal managed in Basel, the European Council was a sui generis institution without any written legal basis, the Clappier-Schulmann-Couzens group met secretly outside of any formal setting, and a vital impulse came from a bilateral, Franco-German framework. These observations stress that black-and-white judgments about Western European cooperation, both from contemporaries ("evil" intergovernmentalism) and historians (all-out transnational history) were, and are, quite misleading. In this concluding section I will compare and contrast the EMS and the snake and examine the role of the European Council, particularly in light of its session in Brussels in December 1978.

From Snake to Rattlesnake

In a nutshell, and as the previous sections made plain, the EMS was almost identical to the snake.[146] In particular, its exchange rate system, like the snake, was based on a bilateral grid of parities. The EMS could be dubbed a "supersnake"—in that it had extended credit facilities—or the "rattlesnake"—because the divergence indicator was meant to act as a warning device when the snake margins were threatened.[147] The four features giving some apparent novelty to the EMS—the divergence indicator, the EMF, the credit mechanisms, and the ECU—were more an example of good political and monetary marketing than genuine new advances. The divergence indicator was flawed from the beginning, since it involved no obligation to intervene.[148] The ECU was merely a rechristened EUA. And even more important, the DM, rather than the ECU, was at the center of the system. The EMF discussions had been postponed and, given the Bundesbank's opposition, were unlikely to ever start. Finally the credit mechanisms, much more developed than under the snake, were nevertheless a mere swap agreement between central banks. It therefore did not imply the loss of their ownership but only a change in their denomination, and thereby a change in the risk carried by their owners. This was quite far off from the dreams of a permanent supranational mechanism pooling the EEC member states' reserves.

Moreover, many of the features contained in the EMS were essentially revamped versions of earlier, ill-fated proposals. This is not only true for the Duisenberg initiative and the divergence indicator but also for the Geens/van Ypersele requests to extend credit mechanisms, and the Fourcade attempt at enlarging the snake to all EEC currencies. Hence, to paraphrase the Hague's 1969 summit motto, the EMS was about the "widening, deepening, and acceleration" of the mechanisms of monetary cooperation launched a few years before, rather than the original new step, emerging ex nihilo, that good political marketing later framed it as. The central *problématiques* to monetary cooperation in Europe remained constant over the 1970s. This is arguably true up until the present day. The proposal for a European IMF, for example, recently resurfaced in the EU.[149]

The similarity of the EMS to the snake further stresses the importance of carefully distinguishing the various currency plans discussed in 1978. These are usually described with the catchall expression "EMS negotiations." Nevertheless, there are at least three steps to be distinguished during the 1978–1979 period: the Schmidt currency plan of early 1978, the Bremen Annex of July 1978, and the March 1979 EMS. The EMS was not a scheme worked out between Schmidt and Giscard. The Bremen Annex was. The EMS was mainly the work of the EEC specialized committees, in which the Bundesbank had the strongest position, thereby explaining the snakelike shape of the March 1979 EMS.

Why, then, does the EMS matter? The EMS was admittedly, in technical terms, not the beginning of a new era. It was the end of an effort that started with high hopes—EMU by 1980—and finished with a merely improved exchange rate system. The EMS mattered because, unlike the snake, it was based on a wider political economy consensus. As the general conclusion will show, the evident weakness of this was that it was based on a convergence in policy beliefs rather than policy outcomes. The EMS constituted a middle-way option between the monetarists and the economists: it created a monetary constraint and called for economic convergence. The EMS also managed, thanks to a strong political impetus, to integrate all but one EEC currency within a single EEC mechanism. Overall, as Ungerer put it, it is probably best to characterize the snake as "a common exchange rate system" and the EMS as "a monetary policy system."[150] The EMS marked the consecration of a new economic and monetary consensus, largely influenced by stability-oriented economic policies aimed at fighting inflation, and it also marked the revival of the goal of EMU for the EEC.

Was the ECU merely a smoke screen? After all, the real technical rupture occurred in 1975, not in 1978, and the acronym was conceived even earlier. Moreover, as Michael Bordo and Anna Schwartz recall, the devising of a composite currency did not appear with the ECU. The electrum—a coin made of three-quarters gold, one-quarter silver, used in Asia Minor circa the sixth century BC—was a case in point.[151] Closer to the present day, composite currencies flourished as a response to the advent of floating rates. The EIB Eurco bonds were another case in point.[152] Bordo and Schwartz's paper even traced the entire evolution of these composite units, showing that they were not a strictly European phenomenon: "The country basket concept of the Eurco was subsequently applied to the SDR in June 1974, the Arab-currency Related Unit (ARCRU) in November 1974, the Asian Monetary Unit (AMU) in December 1974, and the European Unit of Account (EUA), the immediate predecessor of the ECU, in March 1975."[153] The ECU was hence, in technical terms, at the end of a worldwide trend. A second important point is that the source of financial innovation came from financial markets not from governments.[154] It stemmed from the fact that, with the end of a fixed-parity international monetary regime, banks wanted to restore and maintain investment confidence and thought that a basket of European currencies would be the right answer. This was particularly true in the case of the ECU. Not only did banks very early on outline the idea of a composite currency, but even the acronym came from them. Yet the conscious parallel came from politicians (and unsurprisingly

French politicians, Ortoli and Giscard), and, in more general terms, the political dimension of the EUA/ECU emerged only with the creation of the EMS and was peculiar to the European context. With the EMS, the ECU became, as Bordo and Schwartz put it, "an embryonic form of money, closer to historical imaginary monies than to existing currencies that the world has known."[155] Some could think that it would become a full-fledged currency in the long run, in a world system dominated by three currencies (dollar, ECU, and yen).[156] Schmidt hoped that it would help the DM avoid taking too much weight in the international monetary system.[157] Giscard announced in 1978 that he would soon present minted ECUs. The ECU was therefore something more than a mere European SDR: it contained a dream that it might develop into a European common or single currency. The impact of its inception was therefore highly psychological.

The Role of the European Council and the Bypassing of the Commission

A further irony of the EMS creation was that the Commission had been completely bypassed during the negotiations at a time when it tried to reassert itself on this very topic. Every year examined in the preceding chapters, without exception, had been marked by a Commission proposal.[158] Yet the problem was that even if the Commission (and its DG II) was expert on these issues, both Giscard and Schmidt were too. And even more important, they considered themselves the primary EEC experts on monetary matters. Was the bypassing of the Commission due to the European Council's emergence? Not really, since the situation would be reversed in the 1980s, with a Commission president, Jacques Delors, who was much more competent on economic and monetary affairs than the French and German leaders of the time, and thus able to reassert the Commission's leadership.

The Brussels meeting of December 1978 further underlined the difficult balance that the European Council needed to strike. Giscard's unexpected and quite inexplicable sudden behavior, although only for a short while, put at risk the entire EMS endeavor. This underlined once more that the European Council depended strongly on interpersonal relations. When a head of government is making a mistake, it is difficult to change his mind, and only his close counterparts—such as Schmidt in December 1978, although he did not dare do so—can reverse the course of events. Yet, paradoxically, the swift overcoming of the Italian and Irish doubts simultaneously further underscored the initial critical political impetus provided by earlier European Councils. This shows that the behavior of an individual head of government was not necessarily fatal to the whole exercise. The European Council was, though imperfectly, able to provide some form of EEC collective leadership.

THE EMERGENCE OF A EUROPEAN BLOC

> The salient feature of this enterprise [the EMS] . . . is no doubt the exchange rate system of fixed but adjustable parities. All the rest are flanking measures to support and embellish this exchange rate system. It is quite remarkable that exchange rate policy is the chosen instrument for a political demonstration of European unity and stability.
>
> —Otmar Emminger

> But there is, of course, much more to the idea of a European Monetary System than the immediate intervention arrangements. Over the long perspective it looks increasingly clear that the continuing relative shift in economic power between the United States on the one hand, and the EEC countries taken as a whole on the other, is being insufficiently reflected in political, institutional and monetary arrangements.
>
> —Gordon Richardson

There is a striking contrast between the EMS's lack of technical originality and its political, political-psychological, political-economy dimension and later influence. The political dimension of the EMS was indeed so strong that it managed to create the perception over the long run that the EMS was a truly new and innovative mechanism. Since the 1960s, the CAP had been the EEC's flagship policy, although its influence was admittedly progressively diminishing.[1] With the inception of the EMS, monetary cooperation and integration moved to the very top of the EEC's political agenda, partly replacing the CAP as the EEC's flagship endeavor, and becoming a privileged instrument of political affirmation of the EEC vis-à-vis the outside world. Monetary cooperation thus became the new focus the EEC had been looking for since the Hague summit in 1969. Yet, however significant this was for the 1970s—and in the decades to come—the conclusion of such a multilateral study cannot solely focus on the financial dimension of European cooperation, and I will instead try to examine its wider implications. In doing so, in this concluding chapter I will fulfill three main tasks. First, I will relate the book's findings to wider historiographical issues. Second, I will place the book in the perspective of the various ways in which political scientists conceptualize European integration, with the hope that such a perspective will give some transdisciplinary value to this historical study. And third, I will outline the five main implications of the EMS creation. Based on these conclusions, I will provide an explanation of the creation of the EMS that is different from the existing historical literature and the literature on political science.

The Interaction of Transnational, Supranational, and Intergovernmental Phenomena

In contrast to the conventional accounts of the EMS negotiations, which focus solely on the year 1978, I have presented a different way of understanding the creation of the EMS by highlighting longer-term processes. The scholarship on the EMS inception primarily stresses the role of personalities (Schmidt, Giscard, and Jenkins), one institution (the Bundesbank), or specific meetings (the three European Councils of 1978, the Aachen summit, or the Group of Three). Of course, as I have shown, all these actors, institutions, and meetings mattered, to varying degrees, in the overall conception of the EMS. But from the longer-term view I have taken in the book, it is possible to advance another explanation of the creation of the EMS. In examining the prehistory of the negotiations, I have uncovered two important features: the transnational learning process amid a transnationally connected monetary elite and the impact of the emergence of the European Council in the EEC's institutional setup. These constitute the intellectual and technical roots, as well as the political and institutional origins, of the monetary scheme that entered into force in March 1979.

A Transnational Learning Process in a Transnationally Connected Monetary Elite

It has been argued that the lack of technical originality of the EMS can largely be explained by the spread of a Bundesbank-inspired consensus on a snake-like system among a transnationally connected monetary elite. Regarding the transnational learning process idea, I have tried to go beyond a purely abstract, commonsensical, and overly theoretical approach of policy learning by providing some flesh to the claim that policymakers did have many competing ideas in mind while discussing European monetary cooperation in the mid- to late 1970s. As Emanuel Adler and Peter Haas put it, "'failed ideas' do not become extinct but are merely shelved for future reference."[2] It is relatively easy, however, to have such an intuition; it is much more difficult to find tangible, explicit, and permanent cross-references to failed ideas. On the contrary, I have underlined the Socratic way in which various European monetary authorities tried to think about monetary cooperation.[3] From the failure of the Werner Plan until the creation of the EMS, monetary discussions were based on asking and trying to answer questions as to why, how, and to what extent states should pursue monetary cooperation in Europe. For example, in April 1978, in examining how monetary stability could be realized, the European Commission listed and compared the ill-fated plans of the period from 1974 to 1978—namely, the March 1975 agreement on the dollar policy, and the Fourcade, Duisenberg, and van Ypersele proposals.[4] New plans—and particularly the EMS—did not emerge ex nihilo but instead flourished on prepared ground.

This learning process had two main dimensions: sociological and technical. The first dimension, as we saw in chapter 1, began well before 1974 and would carry on in the years to come. Yet the period starting with the failure of the Werner Plan up to the creation of the EMS forms a coherent whole and provides a very good case study of socialization and mutual exchanges of information. The second dimension of this learning process was about the content of monetary policy—or, put differently, what was to be done after the failure of the Werner Plan. According to Adler and Haas, "Such a process of policy evolution has four primary steps: policy innovation, diffusion, selection and persistence."[5] I have underlined each of these steps, in analyzing the proposals, the extent to which they were discussed and implemented (or not), and crucially, the extent to which they were later recycled. Policy innovations were numerous, their diffusion—with the exception of the "parallel currency" approach—was extensive among the European monetary elite, the selection could be easily witnessed in the monetary discussions, and their persistence was quite striking, as the EMS negotiations have shown.

I have stressed not only the importance of the specialized committees—the Monetary Committee, the Committee of Governors, the EPC—for doing the groundwork, for being a place of socialization for an economic and monetary elite, and for facilitating the exchange of ideas but also the importance of their own subgroups (alternates of both committees, specialized groups) in starting this groundwork. An example helps us see their importance better than a long theoretical speech: the very first traces of what would become the so-called Belgian compromise were discernible in the Heyvaert Group discussions.[6] Monetary cooperation in the EEC was thus a complex but quite logical pyramid system, going from the groundwork of alternates to specialized committees, up to the top-level European Council cooperation.

The specialized committees were both a network already built and a group of network builders. A striking feature of European monetary cooperation was that the same names were always appearing and with numerous interconnections.

There were, however, two clearly different strands: academics and "practitioners." Monetary cooperation thus witnessed an impressive game of musical chairs within this monetary elite, with officials moving regularly from one committee to another. It was not unusual for a central bank governor attending the Committee of Governors meetings to have previously attended those of the Monetary Committee. Indeed, the Monetary Committee gathered representatives of finance ministries and the number two of a central bank—a post often occupied by a central banker prior to becoming governor. This applied, for instance, to de La Genière, Emminger, Pöhl, and de Larosière. To detail but one example, Pöhl had been secretary of state in the German Finance Ministry (1972–1977), chairman of the Monetary Committee (February 1976–December 1977), vice president of the Bundesbank (June 1977–December 1979), and then Bundesbank president (1980–1991). Many of these names also had both national and EEC experience (in the Commission, in particular), as in the case of Barre, Schulmann, Marjolin, and Ortoli. And these transnational connections quite obviously were not limited to within Europe. On the occasion of G7 meetings, each head of government traditionally nominated one special representative for the *travaux préparatoires* to the summit. It is noticeable that in the French case, Barre and Clappier were successively the special representatives chosen by Giscard.[7] From an even longer-term perspective, the 1970s also witnessed the emergence of a new generation of European policymakers. Jacques Delors (who was a member of the Conseil général de la Banque de France in the second half of the 1970s), Wim Duisenberg (the first ECB president), Jean-Claude Trichet (the second ECB president, who entered Giscard's cabinet in the late 1970s), Karl-Otto Pöhl, and Jacques de Larosière, to name but a few, would all remain on the European and global monetary scene for the next couple of decades, and would reach more senior positions. It is also noticeable that both Schmidt and Giscard were former members of this monetary elite but had, from the mid-1970s, moved to the head-of-government level.

What did this monetary elite learn? On a sociological note, the second half of the 1970s provided a good example of a longer-term trend toward increasing cooperation among this European monetary elite. It involved the tentative building of a common monetary language and the exchange, adoption, or rejection of monetary policy techniques (monetary targeting, for example). This close-knit community allowed a continuum of expert cooperation, consultation, and harmonization of national policies. This is not to say, however, that this would lead to an *engrenage* from mere cooperation to proper integration. This is rather to observe the development of a habit of cooperation, in both formal and informal settings. One should indeed make it plain that if the specialized committees shared strong technical expertise in monetary matters and were the privileged forum of socialization for this monetary elite, they did not necessarily share the same interpretation of monetary formula and remedies. There were sometimes very stark differences of interpretation, between, for instance, the economists and the monetarists, or between the Keynesians and the Friedmanites.

What was the actual content of this monetary policy learning? It centered on perennial features, quite general on the one hand (where, how, and to what extent was monetary stability to be achieved?), and more specific on the other (systematic comparison of more specific technical ideas, e.g., place of the numéraire in an exchange rate system, identification of the divergent currency, credit support mechanisms). Crucially, they progressively learned to follow the Bundesbank interpretation of monetary policy, and by extension the stability-oriented economic policy of the German government. This consensus was the result of a commonly shared experience (the DM-based snake) as well as the inability of the other proposals to set out a viable alternative (an ECU-based system, a parallel currency, a system of target zones). It is further noticeable that this commonly shared experience went well beyond the borders of the EEC. Austria, Norway, Switzerland, and Sweden were all interested in and formally or informally associated with the snake, thereby underscoring the importance of talking about European—not only EEC—monetary cooperation.[8] They set up a monetary cooperation strand along the Bundesbank line, and the EMS marked the firm anchoring of this monetary policy system committed to stability. The EMS challenge—and arguably the challenge of European monetary cooperation up to today—was that it would oblige a country to remain cost competitive without having the option of currency depreciation (though changes remained possible in the EMS by mutual agreement). EEC member states would have to learn (and try to apply) the Bundesbank-inspired model—or leave the EMS.

This consensus had one instrument: the snake. Ironically, if the EMS marked a departure from the step-by-step approach outlined in the Werner Plan, it did so by using the Werner Plan's product, the snake. Monetary cooperation in Europe in the second half of the 1970s was therefore the story of a protracted enlargement of this exchange rate mechanism. In similar fashion as for EEC enlargements, any candidate for snake membership had to digest a corpus of rules (adjustment of economic policies) prior to entry, and in return the EEC could offer some financial assistance for the less developed countries or delay the application of a certain number of mechanisms. Importantly, this consensus almost exclusively focused on the monetary dimension of EMU. Its redistributive aspect was completely left out. The failure of the EMS concurrent studies, the burying of the 1977 MacDougall Report, as well as the perennial Franco-Italo-Irish-British lost quest for more "symmetry" in the exchange rate system showed an important feature of the Bundesbank-inspired consensus: economic policy was primarily the responsibility of each and every EEC member state alone, and the EEC as such ought not to organize any significant transfer of resources of a federalist type. The EMS remained a fundamentally intergovernmental cooperative mechanism. This thinking finds a striking echo in today's problems of the eurozone.[9]

That the EMS was the product of a Bundesbank-inspired consensus was patent. But why did the Bundesbank interpretation "win" over the others? A first obvious answer was that the snake—a deutsche mark zone—was an evident example of successful monetary cooperation. And the Bundesbank itself was the institution operating the most successful policy in Europe, hence leading by the example. It is known that Giscard and Barre wanted to follow the German economic model. De La Genière gave an even more striking example of this during a training seminar at the Banque de France. Asked what the criteria of a successful monetary policy were, de La Genière simply replied: "I think that you can go and look for them in Germany," before detailing the ingredients of that success.[10] This exchange was an excellent example of the transnational learning process: not only did a Banque de France official explicitly point at Germany as *the* example to follow but he did so in a training session at the central bank, thereby showing what he thought the intellectual template of the next generation should be. The impact of the transnational habits of cooperation among central bankers had here a strong impact. One of the arguments of the defenders of the parity-grid option over the ECU-based one in the EMS negotiations had been that the snake system had been in operation for quite a few years and that it was now well understood by those actively involved. Hence, the strength of the successful transnational working habit proved stronger than the will to adjust or reform it. A monetary proposal from a non-snake member, like the Fourcade memorandum, was unlikely to appear viable in the eyes of the snake members. They naturally were in a position of strength since they were members of a successful ongoing experiment in close monetary cooperation—however limited, imperfect, or strict it may be. But then why did a proposal emanating from a snake member—the Duisenberg initiative—fail?

A second, more realistic answer explaining the Bundesbank-inspired consensus rests with the German central bank's peculiar institutional status within the German political system. If the European monetary consensus revolved around the Bundesbank, it was indeed very prosaically because the Bundesbank was the only institution in the EEC in charge of monetary issues independent from its national government and, moreover, was from the richest EEC member state. As a consequence, any change in Europe-wide monetary policy would have to gain the agreement of an independent German central bank. And it was unlikely that the Bundesbank would ever be convinced, let alone constrained, by an external plan or actor. Rather, any further monetary cooperation in Europe would have to adapt its rules to the Bundesbank's conception of monetary policy, so as to be able to obtain its participation—thereby explaining the failure of a proposal coming from a snake member like that of Duisenberg.

Yet the Bundesbank's centrality, the progressive formation of a consensus around its interpretation of monetary policy, cannot alone explain the creation of the EMS. This transnationally connected monetary elite was indeed largely incapable of exercising influence by itself. A pure Bundesbank line would have been to maintain the snake as it was—certainly not to devise a new European scheme. It is here that one must go beyond a purely transnational approach and pay attention to a fundamental variable, that of the political impetus provided by the European Council.

The Emergence of the European Council in the EEC's Institutional Setup

The second major trend in European monetary cooperation in the second half of the 1970s was the ability of the newly created European Council to provide the political impetus needed to create a new European scheme. European monetary cooperation, culminating in the creation of the EMS, provides the first best case study of the impact of the European Council on the EEC's institutional setup. In contrast to the transnational learning process, the emergence of institutionalized summitry was peculiar to the mid-1970s, both at the European (European Council) and international level (G7). There is, however, an interesting parallel to draw with the monetary elite's learning process. The story of the emergence of the European Council in the EEC's institutional setup was indeed an institutional learning process among a tiny elite of European heads of government and the various ministers and civil servants involved in the process. While the specialized committees set a pattern of regular expert cooperation, the European Council set a pattern of regular heads of government cooperation. The 1960s had been a period of learning how to use the European Community's institutions or for EEC institutions to find and affirm their own place. Similarly, from the mid-1970s onward, EEC member states and institutions learned how to deal with a newcomer, the European Council. In addition to a transnational monetary learning process, there was also an institutional learning process. In this book I have examined more specifically the impact of the European Council in its economic and monetary dimension, but this impact went well beyond monetary issues.[11]

The European Council quickly affirmed its centrality in economic and monetary affairs. This centrality was twofold: the European Council provided a forum of socialization for EEC heads of government where they could freely exchange their views, and it provided a new entry to the EEC decision-making system. In the EMS case in particular, the existence of a sui generis and hybrid institution such as the European Council—part *communautaire*, part intergovernmental— gave an EEC legitimacy to what had originally been a semisecret and bilateral initiative.[12] Prior to 1977, the European Council's existence had had the minimum but crucial effect of keeping the objective of close European cooperation relatively high on the agenda, at a time when exclusively national individual measures could have predominated. Of course, nonconcerted individual national measures still existed, and concerted measures were not always implemented. The French economic plan of late 1975 was implemented with only superficial coordination, and had disastrous consequences at the European level of cooperation (the French franc having to leave the snake), and the German agreement to relaunch activity at the Bonn G7 was mostly a cosmetic measure aimed at calming down the United States and Britain, in order not to endanger the EMS negotiations.[13] There was, however, a longer-term process in the making, namely, the progressive affirmation of an institutional instrument—the European Council— that could be used in the future.

Why did the European Council acquire such centrality? First, because it was strongly supported by the biggest member states (and most obviously Giscard and Schmidt), accepted by the smaller ones, and could benefit from the Commission presidents' (both Ortoli's and Jenkins's) blessing. Second, because the international economic and monetary crisis prompted EEC heads of government to look for a more coherent position vis-à-vis the outside world. The international crisis encouraged the formation of a European bloc—not only monetary but also political and institutional—however tentative and limited it might be. Yet the political impetus provided by the European Council does not alone explain why the EMS, a snakelike system, was created. What matters therefore was the *interaction* of the two strands of development.

The Crux of the Problem: The Interaction of the Transnational, Supranational, and Intergovernmental Phenomena

The central conclusion of this book is that the EMS creation is explained only by analyzing the interaction of transnational, supranational, and intergovernmental phenomena, rather than by taking them separately. In short, the European Council's political impetus explains why reheated old ideas became a palatable dish for EEC heads of government, while the slow formation of a transnational consensus among a European monetary elite along a Bundesbank-inspired line explains the absence of novelty in the EMS. The heroic version, of the Schmidt-Giscard couple overcoming the bitter resistance of their own national administrations, is therefore largely mythical, in the sense that the eventual outcome of the negotiations—a near-snake arrangement—was precisely the *only* outcome desired by these very administrations. The only point on which these administrations gave ground was the creation of something *seemingly* new and the credit system. Moreover, what mattered at the head-of-government level was a more complex phenomenon, namely, the role and influence of an institution rather than the actions, alone, of two leaders. To be sure, the EMS initiative initially started outside the EEC framework. Yet the European Council offered the ideal vehicle to reintroduce this initiative into the EEC system. Since the European Council was indeed spread over the two systems—*communautaire* and intergovernmental— it helped progressively reintroduce an intergovernmental—even bilateral— initiative into the EEC machinery, in order to finally adopt a new EEC-wide monetary system. Similarly, an exclusive focus on transnational or supranational developments, witnessing the slow formation of European polity, would be deeply misleading. The European transnational monetary elite was not willing to devise a new monetary scheme, and the nonstate actors—such as the academic economists advocating the inception of a parallel currency—were incapable of exercising influence beyond the European Commission (and, to a lesser extent, the Banca d'Italia). The protracted formation of a common European monetary language, the development of habits of cooperation, however important they were, could not, alone, create the EMS.

Hence, explaining the creation of the EMS centers on an understanding of the interaction of the three strands of development, the study of which unfortunately tends to be increasingly compartmentalized among historians. The state did not disappear from international relations in the 1970s (or before), and the role of governments—and heads of government in particular—should not be systematically downplayed, as it is sometimes done too easily. If part of the historiography of European integration was indeed an overreaction to the earlier, state-centric, historical studies, current developments in the historical discipline should not themselves overreact to the shortcomings of what they—rightly—consider to have earlier been an overly state-centric approach to European history. The same causes will have the same effects: a partial analysis of events. Historians of the mid-1970s onward indeed face an additional challenge compared to historians of earlier periods: namely, coming to grips with the role and influence of institutionalized summitry, both at the European and at the international level. This new "way of life"—which, according to the policy areas, of course more or less mattered—deserves careful historical attention and will surely go well beyond a mere traditional diplomatic history.[14] Moreover, the interaction of the three also helps us better understand the tentative emergence of a European bloc, in its political and monetary dimensions—or in short, why Europe was not just "made of money." If the EMS is both a political and an economic-monetary event of historical significance, it is because the European Council's political leadership in its creation gave more political weight to an initiative aimed at being an answer to the global economic and monetary crisis. In a nutshell, the European Council was an attempt to fill the EEC political leadership vacuum, just as the EMS was an attempt to fill the European monetary leadership vacuum. In this light, the traditional oppositions in the historiography appear somewhat superficial. In the story of monetary cooperation in the second half of the 1970s, a caricatural opposition of intergovernmentalism versus *communautaire* phenomena, nation-state versus supranational/transnational, economic versus political endeavors is all-too simplistic. It is the combination of all that helps explain the peculiarity of the way in which European governments chose to cooperate monetarily—and it is striking a good balance between these various components that is a significant challenge for future historical works.

The Perspective of Political Science Debates

Political scientists have been facing similar challenges, and consequently a myriad of theories explaining the creation of the EMS, EMU, and European integration in general has blossomed over the past decades.[15] There is no space here to recount all of them in detail. For the sake of clarity—and with the hope that it will not be seen as an oversimplification—in this section I will compare and contrast my findings with what can be seen as the main strands of political science interpretation of European (monetary) cooperation and integration: namely, constructivism, the "international monetary thesis," neofunctionalism, and liberal intergovernmentalism. In the final section I will examine how the concept of "epistemic communities" could be related to the transnational networks identified in this book.

In short, the constructivist approach stresses the role of ideas in the furthering of monetary cooperation. Kathleen McNamara argues, for example, that the critical foundation of the EMS (and EMU) was an ideational consensus in Europe on neoliberal economic policies.[16] Of course—and as I have shown—a new stability-oriented economic policy consensus was progressively formed in the mid-1970s in Europe. Yet the very reason why this consensus revolved around a Bundesbank-led interpretation is much more prosaic than a story of ideas: it is that the Bundesbank was both the most powerful and the most independent Western European central bank, and that, as a consequence, any Europe-wide consensus was bound to follow a Bundesbank line of interpretation. In addition, what permitted the avoidance of a new failure were non-"ideational" events, such as the appointment of Raymond Barre (stemming from a domestic political problem) and external incentive for action (the dollar's decline). Moreover, although I have shown that the EMS was indeed an example of ideational consensus, this alone does not explain why the EMS was created. The snake could have remained in place. The very reason why a seemingly brand-new scheme was set up was fundamentally political, and partly stemmed from the influence of a new institution instead of ideas—the European Council.

One reason why a new monetary system was needed was the fall of the dollar. Randall Henning has presented the EMS—and many other European monetary cooperation landmarks—as a reaction to US policy and the dollar's trajectory.[17] This "international monetary thesis," instead of focusing on internal European debates, argues that "differences with the U.S. administration were most critical in shifting the *German* calculus of the costs and benefits of regional monetary integration."[18] The theme of US policy and the dollar's fluctuations has emerged in many places in the previous chapters, from the attempt at creating a dollar policy in 1975 to the Schmidt plan in early 1978. And it indeed confirmed that the decisive trigger for action, in particular on the side of the German government—while others, like the Dutch or the French, would have been willing to act earlier—was the dollar's fall. Yet this point of view was that of the German *government*, not the Bundesbank. The "international monetary thesis" fails to explain why the EMS was a near-snake arrangement. Confronted with the dollar's fall, the reaction of the German monetary authority was certainly not to devise a brand-new European monetary scheme. And once a new scheme did start being discussed, it had been carefully molded as closely as possible to the snake model, as I have shown in the previous chapters. Furthermore, domestic politics still played a great role: had the French left won the March 1978 general election, the EMS certainly would not have been created, as Schmidt himself explained. Hence if the dollar's fall certainly constituted a decisive trigger for action, other preconditions—in particular domestic—were needed for the EMS move. Most important, the reasons for the EMS similarity to the snake, and for its subsequent political significance, are fundamentally European-centered.

The neofunctionalist approach purports, in short, that integration nurtured further integration.[19] There would have existed a spillover effect, or *engrenage*, from one policy area to the other. The case of the EMS could well apply to this theory, in that the furthering of monetary cooperation was an attempt at safeguarding earlier EEC achievements, such as the CAP (in particular its pricing system) and intra-EEC trade. Yet this would explain only part of the story. For a start, the need to preserve the CAP pricing system did not emerge in 1978, but as soon as the international fixed exchange rate system collapsed; and intra-EEC trade was not so obviously undermined by currency fluctuations.[20] More important, the spillover theory overlooks the impact of the ideational consensus discussed above. And like constructivists, it fails to perceive the role of the European Council in pushing for the creation of the EMS. Put differently, the spillover approach explains the creation of the snake but does not explain why a seemingly new system, akin to the snake, needed to be created.

In order to underline that the EEC's developments did not owe so much to a spillover effect happening at the EEC level, it would probably help at this stage to make a further point on the impact of purely domestic factors. Indeed, despite the creation of habits of consultation and cooperation about national economic policies among ever-increasingly interdependent EEC economies, it is noticeable that the actual outcome of this cooperation remained extremely dependent on each member state's domestic political context. The nomination of Barre as French prime minister, as well as his reappointment in early 1978, was arguably one of the necessary preconditions to the EMS.[21] To paraphrase Jean Boissonat, "Barrism" was necessary for the EMS, and the EMS was necessary for "Barrism" to last.[22] His appointment represented not only the adoption of and the strong commitment to stability-oriented economic policies but also the apparition of someone trusted by the German government. Another case in point was the Pandolfi Plan, which made explicit use of European political rhetoric. Conversely, the coming of general elections in France induced the implementation of a new economic policy at odds with the official European policy discourse of the French government in 1975, and eventually resulted in the French franc leaving the snake.[23] The durability of the scheme was based on the ability of each member state to adapt its own domestic economic policy to validate a semifixed exchange rate with the deutsche mark and hence to follow German economic policy, rather than any binding supranational mechanism. For example, the Trésor-Bundesbank understanding about the need to pursue stability-oriented economic policies over virtually the entire second half of the 1970s remained stuck at a technical level and was permanently dependent on domestic political considerations. In a sense, the EMS itself nurtured the importance of the domestic dimension of European cooperation. In the absence of truly EEC redistributive mechanisms, the primary responsibility for EEC economic and monetary convergence rested on national authorities. The critical foundation of the EMS was therefore very fragile. Were one country to reverse its course, the entire European arrangement could be threatened. However fascinating the EEC was in the 1970s as an incipient trans- and supranational polity, the fundamental political and economic choices remained for the most part nationally rooted, and they would remain so for many years to come.

Moreover, it is particularly fascinating to observe at the European level the strong impact of some domestic constitutional features very peculiar to the three biggest EEC member states. In France, the president has virtually free reign over foreign policy, according to a peculiarity of the French presidency in the theory and practice of the Fifth Republic. Giscard was hence able to easily bypass his own domestic political and administrative opposition to the EMS. The British prime minister—as much as the German chancellor—by contrast could not. Even more important, the unfixed nature of the date of British general elections—a peculiar feature of the British political system—rendered the British government's task to negotiate the EMS without electoral afterthoughts absolutely impossible. During a large part of the EMS negotiations, many British policymakers truly believed that a general election would take place in the fall of 1978—which proved not to be the case. Finally, the constitutional independence of the Bundesbank—a feature specific to the German system in the 1970s—coupled with a perennial German aversion to inflation, made the German central bank the most central actor on the European stage during the EMS negotiations, to such an extent that it was able to mold the scheme according to its own preferences. Overall, there-fore, in explaining the EMS decision, these domestic features have much more importance than a would-be spillover effect alone.

In the liberal intergovernmental approach, the critical actors are seen as being the states. According to Andrew Moravcsik, the EMS was the outcome of inter-state bargaining, in which the German conception won over the French one.[24] Admittedly, as I have shown, the EMS creation was largely intergovernmental. Nevertheless, such an approach tells only half the story. It does explain why the EMS was created, but it does not come to grips with the fact that the EMS was not much different from the snake. And the lack of originality of the EMS precisely stemmed from nonintergovernmental bargaining, namely, the role of the trans-nationally connected monetary elite. To be sure, European monetary authorities had been bypassed in the initial stages of the EMS negotiations. Schmidt and Giscard thus followed a completely different strategy from the Commission pres-ident, Jacques Delors, who decided very early on to directly involve central bank-ers in the discussions of the late 1980s.[25] Yet once the actual negotiations started, the Bundesbank became the central actor on the European stage and, given its independence from the German government, was able to adjust the outcome of the negotiations to its own preferences. Moreover, when states were involved, the critical aspect of their bargaining was the impact of the forum where it happened—the European Council—rather than states individually. The Euro-pean Council had, of course, not a life of its own, but it was not entirely subservi-ent to the states either. It created a new type of momentum, the implications of which were *both* intergovernmental and *communautaire*.

A further, and more problematic, point is that the various actors involved in the monetary discussions of the second half of the 1970s did not always act rationally on the basis of their "national interests"—unlike what a liberal-intergovernmental interpretation purports. Quite the contrary, the economic and financial rationality, as outlined by French, British, German, or Italian monetary authorities, commended *not* joining the EMS (or, at the very least, argued that joining on 1 January 1979 would be too soon). A case in point was Giscard's belief in (semifixed) exchange rates. His belief arose out of pure conviction rather than out of an exclusively rational perception of future benefits.[26] As far as benefits were concerned, Giscard, both in 1975 and 1978, figured that the political advantages outweighed the economic and financial risks. His gamble proved to be deeply mistaken in 1975 (as the Trésor had *rationally* predicted),[27] and partly successful in 1978. And in 1978, one of the critical factors on the French side of the EMS negotiations was the presence of Bernard Clappier, a committed pro-European. The chief French EMS negotiator was well aware of the EMS technical complexity, both in theory and in practice.[28] Clappier did not seem to attach much importance to the fact that the EMS would not differ significantly—if at all—from the snake. He did not even seem to be particularly convinced of the durability of the scheme. Why then did he support the EMS? Arguably, his first and basic motivation was to take a further step in European (monetary) cooperation, be it a bold one or not. It should not be forgotten that Clappier had been a strong supporter of the integration process since the beginning of his career—he was, for instance, in Robert Schuman's cabinet during the elaboration of the Schuman Plan in May 1950. Very clearly, therefore, an exclusive focus on French "material interests" would not fully explain the French decision to opt for the EMS.

Similarly, trust played a much greater role in the EMS creation than the convergence of economic "interests." Indeed, the second half of the 1970s witnessed a convergence in policy beliefs rather than in policy outcomes, as a constructivist approach rightly suggests. In 1978, there was still an important difference in the inflation rates of, for example, France and Britain on the one hand, and Germany on the other.[29] Yet what made French participation in the EMS possible was a *perception* that in their overall trend, inflation rates were now no longer diverging but rather converging. Moreover, this trend was perceived to be happening on a sound basis (the Barre government's anti-inflationary stance), in which both the French president and the German chancellor placed much confidence. In short, the German government's *trust* in the French government's economic policy orientation made up for the lack of tangible policy results. The EMS creation therefore cannot be reduced to mere rational economic interests and interstate bargaining.

Finally, an interesting heuristic device, originally coming from political science, is of particular relevance for the study, namely, that of the epistemic communities. Peter Haas defined epistemic communities as "a network of professionals with recognized expertise and competence in a particular domain and an authoritative claim to policy-relevant knowledge within that domain or issue-area."[30] To sum up, Haas identifies four criteria needed to form an epistemic community: a shared set of normative beliefs, shared causal beliefs, shared notions of validity, and a common policy enterprise.

Of the numerous transnational networks examined in this book—central bankers, academic economists, finance ministers, economic advisers—the central bankers are probably the first to call for a comparison. Although they did share technical expertise, they did not, however, share a common "cause-and-effect understanding" of monetary policy—which is an important dimension of epistemic communities as set out by Adler and Haas.[31] In particular, they did not all give the same priority to the fight against inflation. Nevertheless, the story of European monetary cooperation in the second half of the 1970s was that of the slow formation of a consensus around the snake monetary policy option, focusing on low inflation rates and stability-oriented economic policies. Hence, if EEC central bankers do not fully correspond, as such, to an epistemic community, the snake central bankers alone come much closer to Haas's definition.

Even more interesting was the case of the academic economists advocating the creation of a parallel currency. This informal transnational network corresponded very well indeed to the definition of an epistemic community. They were recognized experts, they shared a similar basic conception of monetary policy, and, crucially, had a common goal: the creation of a parallel currency. They were, however, totally unable to exercise influence by themselves. Their proposals never really reached the attention of policymakers. Their influence was limited to articles in the international press—the Times Group Proposal, the All Saints' Day Manifesto in *The Economist*—that often centered around either Robert Triffin or Robert Mundell and were often informally helped by one institution (the DG II in the Commission).[32] Although successive reports issued by groups set up by the Commission duly contained the usual disclaimer—"the opinions expressed in this report remain the sole responsibility of the group and not that of the Commission and its services"—it does not take a monetary expert to observe that all the groups set up by the Commission came to similar conclusions, and that they often benefited from the DG II secretariat. Although officially denied, there must have been some kind of intellectual link between the two. Why did this epistemic community fail to influence European decision making? Certainly because this community, mainly composed of academics, completely failed to perceive the practical difficulties of such an idea. The only time when the parallel currency approach got closer to the decision maker was when Jenkins talked about monetary union in 1977. Michael Emerson, former official in the DG II and member of Jenkins's cabinet, was behind the proposal, and had already been indirectly involved in the drafting of other studies, like the MacDougall Report.[33] And it is noticeable that the few traces found of an analysis of this type of proposal for a parallel currency were only negative.[34] What a "parallel currency" exactly involves and implies is scarcely intelligible to the general public, and when it is, it is quite difficult to see how it could be implemented in concrete terms. Besides theoretical disagreements, therefore, European decision makers probably thought they would find themselves unable to explain this to the public.

The Emergence of a New Agenda

The monetary discussions of the second half of the 1970s had a number of important effects on the development of the EEC. At least five important themes emerged, all of which gained considerable importance in the following years.

Two-Tier Europe and British "Self-Exclusion"

Monetary cooperation in the 1970s marked the beginning of British self-exclusion from the advancement of EEC cooperation. The British de facto exclusion from the Franco-German tandem already had roots in 1974. Ever since Wilson's return to office, his skeptical stance about European cooperation cleared the way for increased Franco-German cooperation. Simultaneously, this reinforced Franco-German tandem clarified to the British government that, since a triumvirate was unthinkable, it would increasingly be isolated. The EMS transformed this de facto exclusion from bilateral initiatives into an enduring self-exclusion. Observing the British self-exclusion is not to suggest, however, that the British government was wrong in doing so. At the time, many actors who would have liked Britain to take part in the ERM actually showed much understanding for the British decision (although the British government largely failed to perceive the Franco-German tandem's Anglophilia). Giscard and Schmidt, although strong backers of British participation, never showed any personal vexation at the British "half-way house."[35] While both were certainly skeptical about the official rationale of the decision—preference for a global (economic) solution over a regional (monetary) one—they understood Callaghan's electoral considerations. The best example of this was a conversation between Callaghan and Barre on 24 November 1978 reported by Froment-Meurice. To the British prime minister who had just explained his reasons for opting out of the EMS (in particular, the need to be able to let the sterling exchange rate go down), Barre replied: "If I were you, I would do the same."[36] Though coincidental, it is, however, notable that the British government had had to cope with international economic and monetary disturbances ever since its entry into the EEC. This external perturbing factor certainly did not help its adaptation in the Community.

The corollary to British nonparticipation in the ERM and, more generally, to the difficulties encountered in trying to apply a single monetary scheme to all EEC member states contributed to the emergence of the more general theme of a "two-tier Europe." The possibility of a "two-tier" or "two-speed" Europe had already been explicitly mentioned by Tindemans in his 1976 report. The EEC of the 1970s—as much as today's EU—had difficulties "digesting" its first en-largement, and the prospect of the second one was not more promising. The furthering of European (monetary) cooperation could therefore not be done at the same pace for all member states. This was particularly true in the absence of any substantial redistributive mechanism that the EMS concurrent studies were meant to bring about. The EMS, with three EEC members benefiting from some kind of special treatment—wider fluctuation margins for Ireland and Italy, participation in the ECU but not the ERM for Britain—showed that such a dif-ferentiated integration was feasible. Moreover, it showed that although the EMS was an EEC mechanism, all EEC member states were not obliged to take full part in it. This would remain a constant feature of the development of the EEC in the following years: belonging to the EEC/EU does not necessarily mean belonging to the EMS/euro. This would, in a sense, confirm the option presciently outlined by Tindemans in the mid-1970s.

Civil Society's Relative Exclusion and Public Opinion's Reintegration

A second important theme emerging from monetary discussions in the second half of the 1970s was the evolution of the place of civil society in European inte-gration. Indeed, if civil society had largely been left out of monetary discussions, it paradoxically found a way back in by the front door, through the European Council's extreme exposure to public media, and thereby to public opinion. True, this exposure did not impact the EMS negotiations—or did so only by rein-forcing the need to nurture a European integration mythology by presenting something seemingly new. This was, however, not at all comparable to what hap-pened in the 1990s, 2000s, and even today. Civil society's absence from monetary debates was largely understandable. The discussions over the technical details of an exchange rate mechanism had little attraction for nonspecialists. If the basic rationale of a European monetary union could easily be summed up in sweeping statements such as "Europe will be made or not made through [a common] cur-rency,"[37] selling the significance of the "parity-grid versus ECU-based exchange rate system" debate to the general public was a much more difficult task. This is the very reason why presentations of the EMS focused on the ECU: it was easy for the general public to understand (particularly in France) since it could be easily presented as an embryonic European common currency—an "imaginary money" as Bordo and Schwartz put it. The influence of civil society and public opinion was thus rather indirect, and also paradoxically increased thanks to the inception of the European Council. The paradox of the institutionalization of European summitry was indeed that, by routinizing heads of government meetings in the EEC, this top-level dining club attracted considerably more media attention.

The way in which the EMS was negotiated also nurtured the democratic deficit argument. The centrality of the European Council in the monetary negotiations—heads of government meetings are perennially accused of being antidemocratic—the secret discussions of the Schulmann-Clappier-Couzens group, the secret and expert discussions of central bank governors, all nurtured the sentiment that the EEC's functioning was not democratic. This situation was, however, full of paradoxes. Why would a democratically elected head of government suddenly turn antidemocratic just because he met up with his EEC counterparts in Brussels? And why would expert cooperation—in many ways a side effect of representative government—be necessarily antidemocratic? The prospect of the European Parliament's first direct elections would offer a temporary smoke screen to this somewhat paradoxical situation. Nevertheless, the increasing centrality of the European Council in the EEC institutional system, as well as the future of the EMS, would further nurture the democratic deficit debate.

The Passive Role of the United States and the Implicit Presence of the Cold War

As far as international factors are concerned, I have mostly stressed the impact of international monetary discussions, and in particular the very conscious parallels between IMF mechanisms and European monetary discussions. The decline of the dollar gave an extra sense of urgency to European debates, the SDR bore striking resemblance to the EUA/ECU, the system of target zones proposed by Duisenberg in 1976 was inspired by the IMF "guidelines for floating," and the EMF was meant to be built on the IMF model. Each and every time a European specificity was meant to be added, but the technical resemblance was striking.

Since the end of the Second World War, the United States had played an active role in promoting Western European cooperation, and—and because—the link between European integration and the cold war was largely explicit. The monetary discussions of the second half of the 1970s showed a reversal of this situation: the United States had a passive role and the cold war link was implicit, and even internalized by policymakers.

The emergence of a European bloc was not due to any positive action taken by the United States, but rather by its absence—not to say its "malign neglect," as Schmidt put it. The US role in the EMS lay in the dollar's decline, which provided an external impetus for European action.[38] It was, however, no conscious impetus given by Washington. The EMS was rather, as Ludlow put it, "an act of self-defence" by Schmidt against his perception of the Carter administration's "malign neglect."[39] It was of less importance for Giscard, although besides the *"privilège exorbitant du dollar"* he denounced in the 1960s, the French disliked in principle a world monetary system dominated by the US currency, a bit like the way they disliked the NATO integrated command dominated by US generals. The United States did not influence the course of the EMS technical negotiations either. As Schulmann put it: "On the Bremen monetary proposals, all that was conceded to the Americans was that they should be informed."[40] The EMS story was thus the exact opposite of the "empire by invitation" role traditionally attributed to the United States in the late 1940s–early 1950s.[41] Not only did Europe no longer issue any kind of invitation but it instead showed (or tried to) that it could organize itself on its own. The British uneasiness about the overall EMS political enterprise stemmed in part from this tentative emergence of a distinctive European bloc.

Understanding the EMS as part of a wider political ambition aimed at making a European (currency) bloc emerge also helps explain the relationship between European monetary stability and the ongoing cold war. Of course, there was virtually no explicit reference to the cold war in the EMS negotiations—nor before, in the discussion of the various ill-fated monetary initiatives. Yet as Schmidt's intervention at the Bundesbank made plain, the EMS was understood as part of a wider trend of anchoring the Federal Republic in the West.[42] Monetary policy, as Schmidt often recalled, was a crucial element of foreign policy. The EMS thus marked the political affirmation of West German foreign policy. As Ludlow writes, "The EMS was arguably the first major act of German leadership in the history of the European Community."[43] The European Council was here instrumental in providing the "European mantle" mentioned by Schmidt to the West German initiative. The overall shift in 1977 was therefore of tremendous importance. France got even closer to Germany, and Germany moved away from the United States and was willing to provide a European answer to global problems by making effective use of the Franco-German tandem and of the EEC institutions and policies. Even more important, the EMS was regarded as a contribution to the emergence of a European bloc in the cold war. In talking about monetary stability, Matthöfer made the only direct reference (by any official of any country) to the cold war in a monetary discussion. In a meeting with Schmidt and Healey in April 1978, he thus explained that "what mattered was a 'grand concept of Europe' with moves towards a unified currency. In that direction lay greater political and economic stability in Europe and a defence against spreading communism throughout the Mediterranean countries."[44] Interestingly, Matthöfer stressed the political and economic dimension of the Soviet threat rather than the military one. A primarily economic response like the EMS was, in that sense, a contribution to Western European prosperity, itself aimed at defeating the spread of communism in the Mediterranean, as had been the case in the 1940s and 1950s in Western Europe. Similarly, in another meeting with Healey in October 1978, Matthöfer was reported as saying that "the issue [the EMS] went wider than that. Europe could only survive in a world dominated by the US and Soviet bloc if it had a unified market, with ultimately a unified currency. EMS was an important first step in that direction."[45] Monetary stability was in that sense one of the *forces profondes* able to contribute symbolically, psychologically, politically, and economically to the emergence of a European bloc in the midst of the cold war.

The Affirmation of a European Monetary Regionalism

The emergence of a European monetary identity, the affirmation of a European "monetary regionalism," is a longer-term process, for which the European monetary discussions between 1974 and 1979 provide an excellent case study.[46] The second half of the 1970s indeed witnessed a (political) ambition aimed at (slowly) creating a European monetary identity. A first landmark was the creation of the EUA in 1975,[47] followed four years later by the ECU. And the EUA-ECU discussions were indeed excellent examples of the will to build a European monetary identity. This emerging identity was limited, however. Economic and monetary questions were far from being "communautarized." All attempts by the Commission, but also by some member states, such as the Netherlands, to insist on the coordination of economic policies at the EEC level, or even the attempt at the *communautarisation* of such a coordination, revealed that it was impossible. Coordination of economic policies could only be the result of the will of individual governments to do so. EEC constraints did not seem to work—there was not even an attempt to properly implement them, as was the case of the 1974 directive on economic coordination. The story of European monetary cooperation between 1974 and 1979 was, however, the story of bringing the snake explicitly under the EEC framework. If the EMS was not managed in a supranational framework—the EMF was still far off—it was, at least, an EEC mechanism. Admittedly, it was and remained a deutsche mark zone. But while it was felt that the snake was unable to gather all EEC currencies, the EMS, by contrast, became an instrument, a political symbol, for *EEC* monetary cooperation and integration. In short, the EMS emerged as the vehicle for monetary cooperation and integration in the EEC that the snake had been unable to become. And here the ECU played a crucial psychological role. Interestingly, the European monetary identity of the mid- to late 1970s was in part built against the dollar (and its decline). Fourcade envisaged the inception of an EEC dollar policy, and Schmidt revived European monetary cooperation because he was upset by the dollar's fall. The dollar was therefore a perennial issue in European monetary cooperation, which in turn nurtured British skepticism about the EMS enterprise.

If the second half of the 1970s witnessed the tentative emergence of a European monetary identity, did it witness the emergence of a distinctive European monetary policy—or, put differently, a distinctive interpretation of monetarism? The monetary discussions of the 1970s indeed witnessed the progressive diffusion of monetarist (Friedmanite), neoliberal ideas in Western Europe—a diffusion to which I have regularly alluded. On numerous occasions, discussions among heads of government or central bankers underscored that many European policymakers, in the second half of the 1970s, did not take monetarist interpretations in their entirety. They provided a qualified interpretation that would soon be swept away by more radical interpretations from both the Thatcher and Mitterrand governments.

The diffusion of these ideas was in fact a two-sided coin. On the one hand, the EMS undoubtedly marked a departure from the Keynesian template in that it moved the focus away from domestic consumption to monetary stability. In other words, the option of stimulating domestic demand in order to reduce unemployment was now understood as being counterproductive, since it tended to create a balance of payments deficit, a downward move of the exchange rate, and increased inflation. One of the roots of the problem was therefore an excessive demand for consumption. Coupled with oil price increases, this created balance of payment deficits and thereby made the economies—and a currency's exchange rate—vulnerable to shifts in confidence.[48] The central idea became to lower and control inflation. In that sense, the economic policy consensus progressively came closer to monetarist, neoliberal thinking, but still with many national nuances across European countries.

But what causes this inflation? A strict monetarist answer would be the increase of the money supply. And here the interpretation of various European monetary authorities varied. Admittedly, the adoption of quantitative monetary targets was a good indication that European monetary authorities saw a link between the growth of the money supply and inflation.[49] But some of them did not think that there was only one link. For instance, in October 1978, Clappier explained that although the Banque de France considered monetary policy to be an important aspect in the fight against inflation, it did not feel bound to a specific doctrine.[50] One could also mention one section of Emminger's memoirs, tellingly titled "Does the market really know everything better?"[51] Schmidt summarized well the paradox of this economic policy consensus and the distinctiveness of the EMS option: "An orthodox Keynesian should seek flexible exchange rates instead of the EMS—an orthodox monetarist, however, exactly the same."[52] The debate between focusing on the setting of an intermediary objective (growth of money supply, of monetarist inspiration) or of a final objective (inflation target) was thus not so clear-cut in the 1970s: the European reception of monetarism was far from monolithic, presented some distinctive European answers, and was certainly much more qualified in its response than the later example of Thatcher in 1979, who explicitly sought to implement monetarism, or, the other way around, Mitterrand in 1981.

The Emergence of the 1980s–1990s Agenda

A last theme, perhaps the most important, was the emergence of the Single European Act (SEA)/Maastricht agenda. Admittedly, in the late 1960s and early 1970s, the Werner Plan discussions had already pointed somewhat in that direction. In 1977–1979, however, not only did monetary cooperation arrive at the top the EEC's agenda with the EMS creation but also explicit and implicit references to the need for completing the single market emerged. The implicit link was theoretically clear. The OCA theory or the Marjolin Report underscored the numerous prerequisites that the EEC still had to fulfill in order to become a viable currency area.[53] And these prerequisites bore some resemblance to the single-market program in wishing to eliminate the remaining barriers not only to trade but also to the free circulation of people, capital, and services. The explicit links are less numerous. The obvious one was the 1977 Ortoli proposals recommending, textually, the completion of a "single market."[54] The 1975 Marjolin Report was another case in point. In suggesting that EEC governments had not realized the far-reaching implications of a full EMU, it indirectly outlined the steps yet to be taken. The completion of a single market would be one of these, although it was not explicitly mentioned. It thus became clear that further monetary cooperation would have to go hand in hand with further economic and political cooperation for the EEC to become a less imperfect currency area. In the mid- to late 1970s, as before, and up to the present day, the difficulties lay in fundamentally inconsistent economic and monetary policies, and the crux of the problem rests on how to render them consistent. And this undoubtedly constitutes the central challenge to making the EMS a durable attempt at a European bloc.

Acknowledgments

This book could not have been written without the help of many people and institutions. My first thanks go to Harold James, who kindly and constantly supported and advised me over the past few years. I also benefited from discussions with many colleagues, at different stages of my project and in different manners: Robert Boyce, Éric Bussière, Philippe Buton, Benoît Challand, Ken Endo, Giovanni Federico, Olivier Feiertag, Mark Gilbert, Karen Gram-Skjoldager, Fernando Guirao, Yuichi Hosoya, Wolfram Kaiser, Stine Knudsen, Johnny Laursen, Brigitte Leucht, Andy Moravcsik, Serge Noiret, Kiran Patel, Morten Rasmussen, Federico Romero, Sarah Snyder, Kristina Spohr Readman, David Stevenson, Guido Thiemeyer, Maurice Vaïsse, Antonio Varsori, Antoine Vauchez, Arne Westad and Pascaline Winand.

I thank the "Florentines": Mauro Campus, Lucia Coppolaro, Paola di Credico, Gabriele D'Ottavio, Eleonore Eckmann, Mathieu Grenet, Georg von Graevenitz, Aoife Keogh, Jacob Krumrey, Pierre-Yves Lacour, Delphine Lauwers, Franck Lecomte, Marion Lemaignan, Mario, Valérie Mathevon, M'hamed Oualdi, Sabatino, Vivanda, Martin Wall, Giuseppe Zaccara; the "Londoners": Emma de Angelis, Wallyd Benchikh, Eirini Karamouzi; the "Parisians": Vincent Duchaussoy, Mathieu Duhamel, Théodore Efthymiou, Jean-Romain Fayard, Pierre-Étienne Minonzio, Pierre Skorov; the "Bruxellois": Édouard Meier and Marion Santini; many thanks to the RICHIE band, and in particular Marloes Beers, Frédéric Clavert, Garret Martin, Guia Migani, Matthieu Osmont, and Christian Wenkel. It has been a pleasure working with Cornell University Press. Many thanks to Roger Haydon and Susan Specter for their advice and support, to the series editors, to Marie Flaherty-Jones for wonderful copyediting, and to the two anonymous reviewers for all their advice and guidance. Special thanks go to Liz and Michael Benning-Ladurner, Marie-Julie Chenard, Daniel Furby, Michael Geary, Angela Romano, Federico Romero and Laurent Warlouzet for long discussions and, even more important, last-minute help. Thanks also to Piers Ludlow—not only did he manage to awake my interest in European integration history (CAP included, which is no small feat) but he continuously encouraged me to carry on, supported my decision to go to Florence, represented a great *shadow supervisor* during my stay in Tuscany, and bravely read and commented on my successive Frenglish drafts. And finally thanks to my mother, godmother, and Jean-Pierre

Melin, for their constant support. Mistakes, approximations and omissions remain mine.

Many research institutions made this research possible. The European University Institute and the French government provided early funding. The EUI was, in addition, an ideal setting for academic research, while the Centre for Diplomacy and Strategy (LSE IDEAS) and the LSE International History Department provided a great academic home for the last stages of my research. Special thanks go to Maurice Pinto for his kind and enthusiastic support, without which I would not have been able to revise this manuscript.

Such extensive archival research would also have been impossible without help from the staff of the various archives I visited. In particular I thank Jocelyne Collonval (Archives de la Commission), Agnès D'Angio-Barros (Centre des Archives économiques et financières), Jean-Philippe Dumas (Archives du Ministère des Affaires étrangères), Grégoire Eldin (Archives du Ministère des Affaires étrangères), Mareike Fossenberger (das Politische Archiv des Auswärtigen Amtes), Pascal Geneste (Archives nationales), Frédérik Grélard (Archives historiques de la Banque de France), Barbara Groß (Bundesarchiv, Koblenz), Birgit Kmezik (das Politische Archiv des Auswärtigen Amtes), Michael Leumann (Historisches Archiv der deutschen Bundesbank), B. Limberg (Bundesarchiv, Koblenz), Jean-Marie Palayret (Historical Archives of the European Union, Florence), Tom Quinlan (Irish National Archives), Anna Rita Rigano (Archivio Storico della Banca d'Italia), Jeanette Sherry (Bank of England Archive), and Christoph Stamm (Helmut-Schmidt-Archiv, Bonn). I also thank the Commission d'Accès aux Documents administratifs (CADA), which has been remarkably efficient in the treatment of my appeals regarding denied requests for access.

A Note on Sources Cited in the Notes

Because this book uses an extremely wide range of archival material—eighteen archives in six countries—it is necessary to clarify here how sources have been collected, used, and quoted.

Most of the documents consulted are publicly accessible. Only a few required application for a derogation (Giscard papers, Banca d'Italia, Helmut-Schmidt-Archiv). Given that the period studied is very close to the thirty-year rule applied in most European archives, some of the references given are to a temporary number (*Zwischenarchiv, Intermédiaire*), because the documents were not yet fully inventoried at the time of consultation.

All the available sources of the EEC member states of the early to mid-1970s— with the exception of the Netherlands, Belgium, Luxembourg, and Denmark, for reasons of availability and/or linguistic ability—have been used. Finance ministries, treasuries, central banks, foreign ministries, prime ministers/president papers, and, where available, some personal papers (Émile Noël, Otmar Emminger, Paolo Baffi) have been consulted. The documents consist of correspondence, internal notes, briefings, and most important, records of conversation (some official, some by a notetaker or a [prime] minister himself).

For obvious reasons of space, not all documents seen could be referred to in the notes. Hence if only one source is given, it does not mean that others have not been consulted. Rather, it means that the others confirmed, in substance, the information contained in the only source quoted. This strategy helped me avoid multiple references, though it superficially gives the impression that the source is exclusively from one country. Where accounts differed, the difference is analyzed in the text or the note itself. Sometimes a document was located in an archive other than the one in which it was originally housed (e.g., a report of the Monetary Committee in The National Archives rather than in an EEC archive). This does not mean, of course, that the document consulted was not the original (e.g., the original report issued by the Monetary Committee).

To this archival material that can only be seen on-site, I have added collections that are available online: the European Central Bank Archives (which contains the *procès-verbaux* of the Committee of Governors meetings), the Thatcher Archives, the British Diplomatic Oral History Programme, the Gerald R. Ford Presidential Digital Library, and the European Oral History Programme.

English translations are mine unless otherwise noted.

Notes

INTRODUCTION

Epigraph. Helmut Schmidt, BdF, 1489200205/288, text of a planned intervention at a conference of the European League for Economic Cooperation, 30 November 1984.

1. Coppolaro, "Trade"; Ludlow, "The Emergence"; Chenard, "Seeking"; Romano, *From Détente.*
2. Mourlon-Druol, "Filling the EEC Leadership Vacuum?"
3. Chopin, "Le Parlement européen."
4. Kaiser and Meyer, "Non-State Actors."
5. Rasmussen, "Joining"; Geary, *Inconvenient*; Wall, "Ireland"; Karamouzi, "Greece"; Furby, "Revival"; Trouvé, *L'Espagne.*
6. See, for instance, Varsori, "Alle origini"; Varsori, *Alle origini*; Knipping and Schön-wald, *Aufbruch*; Migani and Varsori, *Europe*; Mourlon-Druol, "Managing"; Migani, "La politica"; Garavini, *Dopo.*
7. Such a reading can be found in Dinan, *Europe*, 173–74; Gerbet, *La construction*, 293–97; Apel, *European*; Saint-Périer, "VGE"; Thiemeyer, "H. Schmidt und die Gründ-ung"; Frank, "Les problèmes"; Gillingham, *European*, 134; Bossuat, *Faire*, 150–53; Wein-achter, *VGE*, 131–40; Olivi, *L'Europa*, 181–83 and 189–97; Ikemoto, *European* (except for a cursory reference to the Fourcade memorandum and the Tindemans Report); Waechter, *Schmidt und Giscard*, 107–23.
8. The few exceptions to this rule are Ungerer, *Concise History*; Tsoukalis, *Politics*; Dyson, *Elusive*. Peter Ludlow's detailed study of the EMS negotiations falls into both cat-egories, since it focuses mainly on the year 1978 but does mention the ill-fated proposals of the years 1974–1977, and only cursorily suggests their influence over the EMS negotia-tions, which is an exception compared to the rest of the EMS literature (Ludlow, *Making*). David Marsh's 2009 study also mentions some of the ill-fated earlier plans, but focuses more on high politics (Marsh, *Euro*, 71–88).
9. Milward, *European Rescue*; Varsori, "La storiografia."
10. Kaiser, *Christian*; Kaiser, Leucht, and Rasmussen, *History*; Knudsen, *Farmers*; Lud-low, *European.*
11. Kaiser, "History Meets Politics."
12. Renouvin and Duroselle, *Introduction*; Di Nolfo, *Storia*; Varsori, *La Cenerentola.*
13. Bloch, *Esquisse*; Bussière and Dumoulin, *Milieux*; Bussière, Dumoulin, and Schirmann, *Milieux*; Bussière, "L'intégration"; Cassis, "La communauté"; Feiertag and Margairaz, *Politiques*; Feiertag, "Introduction"; Petrini, *Liberismo*; Ciampani, *L'altra.*
14. See, for instance, Saint-Périer "VGE"; Thiemeyer, "Schmidt und die Gründung."
15. Mundell, "Theory." See chapter 1.
16. See the note on sources.
17. Badie and Smouts, *Le retournement.* See also Clavin, "Defining."
18. Bloch, *Esquisse*; Bussière and Feiertag, "Méthode"; Girault, "Le difficile mariage."
19. Schmidt, *Menschen und Mächte*, 196. Schmidt constantly reaffirmed this point, notably during his speech at the Bundesbank's central council on 30 November 1978. See chapter 8.

20. Frank, *La hantise.*

21. Giscard thus announced the return of the French franc in the snake on 9 May 1975, that is, on the occasion of the Schuman Plan's anniversary; see chapter 2; Schmidt reflected numerous times on German history during his speech at the Bundesbank's central council on 30 November 1978; see chapter 8.

22. This point goes against what is often suggested not only in textbooks but also in the specialized literature. See, for instance, Weinachter, *VGE*; Waechter, *Schmidt und Giscard.*

23. Haas, "Introduction"; Verdun, "Role"; Clavert and Feiertag (eds), "Les banquiers centraux."

24. Emminger, *Verteidigung,* 207.

25. Boyce, *Great,* 5. Original emphasis.

26. James, "Vulnerability," 94.

27. Similarly, for the sake of convenience, "Germany" hereafter refers to West Germany.

28. Bouneau, Burigana, and Varsori, *Les trajectoires.*

29. On these *jeux d'échelle* in international history, see, for instance, Frank, "Penser," 63–64.

30. Mourlon-Druol, "Filling the EEC Leadership Vacuum?"

31. EPU members had set up a "European Unit of Account" on 1 July 1950. See Fountain, "European."

32. For the reform of the EUA, see chapter 2; for its renaming, see chapters 7 and 8.

33. Gilbert, "Narrating," 641.

34. Bitsch, *Histoire,* 212.

35. European governments might have opted for (and did opt for) isolation, national solutions, or simply neutrality rather than (further) cooperation.

36. Gilbert, "Narrating," 641.

37. Cooper, "Almost."

38. "Normally" since the euro is the obvious exception to this rule.

39. See chapter 1.

40. See, for instance, Warlouzet, *Le choix*; Wilkens, "Une tentative"; and chapter 1.

41. Ludlow, "Political," 5.

1. EUROPEAN MONETARY COOPERATION, 1945–1974

Epigraph. Valéry Giscard d'Estaing, AMAE, DAEF 971bis, "Les étapes et les difficultés de l'organisation monétaire de l'Europe," speech given at the École Centrale, 25 January 1974.

1. Mundell, "Theory."

2. McKinnon, "OCAs"; Kenen, "Theory"; Ingram, "Comment"; Haberler, "International Monetary System"; Fleming, "On Exchange Rate"; Kindleberger, "International."

3. See chapter 2. For an analysis of contemporary developments, see Mourlon-Druol, "Euro Crisis."

4. Goodhart, "Monetary," and Goodhart, "Problems"; Lucas, "Econometric."

5. BdF, 1035199602/3, R. de La Genière, "La monnaie," speech made in November 1979.

6. TNA, FCO30/2245, Bone to Cambridge, dinner discussion with Professor Mundell, 3 April 1974.

7. Magnifico, *L'Europe.*

8. Magnifico, *European.*

9. See, for instance, Cobham, "Strategies."

10. Eichengreen, "When," 3.

11. Kruse, *Monetary,* 63.

12. Eichengreen, "When," 3.

13. Ungerer, *Concise History*, 84.

14. Wilkens, "Une tentative," 84.

15. Marsh, *Euro*, 74.

16. Ibid., 288 n. 99.

17. See Bottex, "La mise."

18. BoE, 7A3/12, Monetary Committee, Committee of Governors, Mandate of the working party "Harmonisation of monetary policy instruments," February 1974.

19. See chapters 2–5 in particular.

20. Mourlon-Druol, "Filling the EEC Leadership Vacuum?"

21. Although the impact of the Court of Justice did not go unnoticed. See, for instance, BoE, 6A404/6, Palliser to Butler, Note by Watts, "The influence of the Court of Justice on the development of the Community," 10 September 1975.

22. Simon, *Le système*.

23. The Jacques Vabre case of the French *Cour de Cassation*, on 24 May 1975, interestingly underlined that national courts were beginning to take into account ECJ jurisprudence.

24. See Treaty establishing the EEC; Ungerer, *Concise History*, 45–56.

25. EEC Treaty, articles 67–73.

26. Both in the Commission and also later on with the Marjolin Report. See chapter 2.

27. See, for instance, Feiertag, "Banques centrales"; Clavert, *Schacht*.

28. Tsoukalis, *Politics and Economics*.

29. Ungerer, *Concise History*, 57–66.

30. See Warlouzet, *Le choix*, chapter 6.2.

31. Ibid.

32. Ungerer, *Concise History*, 62.

33. BdF, 1489200205/272, Bref historique de l'association de pays tiers au "serpent," 25 March 1975.

34. Sweden applied for membership in May 1972, but following the crisis of that year (British pound sterling and Danish krona left), joined only in March 1973.

35. BdF, Bureau d'information des CE, "Appel solennel de la Commission européenne aux Chefs d'État ou de Gouvernement et, à travers eux, à tous les Européens," 31 January 1974.

36. Quoted in Weinachter, *VGE*, 69.

37. AMAE, DAEF973, Circulaire no. 384, Entretiens entre V. Giscard d'Estaing et H. Schmidt, 1 June 1974.

38. See Ludlow, *European Community*, 184–85.

39. HAEU, EN599, Handwritten notes during the informal dinner at the Élysée, 14 September 1974.

40. Mourlon-Druol, "Filling the EEC Leadership Vacuum?"

41. See AMAE, DE3790, Telegram no. 402–05, mémoire du gouvernement luxembourgeois, 25 September 1974.

42. AN, Paris, 5AG3/921, Robin to Giscard, Communication italienne, 18 November 1974; AN, Paris, 5AG3 921, Robin to Pierre-Brossolette, 26 November 1974.

43. AMAE, DE3790, Telegram no. 4347–4360 of Burin des Roziers, 8 November 1974.

44. Urwin, *Community*, 174.

45. See chapter 3.

46. HAEU, EN71, Note: observations sur les déclarations de M. Brandt (Paris, 19 November 1974).

47. Ibid.

48. *AAPD 1974*, document 162.

49. HAEU, EN599, Handwritten notes on the "dîner de travail des ministres des affaires étrangères," 16 September 1974.

50. CMA, CM2 1974 576, Draft resolution of the Council and the Representatives of the Governments of the Member States on the implementation of a second stage of EMU in the Community, 8 January 1974.

51. CMA, CM2 1974 575, Décision du Conseil relative à la réalisation d'un degré élevé de convergence des politiques économiques des États membres de la CEE, and CMA, CM2 1974 575, Décision instituant un Comité de politique économique.

52. Ungerer, *Concise History*, 136.

53. To be fair, the French government insisted that this leaving was temporary and that it would be reconsidered within six months, but the decision was quite symbolic.

54. Grygowski, *Les États-Unis*, 285.

55. AMAE, DAEF971bis, Note of Chenu: La Grande-Bretagne et l'UEM, 10 April 1974.

56. See, for example, TNA, T354/115, Fogarty to Airey, Float, vacuum and EMU, 25 January 1974.

57. TNA, FCO30/2245, Bostock to Bailey, Morel, a European investment instrument, and the snake, 13 February 1974.

58. Ibid., Thomas to Littler, French thinking on current monetary problems, 7 March 1974. See also ibid., Littler to Thomas, French thinking on current monetary problems, 3 April 1974.

59. AMAE, DE3774, Note au Comité d'action pour les États-Unis d'Europe du professeur Triffin, 18 January 1972.

60. AMAE, DE3774, Article by Triffin on EMU, no title, no date (presumably 1973/1974).

61. AMAE, DAEF977, Chenu, propositions monétaires du professeur Triffin, 2 April 1974.

62. AMAE, DAEF976, Note sur les problèmes monétaires européens, mid-1974.

63. On Giscard's advisers in more general terms, see Tristram, "Un instrument"; see also Cohen, *Les conseillers*.

64. See, for instance, the chapter titled "Une politique étrangère élyséenne," in Vaïsse, *La puissance*.

65. Helmut Schmidt, "Die deutsche und die japanische Währungsreform nach Weltkrieg II: Ein Vergleich" (master's thesis, University of Hamburg, 1949); Giscard, *La France*.

66. Febvre, *Encyclopédie*.

67. Jenkins, *European Diary*, 279.

68. TNA, T354/355, Bayne to Fogarty, International and European Monetary Questions, 16 July 1975.

69. AMAE, DAEF976, "La réforme du système monétaire international," speech of V. Giscard d'Estaing at the annual assembly of IMF and IRBD governors, 25 September 1973; Schmidt, *Menschen und Mächte*, 196.

70. HAEU, EN854, Noël, "Quelques réflexions sur la préparation, le déroulement et les répercussions de la réunion tenue à Paris par les Chefs de Gouvernement (9–10 décembre 1974)," 9 April 1975.

71. See *AAPD 1974*, document 206; Weinachter, *VGE*, 69.

72. AMAE, DAEF973, Circulaire no. 384, Entretiens entre M. Giscard d'Estaing et M. Helmut Schmidt, 1 June 1974; *AAPD 1974*, document 157. For the French side, see AMAE, DAEF973, Telegram no. 2369/76 de Morizet, rencontre franco-allemande, 4 June 1974.

73. *AAPD 1974*, document 162.

74. AdsD, HSA, 1/HSAA006638, Note, unsigned, Ihr Treffen mit Präsident Giscard d'Estaing, 30 May 1974.

75. Quoted in Weinachter, *VGE*, 132.

2. SHIFTING AWAY FROM THE WERNER APPROACH, MAY 1974–MAY 1975

Epigraphs. Jean-Yves Haberer, BdF, 1489200205/287, "Les problèmes de l'identité monétaire européenne," speech given at the Institut Auguste Comte pour les Sciences de l'action, 9 March 1981. Helmut Schmidt, *Kontinuität und Konzentration*, (Bonn-Bad Godersberg: Verlag Neue Gesellschaft GmbH, 1976), 17 January 1975, 146–47.

1. Bothorel, *Le pharaon*, 99; Goodman, *Monetary*, 115–16; Fourcade, *Et si nous parlions*, 137.

2. *AAPD 1974*, document 205.

3. Ibid., document 206.

4. Ibid., document 247.

5. TNA, PREM16/99, Record of a conversation between the PM and the German chancellor, 19 June 1974.

6. AdsD, HSA, 1/HSAA006594, Schmidt to Rumor, 23 July 1974.

7. Goodman, *Monetary*, 73.

8. *AAPD 1974*, document 181; AdsD, HSA, 1/HSAA006594, Schmidt to Rumor, 23 July 1974.

9. AMAE, DAEF972, Telegram no. 3016–3040 of Burin des Roziers, Conseil du 15 juillet, 20 July 1974.

10. See Weinachter, *VGE*, 132; and AN, Paris, 5AG3/2697, de Larosière to Fourcade, Éventuelle relance de l'Europe monétaire, 29 August 1974.

11. CMA, Intermediate 1974 29364, Prise de position de l'UNICE sur la relance européenne, 5 June 1974.

12. CMA, CM2 1974–615, Texts adopted by the Central Council of the ELEC, 13 May 1974.

13. BdF, 1489200205/258, Brandon Rhys Williams, "L'UEM—et ensuite?" 22 May 1974.

14. HAEU, EN71, Déclaration commune du Président du Conseil et du Président de la Commission, February 1974.

15. ECHA, BAC190–1999 61.

16. Ibid.

17. AMAE, DAEF972, Commission to Council, "Mesures urgentes en matière économique et monétaire," 5 June 1974.

18. BAK, B126/65702, Jaeckel, Mitteilung der Kommission an den Rat vom 5.6, 6 June 1974.

19. ECHA, Collection des discours, "The Personality of Europe and EMU," speech of Ortoli in New York, 26 September 1974.

20. Ibid.

21. Giscard, *Le pouvoir et la vie*, 3:247.

22. BoE, 8A406/2, Allen to Coleby, ECSC loan in "European Currency Unit," 24 November 1970. The same acronym appeared in an article in *Le Monde* on 19 December 1972, arguing for the creation of a European Currency Unit, ECU.

23. BoE, 8A406/2, Pirie to Burges-Watson, ECSC loan in European Monetary Units, 1 December 1970.

24. TNA, T233/2586, White, Weld & Co. Limited to Gas Council, 8 July 1971.

25. BoE, C159/1, N.M. Rothschild & Sons Limited to Bank of England, The "CECU" Unit, 2 August 1971.

26. Ibid., The "Euro-Unit," 16 May 1973.

27. Ibid., Explanatory memorandum: the European Composite Unit ("Eurco"), 8 June 1973.

28. BoE, C159/1, Barclays Bank International Ltd. to Bank of England, "Commercial Use of a European Monetary Unit Eurco-Index," 20 August 1973.

29. BoE, C159/2, Press release—EIB, 15 January 1974.

30. BoE, C159/2, Davison to Byatt, Currency Cocktails: The B-Unit and the Commercial Eurco, 4 February 1974.

31. BoE, C159/1, G.M.G. to Sangster, Proposed E.I.B. Issue in Euro-Units, 22 June 1973.

32. Cairncross, Giersch, Lamfalussy, Petrilli, and Uri, *Economic Policy*. For a more general discussion of the parallel currency approach, but still linked to the Kiel Institute, see also Vaubel, *Strategies*.

33. TNA, FCO30/2269, Giersch, "Economic Policy for the EC: The Way Forward," 4 December 1974.

34. Marjolin Report, Individual Contributions, Annex II, Giersch, "The Case for a European Parallel Currency."

35. TNA, FCO30/2269, Giersch, "Economic Policy."

36. See chapter 5.

37. The Fourcade memorandum is only cursorily mentioned in Tsoukalis, *Politics and Economics*, 156–57, as well as in Marsh, *Euro*, 74–75. Saint-Périer mentions only the first Fourcade memorandum, of September 1974, and essentially focuses on the Franco-German dimension; see "VGE," 38–66; Saint-Périer, "La France," 51–58.

38. BdF, PVCG tome 165, Discours du Gouverneur Wormser, 20 June 1974.

39. AMAE, DAEF976, Déclaration de M. Fourcade au Conseil des Ministres de la CEE du 15 juillet au sujet du maintien d'un flottement autonome pour le franc.

40. AN, Paris, 5AG3/2697, de Larosière to Fourcade, Éventuelle relance de l'Europe monétaire, 29 August 1974.

41. Ibid.

42. AN, Paris, 5AG3/897, Réunion de Champs-sur-Marne (7/8 septembre 1974), Communication de M. Fourcade; and AN, Paris, 5AG3/2697, Ruault to Giscard, Préparation du Conseil des Ministres du 16 septembre, 11 September 1974.

43. AMAE, DAEF971bis, Communication du président du Conseil des Communautés sur la relance monétaire européenne, 16 September 1974.

44. CAEF, B0050416, Note DGSE, Aspects techniques d'une nouvelle définition de l'unité de compte européenne, 16 September 1974. The SDR (Special Drawing Right), created in 1969, became the IMF unit of account in 1972.

45. See chapter 7.

46. ECHA, BAC565–1995 355, Déclaration de M. Haberer devant le Comité monétaire le 10 octobre 1974.

47. ASBI, Banca d'Italia, Studi, Serie CEI—Economia internazionale, 617, Rinaldo Ossola, Towards new EEC exchange rate arrangements, 18 October 1974, and 642, Barattieri to Ossola, La fluttuazione concertata, 24 September 1974.

48. ECHA, BAC565–1995 355, Commission of the EC, DG for Economic and Social Affairs, Note on concerted floating, not, presumably October 1974. Original emphasis.

49. ECHA, BAC565–1995 355, Note sur un nouveau régime de fluctuation des monnaies européennes, presumably 10 October 1974; and AN, 5AG3/2697, Direction du Trésor, unsigned, "Esquisse d'un nouveau régime de fluctuation des monnaies européennes," 29 August 1974.

50. ECHA, BAC565–1995 355, Note sur l'unité de compte européenne présentée par les membres français, 10 October 1974.

51. James, *International*, 165–74.

52. Ibid., 300.

53. See ECB, PV 85ème séance du Comité des Gouverneurs, 12 December 1974; ECHA, BAC565–1995 357, Report of the Monetary Committee on the problem of the European Unit of Account, 28 November 1974; ECHA, BAC565–1995 358–359, Report of the Monetary Committee on joint floating, 4 December 1974; ECHA, BAC190–1999 62,

Groupe d'experts présidé par M. Heyvaert, Propositions françaises relatives à l'unité de compte monétaire européenne, no. 27, 3 December 1974.

54. AN, Paris, 5AG3/908, Fourcade to Giscard, Préparation du sommet européen, 2 December 1974; AN, Paris, 5AG3/908, Dutet to Giscard, Réunion des Chefs de gouvernements de la CEE: questions économiques et financières, 7 December 1974.

55. ECB, PV 84ème séance du Comité des Gouverneurs, 30 September 1974.

56. Ibid.

57. The expression was coined by Jacques van Ypersele; see *EMS*, 44. AMAE, DAEF977, Groupe d'experts Théron, Rapport préliminaire sur les propositions françaises d'adaptation du dispositif de change intracommunautaire, no. 23, 6 November 1974.

58. BAK, B126/65702, Note of Glomb, TO-Punkt 5: "Konzertiertes Floating," 2 December 1974.

59. ECB, PV 85ème séance du Comité des Gouverneurs, 12 November 1974.

60. ECHA, BAC565–1995 358–359, Report of the Monetary Committee on joint floating, 4 December 1974.

61. ECHA, BAC190/1999 62, Propositions françaises relatives à l'unité de compte monétaire européenne, Rapport du groupe d'experts présidé par M. Heyvaert no. 27.

62. BdF, 1489200205/367, Banque nationale de Belgique, Groupe d'experts présidé par M. Heyvaert. La définition et le rôle de l'UCME selon le plan Fourcade, 20 November 1974.

63. See chapter 7.

64. For more details, see Saint-Périer, "VGE."

65. ECHA, BAC565–1995 357, Report of the Monetary Committee on the problem of the European Unit of Account, 28 November 1974.

66. ECHA, BAC190–1999 62, Groupe d'experts présidé par M. Heyvaert, Propositions françaises relatives à l'UCME, no. 27, 3 December 1974.

67. ECHA, BAC565–1995 358–359, Report of the Monetary Committee on the problem of the unit of account, 4 December 1974.

68. CMA, CM21974 585, Commission Communication to the Council, Guidelines in respect of the unit of account, 13 December 1974.

69. AMAE, DAEF972, Telegram no. 4662/4684 of Burin des Roziers, Conseil des Ministres du 18 novembre 1974, 22 November 1974.

70. HAEU, EN599, Handwritten notes during the informal dinner at the Élysée, 14 September 1974.

71. Ibid; HAEU, EN599, Ausführungen des Bundeskanzlers in Paris am 14. September 1974; AdsD, HSA, 1/HSAA009361, Note of Massion, Auswärtiger Ausschuss am 25. September, 24 September 1974.

72. HAEU, EN854, É. Noël, "Quelques réflexions sur la préparation, le déroulement et les répercussions de la réunion tenue à Paris par les Chefs de Gouvernement (9–10 décembre 1974)," 9 April 1975.

73. AN, Paris, 5AG3/908, Dutet to Giscard, Sommet européen, questions économiques, 8 November 1974.

74. HAEU, EN868, Deuxième rapport du groupe ad hoc aux Ministres des Affaires étrangères, 21 November 1974.

75. HAEU, EN869, Rapport des Ministres des Affaires étrangères, 5 December 1974.

76. AMAE, DE3790, Telegram no. 4766–4792 of Burin des Roziers, préparation de la réunion des Chefs de Gouvernement, 27 November 1974.

77. HAEU, EN65, Note, contribution de la Commission à l'élaboration d'une présentation analytique du rapport aux chefs de gouvernement, not signed, 3 December 1974.

78. See, for instance, NAI, DFA, 2004/4/487, Report of Meeting of Interdepartmental Group on EMU held on 13 January 1975; and ASBI, Banca d'Italia, Studi, Serie CEI—

Economia internazionale, 605, Telegram of the Italian representation at the EEC, Consiglio dei Ministri Finanziari della Communità, 16 September 1974.

79. See chapters 7 and 8.

80. HAEU, EN854, É. Noël, "Quelques réflexions sur la préparation, le déroulement et les répercussions de la réunion tenue à Paris par les Chefs de Gouvernement (9–10 décembre 1974)," 9 April 1975.

81. CMA, CM21974 47, Summary of decisions taken by the Council at its meeting held on 18 November 1974.

82. AMAE, DAEF972, Telegram no. 4662/4684 de Burin des Roziers, Conseil des Ministres du 18 novembre 1974, 22 November 1974.

83. AN, Paris, 5AG3/908, Fourcade to Giscard, Préparation du Sommet européen, 2 December 1974.

84. CAEF, B0050483, de Larosière to Fourcade, Préparation de la réunion des Chefs de Gouvernement des États membres de la Communauté. Rapport du Groupe ad hoc et UEM, 29 November 1974.

85. BoE, 4A149/17, Thomas, Record of conversation: French thoughts on the Council of Ministers (Finance) on 16 September, 26 August 1974.

86. AMAE, DE973, Circulaire no. 954, Réunion des Chefs de Gouvernement Paris 9–10 décembre 1974—Problèmes "de substance," 14 December 1974.

87. TNA, PREM16/382, Records of the meetings of heads of state and government together with foreign ministers on 9 December, 13 December 1974.

88. TNA, FCO30/2046, Record of a meeting of heads of government/state and foreign ministers at the Quai d'Orsay, Paris, 10 December 1974.

89. CMA, CM2 1974 111, Meeting of the heads of government of the Community, Paris, 9–10 December 1974, final communiqué. This statement admittedly was slightly ambiguous, since the Paris Conference's precise objective was EMU by 1980. The explicit absence of the year from the statement was, however, widely interpreted as the dropping of the 1980 objective.

90. AMAE, DAEF972, Telegram no. 5303/5324 of Burin des Roziers, Conseil du 19 décembre, 20 December 1974.

91. CMA, CM2 1974 107, Le secrétaire général, 13 December 1974, no title, unsigned.

92. NAI, DT, 2005/145/734, Report of meeting of interdepartmental group on EMU, 13 January 1975.

93. ECB, PV 86ème séance du Comité des gouverneurs, 10 December 1974.

94. ECHA, BAC190/1999 63, Introduction of a common exchange policy (highly confidential), meeting held in Washington with the authorities of the Federal Reserve Board and the Federal Reserve Bank of New York, summary report.

95. ECB, PV 90ème séance du Comité des gouverneurs, 8 April 1975.

96. ECHA, BAC190/1999 62, Note without title, 15 January 1975.

97. ECB, PV 87ème séance du Comité des gouverneurs, 15 January 1975. Interestingly, a verbal understanding between Schmidt and the Bundesbank in 1978 over the EMS would have similar implications—that is, of depriving the new mechanism of any real constraint. See chapter 8.

98. ECB, PV 86ème séance du Comité des gouverneurs, 10 December 1974.

99. BdF, 1489200205/57, Heyvaert Group, report no. 45, Coordination des politiques de change des banques centrales de la CEE à l'égard du dollar, 4 December 1979; BdF, 1489200205/239, Committee of Governors, Examen des politiques d'intervention appliquées par les banques centrales européennes depuis l'arrangement du 12 mars 1975, 2 December 1975.

100. ECHA, BAC565/1995 362, Rapport du Comité monétaire au Conseil et à la Commission sur l'unité de compte, 4 March 1975.

101. AMAE, DAEF972, Telegram no. 1034–1046 of Burin des Roziers, Conseil du 18 mars, 21 March 1975.

102. AN, Fontainebleau, 19900451, Article 55, SGCI, Conseil des CE, session du 18 mars 1975, unité de compte, 17 March 1975.

103. CMA, CM2 1975 36, Note, summary of decisions taken by the Council on 18 March 1975 in Brussels, 21 April 1975; see also AMAE, DAEF1555, Fiche non signée, L'unité de compte européenne, 24 April 1978.

104. CAEF, B0050484, Note on EMU, unsigned, 6 March 1975.

105. Robichek and Eaker, "Debt," 11–18.

106. AN, Fontainebleau, 19900451, Article 51, L'AGEFI, "Eurco: Nouvelle unité monétaire, devrait constituer une étape vers la création d'un marché européen des capitaux," 11 September 1973.

107. BdF, 1489200205/367, Note DGSE, Application de l'UCE: Réalisations, projets et perspectives, 10 February 1977.

108. De La Genière made a similar remark in December 1974. See Saint-Périer, "VGE," 57.

109. AN, Fontainebleau, 19900568, Article 398, Telegram no. 754–61 of Beaumarchais, Lendemains du sommet de Dublin, 13 March 1975.

110. AN, Paris, 5AG3/908, SGCI, Document de travail, Suites données au communiqué final de la réunion des chefs de gouvernement à Paris, 7 March 1975.

111. Robert Marjolin et al. *Report of the Study Group "Economic and Monetary Union 1980."* Brussels: Commission of the European Communities, 1975. The members of the Marjolin study group were R. Marjolin (chairman), F. Bobba, H.W.J. Bosman, G. Brouwers, L. Camu, B. Clappier (until June 1974, when he was appointed at the Banque de France), I. Foighel, F. Forte, H. Giersch, P. Lynch, D. MacDougall, H. Markmann, F. Peeters, A. Shonfield, and N. Thygesen.

112. Marjolin, *Report*, 1.

113. ECHA, Collection des discours, Allocution du président Ortoli au XIIème Congrès annuel de l'Association des Journalistes Européens, Mayence, 13 September 1974.

114. Marjolin, *Report*, 2–5.

115. Ibid., 11–27.

116. This fund should not be confused with the "Exchange Stabilisation Account" mentioned in the Kiel Report.

117. Marjolin, *Report*, 27–35.

118. Bothorel, *Le pharaon*, 101; Mourlon-Druol, "Economist."

119. Goodman, *Monetary Sovereignty*, 116; and Bothorel, *Le pharaon*, 139.

120. AN, Paris, 5AG3/2641, Ruault to Giscard, Conseil restreint du 20 décembre; Politique conjoncturelle, 16 December 1974; see also AN, Paris, 5AG3/2641, Sérisé to Giscard, 16 December 1974.

121. ECB, PV 88ème séance du Comité des gouverneurs, 11 February 1975.

122. AMAE, DAEF972, Telegram no. 1675–1686 of Cazimajou, Conseil du 20 mai.

123. CAEF, Fonds Cabinet, 1A256, Note of Bauchard, Rentrée du franc dans le serpent communautaire, 12 May 1975.

124. AdsD, HSA, 1/HSAA006590, Note of Sanne, Gespräch des Bundeskanzlers und des Bundesaußenministers mit Premierminister Wilson und Außenminister Callaghan am 29. Mai 1975, 2 June 1975.

125. Both of these points are absent from Saint-Périer's analysis; see "VGE," 68–72 (for the return of the French franc in the snake) and 38–66 (for the first Fourcade memorandum).

126. CAEF, B0050484, de Larosière to Fourcade, Réflexions sur une rentrée éventuelle du franc dans le "serpent," 18 April 1975.

127. Ibid.

128. BdF, 1489200205/273, Note DGSE, Retour éventuel du franc dans le système de communautaire de change, 9 December 1974; BdF, 1489200205/273, Note DGSE, Retour éventuel du franc dans le système communautaire de change, March 1975.

129. TNA, FCO30/2801, Arculus to Rawlinson, Note of a conversation between Davies, Fourcade, and de Larosière, 9 September 1975.

130. AMAE, DAEF977, SGCI, Conseil des CE, session du 20 mai 1975, retour du franc dans le "serpent" et système communautaire de change, 16 May 1975.

131. CAEF, B0050484, Aide-mémoire sur le fonctionnement du mécanisme européen de rétrécissement des marges, 20 May 1975.

132. TNA, FCO30/2800, French memorandum on the operation of the European mechanism of narrowed margins, 20 May 1975.

133. AMAE, DAEF976, Telegram no. 289/292 of Lissac, Réflexions danoises sur le serpent monétaire européen, 17 April 1975.

134. ASBI, Banca d'Italia, Studi, Serie CEI—Economia internazionale, 634, Note, Confronti tra il pro-memoria francese del 20 maggio 1975 sul funzionamento del meccanismo europeo di restringimento del margini e vecchie proposte italiane sull'argomento, 4 June 1975.

135. ECHA, BAC565/1995 364, Committee of Governors, Report on the French suggestions for adaptation of the Community exchange rate system, 3 June 1975.

136. AdsD, HSA, 1/HSAA009014, Aktuelle Fragen der Währungs-und Bankenpolitik, Address of Pöhl on 4 June 1975.

137. TNA, FCO30/2800, French memorandum on the operation of the European mechanism of narrowed margins, 20 May 1975.

138. AMAE, DAEF976, Note pour le cabinet du ministre de la Direction des Affaires juridiques, Caractère communautaire du "serpent," 16 July 1975.

139. ECB, PV 89ème séance du Comité des Gouverneurs, 11 March 1975.

140. ECB, PV 92ème séance du Comité des Gouverneurs, 8 June 1975.

141. HAEU, Collection des discours, "The Personality of Europe and EMU," speech by Ortoli in New York, 26 September 1974.

142. BB, B330/DRS142, Protokoll der 413. Sitzung des ZBR, 22 May 1974; CAEF, B0050484, Note sur l'UEM, unsigned, 6 March 1975; NAI, DFA, 2004/4/487, Report of meeting of Interdepartmental Group on EMU held on 13 January 1975.

143. Marjolin, *Report*, 17.

144. Marjolin, *Report*, Individual Contributions, Annex II, 77.

145. BAK, B136/7910, Note of Everling, Gipfelkonferenz in Paris, Besuch von Herrn Delarosière am 4. Dezember 1974, 4 December 1974; CAEF, B0050483, de Larosière to Fourcade, 6 December 1974.

146. AdsD, HSA, 1/HSAA006645, note unsigned, Thematik und Ausgangslage des Treffens, 6 November 1974.

147. *AAPD 1974*, document 162.

148. On this, see McNamara, *Currency*.

149. ECHA, BAC565/1995 359, Compte-rendu succinct, 322ème session du Conseil consacrée aux "questions économiques et financières," 19 November 1974.

150. CMA, CM2 1974 35, Summary of decisions taken by the Council on 16 September 1974.

151. CMA, CM2 1974 63, Summary of decisions taken by the Council on 19 December 1974.

152. CMA, CM2 1974 44, Press release, 310th meeting of the Council of Economics and Finance, 21 October 1974.

153. NAI, DT, 2005/7/513, Meeting with Mr. Wilson in Dublin on 21 November 1974.

154. TNA, FCO30/2800, Bayne to Spreckley, President Giscard on Britain and EMU, 23 May 1975.

155. TNA, PREM16/99, Record of a conversation between the PM and Herr Schmidt, 19 June 1974.

156. TNA, T355/194, Balfour to Fogarty, Basel—10/11 December, 12 December 1974.

157. TNA, T354/425, Record of a lunch held at 11 Downing Street on Monday, 3 February 1975.

158. BdF, PVCG tome 166, Intervention de MM. de Larosière et de Lattre, 19 June 1975. Emphasis added.

159. BoE, OV34/99, Freeland to Thomson, C.A. Freeland—visit to the Bundesbank, EEC and OECD, 31 May 1974.

160. CAEF, B0050483, de Larosière to Fourcade, 6 December 1974.

161. By way of example, see BoE, 7A3/9, Objectives and instruments of monetary policy in the Netherlands, 7 January 1975; Objectives and instruments of monetary policy in Denmark, 9 January 1975; Memorandum on monetary policy in Belgium, 20 January 1975; Note on the objectives and methods of monetary policy in the United Kingdom, undated (presumably early 1975), etc. All notes were produced by the respective central bank.

162. BoE, 7A3/9, Commission of the EEC, DG for economic and financial affairs, Summary of memoranda concerning the monetary policy pursued by the Member States of the EC, 19 February 1975.

163. BoE, 7A3/12, Comité monétaire and Comité des gouverneurs, Groupe de travail présidé par M. Bastiaanse, Rapport intérimaire du groupe de travail sur l'harmonisation des instruments de la politique monétaire, 24 June 1976.

164. Commission of the EC, Report of the study group on the role of public finance in European integration, April 1977; TNA, FCO30/2802, Carey to Littler, Study group on the role of public finance in European economic integration, 9 December 1975.

165. TNA, FCO30/2800, Bostock to Fogarty, EMU, 13 February 1975. For Jenkins's ideas of monetary union, see chapter 5.

166. CAEF, B0050427, de Larosière to Fourcade, Le "rapport Marjolin" et les thèses françaises en matière de politique monétaire européenne, undated.

3. EMU OFF THE AGENDA? JUNE 1975–JUNE 1976

Epigraph. Otmar Emminger, *D-Mark*, 357.

1. See, for instance, a note of the Italian Foreign Ministry in CMA, CM21975/125, Ministero degli Affari Esteri, Consiglio Europeo del 16–17 Luglio, Prospettive di sviluppo della Comunità a seguito del referendum britannico (elementi per un intervento del Presidente del Consiglio), undated, unsigned. See also the title of an entire part of Giscard's overall dossier for the Brussels European Council: AN, Paris, 5AG3/909, Chemise "Avenir de la construction européenne après le référendum britannique."

2. AN, Paris, 5AG3/909, Compte-rendu du Conseil européen de Bruxelles, 16/17 juillet 1975.

3. Ibid., Robin to Giscard, Avenir de la construction européenne après le référendum britannique, 10 July 1975.

4. *AAPD 1975*, document 175.

5. AMAE, DE3775, Télégramme circulaire no. 495 of Courcel, Visite à Paris de M. Genscher, 16 June 1975.

6. AN, Paris, 5AG3/909, Chemise "Avenir de la construction européenne après le référendum britannique," July 1975.

7. AN, Paris, 5AG3/909, Robin to Giscard, 10 July 1975.

8. Ibid., Communiqué sur la rentrée du franc français dans le serpent, non signé, non daté.

9. For the Werner-style plan on EMU, see CAEF, 1A256, Mathonnet, Note sur l'avenir monétaire de l'Europe, 2 July 1975.

10. CAEF, B0050484, de Larosière to Giscard, Réflexions sur l'avenir de l'avenir de l'UEM, 2 July 1975.

11. CMA, CM2 1975 368, Ortoli to Cosgrave, 26 June 1975.

12. CMA, CM2 1975 368, Commission of the EC, Report on European Union, COM (75) 400, 25 June 1975.

13. Ibid., 16. Emphasis added.

14. Ibid., 18–19.

15. Ibid., 20.

16. Ibid., 45.

17. Ibid., 53.

18. AN, Paris, 5AG3/909, Handwritten notes of Dutet, Réunion de préparation du Conseil européen chez J.-R. Bernard (SGCI), 25 June 1975.

19. Ibid., Note introductive de Robin au dossier du Président sur le Conseil européen de Bruxelles, 10 July 1975.

20. Ibid.

21. AN, Paris, 5AG3/909, Telegram no. 1864/1868 of Cazimajou, Conseil européen, 6 June 1975.

22. NAI, DT, 2005/151/537, Notes on European Council meeting of 16–17 July 1975; AN, Paris, 5AG3/909, Robin to Giscard, Conseil européen, 13 June 1975.

23. AN, Fontainebleau, 19900568, Article 398, Compte-rendu du Conseil européen de Bruxelles, 16/17 juillet 1975.

24. TNA, FCO30/2800, Bostock to Bailey, European Council: 16/17 July: Possible DG II Papers, 25 June 1975.

25. For a recent example, see Waechter, *Schmidt und Giscard*.

26. AN, Paris, 5AG3/909, Compte-rendu du Conseil européen de Bruxelles, 16/17 juillet 1975.

27. Bothorel, *Le pharaon*, 138.

28. Saint-Périer, "VGE," 72–75.

29. BAK, B126/65703, Schmidt to Giscard, 25 June 1975.

30. Goodman, *Monetary*, 117.

31. Bothorel, *Le pharaon*, 138–46.

32. Ibid., 143.

33. AN, Paris, 5AG3/2645, Ruault to Giscard, Plan de soutien: Réflexions de caractère général, 20 August 1975.

34. CAEF, 1A304, Programme de développement de l'économie française, Conférence de presse de J.-P. Fourcade, 5 September 1975.

35. CAEF, 1A256, Plan de soutien de l'économie 1975, Exposé des motifs.

36. Frank, "Les problèmes monétaires," 19.

37. Benning, "Economic."

38. AN, Paris, 5AG3/885, Dutet to Giscard, Conférence d'Helsinki: Déjeuner quadripartite, 29 July 1975. Questions économiques et financières; AN, Paris, 5AG3/885, MINEFI, Direction du Trésor, Note unsigned, undated, Schéma d'un retour progressif à un système de parités stables mais ajustables.

39. AMAE, DE3775, Telegram no. 3698/3703 of Wormser, Politique européenne du gouvernement allemand, 23 October 1975.

40. *AAPD 1975*, document 340.

41. TNA, FCO30/2801, Palliser, EMU, diplomatic report no. 326/75, 26 September 1975.

42. NAI, DT, 2006/131/1145, Memorandum presented by Taoiseach for discussion at European Council, Rome, 1–2 December 1975. The Irish memorandum originated from the realization that the German memorandum was harmful to Irish interests; instead of fighting it, the Irish government decided to put forward its own proposals. See NAI, DT, 2005/151/550, Memorandum for government, unsigned, 25 November 1975.

43. TNA, FCO30/3308, Hickman to Fretwell, Irish attitude to EMU, 22 January 1976.

44. AN, Fontainebleau, 19900568, Article 399, Extraits des notes prises en séance par M. Sauvagnargues, 4 December 1975; HAEU, EN1928, Commission des CE, COM(75) 630, La situation économique et sociale dans la Communauté, 25 November 1975.

45. AN, Fontainebleau, 19900568, Article 399, Télégramme circulaire no. 901 de Froment-Meurice, Conseil européen, questions économiques, 3 December 1975.

46. CMA, CM2 1975 127, Office of the President of the European Council, Summary of the conclusions of the meeting of the European Council held in Rome on 1 and 2 December 1975; AN, Fontainebleau, 19900568, Article 399, Télégramme circulaire no. 901 de Froment-Meurice, Conseil européen, questions économiques, 3 December 1975.

47. TNA, PREM16/399, Meeting of the European Council, Rome, 1/2 December 1975, record of discussion, 9 December 1975.

48. Ibid., Denman to Part, European Council Rome 1–2 December 1975, 8 December 1975.

49. Bulletin of the EC, Supplement 1/76, European Union, Report by Leo Tindemans to the European Council.

50. Ibid., 20.

51. Ibid., 22.

52. Ibid.

53. ASBI, Banca d'Italia, Studi, Serie CEI—Economia internazionale, 606, Appunto per il Dr. Palumbo, Alcuni elementi per il nostro discorse all'inizio del semestre italiano, 19 June 1975; and ibid., 593, MAE, Rapporto Tindemans: Elementi per un intervento, UEM, Consiglio europeo del 29–30 novembre 1976.

54. CAEF, B0050484, de Larosière to Fourcade, analyse du rapport Tindemans en ce qui concerne l'UEM, 10 February 1976.

55. BdF, 1489200205/281, Note unsigned, "Esquisse d'une réforme du système de change européen," March 1976.

56. TNA, T384/146, Note of the Bank of England, EMS: Smaller countries, September 1978.

57. Both currencies of course remained members of the snake, which thereby merely swallowed the worm.

58. BdF, 1489200205/273, de Larosière to Fourcade, Compte-rendu des entretiens monétaires de Bruxelles du 14 mars 1976, 16 March 1976.

59. See also BoE, 6A103/5, Note for the record of Jordan-Moss, 17 March 1976.

60. Ibid., Bayne to Jordan-Moss, The franc and the snake: Trésor views, 19 March 1976.

61. TNA, T384/65, Telegram no. 278, Ewart-Biggs to FCO, French proposals for EEC economic and monetary coordination, 19 March 1976.

62. The specific files of the British Treasury do not contain traces of such a proposal by Fourcade (the same applies to other archives). See TNA, T387/86: Joint meeting of EEC Foreign and Finance Ministers, 5 April 1976.

63. ACS, Archivio Aldo Moro, Busta 122, Tesoro, Cooperazione monetaria nella Comunità, 29 March 1976.

64. *AAPD 1976*, document 90.

65. TNA, PREM16/853, Record of a meeting of the European Council, Luxembourg, on 1 and 2 April 1976.

66. HAEU, EN1914, Note du SG, undated, Éléments d'informations sur le "Conseil européen" de Luxembourg, 1er et 2 avril 1976—Intervention de M. Giscard d'Estaing; NAI, 2007/116/423, French draft.

67. AN, Fontainebleau, 19900568, Article 400, Conseil européen de Luxembourg, Compte-rendu résumé, 6 April 1976.

68. Ibid; *AAPD 1976*, document 98.

69. TNA, PREM16/853, Record of a meeting of the European Council, Luxembourg, 1–2 April 1976.

70. Emminger, *D-Mark*, 357.

71. *AAPD 1976*, document 92.

72. AMAE, DE3775, Note de la sous-direction d'Europe occidentale, Les Neuf après Luxembourg: Le Conseil européen mis en cause? 14 April 1976.

73. Ibid.

74. AN, Paris, 5AG3/921–922, Robin to Giscard, Conseil européen, 8 April 1976.

75. *AAPD 1976*, document 98.

76. TNA, PREM16/393, Nairne to Palliser, European Council, 29 July 1975.

77. TNA, PREM16/850, Steering brief by FCO, European Council, Brussels, 12/13 July 1976, 2 July 1976.

78. AMAE, DE3775, Note de la sous-direction d'Europe occidentale, Les Neuf après Luxembourg: Le Conseil européen mis en cause? 14 April 1976.

79. Maurice Delarue, "Paris souhaiterait un 'directoire' européen," *Le Monde*, 10 February 1976; BAK, B136/30664, Massion to Schmidt, Äusserungen Giscards zu einem Direktorium in der EG, 11 February 1976.

80. Henry Peyret, "Un directoire européen," *Le Monde*, 11 February 1976.

81. BAK, B136/30664, Tindemans to Schmidt, 11 February 1976.

82. AMAE, DE3775, Telegram no. 253/57 of Senard, Réactions néerlandaises après le Conseil européen de Luxembourg, 5 April 1976.

83. *AAPD 1975*, document 340.

84. AMAE, DE3775, Telegram no. 3551/3560 of Wormser, Premiers résultats des réflexions du gouvernement fédéral sur le fonctionnement des Communautés, 3 October 1975.

85. AMAE, DAEF3775, Giscard to Thorn, 23 March 1976.

86. AMAE, DAEF1485, Note of Froment-Meurice, Opinion allemande sur le Conseil européen, 25 March 1976. The Dutch and Irish governments were also against any monetary move; see NAI, DFA, 2004/4/487, Note on telephone discussion with Max van der Stoel, 31 March 1976.

87. AN, Fontainebleau, 19900568, Article 400, Conseil européen de Luxembourg, Compte-rendu résumé, 6 April 1976.

88. TNA, PREM16/852, Mitchell to Stowe, European Council: Economic and Monetary Questions, 31 March 1976.

89. CAEF, B0050484, Action économique et monétaire, Communication de la Commission au Conseil européen des 1–2 avril 1976 à Luxembourg.

90. Goodman, *Monetary*, 117.

91. *AAPD 1976*, document 133.

92. "Les déclarations 'irréfléchies' de M. Schmidt sur le gaullisme 'étonnent' M. Chirac," *Le Monde*, 7 May 1976.

93. *AAPD 1976*, document 133.

94. *AAPD 1976*, document 176.

95. AN, Fontainebleau, 19900568, Article 400, Conseil européen de Luxembourg, Compte-rendu résumé, 6 April 1976; NAI, DFA, 2004/4/487, Notes on European Council, 1 April 1976.

96. TNA, PREM16/853, Record of a meeting of the European Council, Luxembourg, 1–2 April 1976.

97. The text of the All Saints' Day Manifesto is reproduced in Fratianni and Peeters, *One Money*, 37–43. The nine signatories of this Manifesto were Giorgio Basevi, Michele Fratianni, Herbert Giersch, Pieter Korteweg, David O'Mahony, Michael Parkin, Theo Peeters, Pascal Salin, and Niels Thygesen.

98. Ibid., 38.

99. Salin, *L'unification*, 276.

100. *Optica Report 1975: Towards Economic Equilibrium and Monetary Unification in Europe*, II/909/75-F final, 16 January 1975.

101. Ibid., 25.

102. Ibid., 41.

103. On the OCA theory, see chapter 1.

104. *Optica Report 1975*, 26.

105. Magnifico, *L'Europe*. See also Magnifico, *L'Euro*.

106. Riboud, *Une monnaie*.

107. For the last version, see Mundell, "Plan." Earlier versions of this plan dated from 1970 and 1973.

108. Robichek and Eaker, "Debt."

109. The difference was actually only in slightly diverging weights of currencies; see ibid., 15.

110. CMA, Intermediate 1976 62044–1, Letters of Marcel Florestan Vanlathem to the EC Council, February 1976.

111. CMA, Commission of the EC, Report on EU, 4.

112. AN, Fontainebleau, 19900568, Article 398, Compte-rendu du Conseil européen de Bruxelles, 16/17 juillet 1975.

113. AN, Paris, 5AG3/885, Compte-rendu de M. Sauvagnargues concernant le Déjeuner Quadripartite de la Conférence d'Helsinki, non daté (presumably around 30 July–1 August 1975).

114. AN, Fontainebleau, 19900568, Article 398, Compte-rendu du Conseil européen de Bruxelles, 16/17 juillet 1975.

115. Mourlon-Druol, "Managing."

116. AN, Paris, 5AG3/886, Handwritten notes of Giscard on the Rambouillet declaration.

117. Tindemans Report, 19.

118. AMAE, DAEF972, Telegram no. 2526–2549 of Soutou, Conseil du 10 juillet, 14 July 1975.

119. *AAPD 1975*, document 268.

120. Mourlon-Druol, "Economist."

121. Fourcade, *Et si nous parlions*, 136.

122. AN, Paris, 5AG3/886, Ministère de l'Economie et des Finances, Note to Giscard, La situation économique française et les perspectives pour 1976, 12 November 1975.

123. PAAA, Zwischenarchiv 105674, Note, Deutsch-französischer Gipfel, 28 July 1975.

124. See for instance "The Snake Must Be Strict," Interview with K.-O. Pöhl, *Newsweek*, 5 April 1976.

125. Tsoukalis, *Politics*, 11–15.

126. CMA, Commission of the EC, Report on EU, 12.

127. TNA, PREM16/853, Telegram no. 103, European Council Luxembourg 1/2 April 1976, 2 April 1976.

128. *AAPD 1975*, document 367; AN, Fontainebleau, 19900568, Article 399, Note unsigned, undated, Amélioration des procédures de décision de la Communauté.

129. BAK, B136/17144, Note of Schmidt, EG-institutionelle Ergebnisse meiner Vier-Augen-Gespräche mit Premierminister Wilson und Staatspräsident Giscard d'Estaing am 24. Juli bzw. 26. Juli 1975, 27 July 1975.

130. ASBI, Banca d'Italia, Studi, Serie CEI—Economia internazionale, 593, Contributo italiano all'elaborazione del rapporto sull'unione europea. Testo consegnato al primo ministro Tindemans a seguito della sua visita a Roma, October 1975.

131. TNA, PREM16/393, Nairne to Palliser, The European Council, 29 July 1975.

132. *AAPD 1976*, document 1.

133. AMAE, DAEF3775, Note de la sous-direction d'Europe occidentale, non signée, Rencontre des directeurs politiques français et allemands, Perspectives du 4ème Conseil européen, 26 September 1975.

134. TNA, PREM16/393, Nairne to Palliser, The European Council, 24 September 1975.

135. TNA, PREM16/393, Record of a discussion at European Council held in Brussels, 16/17 July 1975.

136. TNA, PREM16/399, Meeting of the European Council, Rome, 1/2 Dec. 1975, record of discussion, 9 December 1975.

137. TNA, PREM16/393, Palliser to Nairne, The European Council, 16 September 1975.

138. "The Prime Ministers are the only ministers in national governments who deal with all subjects that are being negotiated in the various Councils and they need to be engaged if the Community is to work properly. Only they can exert the necessary authority over their Ministers to get them to settle the really difficult questions." Butler, *Europe*, 29.

139. TNA, FCO30/2801, Carey to Littler, 24 September 1975.

140. Décision (3289/175/CECA) de la Commission relative à la définition et à la reconversion de l'Unité de compte à utiliser dans les décisions, recommandations, actes et communiqués dans les domaines du Traité instituant la CECA.

141. TNA, PREM16/813, Donoughue to Wilson, Monetary Policy, 23 Dec. 1975, with attached note by the Policy Unit.

142. Schmidt, *Kontinuität*, 139 (declaration made on 17 January 1975).

143. CAEF, B0050484, Note of de Larosière, Le "serpent" monétaire européen, 6 February 1976.

144. BdF, PVCG, tome 166, 4 December 1975.

4. ECONOMIC RAPPROCHEMENT, MONETARY STANDSTILL, JULY 1976–JUNE 1977

Epigraphs. Raymond Barre, "L'Europe face à l'inflation et à la récession," in *L'Europe des crises*, ed. Robert Triffin, Raymond Aron, Raymond Barre, and René Ewalenko (Bruxelles: Bruylant, 1976), 151–52, speech given in October 1975. Helmut Schmidt, Ford Digital Library, National Security Adviser, box 12, memorandum of conversation, Schmidt-Ford, 29 May 1975.

1. HAEU, EN1140, Discussion between Jenkins and Barre in Paris on 28 February 1977, 7 March 1977.

2. BAK, B126/65704, Note of Willmann, Vorschläge von Herrn Oort zum Wechselkurssystem der EG, 18 June 1976; TNA, FCO30/3308, Shepherd to Butler, EMU: Dutch proposals, 21 July 1976; BAK, B126/65776, Oort to Pöhl, European Exchange Rate Policy: A Working Paper, 30 August 1976. See also Oort, "Exchange Rate."

3. BB, N2/264, Oort to Pöhl, 4 June 1976. Original emphasis.

4. TNA, T384/1, Duisenberg to Healey, 6 July 1976.

5. BdF, 1489200205/276, Bank of England, Suppléants des gouverneurs, Note de MM. McMahon et Balfour sur les arrangements de la CEE en matière de change, 6 September

1976; Ibid., DGSE, unsigned note, Réflexions sur la note anglaise relative aux accords de change de la CEE, 10 September 1976.

6. TNA, T384/1, Brief for the EEC Finance Ministers' meeting, 26 July 1976.

7. BdF, 1489200205/257, Note DGSE, Quelques considérations sur les proposi-tions Oort-Duisenberg, 6 September 1976; and ibid., Note of Lacoste, CEE—Politique de change—Les propositions néerlandaises de juin-juillet 1976, 31 August 1976.

8. CAEF, B50427, de Larosière to Barre, Système européen de changes—coordination des politiques économiques des États membres de la CEE, 7 September 1976.

9. CMA, Intermediate 9716, Strengthening of the internal economic and financial coherence of the Community, statement made by Mr. Duisenberg on 26 July 1976; TNA, T384/1, Telegram no. 3991, UK representation in Brussels, Council of Ministers, 26 July 1976; ECHA, BAC 565/1995 no. 386, Note from the Dutch alternates, A system of target zones for exchange rates in the Community, 12 January 1977.

10. ECHA, BAC 565/1995 no. 379, Commission, DG economic and financial affairs, Improving the co-ordination of economic policies, 30 August 1976, and Boyer de la Gi-roday to Burgard and Webb, Travaux en vue de la session de septembre du Comité moné-taire, 27 July 1976.

11. TNA, T384/1, Briefs for the EEC Finance Minister's meeting, 26 July, Annex 2: The "Duisenberg" Initiative.

12. ECHA, BAC 565/1995 no. 380, Detailed minutes of the session of the Monetary Committee on 10 September 1976.

13. CAEF, B0050484, de Larosière to Barre, Propositions néerlandaises sur l'amélioration de la convergence économique dans la CEE, 14 October 1976.

14. CAEF, B50427, de Larosière to Barre, Système européen de changes—coordination des politiques économiques des États membres de la CEE, 7 September 1976.

15. BAK, B126/65704, Note of Flandorffer, Niederländische Vorschläge zur stärkeren Harmonisierung der Wirtschaftspolitik in der Gemeinschaft, 30 August 1976. Otmar Em-minger, who was then vice president of the Bundesbank, also expressed doubt about target zones (both on the world stage and within the EEC) in his memoirs; see *D-Mark*, 351–52.

16. CAEF, B50427, de Larosière to Barre, Système européen de changes—coordina-tion des politiques économiques des États membres de la CEE, 7 September 1976; CAEF, B0050484, de Larosière to Barre, Réunion des suppléants du comité monétaire sur la proposition néerlandaise de zones cibles, 1 February 1977.

17. CMA, Intermediate 1976 9943, Commission of the EC, The Economic Situation in the Community at the End of the Summer 1976, 13 September 1976.

18. Conclusions of the session of the European Council in Brussels, 12 and 13 July 1976.

19. TNA, PREM16/850, Denman to Neale, European Council Brussels 12/13 July, 16 July 1976.

20. Conclusions of the session of the European Council in Brussels, 12 and 13 July 1976.

21. NAI, DT, 2006/133/484, European Council meeting, 12–13 July 1976.

22. TNA, PREM16/850, European Council in Brussels 12/13 July: second session, re-construction from secretary of state's own notes.

23. Giscard, *Le pouvoir et la vie*, 2:420.

24. Ibid., 420–53.

25. Ibid., 453–64.

26. Giscard denies making this statement, saying that he would have described Barre only as *one of* the best French economists (not least because Giscard did not want to ex-clude himself from the list of the best French economists!), but the common memory of

the statement is the first version. For Giscard's point of view, see *Le pouvoir et la vie*, 2:463. On Barre, see Bothorel, *Le pharaon*, 200–209.

27. Barre, *Économie politique*.

28. Barre, *L'expérience*, 102.

29. Mamou, *Une machine*, 103.

30. Barre, *L'expérience*, 77.

31. Ibid., 100.

32. Ibid., 168.

33. TNA, PREM16/1275, Henderson to Owen, 6 April 1977.

34. See also the description given by Giroud, *La comédie*, 244.

35. Ibid., 463.

36. Discours de R. Barre à l'Assemblée nationale, 5 October 1976, http://archives.assemblee-nationale.fr/5/cri/1976-1977-ordinaire1/002.pdf, accessed 6 November 2011.

37. TNA, FCO30/3626, Translation of the French prime minister's interview with *Der Spiegel*, 28 February 1977.

38. Barre, *L'expérience*, 101–2.

39. See again his speech at the National Assembly, and Goodman, *Monetary Sovereignty*, 118–26.

40. BdF, 1035199602/2, Exposé de M. de La Genière sur la politique monétaire à la séance du Conseil général de la Banque de France du 9 mars 1978; BB, B330/017637, Note of Dörner, Geldpolitische Ziele in den EG-Ländern, den USA und der Schweiz und bisherige Erfahrungen, 30 November 1977; and Barre, *L'expérience*, 102.

41. See, for instance, the chapter "Bundestagswahl 1976" in Soell, *Schmidt*, 575–602.

42. On the 1976 IMF episode, see Wass, *Decline*.

43. BoE, ADM3/16, Report and accounts for the year ended 28 February 1977, July 1977.

44. James, *Europe*, 343–45.

45. Discours de R. Barre à l'Assemblée nationale, 5 October 1976; TNA, PREM16/1275, Note of a meeting with PM of France on 11 January 1977.

46. AdsD, HSA, 1/HSAA006587, Note of Massion, Zur Persönlichkeit des französischen Ministerpräsidenten Barre, 3 September 1976; see also Schmidt, *Die Deutschen*, 223.

47. AdsD, HSA, 1/HSAA006587, Aufzeichnung von Veronika Isenberg zur Benennung des neuen französischen Premierministers, 26 August 1976.

48. AN, Paris, 5AG3/2649, Note sur le plan de lutte contre l'inflation du Commissariat général au Plan, 27 August 1976 ; ibid., Projet de note confidentielle, 25 June 1976.

49. Ibid., Ruault to Giscard, Lutte contre l'inflation, 30 June 1976.

50. Giroud, *La comédie*, 253.

51. AN, Paris, 5AG3/911, Compte-rendu résumé du Conseil européen de La Haye, 6 December 1976.

52. TNA, PREM16/851, Record of a meeting of the European Council at The Hague, Statement by the president of the French Republic, 29 November 1976.

53. Ibid., Record of a meeting of the European Council at The Hague, 29 November 1976.

54. AN, Paris, 5AG3/911, Compte-rendu résumé du Conseil européen de La Haye, 6 December 1976.

55. TNA, PREM16/851, Record of a meeting of the European Council at The Hague, 29 November 1976.

56. TNA, PREM16/1253, Steering brief for the Rome European Council, 25–26 March 1977, 17 March 1977.

57. AN, Paris, 5AG3/911, Compte-rendu résumé du Conseil européen de La Haye, 6 December 1976.

58. AN, Fontainebleau, 19900568, Article 400, Conclusions du Conseil européen des 29 et 30 novembre 1976.

59. BoE, OV47/65, Unsigned note to McMahon, 1 April 1976.

60. As far as monetary cooperation is concerned, see, for instance, the report of one of these meetings in AMAE, DAEF1137, de Larosière to Barre, Examen du rapport Tindemans, réunion du 29 juillet 1976 ; see also Froment-Meurice, *Vu du Quai*, 453–54.

61. AN, Paris, 5AG3/911, Giscard to Callaghan (and all other heads of EEC governments), 21 January 1977.

62. AdsD, HSA, 1/HSAA006591, Callaghan to Schmidt, 18 February 1977, van der Stoel to Crosland, 16 December 1976, and Schmidt to Callaghan, 16 March 1977.

63. PAAA, Zwischenarchiv, 121819, van der Stoel to Genscher, with attached memorandum entitled "Organization of the European Council," 15 December 1976.

64. AN, Paris, 5AG3/911, Giscard to Callaghan (and all other EEC heads of government), 21 January 1977.

65. See, for instance, Schmidt's reported tirade following a dinner after the meeting of the European Council of July 1976 in Brussels, in TNA, PREM16/860, Maitland to Wright, European Council, 13 July 1976.

66. ASBI, Banca d'Italia, Studi, Serie CEI—Economia internazionale, 593, MAE, Ristrutturazione della Commissione, Conglio europeo, 29–30 November 1976.

67. TNA, PREM16/860, Maitland to Wright, European Council, 13 July 1976.

68. ECB, PV 108ème séance du Comité des gouverneurs, 8 February 1977.

69. The reinforcement of Franco-German bilateral relations is absent from the literature. Neither Story ("Franco-German"), Ménudier ("VGE"), Miard-Delacroix (*Partenaires*), Waechter (*Schmidt und Giscard*), nor Weinachter (*VGE*) make any mention of it.

70. TNA, FCO30/3626, Note from the British Embassy in Bonn, Paris Summit: Financial Issues, 10 February 1977.

71. Ibid., Telegram no. 108, Franco-German Summit, 7 February 1977.

72. BAK, B102/292805, Note of Everling on the outcome of the Franco-German consultations, 7 February 1977.

73. TNA, FCO30/3626, Bayne to Littler, French views on economic and monetary matters, 9 February 1977.

74. Ibid., Arculus to Butler, Convergence in the European Community, 7 March 1977.

75. HAEU, EN1140, Discussion between Jenkins and Barre in Paris, on Monday, 28 February 1977, 7 March 1977.

76. Text of the joint declaration in TNA, FCO30/3626, Telegram no. 108 from Paris, Franco-German Summit, 7 February 1977.

77. AdsD, HSA, 1/HSAA006689, Note of Zeller, Deutsch-französische Konsultationen der Staats-und Regierungschefs (3. und 4. Februar 1977), 31 January 1977.

78. TNA, FCO30/3626, Bayne to Fretwell, Franco/German relations—Economic aspects, 30 June 1977.

79. BAK, B102/292805, Note of Everling on the outcome of the Franco-German consultations, 7 February 1977.

80. AdsD, HSA, 1/HSAA006689, Note of Zeller, Deutsch-französische Konsultationen der Staats-und Regierungschefs (3. und 4. Februar 1977) in Paris; Gesprächsvorlage, 31 January 1977; TNA, FCO30/3626, Note from the British Embassy in Bonn, Paris Summit, 16 February 1977.

81. CAEF, B50427, de Larosière to Barre, 10 March 1977.

82. See, for instance, TNA, FCO30/3626, Note of the British Embassy in Bonn, Franco-German Summit: Convergence, 24 February 1977.

83. See, for instance, ibid., Butler to Jordan-Moss, Convergence in the EC, 14 March 1977.

84. Ibid., Arculus to Butler, Convergence in the EC, 7 March 1977.

85. HAEU, EN1918, Compte rendu succinct de la 416ème session du Conseil consacrée aux "questions économiques et financières" (Bruxelles, 8 novembre 1976), 10 November 1976; CMA, Intermediate, Summary of decisions of the Finance Council of 8 November 1976.

86. NAI, DF, F1/1/77, Community Exchange Rate System—Duisenberg Proposals, March 1977; TNA, T384/1, Telegram no. 5546 from UK representation in Brussels, EEC Council of Ministers, 8 November 1976.

87. ECB, PV 105ème séance du Comité des gouverneurs, 9 November 1976.

88. On the communication of the Commission of April 1976, see chapter 3.

89. CMA, Intermediate 9716, Monetary Committee, Report to the Council and the Commission, 4 November 1976.

90. ECB, PV 101ème séance du Comité des gouverneurs, 11 May 1976.

91. The report is available in TNA, T384/1, Committee of Governors, Alternates, Report on possible arrangements for contributing to greater exchange rate stability among all Community currencies, 2 November 1976.

92. Ibid., Meeting of EEC Governors, 9 November 1976.

93. Ibid., Committee of Governors, Alternates, Report on possible arrangements for contributing to greater exchange rate stability among all Community currencies, 2 November 1976.

94. ECB, PV 105ème séance du Comité des gouverneurs, 9 November 1976.

95. Ibid., PV 107ème séance du Comité des gouverneurs, 11 January 1977.

96. AdsD, HSA, 1/HSAA006603, Duisenberg to Schmidt, 7 December 1976.

97. Ibid. Original emphasis.

98. AdsD, HSA, 1/HSAA006603, Schmidt to Duisenberg, 20 January 1977.

99. AN, Fontainebleau, 19900568, Article 400, Conseil européen de Luxembourg, Compte-rendu résumé, 6 April 1976; see also *AAPD 1976*, document 98, 456.

100. HAEU, EN1544, Secretariat general of the Commission, Background note on the political situation in France, 22 February 1977.

101. TNA, PREM16/1263, Telegram no. 617 from Wright (Bonn), Franco-German summit (16–17 June), 22 June 1977.

102. CADN, Bonn (ambassade), Sous-série France, Carton 323, Telegram no. 2388/2399 of Henry, Politique intérieure: difficultés de la majorité, 31 May 1977; see also TNA, PREM16/851, Telegram no. 420 of Barnes, Dutch political situation, 25 November 1976.

103. See, for instance, TNA, PREM16/1263, Telegram no. 624 of Wright, FRG Internal scene, 24 June 1977.

104. See AdsD, HSA, 1/HSAA006690, Note of Zeller, 7. Europäischer Rat (25./26. März 1977 in Rom), 23 March 1977; AN, Paris, 5AG3/911, Robin to Giscard, Conseil européen, 22 March 1977; TNA, PREM16/1264, Steering brief by FCO for the European Council in Rome, 22 June 1977.

105. AN, Paris, 5AG3/911, Robin to Giscard, 23 March 1977.

106. BdF, 1489200205/203, Note to Barre, Compte rendu de la 227ème session du Comité Monétaire, 22 February 1977.

107. The strength of the German position led de Larosière to coin the expression "the power of German veto," ibid.

108. AdsD, HSA, 1/HSAA006688, BMF/AA, Zur deutsch-britischen Regierungschefkonsultation am 24. Januar 1977 in Chequers, Schwerpunkte der europäischen Währungspolitik im ersten Halbjahr 1977, 11 January 1977.

109. BdF, 1489200205/203, Secrétariat du Comité monétaire, Projet de compte rendu de la 228ème session du Comité monétaire (3 mars 1977), 11 March 1977; see also ibid., Note to Barre, Compte rendu de la 228ème session du Comité monétaire, 3 March 1977.

110. AMAE, DAEF1486, Télégramme no. 927/946 of Nanteuil, Conseil ECO-FIN du 14 mars, 15 March 1977. For the report of the Committee of Governors, see CMA, Intermediate 9716, Committee of Governors, Report to the Council and the Commission on the feasibility of implementing the Dutch proposals regarding target zones for exchange rates within the Community, 8 March 1977.

111. BB, B330/016427, Note, Tagung des Finanzministerrats am Montag, 14.3.1977, in Brüssel, Duisenberg-Vorschlag (Zielzonen), 15 March 1977; see also TNA, FCO30/3626, Telegram no. 1803, EEC Council of Ministers, 14 March 1977.

112. BdF, 1489200205/203, Note to Barre, 231ème réunion du Comité Monétaire, 9 June 1977.

113. ASBI, Banca d'Italia, Studi, Serie CEI—Economia internazionale, 619, Note of Papadia, Regole di fluttuazione in seno alla CEE come base di un nuovo sistema di cambio intracommunitario, 6 September 1976.

114. BdF, 1489200205/276, Oort to Pöhl, 25 February 1977.

115. Ibid., Rapport du Comité des Gouverneurs, Rapport sur les moyens susceptibles de contribuer à une plus grande stabilité des relations de change intracommunautaire, 3 February 1977.

116. See chapter 8.

117. AAPD 1977, documents 160 and 161; see also TNA, PREM12/1263, Telegram no. 617 of Wright, Franco-German summit (16–17 June), 22 June 1977.

118. BAK, B102/266610, de La Genière to Schlecht, 27 May 1977. Surprisingly, it was no longer a question of involving the foreign ministers.

119. AN, Paris, 5AG3/936, de La Genière to Barre, 10 June 1977.

120. TNA, PREM12/1263, Telegram no. 617 of Wright, Franco-German summit (16–17 June), 22 June 1977.

121. See ECB, PV 109ème séance du Comité des gouverneurs, 8 March 1977; ibid., PV 110ème séance du Comité des gouverneurs, 19 April 1977; ibid., PV 111ème séance du Comité des gouverneurs, 10 May 1977.

122. TNA, FCO30/3626, Bayne to Fretwell, Franco-German relations—Economic aspects, 30 June 1977.

123. TNA, PREM12/1263, Telegram no. 617 of Wright, Franco-German summit (16–17 June), 22 June 1977.

124. ECB, PV 109ème séance du Comité des gouverneurs, 8 March 1977.

125. The British government took over the presidency of the EEC on 1 January 1977; TNA, PREM16/1253, Steering brief by the FCO for the European Council in Rome, 17 March 1977.

126. AAPD 1977, document 79.

127. On the question of representation of the EEC during the G7 summits, see Garavini, "Battle."

128. TNA, FCO30/3626, Address given by V. Giscard d'Estaing, on the occasion of the inauguration of the palace of Europe in Strasbourg, 28 January 1977.

129. Froment-Meurice, Vu du Quai, 473.

130. CAEF, B0054084, Note to Barre, 25 March 1977.

131. BdF, 1489200205/273, Viaud to MINEFI, Le franc et le serpent européen, 11 January 1977.

132. HAEU, EN1544, Brief of Noël for Jenkins's meeting with Barre, 24 February 1977.

133. AN, Fontainebleau, 19900568, Article 401, Session du Conseil européen des 25–26 mars 1977 à Rome, Conclusions de la Présidence.

134. See, for instance, Dinan, Europe, 173.

135. TNA, PREM16/1254, Draft record of the European Council in Rome, 28 March 1977.

136. TNA, PREM16/1263, Transcript of the press conference held by the PM and Mr. Jenkins on 30 June 1977.

137. Commission of the EC, Report of the study group on the role of finance in European integration, April 1977.

138. Ibid., 11.

139. Ibid., 17.

140. ECHA, BAC 565/1995 no. 385, OPTICA Report 1976, Towards economic equilibrium and monetary unification in Europe, 20 December 1976.

141. See, for instance, the Marjolin Report and, even more tellingly, the MacDougall Report.

142. Its last attempt, analyzed in chapter 3, dated back to April 1976.

143. TNA, FCO30/3626, Arculus to Butler, Convergence in the EC, 7 March 1977.

144. BdF, 1489200205/203, Note to Barre, Compte rendu de la 227ème session du Comité Monétaire, 22 February 1977.

145. BoE, 6A103/5, Note on EEC Exchange Rate Arrangements to McMahon, unsigned, 30 July 1976.

146. TNA, FCO30/3626, Brief for 14 February Finance Council, Note for the chancellor on exchange rates and "target zones," not signed, not dated.

147. CAEF, B50424, Note to Giscard, Bilan des travaux du comité monétaire et du Conseil sur les propositions Duisenberg, 17 March 1977.

148. Even though it may be anecdotal, many archives I looked at did have a specific dossier devoted to the Duisenberg initiative, while none had a specific dossier for the Fourcade memorandum.

149. See Mourlon-Druol, "Economist."

150. TNA, FCO30/3626, Boyd to Minister, Paris Summit: Financial Issues, 10 February 1977; see also AMAE, DAEF1127, de Larosière to Barre, Problèmes communautaires—Visite de M. Jenkins, 24 February 1977.

151. HAEU, EN1140, Discussion between Jenkins and Barre in Paris on Monday, 28 February 1977, 7 March 1977.

152. CAEF, B0062158, Note du SGCI, Procédures de concertation communautaires et plan français de lutte contre l'inflation, 17 September 1976.

153. Jenkins, Life, 462.

154. TNA, T384/1, Telegram no. 3391, UK representation in Brussels, Council of Ministers, 26 July 1976.

155. CMA, Intermediate 9716, Note, Strengthening of the internal economic and financial coherence of the Community, statement made by Mr. Duisenberg on 26 July 1976, 28 July 1976. See also the similar reference made in the Commission in HAEU, EN1918, Gautier-Sauvagnac to Ortoli, Réunion ministérielle de La Haye: Situation économique et monétaire, 17 November 1976.

156. BAK, B126/65704, Note unsigned, Fourcade-Vorschläge zur Änderung des europäischen Währungsystems, 3 September 1976; ibid., two notes of Willmann, Vorschläge zum Wechselkurssystem der Gemeinschaft, 7 September 1976. In an even more detailed fashion, see ibid., unsigned note, 220. Tagung des Währungsauschusses in Kopenhagen am 10. September 1976, 23 August 1976. NAI, DFA, 2004/4/487, Common monetary policy, April 1976.

157. CMA, Intermediate 9716, Monetary Committee, Report to the Council and the Commission, 4 November 1976.

158. TNA, T384/1, Committee of Governors, Alternates, Report on possible arrangements for contributing to greater exchange rate stability among all Community currencies, 2 November 1976; see also BoE, 6A103/5, Note to George on EEC Exchange Rate Arrangements, 6 August 1976.

159. TNA, FCO 30/3626, Telegram no. 1803, EEC Council of Ministers, 14 March 1977.

160. BdF, 1489200205/276, Note of Vienney, Réflexions sur les ex-plans de réforme de M. Fourcade et sur les propositions de M. Oort-Duisenberg, 9 September 1976. Even more interestingly, the DG Economic and Financial Affairs of the Commission also regularly did such comparisons; see ibid., Commission, DG Affaires économiques et financières, Confidentiel, Propositions de réforme du système de change communautaire, 25 August 1976.

161. BdF, 1489200206/276, Secrétariat du Comité monétaire, Compte rendu détaillé des discussions intervenues le 10 septembre à Copenhague sur le point 4 de l'ordre du jour "possibilité d'adoption de règles de flottaison au sein de la Communauté," 17 September 1976.

162. Ibid., McMahon to Théron, 6 September 1976.

163. Ibid., Committee of Governors, Alternates, Secretariat, Exchange rate arrangements within the Community (Notes on meeting in Basel on 14 September 1976), 29 September 1976.

164. Werner, L'Europe.

165. CAEF, B50424, Note to Giscard, Bilan des travaux du comité monétaire et du Conseil sur les propositions Duisenberg, 17 March 1977.

166. "Three Steps towards European Monetary Harmonization," Times (London), 26 July 1976. The members of the group signing this proposal were the Earl of Cromer, Bela Balassa, Armin Gutowski, Alexandre Lamfalussy, Giovanni Magnifico, Conrad Oort, Andrew Shonfield, Robert Triffin, Pierre Uri, and Jacques van Ypersele.

167. See TNA, T384/1, Naud to Butler, The Duisenberg Proposals, 20 July 1977. Ungerer, Concise History, 139.

168. See chapter 2.

169. BdF, 1489200205/203, Note to Barre, 220ème session du Comité Monétaire, 10 September 1976; see also CAEF, B0054084, Note to Barre, presumably from de Larosière, 25 March 1977.

170. BB, B330/017637, Note of Dörner, Geldpolitische Ziele in den EG-Ländern, den USA und der Schweiz und bisherige Erfahrungen, 30 November 1977; ECHA, BAC 565/1995 no. 380, Commission, DG affaires économiques et financières, La fixation d'orientations quantitatives pour la politique monétaire à l'intérieur des pays de la Communauté, 9 September 1976.

171. ECB, PV 108ème séance du Comité des gouverneurs, 8 February 1977.

172. BdF, 1489200205/276, Commission des CE, Propositions de réforme du système de change communautaire, 25 August 1976.

173. CAEF, B0050484, de Larosière to the President, UEM, 25 March 1977.

174. Discours de R. Barre à l'Assemblée nationale, 5 October 1976.

175. Mourlon-Druol, "Victory?"

176. AN, Paris, 5AG3/911, Projet d'intervention du président au Conseil européen de La Haye, 29–30 November 1976.

5. CONFLICTING OPTIONS, JULY 1977–MARCH 1978

Epigraph. Helmut Schmidt, MTA, Bundesbank Council meeting with Chancellor Schmidt, 30 November 1978.

1. TNA, FCO30/3627, Présidence belge de la CEE, Propositions sur le plan économique et monétaire, 23 June 1977; CMA, Intermédiaire 9686, Intervention de Gaston Geens au Conseil ECO/FIN du 18 juillet 1977.

2. TNA, FCO30/3626, Statement by Geens, at the Council meeting on Economics and Finance on 18 July 1977.

3. AMAE, DAEF 1553, Telegram no. 2619–24 of Nanteuil, Conseil Eco-Fin du 18 juillet 1977.

4. CMA, Intermédiaire 9686, Intervention de Gaston Geens au Conseil ECO/FIN du 18 juillet 1977.

5. See, for instance, TNA, PREM16/1640, Telegram no. 1088 of Wright, European Council 5/6 December 1977, 30 November 1977.

6. Jenkins, *Life*, 467. Callaghan makes a similar remark in *Time*, 492.

7. Jenkins, *Life*, 463.

8. Ibid. For the whole month of July, his diary is silent on the topic of monetary union (Jenkins, *European*, 124–34).

9. TNA, PREM16/1627, Note of a meeting between PM and Roy Jenkins on 21 July 1977.

10. Ibid., Brief for the PM's meeting with Roy Jenkins, here: EMU, 20 July 1977.

11. HAEU, EN1601, Note on Economic and monetary matters: The role of the Commission. Some suggestions for improvement, unsigned, 13 July 1976. Original emphasis.

12. HAEU, EN130, Ortoli, "Éléments de réflexion sur l'UEM," 15 September 1977.

13. TNA, FCO30/3627, Ortoli, "Points for Consideration with Regard to EMU."

14. See, for instance, Ludlow, "From Deadlock."

15. HAEU, EN130, Ortoli, "Éléments de réflexion sur l'UEM," 15 September 1977.

16. HAEU, EN130, "Les perspectives de l'Union monétaire," note diffusée par le président, 16 September 1977. The Jenkins paper was actually written by a member of his cabinet, Michael Emerson. See TNA 30/3627, Carey to Jordan Moss, EMU, 27 September 1977.

17. Jenkins, *Life*, 467.

18. TNA, FCO30/3627, "The Prospect of Monetary Union."

19. Ibid. See also Jenkins, *Life*, 463–65.

20. See, for instance, Froment-Meurice, *Vu du Quai*, 472–73.

21. TNA30/3627, Carey to Jordan Moss, EMU, 27 September 1977; AN, Paris, 5AG3/912, Dutet to Giscard, Conseil européen de Bruxelles: Question économiques susceptibles d'être évoquées, 9 November 1977; AMAE, DAEF 1553, Note no. 530/CE, Visite du Ministre à Bonn: Approfondissement de la Communauté, UEM, 8 November 1977.

22. Jenkins, *Life*, 465.

23. Grygowski, *Les États-Unis*, 236–37.

24. TNA, FCO30/3627, Commission communication to the Council, "Improving Co-Ordination of the National Economic Policies," 5 October 1977.

25. See, for instance, his meeting with Graf Lambsdorff in BAK, B102/266602, Note of Everling, Gespräch zwischen Lambsdorff und Ortoli, 17 October 1977.

26. TNA, FCO30/3627, Commission communication to the Council, "Improving Co-Ordination of the National Economic Policies," 5 October 1977.

27. Ibid., Telegram no. 6606 from UK representation in Brussels, Ad hoc group of financial counsellors, Commission communication on improving economic policy coordination, 7 November 1977.

28. Ibid., EEC Council of Ministers of 17 October 1977, 19 October 1977.

29. Ibid., Brief on Commission communication to the Council "Improving Co-Ordination of the National Economic Policies," undated, unsigned.

30. Ibid., Braithwaite to Carey, EMU, 6 October 1977.

31. Ibid., Telegram no. 5885 from UK representation in Brussels, Ortoli's visit to the Chancellor of the Exchequer, 6 October 1977.

32. The "proselytizing" metaphor is used by Jenkins in *Life*, 474.

33. R. Jenkins, "Europe's Present Challenge and Future Opportunity" (first Jean Monnet Lecture, European University Institute, Florence, 27 October 1977).

34. Middlemas, *Orchestrating*, 87; Dinan, *Europe*, 173.

35. "Look Before You Leap," *Economist*, 25 November 1977.

36. BB, B330/DRS.142, Protokoll der 495. Sitzung, 3 November 1977.

37. TNA, PREM16/1640, Jones to Cartledge, Treasury comments on Mr. Jenkins' lecture on EMU, 2 December 1977.

38. AN, Fontainebleau, 19900568 article 402, MAE, Note of Froment-Meurice, Entretien avec M. Ortoli, 14 November 1977.

39. See, for instance, BB, B330/17523, Pleines to Jennemann, Die WWU—ein entstehungsgeschichtlicher Abriss, 23 November 1977.

40. ECB, PV 116ème séance du Comité des gouverneurs, 13 December 1977.

41. ASBI, Banca d'Italia, Studi, Serie CEI—Economia internazionale, 621, Commission des CE, DG des affaires économiques et financières, Monnaies parallèles, unités de compte et organisation monétaire européenne, 11 January 1978.

42. ASBI, Segretaria particolare, Pratt., 1497, G. Magnifico, Memo on EMU, 18 November 1977. See also 1498, Masera, Appunto per il direttorio, Prospettive di unificazione economica e monetaria europea, 7 March 1978.

43. *AAPD 1977*, document 277.

44. TNA, PREM16/1640, Telegram no. 1088 of Wright, European Council 5/6 December 1977, 30 November 1977.

45. HAEU, EN1142, Note of Hayden Philipps, Meeting of President Jenkins with Andreotti, 28 October 1977 in Rome, 9 November 1977; HAEU, EN1143, Record of conversation between the president of the European Commission and the French PM, 19 November 1977.

46. Froment-Meurice, *Vu du Quai*, 473.

47. TNA, FCO30/3627, Bailes to Soutar, Meeting of EEC Commissioners at La Roche, 14 October 1977.

48. Ibid., Maud to Butler, The Duisenberg Proposals, 20 July 1977.

49. Ibid., Bailes to Soutar, Meeting of EEC Commissioners at La Roche, 14 October 1977.

50. Ibid., Bayne to Hedley-Miller, France and EMU, 28 October 1977; ibid., Bayne to Jordan-Moss, French economic policy: Germany and Europe, 28 October 1977.

51. AMAE, DAEF1553, Note BB/SF no. 530/CE, Visite du Ministre à Bonn: Approfondissement de la Communauté, UEM, 8 November 1977.

52. TNA, FCO30/3627, Bullard to Goodall, FRG and France, 26 October 1977.

53. CAEF, B50443, de Larosière to Barre/Boulin, Examen par le Comité monétaire de la communication de la Commission, 6 January 1978.

54. BdF, 1489200205/203, de Larosière to Barre/Boulin, 238ème réunion du Comité monétaire, 28 February 1978.

55. AMAE, DE4087, Compte-rendu de la réunion du 8 november 1977 sur la préparation du Conseil européen, 17 November 1977.

56. TNA, FCO30/3482, Telegram no. 738 of Henderson to FCO, Franco/British/German relations, 26 July 1977.

57. TNA, PREM16/1650, Hunt to Cartledge, Follow Up to President Giscard's Visit, 6 February 1978.

58. Wiegrefe, *Das Zerwürfnis*, 206–23; Grygowski, *Les États-Unis*, 244–55.

59. BoE, OV34/99, Boyd to Hall, Next president of the Bundesbank, 26 April 1977. K.-O. Pöhl became vice president. Emminger was regarded as closer to the CDU, while Pöhl was closer to the SPD (and Schmidt), which explains the German chancellor's insistence on his finance minister having the job of number two.

60. ECB, PV 113ème séance du Comité des gouverneurs, 12 July 1977.

61. BdF, 1489200205/203, de Larosière to Barre/Boulin, 235ème réunion du Comité monétaire, 15 November 1977.

62. TNA, FCO30/3627, Wright to Boyd, Call on the president of Deutsche Bundesbank: 11 November 1977, 15 November 1977.

63. BdF, 1489200205/203, de Larosière to Barre/Boulin, 236ème réunion du Comité monétaire, 9 December 1977.

64. ECB, PV 116ème séance du Comité des gouverneurs, 13 December 1977.

65. ECB, PV 119ème séance du Comité des gouverneurs, 14 March 1978.

66. *AAPD 1977*, document 194.

67. AdsD, HSA, Note of Loeck, Gespräch des Bundeskanzlers mit PM Barre am 6. Februar 1978, 8 February 1978.

68. TNA, PREM16/1641, Prime Minister's conversation with R. Jenkins on 31 March 1978.

69. Grygowski, *Les États-Unis*, 249–50.

70. Grygowski, "Les États-Unis," 327–28.

71. TNA, PREM16/1615, US/FRG Joint Communiqué, 13 March 1978.

72. ECB, PV 119ème séance du Comité des gouverneurs, 14 March 1978.

73. HAEU, EN1143, Call of the leader of the opposition in Britain on the President of the European Commission, Brussels, 2 December 1977.

74. James, *International*, 296–97.

75. BdF, 1489200205/203, de Larosière to Barre/Boulin, 239ème réunion du Comité monétaire, 4 April 1978.

76. Gowa, "Hegemons."

77. Jenkins, *Life*, 474.

78. Ibid., 467.

79. *AAPD 1977*, document 271.

80. TNA, FCO30/3627, Bayne to Hedley-Miller, France and EMU, 28 October 1977.

81. Ibid.

82. ECB, PV 114ème séance du Comité des gouverneurs, 13 September 1977.

83. ECB, PV 115ème séance du Comité des gouverneurs, 8 November 1977.

84. ECB, PV 116ème séance du Comité des gouverneurs, 13 December 1977.

85. TNA, FCO30/4003, Note for the record, Monetary Committee: 26 January 1978, 31 January 1978.

86. BdF, 1489200205/203, de Larosière to Barre/Boulin, 238ème réunion du Comité monétaire, 28 February 1978.

87. ECB, PV 119ème séance du Comité des gouverneurs, 14 March 1978.

88. ECHA, BAC 86/1989 no. 75, Commission, Communication on the prospect of EMU, 17 November 1977.

89. Jenkins, *Life*, 468.

90. Ibid., 469. See also Ludlow, "Political," 10–12, and *Making*, 56–58.

91. BAK, B102/266602, Note of Everling, Gespräch zwischen Lambsdorff und Ortoli, 17 October 1977.

92. TNA, FCO30/3627, Telegram no. 7061 of Maitland, Council of Finance Ministers, EMU, 22 November 1977.

93. Ibid; AN, Paris, 5AG3/912, Dutet to Giscard, Conseil européen de Bruxelles: Questions économiques, 1 December 1977; AN, Fontainebleau, 19900568 article 402, SGCI, Note, Les perspectives d'UEM. Communication de la Commission au Conseil, 29 November 1977.

94. AN, Paris, 5AG3/912, Handwritten notes of Robin, undated (but before the European Council).

95. AMAE, DE4087, Note of Froment-Meurice, Conseil européen: Questions économiques, 28 November 1977.

96. AN, Paris, 5AG3/912, Notes manuscrites de Dutet prises lors d'une réunion avec Paye (SGCI), 8 November 1977.

97. BdF, 1489200205/273, Note DGSE, La réintégration du franc français dans le "serpent" est-elle possible et surtout souhaitable? December 1977.

98. TNA, PREM16/1627, The President of the European Commission's call on the PM, 25 Nov. 1977.

99. Ibid., Record of a call by Roy Jenkins on the PM on Friday, 25 November 1977.

100. AdsD, HSA, I/HSAA006708, Zeller to Schmidt, Europäischer Rat in Brüssel, 2 December 1977.

101. TNA, PREM16/1627, The President of the European Commission's call on the PM, 25 Nov. 1977.

102. AN, Fontainebleau, 19890642, article 21, Telegram no. 4848 of Brunet, Entretien avec M. Emminger, 23 November 1977.

103. BdF, 1489200205/256, Note of the Banca d'Italia, Perspectives d'UEM: Considérations générales suggérées par la Communication de la Commission, 7 March 1978. Original emphasis.

104. ASBI, Banca d'Italia, Studi, Serie CEI—Economia internazionale, 595, MAE, Unione economica e monetaria, elementi di intervento, Consiglio europeo, 5–6 December 1977. Surprisingly, some in the European Commission shared this view and insisted on the importance of regional policy in EMU but did not manage to be followed by Jenkins. See ECHA, BAC 86/1989 no. 75, Giolitti to Jenkins and Ortoli, Relance de l'UEM, 11 October 1977.

105. NAI, DF, F001/005/78, A return to monetary cohesion, presumably December 1977; DT, 2007/116/526, EMU, Speaking note for December 1977 European Council.

106. Quotation from *AAPD 1977*, document 345; BAK, B136/11891, Thiele to Schmidt, Pläne der Kommission zur Wiederbelebung der WWU, 12 October 1977.

107. TNA, PREM16/1640, Commission of the European Communities, Opening statement of Roy Jenkins on the short-term outlook and the longer-term objectives of EMU, European Council 5/6 December 1977.

108. Jenkins, *Diary*, 181. That Schmidt seemed to be sleeping is also reported in the Irish record; see NAI, DT, 2007/116/527, European Council, Brussels, 5–6 December 1977.

109. TNA, PREM16/1640, Record of a meeting of the European Council held at the Charlemagne building, Brussels, on 5–6 Dec. 1977; CADN, RPCEE1167, Compte-rendu du Conseil européen de Bruxelles, 5 et 6 décembre 1977.

110. TNA, PREM16/1640, Record of a meeting of the European Council held at the Charlemagne building, Brussels, on 5/6 December 1977; AN, Paris, 5AG3/912, Représentation permanente de la France auprès des Communautés européennes, Conseil européen des 5 et 6 décembre 1977, procès-verbal officieux, 11 January 1978. Admittedly, the Danish government was also not very enthusiastic about the Commission's paper, but this was essentially due to the absence of concrete proposals. AN, Fontainebleau, 19900568 article 402, Telegram no. 705/13 of Gorce, Conseil européen des 5 et 6 décembre, 30 November 1977.

111. TNA, PREM16/1640, Record of a meeting of the European Council held at the Charlemagne building, Brussels, on 5–6 December 1977.

112. AN, Fontainebleau, 19900568 article 402, Conseil européen des 5 et 6 décembre 1977 à Bruxelles, Conclusions de la présidence.

113. Ibid., Conseil des CE, Note d'information sur les travaux de l'Assemblée, Strasbourg, session du 12 au 16 décembre 1977, 21 December 1977.

114. Jenkins, *Life*, 469.

115. ECHA, BAC 86/1989 no. 75, Commission, Action programme for 1978, 8 February 1978.

116. TNA, FCO30/4003, Telegram no. 1013 of Maitland to FCO, Finance Council: 20 February 1978, EMU, 20 February 1978.

117. For both versions, see BB, N2/264, "Rapprocher les monnaies européennes," February 1978, and "Rapprocher les monnaies européennes (2)," 22 March 1978.

118. Ibid., "Rapprocher les monnaies européennes (2)." Surprisingly, van Ypersele omits Fourcade—this is surprising since he did mention Fourcade in the first sketch of his plan; see ibid., "Rapprocher les monnaies européennes."

119. See chapter 2.

120. BB, N2/264, Schlüter to Pöhl, Van Ypersele-Plan für einen engerene Zusammenschluss der europäischen Währungen, 3 April 1978.

121. Ibid., "Rapprocher les monnaies européennes (2)," 22 March 1978.

122. TNA, PREM16/1641, PM's conversation with Jenkins on 31 March 1978.

123. MTA, Bundesbank Council meeting with Chancellor Schmidt, 30 November 1978.

124. AN, Paris, 5AG3/936, Compte-rendu de l'entretien du Président avec H. Schmidt, mardi 19 juillet 1977.

125. TNA, PREM16/1641, PM's conversation with Jenkins on 31 March 1978.

126. Ibid.

127. TNA, PREM16/1627, Record of a call by Jenkins on the PM on Friday, 25 November 1977.

128. See, for instance, Ludlow, *Making*, 63.

129. Marsh, *Euro*, 78–79; Thiemeyer, "Schmidt und die Gründung," 245–68.

130. Soell, *Schmidt*, 691–94; Waechter, *Schmidt und Giscard*. Soell's and Waechter's books are the only two to use Schmidt's private papers in Hamburg. Thiemeyer primarily uses the Schmidt papers held in Bonn, while Marsh does not, but includes material from the Bundesarchiv, the Bundesbank, and the Auswärtiges Amt.

131. See, for instance, Thiemeyer, "Schmidt und die Gründung," 250–52.

132. PREM16/1615, Note of Stowe, Prime Minister's meeting with Chancellor Schmidt, 12 March 1978.

133. Schmidt, *Die Deutschen*, 253.

134. PAAA, Zwischenarchiv 111215, von Dohnanyi to Genscher, Europäische Währungspolitik; Bemerkungen des Bundeskanzlers in der Kabinettsitzung am 15. February 1978, 15 February 1978.

135. See, for instance, Ludlow, *Making*, 63. Virtually all the literature makes a similar point.

136. PAAA, Zwischenarchiv 111215, Reaction of Genscher on the note of von Dohnanyi, 15 February 1978.

137. Schmidt himself made this point during his speech at the Bundesbank central council. See BB, N2/269, Emminger to Schmidt, EWS (Wortprotokoll ZBR-Sitzung), 1 December 1978, 8.

138. Ludlow, *Making*, 82–85. See also the description of the campaign given by Giscard in his memoirs, *Le pouvoir et la vie*, 3:315–39 and 3:769–82.

139. CADN, Bonn (ambassade), Sous-série France, Carton 323, Telegram no. 499/52 of Brunet, 31ème consultation franco-allemande et les relations entre la France et la République fédérale (III), 3 February 1978.

140. See, for instance, AMAE, DAEF1553, Note BB/SF no. 589/CE, Communication de la Commission au Conseil sur l'UEM, 28 November 1977.

141. CMA, Intermédiaire 9766, Intervention du Président, 18 July 1977.

142. NAI, DF, F1/1/77, Convergence of European currencies, The van Ypersele initiative, April 1978.

143. HAEU, EN130, Ortoli, "Éléments de réflexion sur l'UEM," 15 September 1977. Although he did not formally mention Duisenberg, Ortoli wrote: "*Reprise* de l'idée de target zones pour les monnaies ne faisant plus partie du serpent" (emphasis added). Both the concept and the use of the word "*reprise*" leave little doubt as to the fact that Ortoli was referring to the July 1976 Dutch initiative.

144. HAEU, EN1143, Record of conversation between the president of the European Commission and the French PM, 19 November 1977. See also ibid., Call of the leader of the opposition in Britain on the President of the European Commission, Brussels, 2 December 1977.

145. AN, Paris, 5AG3/920, Note of Robin, Audience de M. Jenkins, 22 February 1978.

146. TNA, FCO30/3482, Telegram no. 738 of Henderson, Franco/British/FRG relations, 26 July 1977.

147. NAI, DT 2007/116/47, EMU, Background note for the European Council in London, 29–30 June 1977.

148. HAEU, EN130, Ortoli, "Éléments de réflexion sur l'UEM," 15 September 1977; TNA, FCO30/3628, "The Integration of the Community in the Face of Enlargement," address of R. Jenkins to the Deutsche Gesellschaft für Auswärtige Politik, 8 December 1977.

149. TNA, FCO30/3628, Summary record of interventions by Ortoli and Lambsdorff at 21 November Finance Council. Ortoli made the same remark in a conversation with the German economics minister; see BAK, B102/266602, Note of Everling, Gespräch zwischen Lambsdorff und Ortoli, 17 October 1977.

150. See chapters 2 and 3.

151. BB, B330/DRS.142, Protokoll der 495. Sitzung des ZBR der Deutschen Bundesbank, 3 November 1977; ECHA, BAC 86/1989 no. 75, Éléments de réflexion sur l'UEM, Communication de M. Ortoli, Réunion spéciale de la Commission, 16–18 September 1977, 15 September 1977; NAI, DT 2007/116/525, EMU, 14 November 1977.

152. Grygowski, *Les États-Unis*, 307.

153. See, for instance, TNA, FCO30/3627, Forthcoming Community discussions on economic and monetary policy co-ordination, Memorandum by HM Treasury, 25 October 1977.

154. Ibid., Carey to Jordan Moss, EMU, 27 September 1977.

155. HAEU, EN1143, Record of conversation between the president of the European Commission and the French PM, 19 November 1977; TNA, FCO30/3628, Goodison to Fretwell, EMU: Mr Jenkins' lecture in Florence, 3 November 1977.

156. ECHA, BAC 86/1989 no. 75, Wilson to Rencki, Mr. Jenkins' arguments for monetary union, 1 December 1977.

157. HAEU, EN1143, Call of the leader of the opposition in Britain on the President of the European Communities, Brussels, 2 December 1977.

158. TNA, FCO30/3627, Carey to Jordan Moss, EMU, 27 September 1977.

159. HAEU, EN1142, Note of Philipps, Meeting of Jenkins with Andreotti, 28 October 1977, in Rome, 9 November 1977.

160. ECHA, BAC 86/1989 no. 75, Commission, Communication on the prospect of EMU, 17 November 1977.

161. TNA, PREM16/1640, Commission of the EC, Opening statement of R. Jenkins on the short-term outlook and the longer-term objectives of EMU, European Council 5–6 December 1977.

162. CAEF, B50443, de Larosière to Barre/Boulin, Examen par le Comité monétaire de la communication de la Commission sur l'amélioration de la coordination des politiques économiques nationales, 6 January 1978.

163. *AAPD 1977*, document 345.

164. AN, Paris, 5AG3/912, Représentation permanente de la France auprès des CE, Conseil européen des 5–6 décembre 1977, procès-verbal officieux, 11 January 1978.

165. TNA, PREM16/1640, Discussion between heads of government after dinner on 5 December.

6. A SEMISECRET NEGOTIATION, LATE MARCH–MID-JULY 1978

Epigraph. Roy Jenkins, *Diary*, 7 April 1978.

1. TNA, PREM16/1615, Note of Stowe: PM's meeting with H. Schmidt in Bonn, 12 March 1978.

2. TNA, PREM16/1641, PM's conversation with R. Jenkins on 31 March 1978. This was Jenkins's expression.

3. Giscard, *Le pouvoir,* 3:291.

4. TNA, PREM16/1615, PM's telephone conversation with President Giscard, 4 April 1978.

5. TNA, FCO30/4004, Bayne to Jordan-Moss, European Council, European Monetary Questions, 26 April 1978.

6. Schmidt, *Die Deutschen*, 249.

7. TNA, PREM16/1615, Note of Stowe: PM's meeting with Chancellor Schmidt in Bonn, 12 March 1978.

8. Warlouzet, *Le choix*, chapters 3 and 6. See also Maes and Buyst, "Triffin."

9. Miard-Delacroix, *Partenaires*, 180.

10. TNA, PREM16/1641, PM's conversation with Roy Jenkins on 31 March 1978.

11. Ibid. This point was contradicted by Callaghan's recollection of his conversation with Schmidt on 12 March; according to Callaghan, the German chancellor said that he had discussed his plan so far with Emminger and Horst Schulmann (not Hans Mat-thöfer).

12. TNA, PREM16/1641, PM's conversation with Roy Jenkins on 31 March 1978.

13. TNA, PREM16/1615, Couzens to Wicks, Chancellor Schmidt, the Snake and the pooling of reserves, 6 April 1978.

14. TNA, PREM16/1912, Healey to Callaghan, 3 March 1978, with attached paper on "International Action on Growth, Currency Stability, Energy and Other Matters." See also von Karczewski, "Weltwirtschaft," 377–79.

15. This was explicitly stressed in the paper itself, and Healey further insisted on it in the accompanying letter to Callaghan. See TNA, PREM16/1912, Healey to Callaghan, 3 March 1978.

16. TNA, PREM16/2011, Davies to Lankester, SDRs and Witteveen Proposal, 15 November 1978.

17. See chapter 3.

18. TNA, T381/108, McMahon to Hedley-Miller, European Currency Arrangements: Schmidt/Giscard, 28 June 1978.

19. Jenkins, *Diary*, 242.

20. Ibid.

21. ASBI, Banca d'Italia, Studi, Serie CEI—Economia internazionale, 622, Ministero del Tesoro, Gabinetto del ministro, Note undated (presumably May 1978), Per una maggiore stabilità dei cambi in ambito CEE. For the Irish position, see, for instance, NAI, DF, F1/5/78/PART001, Ministers meeting with President of the Commission, 23 February 1978, 27 February 1978.

22. BB, N2/264, Pöhl to Schmidt, 21 March 1978.

23. BdF, 1489200205/273, Note DGSE, Les chances de réintégration du franc dans le serpent monétaire européen, February 1978.

24. BdF, 1489200205/272, Note DGSE, L'avenir du "serpent" monétaire européen, 12 January 1978.

25. AN, Paris, 5AG3/913, Ruault to Giscard, Situation économique et monétaire intra-européenne, 6 April 1978.

26. BB, N2/264, Emminger to Schmidt, Währungspolitische Fortschritte in Europa, 30 March 1978.

27. It must be noted that in the reference to the Fourcade Plan, only the wider fluctuation margins and the temporary leave of absence of a currency were mentioned, but *not* the possibility of organizing the exchange rate system around the trade-weighted EUA.

28. TNA, FCO30/4004, R. Jenkins, Memorandum for the European Council, 7/8 April 1978, 3 April 1978.

29. TNA, PREM16/1641, PM's conversation with R. Jenkins on 31 March 1978.

30. Though the invitation came from Schmidt, it was Giscard who called Callaghan on 4 April to invite him to this early breakfast. See TNA, PREM 16/1615, PM's conversation with President Giscard on 4 April 1978.

31. TNA, PREM16/1615, Note of Stowe, Proposals for a European currency reserve, 11 April 1978. This is corroborated by Jenkins in *Diary*, 246.

32. Jenkins, *Diary*, 242–43.

33. Ibid., 249. Jenkins unfortunately does not give further details about Tindemans's ideas, and no trace of them has been found in the archives visited.

34. Ibid., 246.

35. TNA, PREM 16/1616, Note of a meeting in the cabinet room on Thursday, 20 April 1978.

36. TNA, PREM16/1615, Note for the record of Stowe, Proposals for a European currency reserve, 11 April 1978; HAEU, EN1144, Notes of Tickell on restricted meeting of the nine heads of state and government, and the president of the European Commission, 7 April 1978, 18 April 1978; NAI, DF, F001/019/78, Notes taken by the Taoiseach at the afternoon dinner session, Copenhagen, 7 April 1978.

37. It seems that heads of government had agreed to keep this exchange on monetary affairs strictly confidential, according to Lynch in NAI, DT, 2008/148/418, Notes on European Council in Copenhagen, April 1978.

38. As is the case also with Schmidt's change of mind in January–February 1978, the literature on the topic does not help portray in more detail the reaction of the heads of government in Copenhagen.

39. TNA, PREM16/1615, The case for more intra-European monetary cooperation, summary of comments made in Copenhagen on 7 April 1978.

40. Jenkins, *Diary*, 247; Ludlow, *Making*, 92–93.

41. Monetary issues were not discussed at all during the official session of the European Council on 8 April; see Jenkins, *Diary*, 249.

42. TNA, PREM16/1615, Note of Couzens, PM's discussion on 8 April with Chancellor Schmidt and President Giscard, 11 April 1978. Original emphasis.

43. Jenkins, *Diary*, 249.

44. HAEU, EN1144, Notes of Tickell on restricted meeting of the nine heads of state and government, and the president of the European Commission, 7 April 1978, 18 April 1978.

45. Schmidt confirms this point in *Die Deutschen*, 256.

46. Froment-Meurice, *Vu du Quai*, 474.

47. Schmidt, *Die Deutschen*, 254.

48. In his memoirs, Schmidt lists the (administrative) obstacles to a European monetary initiative; see ibid., 250–52.

49. European Oral History, INT565, Interview with Michael Butler.

50. Ludlow, *Making*, 104–5.

51. In a longer-term perspective, it is interesting to note that Jacques Delors, with the appointment of the Delors committee, would employ exactly the opposite tactics. Where Schmidt and Giscard openly wanted to bypass traditional national and EEC decision-making channels, Delors would, on the contrary, involve the central bankers from the very beginning. See, for instance, Marsh, *Euro*, 118–24.

52. Naturally, apart from Clappier himself, who belonged to both groups, but this did not interfere in their work.

53. Donald Maitland nicely describes the van Ypersele questionnaire as a "socratic list of questions about the ways and means of bringing more cohesion and stability into Community exchange rate relationships." See TNA, T381/106, Telegram no. 2802 of Maitland, 12 May 1978.

54. BoE, 6A103/6, Committee of Governors, Alternates, Questionnaire on member countries' exchange rate policies, 13 April 1978. See also ASBI, Banca d'Italia, Studi, Serie CEI—Economia internazionale, 640, Towards a greater convergence of foreign exchange policies within the Community, Reflections by the Belgian Presidency, 3 April 1978. Some replies to the questionnaire can be found in BdF, 1489200205/277, DGSE, Réponses des Banques centrales au questionnaire Janson sur les politiques de change des États membres de la CEE, April 1978.

55. For the van Ypersele questionnaire, see BdF, 1489200205/277, DGSE, Relations de change intracommunautaires et sujets connexes, 10 May 1978.

56. See chapter 5.

57. ECB, PV 121ème séance du Comité des gouverneurs, 9 May 1978, Annexe 2: Comité des gouverneurs, suppléants, Recherche d'une meilleure stabilité des relations de change intracommunautaire, 8 May 1978.

58. The French text reads "axes de référence" and not "zones cibles," which would correspond to the exact translation "target zones." Yet given the context, the idea was very close.

59. ECB, PV 121ème séance du Comité des gouverneurs, 9 May 1978.

60. Ibid.

61. BdF, 1489200205/203, Note to Monory, 240ème session du Comité Monétaire, 11 and 12 May 1978. On this meeting, see also TNA, FCO30/4005, Telegram no. 2802 of Maitland, Monetary Committee: 11/12 May, 12 May 1978.

62. CAEF, B0050443, Haberer to Monory, Compte rendu de la 240ème session du Comité monétaire, 19 May 1978. Pöhl himself, reporting this session to the Zentralbankrat of the Bundesbank, stressed that the opinions were "very different" inside the Monetary Committee. See BB, B330/DRS.142, Protokoll der 508. Sitzung, 18 May 1978.

63. BdF, 1489200205/203, Note to Monory, 241ème session du Comité Monétaire, 5–6 June 1978.

64. CMA, Intermédiaire 9688, Report of the Monetary Committee to the Council and the Commission, 9 June 1978.

65. CMA, Intermédiaire 9680, Report of the Committee of Governors to the Council, "Efforts to Ensure Greater Exchange Rate Stability among EEC Member Countries' Currencies," 12 June 1978.

66. See chapter 4.

67. ECB, PV 122ème séance du Comité des gouverneurs, 11 June 1978.

68. See Ludlow, *Making*, 104–17.

69. The three presumably met at other times or simply talked over the phone. Yet had these other contacts been of particular significance, it is doubtless that Couzens (or indeed Clappier or Schulmann) would have recorded them in one way or another. Admittedly, there is also the methodological difficulty of relying extensively on accounts written by the least committed member of the Group of Three. This should be qualified, however: for the 12 May meeting, a record by Schulmann also exists, and the draft schemes of Schulmann and Clappier are the original documents. Whether Couzens's narrative account of the Group of Three discussions was neutral and dispassionate is of course an open question, which I have obviously kept in mind while writing this chapter.

70. Jenkins, *Diary*, 283n.

71. TNA, PREM16/1616, Note of Couzens of a discussion with Schulmann, 21 April 1978.

72. Ibid. Most of Couzens's records of these meetings were addressed to the prime minister and copied to the chancellor of the exchequer, the governor of the Bank of England, and sometimes the foreign secretary.

73. Ibid.

74. TNA, PREM16/1616, Note of a meeting in the cabinet room on Thursday, 20 April 1978.

75. Ibid., Note of Couzens of a discussion with Schulmann, 21 April 1978.

76. Ibid., Note of a meeting in the cabinet room on Thursday, 20 April 1978.

77. Interestingly, van Ypersele had also been reported as having the impression in late May 1978 "that other ideas on this subject [monetary] were being considered on a bilateral or trilateral basis at the highest level, and therefore we might well be working in the Monetary Committee to no useful purpose—or indeed, across the grain of other work." See BoE, 6A103/6, Jordan-Moss to Hancock, EEC exchange rate system, 25 May 1978.

78. On this, see, for instance, TNA, PREM16/1616, Note of a meeting in the cabinet room on Thursday, 20 April 1978.

79. Two accounts of the meeting exist, one by Schulmann, the other by Couzens. For Schulmann's, see TNA, PREM16/1616, Schulmann to Couzens, "Possible Elements of a New Exchange Rate Scheme," 19 May 1978; for Couzens's, see ibid., Couzens to Stowe, Chancellor Schmidt's proposals for European currencies, Note of a meeting at the Bank of France on 12 May 1978, 16 May 1978.

80. See TNA, PREM16/1615, The case for more intra-European monetary cooperation, summary of comments made in Copenhagen on 7 April 1978.

81. TNA, PREM16/1616, Schulmann to Couzens, "Possible Elements of a New Exchange Rate Scheme," 19 May 1978.

82. Ibid., Couzens to Stowe, Chancellor Schmidt's proposals for European currencies, Note of a meeting at the Bank of France on 12 May 1978, 16 May 1978.

83. Ibid., Schulmann to Couzens, "Possible Elements of a New Exchange Rate Scheme," 19 May 1978. This note is described by Schulmann as "I hope . . . a fair record of what was said [in Paris on 12 May] and a useful basis for further discussion." It is not, therefore, a German position-taking, contrary to what its title could suggest.

84. Ibid., Couzens to Stowe, Chancellor Schmidt's proposals for European currencies, Note of a meeting at the Bank of France on 12 May 1978, 16 May 1978.

85. Ibid., Couzens to Stowe, Chancellor Schmidt's proposal for a European currency reform, Record of discussion with Clappier and Schulmann over dinner, Washington, 26 May 1978, 30 May 1978.

86. TNA, PREM16/1634, Couzens to Stowe, European Monetary Co-operation, Discussions in Paris on 14–15 June 1978, 19 June 1978, Annex A: Outline of a scheme by Clappier.

87. Ibid., Annex B: Herr Schulmann's draft for an agreement at Bremen.

88. Ibid., Couzens to Stowe, European Monetary Co-operation, Discussions in Paris on 14–15 June 1978, 19 June 1978.

89. It suggested the following: "Heads of Government wish to see developed for their further consideration a plan for European monetary cooperation with certain defined characteristics. They believe that a plan of the right kind, set in the right framework of cooperation, could contribute both to the reduction of the general level of inflation in the Community and to a higher rate of economic growth." See TNA, T381/108, Couzens to Stowe, Possible UK counter-draft, 29 June 1978.

90. TNA, T385/136, Hedley-Miller to Jordan Moss, European Currency Arrangements. Some features of a possible United Kingdom proposal (building on M. Clappier's ideas), 27 June 1978.

91. TNA, T381/108, Couzens to Stowe, Possible UK counter-draft, 29 June 1978.

92. Butler, *Europe*, 69.

93. TNA, PREM16/1634, Telegram no. 512 of Couzens, European Monetary Reform, 28 June 1978; ibid., Telegram no. 506 of Bullard, Federal Chancellor's meeting with president Giscard d'Estaing, 25 June 1978.

94. Ludlow, *Making*, 105.

95. TNA, PREM16/1634, Telegram no. 512 of Couzens, European Monetary Reform, 28 June 1978.

96. Ibid., Schulmann/Clappier draft, 28 June 1978.

97. BB, B330/DRS.142, Protokoll der 506. Sitzung, 10–11, 20 April 1978.

98. TNA, FCO30/4004, Bayne to Jordan-Moss, Record of conversation, European Council—European Monetary Questions, 19 April 1978.

99. TNA, FCO30/4007, Telegram no. 3026 of Maitland, Finance Council: 22 May, 22 May 1978.

100. AdsD, HSA, I/HSAA006588, Schulmann to Schmidt, Follow-up von Kopenhagen, Brief an Giscard, 8 May 1978.

101. TNA, PREM16/1634, Couzens to Stowe, Annex C: Record of a meeting between the Chancellor of the Exchequer and the French Minister for the Economy, 15 June 1978; ibid., Note of Healey to Callaghan, European currency arrangements, 22 June 1978.

102. On the neutron bomb episode, see Wiegrefe, *Das Zerwürfnis*, 180–205; Spohr Readman, "Germany." See also the account given by the French president in his memoirs, Giscard, *Le pouvoir*, 1–2:126–29.

103. Grygowski, *Les États-Unis*, 313.

104. Giscard, *Le pouvoir*, 1–2:128.

105. Story, "Launching," 397.

106. Giscard, *Le pouvoir*, 1–2:129.

107. ECB, PV 120ème séance du Comité des gouverneurs, 11 April 1978.

108. Ibid.

109. Grygowski, *Les États-Unis*, 260.

110. Ludlow, *Making*, 117–21.

111. Grygowski, "Les États-Unis," 348–51.

112. Ludlow, *Making*, 121–22.

113. Jenkins, *Diary*, 275.

114. See AMAE, DAEF1553, Telegram no. 2801–30 of Nanteuil, Conseil ECO-FIN du 19 juin, 20 June 1978; and TNA, FCO30/4008, Telegram no. 154 of Wright, Finance Council, 19 June, Common strategy: monetary policy, 19 June 1978; PREM16/1634, Healey to Callaghan, Summary of Chancellor of the Exchequer's intervention at the Finance Council in Luxembourg on 19 June, 6 July 1978.

115. CMA, Intermédiaire 9688, Monetary Committee, Conclusions of the Council's debate of 19 June, on possibilities of bringing about greater exchange rate stability in the Community, 27 June 1978. This rather positive consensus should not hide the fact that, naturally, on a number of more specific issues, each minister did not fail to voice his traditional remarks. This was the case, for instance, with Hans Matthöfer, who criticized the target zones concept.

116. AMAE, DAEF1553, Telegram no. 2801–30 of Nanteuil, Conseil Eco-Fin du 19 juin, 20 June 1978.

117. TNA, FCO30/4008, Telegram no. 154 of Wright, Finance Council: 19 June, Common strategy: monetary policy, 19 June 1978.

118. AMAE, DAEF1553, Telegram no. 2801–30 of Nanteuil, Conseil ECO-FIN du 19 juin, 20 June 1978. In listing the points, however, it must be noted that the records are identical and underline the need for a "strong, durable system of reciprocal obligations" that "implied greater convergence and collective discipline."

119. TNA, PREM16/1634, Note of a conversation between the Prime Minister, President Giscard and Chancellor Schmidt on monetary reform in the Rathaus, Bremen, on 6 July 1978 at 18.20.

120. Jenkins, *Diary*, 287.

121. Ibid., 284–86. Of course the Irish were themselves surprised; see NAI, DF, F001/019/78, Memo, 30 June 1978.

122. TNA, PREM16/1634, Discussion by heads of government and the president of the Commission during the evening of 6 July 1978 in the Rathaus.

123. Ibid., Note of a meeting held at 10 Downing Street at 09.30 on 3 July 1978.

124. Ibid., Discussion by heads of government and the president of the Commission during the evening of 6 July 1978 in the Rathaus.

125. NAI, DF, F001/019/78/PART001, Notes taken by the Taoiseach at the after dinner meeting at the Bremen summit, 6 July 1978.

126. MTA, PV de la session du Conseil européen tenue à Brême les 6 et 7 juillet 1978 établi par P. Gueben (General Secretariat of the Council of Ministers), 24 July 1978; Jenkins, *Diary*, 289. The volte-face is best described by Froment-Meurice. He reports Giscard as saying, on 6 April, "This is miraculous; the English accept the paper that will be published in annex"; and the following day: "This is a fiasco, let's stop everything; I'll say it's a failure because of the English" (!). Froment-Meurice, *Vu du Quai*, 476.

127. TNA, PREM16/1642, European Council: Second Session, Transcription of the Owen's notes of the morning session of the European Council on Friday 7 July.

128. NAI, DT, 2008/148/550, Notes by the Minister for Foreign Affairs of the proceedings of the second day, 7 July 1978, of the meeting of the European Council in Bremen.

129. For more details, see Ludlow, *Making*, 127–32.

130. Ibid., 129.

131. James, *International*, 294–96.

132. Ludlow, *Making*, 132.

133. This view was shared by Jenkins and Callaghan. See TNA, PREM16/1634, Record of a discussion between Jenkins and Callaghan, 3 July 1978.

134. TNA, FCO30/4004, R. Jenkins, Memorandum for the European Council, Copenhagen, 7/8 April 1978, 3 April 1978.

135. AdsD, HSA, I/HSAA006588, Schulmann to Schmidt, Follow-up von Kopenhagen, Brief an Giscard, 8 May 1978.

136. BAK, B136/8060, Schmidt to Giscard, 1 June 1978.

137. TNA, FCO30/4008, Note of Prendergast, Giscard/Schmidt meeting at Hamburg, 27 June 1978.

138. Jenkins, *Diary*, 294 and 306.

139. TNA, PREM16/1641, PM's conversation with R. Jenkins on 31 March 1978.

140. TNA, PREM16/1634, Couzens to Stowe, European Monetary Reform, Annex B: Possible UK counter draft, 29 June 1978.

141. See BdF, 1489200205/203, Note to Monory, 240ème session du Comité Monétaire, 11 and 12 May 1978; and ECB, PV 120ème séance du Comité des gouverneurs, 11 April 1978. See also AN, Paris, 5AG3/913, Notes manuscrites de Dutet lors de la réunion chez Paye du 8 juin 1978 pour la préparation du Conseil européen.

142. TNA, T 381/106, Henderson to FCO, European Monetary Questions, 12 May 1978. Fourcade himself, in a symposium in Davos in early February 1978, restated his proposals, in particular that of basing the exchange rate margin on the ECU instead of a

bilateral grid of parities. J.-Ph. Chenaux, "Symposium de Davos: M. Fourcade propose un nouveau système de changes pour l'Europe," *Journal de Genève*, 3 February 1978.

143. TNA, T381/107, Couzens to Hedley-Miller, 5 June 1978.

144. NAI, DF, F1/1/77, DG Economic and Financial Affairs, The achievement of greater stability in exchange rate relationships between the currencies of the EEC member states, 13 April 1978; CMA, Intermédiaire 9688, Report of the Monetary Committee to the Council and the Commission, 9 June 1978.

145. ASBI, Banca d'Italia, Studi, Serie CEI—Economia internazionale, 622, Monetary Committee, K.-O. Pöhl, Improved co-ordination of monetary policy, 5 June 1978.

146. Giscard, *Le pouvoir*, 1–2:143; Froment-Meurice, *Vu du Quai*, 475. See chapter 2 for the real birth of the ECU acronym.

7. CHASING THE GHOSTS OF FAILED NEGOTIATIONS, MID-JULY TO LATE SEPTEMBER 1978

Epigraph. Nigel Lawson, MTA, note to Thatcher, The European Monetary System, 30 October 1978.

1. "Will EMU Lay an Egg?" *Economist*, 19 August 1978.

2. The Bremen Annex marked the *official* start of the EMS negotiations; from Copenhagen until Bremen, the negotiations were very much about the overall philosophy of the new system (if not the opportunity alone to create a new one) more than about its technical and precise working. Furthermore, the competent bodies able to make the final decisions had so far largely been left aside in the discussions. It is not a coincidence that some archives have labeled "EMS negotiations no. X" only the boxes related to European monetary cooperation that contain documents dating from mid-July 1978 onward. See, for instance, PAAA, B202, EWS I (14 July–10 November), EWS II (10 November–27 November), EWS III (-).

3. ECB, PV 123ème séance du Comité des gouverneurs, 11 July 1978.

4. See chapter 3.

5. ECB, PV 123ème séance du Comité des gouverneurs, 11 July 1978.

6. BAK, B126/70439, Note, Sitzung des Währungsauschusses am 18./19.7.1978, 21 July 1978.

7. The timetable set by the Bremen Annex reads as follows: "It [the European Council] agreed to instruct the Finance Ministers at their meeting on 24 July to formulate the necessary guidelines for the competent Community bodies to elaborate by 31 October the provisions necessary for the functioning of such a scheme.... Decisions can then be taken and commitments made at the European Council meeting on 4 and 5 December."

8. ECB, PV 123ème séance du Comité des gouverneurs, 11 July 1978.

9. Jenkins, *Diary*, 324.

10. ECB, PV 123ème séance du Comité des gouverneurs, 11 July 1978.

11. Chapter 5 of Ludlow, *Making*; Middlemas, *Orchestrating*, 88; Gillingham, *European*, 134.

12. Moravcsik, *Choice*, 298.

13. See chapter 6.

14. See chapter 3.

15. ASBI, Banca d'Italia, Studi, Serie CEI—Economia internazionale, 610, Note of Caranza and Saccommani, Consiglio Ecofin del 22/5/78, 24 May 1978, and, ibid., various documents.

16. AMAE, DAEF1557, Dupont to DREE, Réactions du Gouvernement Irlandais au SME, 26 July 1978. See also the almost immediate positive reaction after Copenhagen: NAI, DF, F001/019/78, Horgan to Tanaiste, 20 April 1978.

17. ECB, PV 123ème séance du Comité des gouverneurs, 11 July 1978.

18. BdF, 1489200205/203, Note to Monory, 242ème session du Comité Moné-taire, 18–19 juillet 1978; BAK, B126/70439, Note, Sitzung des Währungsauschusses am 18./19.7.1978, 21 July 1978.

19. CAEF, B0050444, Haberer to Monory, Suites du Conseil Européen de Brême, 20 July 1978.

20. According to the records of the session, neither the British nor the Italian members advanced a precise proportion of "fixed" to "variable" parts.

21. BAK, B126/70439, Note, Stellungnahmen einzelner Delegationen im ECOFIN-Rat am 24.7.78 zum Fragebogen der Präsidentschaft betr. das EWS, 25 July 1978.

22. BB, N2/265, Note, Tagung des EG-Rates der Wirtschafts-und Finanzminister am 24. Juli in Brüssel, EWS, 25 July 1978. Surprisingly, no French record of that meeting was found in the French archives.

23. TNA, FCO30/4009, Fretwell to Butler, 24 July Finance Council: suggested approach to Lautenschlager, 14 July 1978.

24. TNA, FCO30/4029, Bailes to Petrie, EMS and Parliament: the "Eight Principles," 7 November 1978.

25. BB, N2/265, Note, Tagung des EG-Rates der Wirtschafts-und Finanzminister am 24. Juli in Brüssel, 25 July 1978.

26. BAK, B126/70439, Note, Ergebnis des EG-Ministerrats am 24.7.1978, 25 July 1978; Jenkins, *Diary*, 324.

27. BB, N2/265, Erklärung von O. Emminger zu dem Bremer Währungsplan im Bundeskabinett am 12.7.1978, 12 July 1978.

28. BB, B330/DRS.142, 499.-522, Sitzung, 1978, Protokoll der 512. Sitzung, 13 July 1978.

29. BAK, B126/70442, Schlüter to Weber, Schlussfolgerungen aus dem Bremer EG-Gipfel vom 6./7. Juli 1978 im Währungsbereich, Abstimmung der deutschen Verhandlung-sposition zwischen BBk und BMF auf Referentenebene für die kommenden Beratungen, 14 July 1978; BAK, B126/70439, Note of Willmann, Diskussion des Währungsauschusses über das EWS, 14 July 1978.

30. With the obvious exception of Clappier, who contributed to the drafting of the Bremen Annex and sat on the Committee of Governors.

31. The first description is that of P. Ludlow (*Making*, chapter 5), the second of K. McNamara (*Currency*, 127).

32. Marsh, *Euro*, 82.

33. At least four drafts exist, produced on 20 July, 24 July, 8 August, and 23 August. See BdF, 1489200205/282.

34. Ibid., DGSE, Esquisse du nouveau système monétaire européen, 24 July 1978.

35. BdF, 1489200205/347, DGSE, Description sommaire d'un système dont l'ECU constituerait le pilier, 8 August 1978.

36. BAK, B126/70439, Ausgestaltung des EWS, 23 August 1978.

37. BdF, DGSE, Note, SME: Positions françaises et allemandes, 31 August 1978.

38. BB, N2/266, Pöhl an die Mitglieder des Zentralbankrats, Das EWS, 4 August 1978.

39. BAK, B126/70439, Note of Grosche, EWS, 25 August 1978.

40. BdF, 1489200205/347, DGSE, Réflexions sur le nouveau SME, 23 August 1978. Schmidt makes similar points in his memoirs (*Die Deutschen*, 163 and 263).

41. BAK, B126/70440, Willmann to Lahnstein, EWS, 11 September 1978.

42. Ibid; see also BAK, B136/8060, Weber to Ruhfus, Vorbereitung der deutsch-französischen Konsultation am 14./15. September 1978, 18 August 1978.

43. A group on European Monetary Cooperation composed of the ministers directly concerned with the negotiations (plus Couzens), called GEN 136, had been charged with

"supervising the representation of British interests" in the EMS negotiations (Dell, "Britain," 38–39). In addition, the British Treasury itself constituted a "Steering Group" in order to follow the EMS negotiations (including the concurrent studies). This group was composed of Couzens, McMahon (Bank of England), Butler (FCO, head of European Integration Department), and Michael Franklin (head of the European Secretariat in the Cabinet Office).

44. TNA, FCO30/4014, Butler to Couzens, EMS: exchange rate, 30 August 1978.

45. TNA, FCO30/4016, Couzens to Butler, 14 September 1978.

46. PAAA, Zwischenarchiv 122325, Note of Möhler, Deutsch-französische Konsultationen in Aachen, 13 September 1978.

47. European Oral History, interview with Filippo Pandolfi.

48. TNA, FCO30/4015, Galsworthy to Baker, Italian government's draft 3-year plan, 7 September 1978. PAAA, Zwischenarchiv 122325, Note unsigned, Italien: 3-Jahresplan zur Sanierung der italienischen Wirtschaft, 12 October 1978.

49. HAEU, EN1146, Note of Philipps of a discussion between the president of the Commission and the Italian Prime Minister, 8 September 1978, 9 October 1978.

50. See, for instance, BoE, 6A218/1, McMahon/The Governors, EEC Currency Arrangements, 28 June 1978; TNA, FCO30/4014, Sankey to Petrie, EMS: the Netherlands Position; Extract from a memorandum of 21 August 1978 from the Netherlands Minister of Finance to the Second Chamber of Parliament, 25 August 1978; AMAE, DE4088, Telegram no. 1100/03, Gaussot, Les Pays-Bas et le projet de SME, 25 August 1978; TNA, FCO30/4013, Note of Battishill, Visit of Signor Pandolfi and Signor Baffi, 28 July 1978.

51. Ludlow, *Making*, 165.

52. TNA, FCO30/4013, Meeting of the Monetary Committee Alternates, 10–11 August 1978.

53. ECB, Heyvaert Group, Interim Report no. 39 on the EMS, 21 August 1978.

54. BoE, 6A103/6, Sangster to McMahon, Community Exchange Rate Scheme—A Variant, 18 July 1978; see also ibid., Gill to Sangster, The "Sangster Scheme" for European Exchange Rates, 6 July 1978. Broad reference to such a scheme can be found as early as late June/early July 1978.

55. BoE, 6A103/6, Sangster to McMahon, Community Exchange Rate Scheme—A Variant, 18 July 1978.

56. TNA, T 381/111, Hancock to Barratt, Meeting of the Heyvaert Group 31 July–2 August, 7 August 1978.

57. Interestingly, Dyson notices that the Belgian compromise was "consistent with the spirit of the Duisenberg Plan," but does not mention the Sangster Scheme (*Elusive*, 106–7).

58. CMA, Intermédiaire 10159, Interim Report on the EMS, 7 September 1978.

59. CAEF, B0050444, Note des membres belges du Comité monétaire, Lignes directrices de la formule de rapprochement entre les deux systèmes d'intervention basés respectivement sur l'ECU et la grille de parités, 20 September 1978.

60. The divergence indicator has also been called the "rattlesnake." See Ungerer, *Concise History*, 159.

61. See chapters 4 and 5.

62. TNA, FCO30/4012, Bayne to Baker, France and the EMS, 7 August 1978; NAI, DF, F001/019/78/PART001, Meeting held in Department of Finance on 28 August 1978.

63. ECB, PV 124ème séance du Comité des gouverneurs, 12 September 1978.

64. BdF, 1489200205/347, DGSE, Réflexions sur le nouveau SME, 23 August 1978.

65. TNA, FCO30/4026, Bayne to Hedley-Miller, EMS: Views of the governor of the Bank of France, 25 October 1978; MTA, Lawson to Thatcher, France & the EMS, 31 October 1978.

66. ECB, PV 124ème séance du Comité des gouverneurs, 12 September 1978. Lamfalussy showed in various BIS notes that, if indeed technically complex, an ECU-centered EMS would not be impossible to operate. See ASBI, Segretaria particolare, Pratt., 1501, A. Lamfalussy, The use of the ECU as numeraire in the European monetary system, 24 August 1978.

67. NAI, DF, F001/019/78/PART001, Report on meeting with M. Ortoli, 12 September 1978.

68. PAAA, Zwischenarchiv 122325, Note of Fischer, EWS, Besuch des Präsidenten der Kommission der EG, R. Jenkins, in Dublin am 4. September 1978, 6 September 1978.

69. NAI, DF, F1/5/78/PART001, Central Bank of Ireland, The Proposed EMS and Implications for Ireland—A Preliminary Analysis, 22 September 1978.

70. For more details on this break, see Honohan and Murphy, "Breaking."

71. CADN, Rome 54, Telegram no. 1988/93 of Puaux, Visite de M. Jenkins à Rome, 8 September 1978.

72. Jenkins, *Diary*, 308.

73. TNA, FCO30/4016, Note of Fitchew of a dinner at 11 Downing Street on 5 September, 1978, 13 September 1978.

74. TNA, FCO30/4015, Hedley-Miller, Meeting of the Monetary Committee, 6–7 September 1978, 11 September 1978; CMA, Intermédiaire 10159, Interim Report on the EMS, 7 September 1978.

75. CMA, Intermédiaire 10159, Interim Report on the EMS, 7 September 1978.

76. CAEF, B0050444, Bank of England, EMS, Paper for the Heyvaert Group by the Bank of England, July 1978.

77. ECB, PV 124ème séance du Comité des gouverneurs, 12 September 1978.

78. BB, B330/DRS.142, 499.-522, Sitzung, 1978, Protokoll der 515. Sitzung, 7 September 1978, Anlage: Stellungnahme des Zentralbankrat der Deutschen Bundesbank zu den Vorschlagen für ein EWS nach dem Stand vom 6. September 1978.

79. Initial demythologization was carried out by P. Ludlow (*Making*, 182–84); K. Dyson (*Elusive Union*, 104–5) and A. Moravcsik (*Choice*, 298–99) followed this interpretation.

80. Marsh, *Euro*, 82.

81. PAAA, Zwischenarchiv 122325, Note of Kliesow, Gespräch des Bundeskanzlers mit Präsident Giscard, 12 September 1978.

82. BAK, B136/8060, Schulmann to Schmidt, Deutsch-französische Konsultationen, 14 September 1978.

83. CAEF, B0050424, Confidential, Memorandum of understanding, Aachen, 15 September 1978; and BAK, B126/70439, Memorandum of understanding, Aachen, 15 September 1978. Importantly, these two versions are identical! See also PAAA, Zwischenarchiv 122325, Note of Brockdorff, EWS, Deutsch-französischer Gipfel in Aachen, 19 September 1978.

84. CADN, Bonn 324, Compte rendu de la séance plénière, Aix-la-Chapelle, 15 septembre 1978, 11H45.

85. TNA, FCO30/4015, Telegram no. 754 of Henderson, Franco-German summit at Aachen—monetary matters, 18 September 1978.

86. Saint-Périer, "VGE," 167. See also Dyson, *Elusive*, 104.

87. ECB, Committee of Governors, Oral Report to the Council by the Chairman of the Committee, 14 September 1978.

88. AMAE, DAEF1553, Telegram no. 3842/60 of Nanteuil, Conseil Eco-Fin du 18 Septembre, 19 September 1978 ; TNA, FCO30/4016, Telegram no. 5379, ECO/FIN Council: 18 September 1978; BB, B330/DRS.142, 499.-522, Sitzung, 1978, Protokoll der 516. Sitzung, 21 September 1978.

89. CAEF, B0050444, SME, Intervention du ministre prononcée au Conseil Éco/Fin, 18 September 1978.

90. AMAE, DAEF1553, Telegram no. 3842/60 of Nanteuil, Conseil Eco-Fin du 18 Septembre, 19 September 1978. See also TNA, FCO30/4016, Telegram no. 5373, Finance Council Brussels 18 September.

91. PAAA, Zwischenarchiv 122319, Rückschau auf den Rat der Wirtschafts-und Finanzminister am 18. September in Brüssel, 19 September 1978.

92. See chapter 4.

93. For instance, in the Finance Council on 18 September 1978, Pandolfi stressed the absence of a redistributive effect of the EEC budget (characteristic of a budget in a federal system): AMAE, DAEF1553, Telegram no. 3842/60 of Nanteuil, Conseil Eco-Fin du 18 Septembre, 19 September 1978.

94. CMA, Intermédiaire 9774, Mandat au CPE, 27 July 1978; FCO30/4010, Telegram no. 4792, COREPER 27 July 1978, Follow-up to ECO/FIN Council: mandate for EPC on concurrent studies, 27 July 1978.

95. BAK, B126/70439, Note, EWS: Massnahmen zur Stärkung der Wirtschaft der finanziell schwächeren Mitgliedsländer, 14 August 1978; AMAE, DAEF1557, Note BM/SW no. 399/CE, CPE de la Communauté: 11 août 1978: études parallèles au SME, 16 August 1978.

96. AMAE, DAEF1557, Note BM/DS no. 427/CE, Réunion du CPE relative aux études parallèles du SME, 8 September 1978; PAAA, Zwischenarchiv 122325, Note, EWS: Stand der Arbeiten des Wirtschaftspolitischen Ausschusses, 8 September 1978; BdF, 1489200205/288, Note SGCI, Compte-rendu de la réunion du CPE du 6 septembre 1978, 8 September 1978; TNA, FCO30/4015, Note of Appleyard, EMS: Concurrent Studies, EPC Meeting 6 September, 7 September 1978.

97. The Bremen Annex stated that "there will be concurrent studies of the action needed to be taken to strengthen the economies of the less prosperous member countries in the context of such a scheme; such measures will be essential if the zone of monetary stability is to succeed."

98. CAEF, B005048, Note du Trésor, Demandes présentées par le Royaume-Uni au titre des "études parallèles" et éléments pour une réponse française, undated.

99. The Irish government's quest for financial transfers from the EEC was not a new one. It had begun in 1974 with discussion about the creation of a regional fund. See Wall, "Half."

100. TNA, T385/151, Unsigned note to Whalley, A Community Unemployment Benefit Scheme, July 1978.

101. For the Marjolin Report, see chapter 2; for the MacDougall Report, see chapter 4.

102. HAEU, EN1146, Note of Tickell, Record of a meeting between the president of the European Commission and Irish ministers, Dublin, 4 September 1978. See also AMAE, DAEF1557, Telegram no. 276–278 of Marcaggi, Entretien de MM. Jenkins et Lynch sur le futur SME, 5 September 1978.

103. TNA, FCO30/4014, European Commission, Working paper presented to the EPC by the Members nominated by the Commission, Structural Indicators, 24 August 1978.

104. Ludlow, Making, 170–80.

105. CAEF, B005048, Note du Trésor, Demandes présentées par l'Italie au titre des "études parallèles" et éléments pour une réponse française, undated.

106. TNA, FCO30/4015, Petrie to Franklin, The EMS and concurrent studies: Views of other member states, 8 September 1978.

107. TNA, FCO30/4014, EMS concurrent studies: Possible devices for increasing UK net receipts from the Community budget, excluding the CAP, 29 August 1978.

108. Ludlow, Dealing.

109. CAEF, B005048, Note du Trésor, Demandes présentées par le Royaume-Uni au titre des "études parallèles" et éléments pour une réponse française, undated.

110. PAAA, Zwischenarchiv 122325, Note of Möhler, Deutsch-französische Konsultationen in Aachen, 13 September 1978.

111. AMAE, DAEF1557, Note BM/SW, Études "parallèles" au SME, 1 September 1978; CAEF, B005048, Note du Trésor, Demandes présentées par l'Irlande au titre des "études parallèles" et éléments pour une réponse française, undated.

112. BAK, B126/70439, Note, Weiteres Vorgehen im Anschluss an die Tagung des Europäischen Rates vom 6./7. Juli 1978: Leitlinien zur Ausarbeitung des EWS, 21 July 1978.

113. TNA, FCO30/4010, Telegram no. 4792, COREPER 27 July 1978, Follow-up to ECO/FIN Council: Mandate for EPC on concurrent studies, 27 July 1978.

114. HAEU, EN1146, Note of Tickell, Record of a meeting between the president of the European Commission and Irish ministers, Dublin, 4 September 1978.

115. NAI, DFA, 2008/79/1894, Visit by Mr Jenkins to Taoiseach, 4 September 1978; CADN, Rome 54, Telegram no. 1988/93 of Puaux, Visite de M. Jenkins à Rome, 8 September 1978.

116. HAEU, EN1146, Note of Philipps of a discussion between the president of the Commission and the Italian Prime Minister, 8 September 1978, 9 October 1978.

117. AMAE, DAEF1557, Note BM/SW, Etudes "parallèles" au SME, 1 September 1978.

118. Ludlow, *Making*, 180.

119. BAK, B126/70441, Mündlicher Bericht des Vorsitzenden des wirtschaftspolitischen Ausschusses der Europäischen Gemeinschaft für den EG-Rat am 18. September 1978, 15 September 1978.

120. AMAE, DAEF1553, Telegram no. 3842/60 of Nanteuil, Conseil Eco-Fin du 18 Septembre, 19 September 1978.

121. Jenkins made this point during his visits to Dublin and Rome. See HAEU, EN1146, Note of Tickell, Record of a meeting between the president of the European Commission and Irish ministers, Dublin, 4 September 1978; and ibid., Note of Philipps of a discussion between the president of the Commission and the Italian Prime Minister, 8 September 1978, 9 October 1978.

122. Ibid., Note of Philipps of a discussion between the president of the Commission and the Italian Prime Minister, 8 September 1978, 9 October 1978.

123. BdF, 1489200205/347, Note of the DGSE, Réflexions sur le nouveau SME, 23 August 1978.

124. ECB, PV 123ème séance du Comité des gouverneurs, 11 July 1978.

125. Saint-Périer, "VGE," 149; more curiously, Ungerer, *Concise History*, 163.

126. See chapter 2.

127. TNA, FCO30/4016, Telegram no. 5379, ECO/FIN Council: 18 September 1978.

128. Schmidt, *Die Deutschen*, 248.

129. AMAE, DAEF1484, Note BB/SF no. 426/CE, Sommet franco-allemand d'Aix-la-Chapelle. Coordination des priorités pour les présidences allemande et française, 5 September 1978.

130. See chapter 4.

131. AMAE, DAEF1557, Telegram no. 3202–3211 of Sauvagnargues, Coopération monétaire européenne, 22 September 1978.

132. Ibid., Centre d'analyse et de prévision, Note N/391, Les obstacles politiques et économiques sur la voie de la Zone de Stabilité Monétaire européenne, 30 August 1978.

133. BdF, 1489200205/288, Note SGCI, Compte-rendu de la réunion du CPE du 6 septembre 1978, 8 September 1978.

134. TNA, FCO30/4016, Couzens to Butler, 14 September 1978.

135. Jenkins, *Diary*, 307.

8. A FALSE START, OCTOBER 1978–MARCH 1979

Epigraphs. NAI, DFA, 2008/79/1939, notes of Michael O'Kennedy, European Council, Brussels, 4–5 December 1978. Jean-Yves Haberer, CAEF, B0050424, notes, Ultimes remarques sur le Système Monétaire Européen avant le Conseil européen du 4 décembre, 30 November 1978.

1. BB, N2/269, Emminger to Schmidt, EWS (Wortprotokoll ZBR-Sitzung), 1 December 1978.

2. PAAA, Zwischenarchiv 122321, National Bank of Belgium, Combination of the parity grid and the indicator of divergence. Implications of the "Belgian compromise," 23 October 1978.

3. CAEF, B0050424, Confidential, Memorandum of understanding, Aachen, 15 September 1978; BAK, B126/70441, Pöhl to the members of the Bundesbank ZBR, Das EWS, 3 October 1978. Emphasis added.

4. TNA, FCO30/4027, Michell to Jordan-Moss, Monetary Committee Alternates: 27 October 1978, 30 October 1978.

5. TNA, FCO30/4038, Note of a meeting and lunch with M. Ortoli on 13 November 1978, 17 November 1978.

6. TNA, CAB/128/64/17, CM(78)37th meeting, 2 November 1978; AMAE, DAEF1557, Telegram no. 3806/08 of Sauvagnargues, Entretiens avec M. Healey relatifs au SME, 7 November 1978; PAAA, Zwischenarchiv 122325, Telegram no. 2491, EWS, Besprechung Schatzkanzlers Healey mit Monory, 7 November 1978.

7. TNA, FCO30/4022, Telegram no. 280, Finance Council, 16 October 1978.

8. ECB, PV 125ème séance du Comité des gouverneurs, 9 October 1978; CAEF, B0050428, Haberer to Monory, SME. Réunion du Comité Monétaire, 12 October 1978.

9. For more details on the issue of the credit mechanisms, see Ludlow, *Making*, 166–69 and 239–43.

10. ECB, PV 126ème séance du Comité des gouverneurs, 30 October 1978; ASBI, Carte Baffi, Monte Oppio, cart.116, fasc.1, diario Baffi.

11. ECB, PV 127ème séance du Comité des gouverneurs, 14 November 1978; PAAA, Zwischenarchiv 122326, Pöhl to Lahnstein, Treffen der EG-Notenbankgouverneure am 14.11.1978 in Basel, 16 November 1978.

12. TNA, FCO30/4034, Telegram no. 1747, Finance Council, 21 November 1978; AMAE, DAEF1553, Telegram no. 5160–81 of Nanteuil, Conseil ECO-FIN, 21 November 1978.

13. BB, B330/DRS.142, 499.-522, Sitzung, 1978, Protokoll der 517. Sitzung, 5 October 1978.

14. ECB, PV 125ème séance du Comité des gouverneurs, 9 October 1978.

15. ECB, Oral report by the chairman of the Committee of Governors, 13 October 1978.

16. AMAE, DAEF1553, Telegram no. 4476–4500, Conseil ECO-FIN, 17 October 1978.

17. PAAA, Zwischenarchiv 122325, Note of Lautenschlager, Europafragen: Rückschau auf den Rat der EG-Wirtschafts-und Finanzminister am 16. Oktober 1978, 17 October 1978.

18. *AAPD 1978*, document 338.

19. TNA, FCO30/4029, Telegram no. 996, EMS, 5 November 1978; ibid., Telegram no. 931, EMS: Views of the governor of the Bank of France, 3 November 1978; BAK, B136/8060, Schulmann to Schmidt, Ihr Treffen mit Präsident Giscard d'Estaing am 2. November 1978, 31 October 1978.

20. ECB, PV 126ème séance du Comité des gouverneurs, 30 October 1978.

21. ECB, PV 127ème séance du Comité des gouverneurs, 14 November 1978. The annex about the operation of the divergence indicator reads: "If, however, the intervention

commitment seemed too mechanical, it might conceivably be delayed until the crossing of the divergence threshold had been confirmed by five consecutive days of 'divergence.' The delay could be used to trigger consultations." See ECB, Annex 1 to the draft report of the Committee of Governors to the Council on the EMS, 1 November 1978.

22. ECB, PV 127ème séance du Comité des gouverneurs, 14 November 1978.

23. ECB, Draft report of the Committee of Governors to the Council on the EMS, 1 November 1978.

24. ECB, Annex "The operation of the indicator of divergence based on the ECU" to the Draft report of the Committee of Governors to the Council on the EMS, 1 November 1978.

25. TNA, FCO30/4034, Telegram no. 1747, Finance Council 20 November 1978, 21 November 1978; AMAE, DAEF1553, Telegram no. 5160–81 of Nanteuil, Conseil ECO-FIN du 20 novembre 1978, 21 November 1978.

26. In addition to the political pressure to find an agreement in principle on the EMS during the Brussels European Council, it should also be noted that Giscard and Schmidt both added some extra pressure by often publicly insisting that they wanted the new system to be operative on 1 January 1979.

27. AMAE, DAEF1553, Telegram no. 4476–4500, Conseil ECO-FIN, 17 October 1978; ECB, PV 126ème séance du Comité des gouverneurs, 30 October 1978.

28. BAK, B126/70442, Note, EG-Ratstagung (Wirtschafts-und Finanzminister) am 20. November 1978, 14 November 1978; TNA, FCO30/4024, Note of a discussion at the Federal Ministry of Finance on 18th October, 1978, 20 October 1978.

29. AMAE, DAEF1553, Telegram no. 4476–4500, Conseil ECO-FIN, 17 October 1978.

30. TNA, FCO30/4022, Telegram no. 280, Finance Council: 16 October 1978, 16 October 1978.

31. CADN, RPCEE1167, PV (Conseil) de la session du Conseil européen tenue à Bruxelles les 4 et 5 décembre 1978; TNA FCO30/4039, Transcription of Foreign and Commonwealth Secretary's notes, European Council, Brussels, 4 December 1978.

32. TNA, CAB/128/64/16, CM(78)36th meeting, 26 October 1978.

33. Conseil constitutionnel, Décision no. 78–99 DC du 29 décembre 1978, http://www.conseil-constitutionnel.fr/conseil-constitutionnel/francais/les-decisions/acces-par-date/decisions-depuis-1959/1978/78–99-dc/decision-n-78–99-dc-du-29-de-cembre-1978.7697.html, accessed 28 November 2009.

34. See, for instance, NAI, DF, F001/026/78/PART01, Note of a meeting between The Tanaiste and Mr Pandolfi, Dublin, 13 November 1978; TNA, FCO30/4024, Note of a discussion at the Federal Ministry of Finance 18 October 1978, 20 October 1978.

35. See, for instance, ASBI, Carte Baffi, Monte Oppio, cart.116, fasc.1, Note of Baffi, 21 November 1978.

36. ECB, Draft report of the Committee of Governors to the Council on the EMS, 1 November 1978. Emphasis added.

37. ASBI, Segretaria particolare, Pratt., 1501, Banca d'Italia (R. Masera), A Blueprint for the EMS, 26 September 1978.

38. TNA, FCO30/4022, Telegram no. 281, Finance Council: 16 October, 16 October 1978.

39. TNA, FCO30/4021, Telegram no. 390 of Owen, EMS: Finance Council, 16 October, 12 October 1978.

40. TNA, FCO30/4022, Telegram no. 280, Finance Council, 16 October 1978.

41. HAEU, EN1148, Note of Tickell of a Call by the President of the European Commission on the Federal German Chancellor, 27 October 1978, 31 October 1978; BAK, B126/70442, Note of Schulmann über das Gespräch des Herrn Bundeskanzlers mit dem Präsidenten der EG-Kommission am 27. Oktober 1978.

42. HAEU, EN1148, Note by Tickell of a Call by the President of the European Commission on the British PM, 3 November 1978, 15 November 1978.

43. HAEU, EN1148, Note of Tickell of a Call by the President of the European Commission on the Federal German Chancellor, 27 October 1978, 31 October 1978; BAK, B126/70442, Note of Schulmann über das Gespräch des Herrn Bundeskanzlers mit dem Präsidenten der EG-Kommission, 27 October 1978.

44. HAEU, EN1148, Note of Tickell of a Call by the President of the European Commission on the Federal German Chancellor, 27 October 1978, 31 October 1978.

45. MTA, Bundesbank Council meeting with Chancellor Schmidt.

46. CADN, RPCEE1167, PV (Conseil) de la session du Conseil européen tenue à Bruxelles les 4 et 5 décembre 1978.

47. TNA, FCO30/4029, The PM's Discussion with the President of the European Commission at 10 Downing Street on 3 November 1978, 6 November 1978; HAEU, EN1148, Note by Tickell of a call by the President of the European Commission on the British PM, 3 November 1978, 15 November 1978.

48. TNA, FCO30/4029, Telegram no. 504, German/Italian talks in Siena on 1/2 November, EMS, 2 November 1978.

49. BdF, 1489200205/287, SGCI, SME, 16 November 1978.

50. Ludlow and Saint-Périer mention this meeting only very cursorily (*Making*, 198; "VGE," 184–85). Marsh is the first one to mention it in more detail.

51. MTA, Bundesbank Council meeting with Chancellor Schmidt.

52. See chapter 3.

53. BB, N2/267, "Aktuelle Konjunktur-und Währungsprobleme," Ausführungen von O. Emminger, 21 October 1978.

54. TNA, FCO30/4016, Bailes to Shepherd, EMS, 22 September 1978.

55. Ludlow, *Making*, 217–25; Dell, "Britain."

56. The remark about "abandonment" was made by, among others, Sauvagnargues; see AMAE, DAEF1557, Telegram no. 3438/3444 of Sauvagnargues, SME, 11 October 1978.

57. "Right" meaning following the "Eight Principles" he set out in July. See chapter 7.

58. Indeed so negative that Emminger comparatively appeared to have a positive one. See NAI, DF, F001/019/78/PART003, Report of the meeting of Eco/Fin on 20 November 1978.

59. TNA, FCO30/4033, Note of a meeting between the Chancellor of the Exchequer, Signor Pandolfi and Mr Colley on 20 November 1978 in Brussels.

60. TNA, CAB/129/204/21, Green paper on the EMS.

61. TNA, CAB/128/64/21, CM(78)41st meeting, 30 November 1978.

62. TNA, FCO30/4035, Callaghan to Jorgensen (et al.), 30 November 1978.

63. Ludlow, *Making*, 217–18.

64. MTA, Cabinet, Ministerial group on European monetary cooperation, 10 October 1978.

65. TNA, FCO30/4025, EMS: A British Initiative, 19 October 1978.

66. TNA, FCO30/4029, Couzens to Healey, EMS: Trying for a soft landing, 23 October 1978. The "soft landing" analogy was also used later on by Callaghan in a talk with Jenkins. See HAEU, EN1148, Note by Tickell of a call by the President of the European Commission on the British PM, 3 November 1978, 15 November 1978.

67. TNA, FCO30/4028, EMS: Mr Healey's Suggestion for a Possible British Initiative, 30 October 1978.

68. HAEU, EN1148, Note of Tickell, EMS, 31 October 1978; TNA, FCO30/4027, Prendergast to Petrie, EMS, 31 October 1978.

69. TNA, CAB/128/64/17, CM(78)37th meeting, 2 November 1978.

70. TNA, FCO30/4033, Healey to Callaghan, EMS: UK stance in the coming weeks, 13 November 1978.

71. TNA, FCO30/4032, Butler to Walden, EMS: UK stance in the coming weeks, 15 November 1978.

72. TNA, FCO30/4033, Healey to Callaghan, EMS: UK stance in the coming weeks, 13 November 1978.

73. TNA, FCO30/4019, Telegram no. 381 of Owen, EMS, 5 October 1978.

74. AMAE, DAEF1553, Telegram no. 4476–4500, Conseil ECO-FIN, 17 October 1978.

75. HAEU, EN1148, Note of Tickell, Call by the President of the European Commission on the Federal German Chancellor, 27 October 1978, 31 October 1978.

76. TNA, FCO30/4031, Maitland to Franklin, EMS, 10 November 1978. It must be added that Donald Maitland himself seemed quite reluctant to join the EMS—or at least he thought it was too early a step. See British Diplomatic Oral History Programme, interview with Sir Donald Maitland.

77. HAEU, EN1148, Note of Tickell, EMS, 21 November 1978; TNA, FCO30/4036, Discussion with Manfred Lahnstein, 15 November 1978.

78. BAK, B136/8060, Schulmann to Schmidt, Britische Haltung zum geplanten EWS, 16 October 1978.

79. ASBI, Carte Baffi, Monte Oppio, cart.116, fasc.1, diario Baffi.

80. Ibid., cart.117, fasc.2, MAE, Sommario dell'incontro Pandolfi-Matthöfer, Francoforte, 16–17 October 1978; PAAA, Zwischenarchiv 122325, Note of Weber, Besuch des ital. Schatzministers Pandolfi und des Notenbankpräsidenten Baffi am 16./17. Oktober 1978; ibid., Note, Italien; hier: 3-Jahresplan zur Sanierung der italienischen Wirtschaft, 12 October 1978.

81. AMAE, DAEF1557, Telegram no. 2374–2382 of Puaux, L'Italie et le SME, Note pour le dossier des entretiens du 26 octobre, undated; TNA, FCO30/4028, Petrie to Butler, President Giscard's visit to Rome, 25/26 October: Discussions of the EMS, 31 October 1978.

82. *AAPD 1978*, document 337; PREM16/1637, Telegram no. 501–502 Campbell to Butler and Jordan-Moss, German/Italian talks in Siena on 1/2 November, EMS, 2 November 1978.

83. PAAA, Zwischenarchiv 122325, Note of BMF, Italien: währungspolitische Optionen im Hinblick auf einen Beitritt zum EWS, 24 October 1978.

84. TNA, FCO30/4029, Telegram no. 996, EMS, 5 November 1978.

85. Baffi first mentioned the Italian request for wider margins during a session of the Committee of Governors; see ECB, PV 125ème séance du Comité des gouverneurs, 9 October 1978.

86. BB, N2/269, Emminger to Schmidt, EWS (Wortprotokoll ZBR-Sitzung), 1 December 1978.

87. ASBI, Carte Baffi, Monte Oppio, cart.117, fasc.2, MAE, Sommario dell'incontro Pandolfi-Matthöfer, Francoforte, 16–17 October 1978.

88. AMAE, DAEF1557, Telegram no. 350–356 of Dupuy, Irlande et SME, 19 October 1978; BAK, B126/70442, Note, EWS: Probleme im Zusammenhang mit einem möglichen Beitritt Irlands zum EWS, 6 November 1978.

89. NAI, DFA, 2008/79/1907, Murray to Colley, 23 November 1978. That the British decision would not be a major factor in Ireland's own decision making on the EMS was even explicitly told to the British. See NAI, DF, F001/019/78/PART002, Report of meeting with British officials about proposed EMS and associated "concurrent studies," 26 September 1978.

90. AMAE, DAEF1557, Ambassade de France en Irlande, Compte-rendu des entretiens entre M. Colley et M. Monory, 6 November 1978.

91. BAK, B126/70442, EWS: Ergebnis des Gesprächs zwischen Matthöfer und Colley am 9.11.1978, 10 November 1978; PAAA, Zwischenarchiv 122326, Telegram no. 95, Beitritt Irlands zum EWS: Besuch Finanzminister Colley in Bonn am 8. 9. November 1978.

92. Ludlow, *Making*, 251–62.

93. TNA, FCO30/4018, EMS: Concurrent studies, EPC: 2 October 1978; AMAE, DAEF1557, Note BM/GC no. 463/CE, Études parallèles au SME. Réunion du CPE du 2 octobre, 3 October 1978.

94. TNA, FCO30/4018, EMS: Concurrent studies, EPC: 2 October 1978.

95. TNA, FCO30/4027, Petrie to Prendergast, EMS and concurrent studies, 31 October 1978.

96. TNA, FCO30/4024, Telegram no. 6379, EMS and concurrent studies, 25 October 1978.

97. AMAE, DAEF1556, Note SGCI, "Études parallèles" à la mise au point du SME, 8 November 1978; CAEF, B0050424, Note of Haberer, Demandes présentées par l'Irlande au titre des "études parallèles" et éléments pour une réponse française, 28 November 1978.

98. BB, N2/269, Emminger to Schmidt, EWS (Wortprotokoll ZBR-Sitzung), 1 December 1978.

99. TNA, FCO30/4036, Discussion with Manfred Lahnstein, 15 November 1978.

100. HAEU, EN1148, Tickell to Schulmann, 31 October 1978.

101. HAEU, EN1147, Record by Tickell of a conversation between the president of the European Commission and Netherlands Ministers, 3 October 1978, 6 October 1978.

102. TNA, FCO30/4027, Appleyard to Byatt, EMS: Concurrent studies, EPC: 26–27 October 1978, 30 October 1978.

103. CMA, Intermédiaire 10160, EPC, Report to the Council, 13 November 1978.

104. TNA, FCO30/4032, Telegram no. 7066, Finance Council, 20 November: Concurrent studies, 21 November 1978; AMAE, DAEF1553, Telegram no. 5160–81 of Nanteuil, Conseil ECO-FIN du 20 novembre 1978, 21 November 1978.

105. Ludlow, *Making*, 264.

106. CADN, RPCEE1167, PV (Conseil) de la session du Conseil européen tenue à Bruxelles les 4–5 décembre 1978; TNA FCO30/4039, Transcription of Foreign and Commonwealth Secretary's notes, European Council, Brussels, 4 December 1978; *AAPD 1978*, document 380.

107. CADN, RPCEE1167, PV (Conseil) du Conseil européen, 4–5 décembre 1978.

108. Jenkins, *Diary*, 349.

109. HAEU, EN1148, Tickell to Jenkins, European Council, 4–5 December 1978, 8 December 1978.

110. Jenkins, *Diary*, 348.

111. HAEU, EN1148, Tickell to Jenkins, European Council, 4–5 December 1978, 8 December 1978.

112. Ibid.

113. TNA FCO30/4039, Transcription of Foreign and Commonwealth Secretary's notes, European Council, Brussels, 4 December 1978; NAI, DFA, 2008/79/1939, Notes of Michael O'Kennedy, European Council, Brussels, 4/5 December 1978.

114. Jenkins, *Diary*, 352; HAEU, EN1148, Tickell to Jenkins, European Council, 4–5 December 1978, 8 December 1978.

115. HAEU, EN1148, Tickell, Note of conversation between Chancellor Schmidt and the President of the European Commission at one of the intervals in the European Council Brussels, 5 December 1978, 11 December 1978.

116. AMAE, DAEF1488, Telegram no. 2839/49 of Puaux, Réactions italiennes au Conseil européen de Bruxelles, 6 December 1978.

117. NAI, DFA, 2008/79/1939, Notes of Michael O'Kennedy, European Council, Brussels, 4/5 December 1978.
118. Jenkins, *Diary*, 351.
119. HAEU, EN1148, Tickell to Jenkins, European Council, 4 and 5 December 1978, 8 December 1978.
120. CADN, RPCEE1167, PV (Conseil) du Conseil européen, 4–5 décembre 1978.
121. Ibid.
122. HAEU, EN1148, Note of Tickell, Note of conversation between Chancellor Schmidt and the President of the European Commission at one of the intervals in the European Council Brussels, 5 December 1978, 11 December 1978, where Jenkins is reported to have said to Schmidt that "the figures in dispute were peanuts." See also Jenkins, *Diary*, 352.
123. NAI, DF, F001/019/78/PART002, Murray to DF, Note on the EMS and Resource Transfers, 12 October 1978.
124. This point is also made by Jenkins; see *Diary*, 351.
125. HAEU, EN1148, Note of Tickell, Note of conversation between Chancellor Schmidt and the President of the European Commission at one of the intervals in the European Council Brussels, 5 December 1978, 11 December 1978.
126. Ibid., Tickell to Jenkins, European Council, 4 and 5 December 1978, 8 December 1978.
127. ASBI, Carte Baffi, Monte Oppio, cart.116, fasc.1, diario Baffi.
128. Ibid.
129. Jenkins, *Diary*, 351.
130. HAEU, EN1148, Tickell to Jenkins, European Council, 4–5 December 1978, 8 December 1978.
131. Jenkins, *Diary*, 353; CADN, RPCEE 1167, Conférence de presse française, 5 December 1978.
132. TNA, CAB/128/64/22, CM(78)42nd meeting, 7 December 1978.
133. NAI, DT, 2008/148/504, Informal conversation after the conclusion of the Council, November 1978.
134. NAI, DF, F001/026/78/PART01, Visit of the Taoiseach to the FRG, 27–28 November 1978.
135. BAK, B136/8061, Note of Thiele über das Telefongespräch zwischen dem Bundeskanzler und dem irischen Premierminister Lynch am 7. Dezember 1978, 8 December 1978.
136. NAI, DF, F001/026/78, EMS: Summary of discussions in Luxembourg, 12 December 1978; and various documents in NAI, DT, 2008/148/658.
137. NAI, DFA, 2008/79/1939, Message from the Taoiseach to the heads of state or government of the member countries of the European Communities, 15 December 1978.
138. NAI, DT, 2008/148/504, Note to Taoiseach, EMS, summary of discussions in Luxembourg, 12 December 1978.
139. For a full examination, based on Andreotti's papers and other sources, see Varsori, *La Cenerentola*, 314–30.
140. ASBI, Carte Baffi, Monte Oppio, cart.116, fasc.1, diario Baffi.
141. AMAE, DAEF1557, Telegram no. 2888/97 of Puaux, SME, 8 December 1978.
142. ASBI, Carte Baffi, Monte Oppio, cart.116, fasc.1, diario Baffi; BAK, B136/8061, Andreotti to Schmidt, 15 December 1978; AMAE, DAEF1557, Télégramme no. 2933/41 of Puaux, L'Italie et le SME, 11 December 1978.
143. CAEF, B0050444, Compte-rendu du Conseil des Ministres des CE du 18 décembre 1978, 19 December 1978.
144. "The European Council stresses the importance of henceforth avoiding the creation of permanent MCAs and progressively reducing present MCAs in order to reestab-

lish the unity of prices of the common agricultural policy, giving also due consideration to price policy."

145. Ludlow, *Making,* 279–83; *AAPD 1979,* documents 16, 26, and 117.

146. See also Marsh, *Euro,* 87–88.

147. The Banque de France used the expression *"serpent à sonnettes"* in BdF, 1489200205/347, Note of the DGSE, Réflexions sur le nouveau SME, 23 August 1978.

148. Paul Fabra even dubs it *"un gadget"* in "La politique," 150.

149. Manfred Schäfers, "Schäuble denkt an Europäischen Währungsfonds," *Frankfurter Allgemeine Zeitung,* 7 March 2010; Yves Leterme, "Pour une agence européenne de la dette," *Le Monde,* 5 March 2010. See also Mourlon-Druol, "The Euro Crisis."

150. Ungerer, *Concise History,* 166.

151. Bordo and Schwartz, "ECU," 11.

152. See chapter 2.

153. Bordo and Schwartz, "ECU," 12–13.

154. Ibid., 18 and 23.

155. Ibid., 2.

156. HAEU, EN1148, Note by Tickell of a call by the President of the European Commission on the British PM, 3 November 1978, 15 November 1978.

157. BB, N2/269, Emminger to Schmidt, EWS (Wortprotokoll ZBR-Sitzung), 1 December 1978.

158. In 1974, the plan for urgent economic and monetary measures; in 1975, the report on European Union; in 1976, the plan proposed at the Luxembourg European Council; and in 1977, the Jenkins and Ortoli plans—to which could be added the support for the production of various expert reports such as the Optica ones. See chapters 2 through 5.

CONCLUSIONS

Epigraphs. Otmar Emminger, TNA, PREM 16/2011, "The Exchange Rate as an Instrument of Policy," LSE Society Special Lecture, 7 December 1978. Gordon Richardson, MTA, note to Callaghan, 31 October 1978.

1. Ludlow, "Green."

2. Adler and Haas, "Conclusion," 372.

3. See, for instance, comprehensive analysis in BAK, B102/266602, Note of Fest, Europäische Wirtschaftspolitik/WWU, 21 September 1977; BdF, 1489200205/258, Note DGSE, "Principales propositions pour l'UEM depuis le plan Werner de 1970," 8 October 1976.

4. BdF, 1489200205/277, Commission, Recherche d'une plus grande stabilité dans les rapports de change entre les monnaies des États membres de la CEE, 13 April 1978.

5. Adler and Haas, "Conclusion," 373.

6. ECB, Heyvaert Group, no. 39, Interim Report on the EMS, 21 August 1978. For the "Belgian compromise," see chapter 7.

7. Smouts, "Les sommets," 677; and Barre, *L'expérience,* 72–73.

8. Austria, Switzerland, Sweden, and Norway ultimately did not join the EMS. On the Swiss attempt to join the snake, see chapter 3.

9. With the important difference that the currency is now supranationally managed. But there still does not exist a substantial supranational budget. Mourlon-Druol, "Euro Crisis."

10. BdF, 1035199602/2, Institut de Formation, Exposé de M. de La Genière sur la politique monétaire, réponses aux questions posées par les adjoints de direction de la promotion 1977, 29 November 1977.

11. See Mourlon-Druol, "Victory."

12. See chapters 6 and 7.

13. See, respectively, chapters 3 and 6.

14. For first steps in that direction, see Mourlon-Druol, "Managing." The expression "summitry as a way of life" is that of David Reynolds, in *Summits*, chapter 8. See also Mourlon-Druol, "Integrating."

15. For a survey of these numerous studies, see Verdun, "Why EMU Happened."

16. McNamara, *Currency*; see also Marcussen, *Ideas*.

17. Henning, "Systemic."

18. Ibid., 558.

19. Niemann and Schmitter, "Neofunctionalism."

20. The argument according to which exchange rate instability undermines the growth of trade was notably questioned by Otmar Emminger; see *Verteidigung*, 207.

21. See chapter 4.

22. Barre, *L'expérience*, 204.

23. See chapter 3.

24. Moravcsik, *Choice*, 305.

25. Dyson, *Elusive*.

26. BoE, 8A460/4, McMahon to Fogarty, Giscard's Views on Exchange Rates, 15 August 1975.

27. See chapter 3.

28. TNA, FCO30/4026, Bayne to Hedley-Miller, EMS: Views of the governor of the Bank of France, 25 October 1978; MTA, Lawson to Thatcher, France & the EMS, 31 October 1978.

29. Respectively, 9.71%, 8.39%, and 2.54%.

30. Haas, "Introduction," 3.

31. Adler and Haas, "Conclusion," 389.

32. See chapters 2 and 3 in particular.

33. See chapters 2 and 5.

34. The Banque de France and the Trésor were in particular reported to be "concerned" by the Commission's ideas of a parallel currency; see AMAE, DAEF1553, Note of Bochet, UEM, 28 November 1977.

35. See chapter 8.

36. Froment-Meurice, *Vu du Quai*, 478.

37. Rueff, "L'Europe."

38. See chapter 5.

39. Ludlow, *Making*, 129. Kenneth Dyson similarly talks of a "limited, defensive mechanism to improve monetary stability: a 'shock absorber' mechanism to deal with external problems, specifically the US dollar" (*Elusive*, 111).

40. NAI, DFA, 2008/79/1887, Bonn Embassy, The Bonn economic summit: comments by Dr Schulmann of Chancellor Schmidt's office, 25 July 1978.

41. Lundestad, "Empire."

42. See chapter 8.

43. Ludlow, *Making*, 290.

44. TNA, PREM16/1655, Note, Visit of Chancellor Schmidt of the FRG, 23/24 April 1978.

45. TNA, FCO30/4024, Note of a discussion at the Federal Ministry of Finance on 18 October 1978, 20 October 1978.

46. Bussière, "Régionalisme."

47. See chapter 2.

48. John Kenneth Galbraith made such an analysis with respect to Britain; see TNA, PREM16/818, Isaac to principal private secretary, Professor Galbraith, 12 November 1976;

see also ibid., Galbraith to Callaghan, A note on the British economic problem—and remedies, 2 November 1976.

49. See chapter 6.
50. BdF, PV du Conseil général, tome 169, 19 octobre 1978.
51. Emminger, *D-Mark*, 324–27.
52. Schmidt, *Die Deutschen*, 265.
53. See chapters 1 and 2.
54. See chapter 5.

Sources

PRIMARY SOURCES

Unpublished Primary Sources

European Economic Community (EEC)

Council of Ministers Archives, Brussels (CMA)
European Commission Historical Archives, Brussels (ECHA)
Historical Archives of the European Union, Florence (HAEU)

France

Archives du Ministère des Affaires étrangères, La Courneuve (AMAE). Direction Europe/Coopération Économique (DE/CE); Direction des Affaires économiques et financières (DAEF); Fonds PA-AP 373, Jean Sauvagnargues.
Archives historiques de la Banque de France, Paris (BdF). Procès-verbaux du Conseil général (PVCG); Direction générale des Services étrangers, Service des Relations européennes, Sous-fonds Communauté européenne—Union européenne (Cote 1489200205).
Centre des Archives diplomatiques de Nantes (CADN). Postes: Bonn (ambassade), Bruxelles (ambassade, versement 1972–1982), Copenhague, Dublin (ambassade), La Haye (ambassade), Londres (ambassade), Luxembourg (ambassade, 1891–1987), Rome (Inventaire du fonds 1969–1980); Représentations permanentes: Représentation permanente de la France auprès des Communautés européennes à Bruxelles.
Centre des Archives économiques et financières, Savigny-le-Temple (CAEF). Fonds Cabinet; fonds Trésor.
Service interministériel des archives de France: Archives nationales, site de Fontainebleau (AN, Fontainebleau). Services du Premier Ministre/Cabinet du Premier Ministre et services rattachés, Secrétariat Général du Gouvernement/ Secrétariat général du comité interministériel (SGCI).
Service interministériel des archives de France: Archives nationales, site de Paris (AN, Paris). Fonds de la Présidence de la République, V. Giscard d'Estaing (Cote 5AG3); Fonds Jean-René Bernard (Cote 86AJ44).

Germany

Das Bundesarchiv, Koblenz (BAK). Bundeskanzleramt (B136); Bundesministerium der Finanzen (B126); Bundesministerium für Wirtschaft (B102).
Das Politische Archiv des Auswärtigen Amtes, Berlin (PAAA)
(III.) Leitungsebene: B1 Ministerbüro, 1955–2004; B2 Büro Staatsekretäre, 1949–1984.
(IV.) Politische Abteilungen: B21 Europäische Einigung und politische Zusammenarbeit, Europarat, nichtstaatliche europäische Organisationen, WEU, 1972–1992.
(X.) Europa-Abteilung: B200 Europäische Gemeinschaften, Grundsatzfragen, Institutionen, Assoziierungen, Beitritte, innerer Ausbau, Beziehungen zu den Staaten

der EFTA (bis 1975), des Mittelmeerraumes und Afrika und den übrigen AKP-Staaten, 1972–1992; B202 Europäische Wirtschafts- und Währungsunion, Industrie-, Regional-, Sozial-, Energie- und Verkehrspolitik der EG, Internationale Währungspolitik, 1972–1992.

Friedrich Ebert Stiftung, Archiv der sozialen Demokratie, Helmut-Schmidt-Archiv, Bonn (AdsD, HSA)

Historisches Archiv der Deutschen Bundesbank, Frankfurt am Main (BB). Zentralbankrat Protokolle (ZBR); Schriftgut der Dienstelle des Direktoriums (B330); Nachlass Prof. Dr. Otmar Emminger (N2).

Ireland

The National Archives of Ireland, Dublin (NAI). Department of the Taoiseach (DT); Department of Finance (DF); Department of Foreign Affairs (DFA).

Italy

Archivio centrale dello stato, Rome (ACS). Archivio Aldo Moro; Serie presidenza del consiglio dei ministri, 23 November 1974–29 July 1976.

Archivio storico della Banca d'Italia, Rome (ASBI). Segretaria particolare; Banca d'Italia, Studi; Carte Baffi.

United Kingdom

The Bank of England Archive, London (BoE). Administration Department (ADM); Cashier's Department (C); Economic Intelligence Department (EID); Overseas Department (OV); European integration: European Economic Community (4A149).

The National Archives, Kew (TNA). Prime Minister's Office (PREM); Foreign and Commonwealth Office's Files (FCO); Treasury Files (T); Cabinet's Files (CAB).

Published Primary Sources

Archives

Akten zur Auswärtigen Politik der Bundesrepublik Deutschland (AAPD). Munich: Oldenbourg. Years consulted: 1974, 1975, 1976, 1977, 1978, 1979.

British Diplomatic Oral History Programme, http://janus.lib.cam.ac.uk/db/node.xsp?id=EAD%2FGBR%2F0014%2FDOHP.

European Central Bank Archive (ECB), http://www.ecb.int/ecb/history/archive/intro/html/index.en.html.

European Oral History Programme, http://www.eui.eu/HAEU/EN/OralHistory.asp.

Foreign Relations of the United States, 1969–1976. Vol. 31, *Foreign Economic Policy, 1973–1976*. Washington, DC: Department of State, 2009.

The Gerald R. Ford Presidential Digital Library, http://www.fordlibrarymuseum.gov/library/docs.asp.

Margaret Thatcher Archive (MTA), http://www.margaretthatcher.org/archive/thatcher-archive.asp.

Memoirs

Barre, Raymond. *L'expérience du pouvoir: Conversations avec Jean Bothorel*. Paris: Fayard, 2007.

Butler, Michael. *Europe: More Than a Continent*. London: Heinemann, 1986.

Callaghan, Jim. *Time and Chance*. London: Collins, 1987.

Emminger, Otmar. *D-Mark, Dollar, Währungskrisen: Erinnerungen eines ehemaligen Bundesbankpräsidenten*. Stuttgart: Deutsche Verlags-Anstalt, 1987.

Fourcade, Jean-Pierre. *Et si nous parlions de demain . . .* Paris: Fayard, 1979.

Froment-Meurice, Henri. *Vu du Quai: Mémoires 1945–1983*. Paris: Fayard, 1998.

Giroud, Françoise. *La comédie du pouvoir*. Paris: Fayard, 1977.

Giscard d'Estaing, Valéry. *Le pouvoir et la vie*. Vols. 1–2. Paris: Compagnie 12/Le Livre de poche, 1988 and 1991.

———. *Le pouvoir et la vie*. Vol. 3: *Choisir*. Paris: Compagnie 12/Le Livre de Poche, 2006.

Jenkins, Roy. *European Diary 1977–1981*. London: Collins, 1989.

———. *A Life at the Centre*. London: MacMillan, 1991.

Schmidt, Helmut. *Die Deutschen und ihre Nachbarn*. Berlin: Siedler, 1990.

———. *Menschen und Mächte*. Berlin: Siedler, 1987.

SECONDARY SOURCES CITED

Adler, Emanuel, and Haas, Peter M. "Conclusion: Epistemic Communities, World Order, and the Creation of a Reflective Research Program." *International Organization* 46, no. 1 (1992): 367–90.

Apel, Emmanuel. *European Monetary Integration, 1958–2002*. London: Routledge, 1998.

Badie, Bertrand, and Smouts, Marie-Claude. *Le retournement du monde: Sociologie de la scène internationale*. Paris: Presses de la Fondation nationale de Sciences politiques and Dalloz, 1992.

Barre, Raymond. *Économie politique*. Paris: Presses Universitaires de France, 1959.

———. "L'Europe face à l'inflation et à la recession." In *L'Europe des crises*, edited by Robert Triffin, Raymond Aron, Raymond Barre, and René Ewalenko, 143–62. Brussels: Bruylant, 1976.

Benning, Elizabeth. "Economic Power and Political Leadership: The Federal Republic, the West and the Re-Shaping of the International Economic System, 1972–76." PhD diss., London School of Economics and Political Science, 2011.

Bitsch, Marie-Thérèse. *Histoire de la construction européenne*. Brussels: Éditions Complexe, 2004.

Bloch, March. *Esquisse d'une histoire monétaire de l'Europe*. Paris: Cahiers des Annales, Armand Colin, 1954.

Bordo, Michael D., and Schwartz, Anna J. "The ECU: An Imaginary or Embryonic Form of Money; What Can We Learn from History?" Working Paper no. 2345, National Bureau of Economic Research, 1987.

Bossuat, Gérard. *Faire l'Europe sans défaire la France: 60 ans de politique d'unité européenne des gouvernements et des présidents de la République française (1943–2003)*. Brussels: P.I.E. Peter Lang, 2005.

Bothorel, Jean. *Le pharaon: Histoire du septennat giscardien, 19 mai 1974–22 mars 1978*. Paris: Grasset, 1983.

Bottex, Agnès. "La mise en place des institutions monétaires européennes (1957–1964)." *Histoire, économie et sociétés* 4 (1999): 753–74.

Bouneau, Christophe, Burigana, David, and Varsori, Antonio, eds. *Les trajectoires de l'innovation technologique et la construction européenne: Des voies de structuration durable?* Brussels: Peter Lang, 2010.

Boyce, Robert. *The Great Interwar Crisis and the Collapse of Globalization*. Basingstoke: Palgrave MacMillan, 2009.

Bussière, Éric. "L'intégration économique de l'Europe au XXe siècle: processus et acteurs." *Entreprises et histoires* 33 (2003): 12–24.

——. "Régionalisme monétaire et identité européenne depuis le traité de Rome." *Relations internationales* 139, no. 3 (2009): 25–36.

Bussière, Éric, and Dumoulin, Michel. *Milieux économiques et intégration européenne en Europe occidentale au XXème siècle*. Arras: Artois Presses Université, 1998.

Bussière, Éric, Dumoulin, Michel, and Schirmann, Sylvain. *Milieux économiques et intégration européenne au XXème siècle: La crise des années 1970; De la conférence de La Haye à la veille de la relance des années 1980*. Brussels: Peter Lang, 2006.

Bussière, Éric, and Feiertag, Olivier. "Méthode, problèmes et premiers résultats d'une histoire des relations monétaires internationales au XXe siècle." In *Banques centrales et convergences monétaires en Europe (1920–1971)*, edited by É. Bussière and O. Feiertag, Special Issue, *Histoire, Économie et Sociétés* 4 (1999): 675–80.

Cairncross, Alec, Giersch, Herbert, Lamfalussy, Alexandre, Petrilli, Giuseppe, and Uri, Pierre. *Economic Policy for the European Community: The Way Forward*. London: Macmillan for the Institut für Weltwirtschaft an der Universität Kiel, 1974.

Cassis, Youssef. "La communauté des gouverneurs des banques centrales européennes depuis la fin de la Seconde Guerre mondiale." In *Politiques et pratiques des banques d'émission en Europe (XVIIe–XXe siècle)*, edited by Olivier Feiertag and Michel Margairaz, 753–65. Paris: Albin Michel, 2003.

Chassaigne, Philippe. *Les années 1970: Fin d'un monde et origine de notre modernité*. Paris: Armand Colin, 2008.

Chenard, Marie-Julie. "Seeking Détente and Deepening Integration: The Case of China, 1975–1978." *Journal of European Integration History* (forthcoming 2012).

Chopin, Thierry. "Le Parlement européen." In *Les années Giscard: Valéry Giscard d'Estaing et l'Europe, 1974–1981*, edited by Serge Berstein and Jean-François Sirinelli, 153–89. Paris: Armand Colin, 2006.

Ciampani, Andrea, ed. *L'altra via per l'Europa: Forze sociali e organizzazione degli interessi nell'integrazione europea 1947–1957*. Milan: FrancoAngeli, 1995.

Clavert, Frédéric. *Hjalmar Schacht, financier et diplomate (1930–1950)*. Brussels: Peter Lang, 2009.

Clavert, Frédéric, and Feiertag, Olivier. "Les banquiers centraux et la construction européenne." Special issue of *Histoire, Économie et Société* 30, no. 4 (2011).

Clavin, Patricia. "Defining Transnationalism." *Contemporary European History* 14, no. 4 (2005): 421–39.

Cobham, David. "Strategies for Monetary Integration Revisited." *Journal of Common Market Studies* 27, no. 3 (March 1989): 203–17.

Cohen, Samy. *Les conseillers du président: De Charles de Gaulle à Valéry Giscard d'Estaing*. Paris: Presses Universitaires de France, 1980.

Cooper, Richard. "Almost a Century of Central Bank Cooperation." Working Paper no. 198, BIS, February 2006.

Coppolaro, Lucia. "Trade and Politics across the Atlantic: The European Economic Community and the United States of America in the GATT Negotiations of the Kennedy Round (1962–1967)." PhD diss., European University Institute, 2006.

Dell, Edmund. "Britain and the Origins of the European Monetary System." *Contemporary European History* 3, no. 1 (1994): 1–60.

Di Nolfo, Ennio. *Storia delle relazioni internazionali, 1918–1999*. Rome: Editori Laterza, 2000.

Dinan, Desmond. *Europe Recast: A History of European Union*. London: Lynne Rienner, 2004.

Dyson, Kenneth. *Elusive Union: The Process of Economic and Monetary Union in Europe.* London: Longman, 1994.

Eichengreen, Barry. "When to Dollarize." Paper presented at a conference on dollarization hosted by the Federal Reserve Bank of Dallas, 6–7 March 2000.

Emminger, Otmar. "The Exchange Rate as an Instrument of Policy." *Lloyds Bank Review* 133 (July 1979): 1–22.

——. *Verteidigung der DM: Plädoyers für stabiles Geld.* Fritz Knapp Verlag: Frankfurt am Main, 1980.

Fabra, Paul. "La politique monétaire internationale du président Giscard d'Estaing." In *La politique extérieure de Valéry Giscard d'Estaing,* edited by Samy Cohen and Marie-Claude Smouts, 138–50. Paris: Presses de la Fondation Nationale des Sciences Politiques, 1985.

Febvre, Lucien, ed. *Encyclopédie française.* Paris: Société de Gestion de l'Encyclopédie française, 1937.

Feiertag, Olivier. "Banques centrales et relations internationales au XXe siècle: Le problème historique de la coopération monétaire international." *Relations internationales* 100 (Winter 1999): 355–76.

——. "Introduction: Pour une histoire de l'autorité monétaire des banques centrales." In *Mesurer la monnaie: Banques centrales et construction de l'autorité monétaire (XIXe–XXe siècle),* edited by Olivier Feiertag, 13–26. Paris: Albin Michel, 2005.

Feiertag, Olivier, and Margairaz, Michel, eds. *Politiques et pratiques des banques d'émission en Europe (XVIIe–XXe siècle).* Paris: Albin Michel, 2003.

Fleming, Marcus. "On Exchange Rate Unification." *Economic Journal* 81 (September 1971): 467–88.

Fountain, John. "European Units of Account." *Financial Analyst Journal* 20, no. 1 (1964): 102–3.

Frank, Robert. *La hantise du déclin.* Paris: Belin, 1994.

——. "Les problèmes monétaires et la création du SME." In *Les années Giscard: Valéry Giscard d'Estaing et l'Europe, 1974–1981,* edited by Serge Berstein and Jean-François Sirinelli, 13–26. Paris: Armand Colin, 2006.

——. "Penser historiquement les relations internationales." *Annuaire français des relations internationales* 4 (2003): 42–65.

Fratianni, Michele, and Peeters, Theo, eds. *One Money for Europe.* London: MacMillan, 1978.

Furby, Daniel. "The Revival and Success of Britain's Second Application for Membership of the European Economic Community, 1968–71." PhD diss., Queen Mary University, 2010.

Garavini, Giuliano. *Dopo gli imperi: L'integrazione europea nello scontro Nord-Sud.* Firenze: Le Monnier, 2009.

——. "The Battle for the Participation of the European Community in the G7 (1975–7)." *Journal of European Integration History* 2, no. 1 (2006): 141–58.

Geary, Michael. *An Inconvenient Wait: Ireland's Quest for Membership of the EEC, 1957–73.* Dublin: Institute of Public Administration, 2009.

Gerbet, Pierre. *La construction de l'Europe.* Paris: Imprimerie nationale, 2007.

Gilbert, Mark. "Narrating the Process: Questioning the Progressive Story of European Integration." *Journal of Common Market Studies* 46, no. 3 (2008): 641–62.

Gillingham, John. *European Integration 1950–2003: Superstate or New Market Economy?* Cambridge: Cambridge University Press, 2003.

Girault, René. "Le difficile mariage de deux histoires: Économie et relations internationales dans le monde contemporain." *Relations internationales* 41 (1985): 13–28.

Giscard d'Estaing, Edmond. *La France et l'unification économique de l'Europe*. Paris: Éditions M.-Th. Génin, 1953.

Gold, Joseph. "A New Universal and a New Regional Monetary Asset: SDR and ECU." In *Legal and Institutional Aspects of the International Monetary System: Selected Essays*, edited by Joseph Gold, 659–722. Washington, DC: IMF, 1984.

Goodhart, Charles. "Monetary Relationships: A View from Threadneedle Street." *Papers in Monetary Economics* 1, Reserve Bank of Australia, 1975.

———. "Problems of Monetary Management: The UK Experience." *Papers in Monetary Economics* 1, Reserve Bank of Australia, 1975.

Goodman, John B. *Monetary Sovereignty: The Politics of Central Banking in Western Europe*. Ithaca, NY: Cornell University Press, 1992.

Gowa, Joanne. "Hegemons, IOs, and Markets: The Case of the Substitution Account." *International Organization* 38, no. 4 (Autumn 1984): 661–83.

Griffiths, Richard. "A Dismal Decade? European Integration in the 1970s." In *Origins and Evolution of the European Union*, edited by Desmond Dinan, 169–90. Oxford: Oxford University Press, 2006.

Gros, Daniel. "Paradigms for the Monetary Union of Europe." *Journal of Common Market Studies* 27, no. 3 (March 1989): 219–30.

Gros, Daniel, and Thygesen, Niels. *European Monetary Integration*. London: Longman, 1992.

Grygowski, Dimitri. "Les États-Unis et la création du SME: Un test de la politique étrangère américaine vis-à-vis de la construction européenne." In *Quelle(s) Europe(s)? Nouvelles approches en histoire de l'intégration européenne. Which Europe(s)? New approaches in European integration history*, edited by Katrin Rücker and Laurent Warlouzet, 169–79. Brussels: Peter Lang, 2006.

———. "Les États-Unis et l'unification monétaire de l'Europe, 1968–1998." PhD diss., Cergy-Pontoise University, 2007.

———. *Les États-Unis et l'unification monétaire de l'Europe*. Brussels: Peter Lang, 2009.

Haas, Peter M. "Introduction: Epistemic Communities and International Policy Coordination." *International Organization* 46, no. 1 (1992): 1–36.

Haberler, Gottfried. "The International Monetary System: Some Developments and Discussions." In *Approaches to Greater Flexibility of Exchange Rates*, edited by George N. Halm, 115–23. Princeton, NJ: Princeton University Press, 1970.

Henning, C. Randall. "Systemic Conflict and Regional Monetary Integration: The Case of Europe." *International Organization* 52, no. 3 (Summer 1998): 537–73.

Honohan, Patrick, and Murphy, Gavin. "Breaking the Sterling Link: Ireland's Decision to Enter the EMS." Institute for International Integration Studies, Trinity College Dublin, no. 317, February 2010.

Ikemoto, Daisuke. *European Monetary Integration 1970–79. British and French Experiences*. Basingstoke: Palgrave Macmillan, 2011.

Ingram, James. "Comment: The Optimum Currency Problem." In *Monetary Problems of the International Economy*, edited by R. Mundell and A. Swoboda, 95–100. Chicago: University of Chicago Press, 1969.

James, Harold. *Europe Reborn: A History, 1914–2000*. London: Pearson, 2003.

———. *International Monetary Cooperation since Bretton Woods*. Oxford: Oxford University Press, 1996.

———. *Rambouillet, 15. November 1975: Die Globalisierung der Wirtschaft*. Munich: DTV, 1997.

———. "The Vulnerability of Globalization." *German Historical Institute Bulletin* 35 (2004): 85–95.

Kaiser, Wolfram. *Christian Democracy and the Origins of the European Union*. Cambridge: Cambridge University Press, 2007.

——. "History Meets Politics: Overcoming Interdisciplinary Volapük in Research on the EU." *Journal of European Public Policy* 15, no. 2 (March 2008): 300–13.

Kaiser, Wolfram, Leucht, Brigitte, and Rasmussen, Morten, eds. *The History of the European Union: Origins of a Trans- and Supranational Polity, 1950–72*. London: Routledge, 2009.

Kaiser, Wolfram, and Meyer, Jan-Henrik, eds. "Non-State Actors in European Integration in the 1970s: Towards a Polity of Transnational Contestation." *Comparativ* 20, no. 3 (2010): 7–104.

Karamouzi, Eirini. "Greece's Path to EEC membership, 1974–1979: The View from Brussels." PhD diss., London School of Economics and Political Science, 2011.

Kenen, Peter B. "The Theory of Optimum Currency Areas: An Eclectic View." In *Monetary Problems of the International Economy*, edited by R. Mundell and A. Swoboda, 41–60. Chicago: University of Chicago Press, 1969.

Kindleberger, Charles P. "International Public Goods without International Government." *American Economic Review* 76, no. 1 (March 1986): 1–13.

Knipping, Franz, and Schönwald, Matthias, eds. *Aufbruch zum Europa der zweiten Generation: Die europäische Einigung, 1969–1984*. Trier: Wissenschaftlicher Verlag Trier, 2004.

Knudsen, Ann-Christina L. *Farmers on Welfare: The Making of Europe's Common Agricultural Policy*. Ithaca, NY: Cornell University Press, 2009.

Kruse, D. C. *Monetary Integration in Western Europe: EMU, EMS and beyond*. London: Butterworths, 1980.

Lucas, Robert. "Econometric Policy Evaluation: A Critique." In *The Phillips Curve and Labor Markets, Carnegie-Rochester Conference Series on Public Policy*, vol. 1, edited by K. Brunner and A. Meltzer, 19–46. Amsterdam: North-Holland, 1976.

Ludlow, N. Piers. *Dealing with Britain: The Six and the First UK Application to the EEC*. Cambridge: Cambridge University Press, 1997.

——. "The Emergence of a Commercial Heavy-Weight: The Kennedy Round Negotiations and the European Community of the 1960s." *Diplomacy and Statecraft* 18 (2007): 351–68.

——. *The European Community and the Crises of the 1960s: Negotiating the Gaullist Challenge*. London: Routledge, 2005.

——. "From Deadlock to Dynamism: The European Community in the 1980s." In *Origins and Evolution of the European Union*, edited by Desmond Dinan, 218–23. Oxford: Oxford University Press, 2006.

——. "The Green Heart of Europe: The Rise and Fall of the CAP as the Community's Central Policy, 1958–1985." In *Fertile Ground for Europe? The History of European Integration and the Common Agricultural Policy since 1945*, edited by Kiran Patel, 79–98. Baden Baden: Nomos, 2009.

Ludlow, Peter. *The Making of the European Monetary System: A Case Study of the Politics of the European Community*. London: Butterworth Scientific, 1982.

——. "The Political and Diplomatic Origins of the European Monetary System." Occasional Paper no. 32 of the Research Institute, John Hopkins University, Bologna Center, June 1980.

Lundestad, Geir. "Empire by Invitation? The United States and Western Europe, 1945–1952." *Journal of Peace Research* 23, no. 3 (1986): 263–77.

Maes, Ivo, and Buyst, Erik. "Triffin, the European Commision and the Project of a European Reserve Fund." In *Réseaux économiques et construction européenne/*

Economic networks and European integration, edited by Michel Dumoulin, 431–44. Brussels: Peter Lang, 2004.

Magnifico, Giovanni. *European Monetary Unification*. London: MacMillan, 1973.

——. *L'Euro: Ragioni e lezioni di un successo sofferto*. Rome: Luiss University Press, 2005.

——. *L'Europe par la monnaie*. Paris: Lavauzelle, 1974.

Mamou, Yves. *Une machine de pouvoir: La direction du Trésor*. Paris: La Découverte, 1988.

Marcussen, Martin. *Ideas and Elites: The Social Construction of Economic and Monetary Union*. Viborg: Aalborg University Press, 2000.

Marsh, David. *The Euro: The Politics of the New Global Currency*. New Haven, CT: Yale University Press, 2009.

McKinnon, Ronald. "Optimal Currency Areas." *American Economic Review* 53 (September 1963): 717–24.

McNamara, Kathleen. *The Currency of Ideas: Monetary Politics in the European Union*. Ithaca, NY: Cornell University Press, 1998.

Ménudier, Henri. "Valéry Giscard d'Estaing et les relations franco-allemandes (1974–1981)." In *La politique extérieure de Valéry Giscard d'Estaing*, edited by Samy Cohen and Marie-Claude Smouts, 66–85. Paris: Presses de la Fondation Nationale des Sciences Politiques, 1985.

Miard-Delacroix, Hélène. *Partenaires de choix? Le chancelier Helmut Schmidt et la France (1974–1982)*. Bern: P. Lang, 1993.

Middlemas, Keith. *Orchestrating Europe: The Informal Politics of the European Union 1973–95*. London: Fontana, 1995.

Migani, Guia. "La politica di cooperazione allo sviluppo della CEE: dall'associazione alla partnership (1957–1975)." *Memoria e ricerca* 30 (2009): 27–36.

Migani, Guia, and Varsori, Antonio. *Europe in the International Arena during the 1970s: Entering a Different World*. Brussels: Peter Lang, 2011.

Milward, Alan. *The European Rescue of the Nation-State*. London: Routledge, 1992.

Moravcsik, Andrew. *The Choice for Europe: Social Purpose and State Power from Messina to Maastricht*. Ithaca, NY: Cornell University Press, 1999.

Mourlon-Druol, Emmanuel. "Economist or Monetarist? The Difficult Creation of an Internal French Consensus about European Monetary Integration (1974–1976)." In *Les deux Europes*, edited by Michele Affinito, Guia Migani, and Christian Wenkel, 213–24. Brussels: Peter Lang, 2009.

——. "The Euro Crisis: A Historical Perspective." Strategic Update, LSE IDEAS, June 2011.

——. "Filling the EEC Leadership Vacuum? The Creation of the European Council in 1974." *Cold War History* 10, no. 3 (2010): 315–39.

——. "Integrating an International Political Economy Dimension into European Integration History: The Challenges of the 1970s." *Journal of European Integration History* 17, no. 2 (2011): 335–41.

——. "'Managing from the Top': Globalization and the Banalization Summitry, 1974–1977." Paper presented at the LSE Cold War History Seminar, 2 March 2011.

——. "The Victory of the Intergovernmental Method? The Emergence of the European Council in the EEC's Institutional Set-Up, 1974–1977." In *The Road Europe Travelled Along: The Evolution of the EEC/EU Institutions and Policies*, edited by Daniela Preda and Daniele Pasquinucci, 27–40. Brussels: Peter Lang, 2010.

Mundell, Robert A. "Plan pour une monnaie européenne." In *L'unification monétaire européenne*, edited by Pascal Salin. Paris: Calmann-Levy, 1974.

———. "A Theory of Optimum Currency Areas." *American Economic Review* 51, no. 4 (September 1961): 657–65.

Niemann, Arne, with Schmitter, Philippe. "Neofunctionalism." In *European Integration Theory*, edited by Thomas Dietz and Antje Wiener, 45–66. Oxford: Oxford University Press, 2009.

Olivi, Bino. *L'Europa difficile: Storia politica dell'integrazione europea 1948–2000*. Bologna: Il Mulino, 2001.

Oort, Conrad. "Exchange Rate Policy in the European Communities." *Common Market Law Review* 13, no. 3 (1976): 301–14.

Petrini, Francesco. *Il liberismo a una dimensione: La Confindustria e l'integrazione europea, 1947–1957*. Milan: FrancoAngeli, 2005.

Rasmussen, Morten. "Joining the European Communities: Denmark's Road to EC-membership, 1961–1973." PhD diss., European University Institute, 2004.

Renouvin, Pierre, and Duroselle, Jean-Baptiste. *Introduction à l'histoire des relations internationales*. Paris: Armand Colin, 1964.

Reynolds, David. *Summits: Six Meetings That Shaped the Twentieth Century*. New York: Basic Books, 2007.

Riboud, Jacques. *Une monnaie pour l'Europe: L'Eurostable*. Paris: Editions de la Revue Politique et Parlementaire, 1975.

Robichek, Alexander A., and Eaker, Mark R. "Debt Denomination and Exchange Risk in International Capital Markets." *Financial Management* 5, no. 3 (Autumn 1976): 11–18.

Romano, Angela. *From Détente in Europe to European Détente: How the West Shaped the Helsinki CSCE*. Brussels: PIE-Peter Lang, 2009.

Rueff, Jacques. "L'Europe se fera par la monnaie ou ne se fera pas." *Revue Synthèses* 45 (1950).

Saint-Périer, Amaury de. "La France et la sauvegarde du système communautaire de change de 1974 à 1977." In *Milieux économiques et intégration européenne au XXe siècle: La crise des années 1970; De la conférence de La Haye à la veille de la relance des années 1980*, edited by Michel Dumoulin, Sylvain Schirmann, and Éric Bussière, 51–58. Brussels: P.I.E. Peter Lang, 2006.

———. "Valéry Giscard d'Estaing, la France et l'Europe monétaire de 1974 à 1981: La persévérance recompense." PhD diss., Paris-Sorbonne University, 2008.

Salin, Pascal, ed. *L'unification monétaire européenne*. Paris: Calmann-Levy, 1974.

Schmidt, Helmut. *Kontinuität und Konzentration*. Bonn-Bad Godersberg: Verlag Neue Gesellschaft GmbH, 1976.

Simon, Denys. *Le système juridique communautaire*. Paris: Presses Universitaires de France, 3rd ed., 2001

Simonian, Haig. *The Privileged Partnership: Franco-German Relations in the European Community 1969–1984*. Oxford: Clarendon, 1985.

Smouts, Marie-Claude. "Les sommets des pays industrialisés." *Annuaire de droit international* (1979): 668–85.

Soell, Hartmut. *Helmut Schmidt, 1969 bis heute, Macht und Verantwortung*. Munich: Deutsche Verlags-Anstalt, 2008.

Spohr Readman, Kristina. "Germany and the Politics of the Neutron Bomb." *Diplomacy & Statecraft* 21, no. 2 (2010): 259–85.

Story, Jonathan. "The Franco-German Alliance within the Community." *The World Today*, June 1980: 209–17.

———. "The Launching of the EMS: An Analysis of Change in Foreign Economic Policy." *Political Studies* 36 (1988): 397–412.

Taulègne, Béatrice. *Le Conseil européen*. Paris: Presses Universitaires de France, 1993.

Thiemeyer, Guido. "Helmut Schmidt und die Gründung des Europäisches Währungs-systems 1973–1979." In *Aufbruch zum Europa der zweiten Generation: Die europäische Einigung 1969–1984*, edited by Franz Knipping and Matthias Schön-wald, 245–68. Trier: Wissenschaftlicher Verlag Trier, 2004.

Tristram, Frédéric. "Un instrument politique mal assumé? L'entourage de Valéry Gis-card d'Estaing à l'Élysée de 1974 à 1981." *Histoire@Politique: Politique, culture, société* 8 (May–August 2009), http://www.histoire-politique.fr/index2.php?num ero=08&rub=dossier&item=80.

Trouvé, Matthieu. *L'Espagne et l'Europe: De la dictature de Franco à l'Union européenne.* Brussels: P.I.E. Peter Lang, 2008.

Tsoukalis, Loukas. *The Politics and Economics of European Monetary Integration.* Lon-don: George Allen & Unwin, 1977.

Ungerer, Horst. *A Concise History of European Monetary Integration: From EPU to EMU.* Westport, CT: Quorum Books, 1997.

——. "The European Monetary System and the International Monetary System." *Jour-nal of Common Market Studies* 27, no. 3 (March 1989): 231–48.

Urwin, Derek. *The Community of Europe: A History of European Integration since 1945.* London: Longman, 1995.

Vaïsse, Maurice. *La puissance ou l'influence? La France dans le monde depuis 1958.* Paris: Fayard, 2009.

van Ypersele, Jacques. *The European Monetary System: Origins, Operation, and Out-look.* Brussels: Commission of the European Communities, 1984.

——. "Le nouveau système monétaire européen." *Revue de la Banque* 2 (1979): 247–70.

Varsori, Antonio, ed. *Alle origini del presente: L'Europa occidentale nella crisi degli anni Settanta.* Milan: FrancoAngeli, 2007.

——. "Alle origini di un modello sociale europeo: la Comunità europea e la nascita di una politica sociale (1969–1974)." *Ventunesimo Secolo* 5, no. 9 (2006): 17–47.

——. *La Cenerentola d'Europa? L'Italia e l'integrazione europea dal 1947 a oggi.* Soveria Manelli: Rubbettino, 2010.

——. "La storiografia sull'integrazione europea." *Europa Europe* 10, no. 1 (2001): 69–93.

Vaubel, Roland. *Strategies for Currency Unification: The Economics of Currency Compe-tition and the Case for a European Parallel Currency.* Tübingen: Mohr, 1978.

Verdun, Amy. "The Role of the Delors Committee in the Creation of EMU: An Epis-temic Community?" *Journal of European Public Policy* 6, no. 2 (1999): 317.

——. "Why EMU Happened: A Survey of Theoretical Explanations." In *Before and Be-yond EMU: Historical Lessons and Future Prospects*, edited by Patrick M. Crow-ley, 71–98. London: Routledge, 2002.

von Karczewski, Johannes. *"Weltwirtschaft ist unser Schicksal": Helmut Schmidt und die Schaffung der Weltwirtschaftsgipfel.* Bonn: Dietz Verlag, 2008.

Waechter, Matthias. *Helmut Schmidt und Valéry Giscard d'Estaing: Auf der Suche nach Stabilität in der Krise der 70er Jahre.* Bremen: Edition Temmen, Studien der Helmut und Loki Schmidt-Stiftung, 2011.

Wall, Martin. "'Half a loaf was better than no bread': Ireland and the Creation of the European Regional Development Fund." *Journal of the Trinity History Postgrad-uate Seminar Series* 1, (2009): 44–52.

——. "Ireland and the European Community 1973–1977." PhD diss., University Col-lege Cork, 2011.

Warlouzet, Laurent. *Le choix de la CEE par la France: L'Europe économique en débat de Mendès-France à de Gaulle (1955–1969).* Paris: CHEFF, 2011.

Wass, Douglas. *Decline to Fall: The Making of British Macro-Economic Policy and the 1976 IMF Crisis*. Oxford: Oxford University Press, 2008.

Weinachter, Michèle. *Valéry Giscard d'Estaing et l'Allemagne: Le double rêve inachevé*. Paris: Harmattan, 2004.

Werner, Pierre. *L'Europe monétaire reconsidérée*. Lausanne: Centre de recherches européennes, 1977.

Wiegrefe, Klaus. *Das Zerwürfnis: Helmut Schmidt, Jimmy Carter und die Krise der deutsch-amerikanischen Beziehungen*. Berlin: Propyläen Verlag, 2005.

Wilkens, Andreas. "Une tentative prématurée? L'Allemagne, la France et les balbutiements de l'Europe monétaire (1969–1974)." In *Dynamiques européennes: Nouvel espace, nouveaux acteurs, 1969–1981*, edited by Élisabeth du Réau and Robert Frank, 77–104. Paris: Publications de la Sorbonne, 2002.

Index